# Transnational Modern Languages: A Handbook

# Transnational Modern Languages

Transnational Modern Languages promotes a model of Modern Languages not as the inquiry into separate national traditions, but as the study of languages, cultures and their interactions. The series aims to demonstrate the value – practical and commercial, as well as academic and cultural – of modern language study when conceived as transnational cultural enquiry.

The texts in the series are specifically targeted at a student audience. They address how work on the transnational and the transcultural broadens the confines of Modern Languages; opens an extensive range of objects of research to analysis; deploys a complex set of methodologies; and can be accomplished through the exposition of clearly articulated examples.

The series is anchored by *Transnational Modern Languages: A Handbook*, ed. Jenny Burns (Warwick) and Derek Duncan (St. Andrews), which sets out the theoretical and conceptual scope of the series, the type of research on which it is based and the kinds of questions that it asks. Following on from the *Handbook*, the series includes a text for the study of the following Modern Languages:

*Transnational French Studies*, ed. Charles Forsdick (Liverpool) and Claire Launchbury (Leeds)

*Transnational German Studies*, ed. Rebecca Braun (Lancaster) and Benedict Schofield (King's College London)

*Transnational Spanish Studies*, ed. Catherine Davies (IMLR) and Rory O'Bryen (Cambridge)

*Transnational Italian Studies*, ed. Charles Burdett (Durham) and Loredana Polezzi (Cardiff)

*Transnational Portuguese Studies*, ed. Hilary Owen (Manchester/Oxford) and Claire Williams (Oxford)

*Transnational Russian Studies*, ed. Andy Byford (Durham), Connor Doak (Bristol) and Stephen Hutchings (Manchester)

# Transnational Modern Languages

## A Handbook

*edited by*

*Jennifer Burns and Derek Duncan*

LIVERPOOL UNIVERSITY PRESS

First published 2022 by
Liverpool University Press
4 Cambridge Street
Liverpool
L69 7ZU





British Library Cataloguing-in-Publication data
A British Library CIP record is available

ISBN 978-1-80034-849-3

Typeset by Carnegie Book Production, Lancaster
Printed in the UK by CPI Group (UK) Ltd, Croydon CR0 4YY

# Contents

# An Introduction

*Jennifer Burns and Derek Duncan*

Myriam Gurba's 'nonfiction novel' *Mean* (2017) is a humorous and dark account of growing up queer and Chicana in California in the 1990s.[1] The book's first-person narrator explores contemporary racism, homophobia, and misogyny in a text that shows little respect for the formal boundaries of fiction or life-writing. The memoir is also part ghost story and part crime fiction, as it recounts in non-chronological order the narrator's own experience of sexual violence, and her traumatic haunting by the woman brutally murdered by the same assailant. 'Mean' is how the narrator characterizes the robust humour she adopts to speak back to an often-hostile world: for a young Chicana lesbian, the world itself is a very 'mean' place. While most reviewers of the book praised Gurba's original and incisive social critique, none of them made much of the narrator's queer monolingualism: 'I began as an only child with an only language. This language was English and Spanish' (p. 4). She also grows up knowing some Nahuatl and Polish. Much of the violence the narrator experiences as a child is caused by derogatory cultural responses to her linguistic versatility. Her nursery teachers attempt to correct her creative fusion of Spanish and English, and the management of Spanish is a constant focus of discipline throughout her education. Yet as an adult reflecting on the response of her nursery teachers to her unconventional bilingualism, she understands its added value: 'They didn't get that my first language was double theirs' (p. 5). Language, too, is the site of complex identity formation. The narrator ironically self-identifies as 'Molack' (part Mexican and part Polish), but is the target of racially abusive terms such as 'wetback' and 'chola'. Language is also the platform from which she experiences, and experiments

[1] Myriam Gurba, *Mean* (Minneapolis and Brooklyn: Coffee House Press, 2017).

with, cultural difference as advocate and connoisseur. Her literary interests challenge demeaning stereotypes of illiterate Mexicans, although she knows that her middle-class educational privilege makes her 'whiter' than most. Cyndi Lauper, Kazuo Ishiguro, Gertrude Stein, Michael Jackson, Van Halen, Walter Benjamin, and Anne Frank are only a few of the names who feature in her idiosyncratic cultural catalogue. The lives and work of feminist artists Hannah Wilke and Ana Mendieta who documented the multiple, varied forms of violence enacted on the female body offer uncanny parallels to the narrator's own experience. And if 'meanness' started off as little more than a jokey exchange with her father, the Black and Hispanic drag queens in Jennie Livingston's film *Paris is Burning* (1990) offer her the fullest expression of 'mean' as cultural critique. To be 'mean' is to be acutely aware of borders and their enforcement, but also to know how to find the resources to transgress them creatively and with purpose. 'Meanness' or indeed 'queerness' protests against white, American middle-class norms of race, ethnicity, class, and embodiment that find material form in languages and cultures.

Set entirely in the US, *Mean* is a thoroughly transnational text, and an ironic retort to the view that knowledge of two or more languages is an impairment, and monolingualism a marker of accomplishment. It celebrates cultural diversity yet warns of the dangers of being different. *Mean* reflects on the mobility and fluidity of languages and cultures as sources of enrichment but not as safe spaces. It is an essay on how to think critically and creatively across conventional boundaries of language and culture, but not necessarily on how to emerge unscathed from the formations of power in which mobility is entangled. *Mean* is what *A Handbook* is all about.

Like Gurba, the authors in *A Handbook* offer an original take on a familiar term to suggest how it might work as a tool for thinking about languages and cultures transnationally. Each essay starts from and works with a keyword as an example of transnational critical practice reflecting on the ways in which languages, cultures and the people who inhabit them connect and intersect. The authors attempt to think themselves as transnational subjects asking what it means to write critically across linguistic and cultural borders. They do not simply try to describe or account for transnational phenomena as something external to them, but involve themselves in the process of transnational knowledge production, or world-making.

The essays in *A Handbook* are written in English, but contain words from other languages. Many are written by people whose first language is English, but many are not. Some are written by teachers and researchers working in Departments or Schools of Modern Languages, others by scholars in other disciplines attentive to how the work of cultural and linguistic crossing matters. *A Handbook*'s authors mostly don't live and work in places where the languages they write about are most commonly spoken. The chronological scope of the essays goes from the Middle Ages to the present day and the geographical spread is equally broad. Some of the contributors focus on processes of human mobility to emphasize the consequences or legacies of transnational displacements. Others identify instances of the transnational in particular localities and bring out its transformative effects in apparently settled communities. In a few cases, authors bring transnational thinking to bear on questions that do not seem, at first glance, to have much to do with the issues of migration and demographic change with which transnationalism as a concept has been commonly associated.

Each essay in *A Handbook* expresses and is underpinned by the lived experience of its author and their particular history of cultural and linguistic connectedness. Some quite explicitly make biographical connections between writer and subject matter, while others are more reticent about bringing that link to the fore. In other respects, too, the essays diverge in terms of style. Some adopt an almost conversational tone, reflecting directly on both the research and writing process, while others appear to retain a more distanced perspective. Yet each articulates the active, real-time and human practice of work in Modern Languages and offers suggestions on how to operate across languages and cultures in everyday life and professional practice.

One of *A Handbook*'s most striking features is that its authors create a field of study as they go along. They do not attempt to analyse a pre-existing body of work or explicate a pre-determined area of disciplinary knowledge. Each keyword serves as a prompt to think about how languages, cultures, objects, and modes of critical enquiry come into contact with one another in one particular instance from one particular perspective. They touch, influence, and irritate in ways that are unpredictable and surprising. What counts in these essays is not the detail of these contacts, but rather the fact that these contacts took place, are identifiable, and that they made a difference to interpretations of language and culture seen solely in national, or singular terms. A different researcher working with a different set of linguistic and cultural co-ordinates would have made different transnational connections as they worked with their chosen keyword. There is no ambition to define, or lay claim to, the term itself. One of the functions of the keyword is to foreground the creative and intellectual agency of the researcher in calling on disciplinary expertise and subjective experience as platforms from which to engage in the critical exploration of connectivity. In consequence, the authors openly display the ways in which knowledge is actively produced, inviting their readers to draw on their own, varied, and possibly idiosyncratic linguistic and cultural toolkit to devise patterns of cultural connectedness that are transnational both in terms of the constellations they describe, but more particularly in terms of the critical imagination they bring to bear on their identification and analysis of how patterns of transnational connectivity put pressure on bounded understandings of national cultures and allow for more inclusive and flexible forms of cultural and linguistic cohabitation.

This form of creative critical practice extends to and includes the readers of this *Handbook*. The essays are not grouped in sections nor placed in a specific order and instead invite readers to plot their own itineraries through the materials, tracing and developing different connections between keywords according to resonances in the content or approach of the essays and according also to their own work and thinking at any one time of reading. As this suggests, readers may read different clusters of essays in different combinations at different times in their use of *A Handbook* and of the other volumes in the series; they may read two or three essays repeatedly and another never; an essay that may suggest little to them on first reading may acquire sharpened significance on second and subsequent readings when placed in relation to another essay in *A Handbook* or to a book, sound, film, phrase, object, or encounter experienced elsewhere. At different points in a study or research programme, different kinds of reading might be used along a spectrum from distant readings of multiple essays to map lateral connections and inspire flexible methods of critical analysis, to minute and intimate readings of a single essay as a critical counterpart in developing an analytical response to a specific question, task, or project. If *A Handbook* is to achieve its aims, it will very simply be kept to hand throughout an extended itinerary of engagement with the range of materials, experiences and ideas that populate work in and beyond Modern Languages.

Definitions are avoided in *A Handbook* and their place is taken by demonstrations of active critical practice. The list of keywords themselves has no ambition to demarcate the intellectual field of Modern Languages nor to explain it exhaustively. The motivation that drove the selection of keywords was to prompt questions and creative reflection rather than instant and assured recognition. With this in mind, certain terms that researchers in Modern Languages regard as core to their current and forward-looking thinking may seem to be absent. 'Race', 'gender', 'visual culture', and 'memory', for instance, are terms that have long been prominent in research and in the curriculum in Modern Languages and related degrees, and will continue to be at the forefront of enquiry. As this implies, they are terms that critical practitioners of languages 'know', and also know to be shifting in terms of their range, conceptual re-tuning, and the objects of critical analysis that they engage. Other handbooks, readers, and introductory volumes furnish extensive and inclusive explorations of these terms. In *A Handbook*, they instead inhabit various other keywords and the essays that discuss them, offering dynamic and perhaps disruptive evidence of the insistence of questions of race, for example, in activities or experiences where it is not instinctively known to be a pertinent category of understanding.

'Transnational' is similarly everywhere in *A Handbook* and in all of the volumes in the series that it accompanies but nowhere as a keyword in this collection. The purpose of the series is to demonstrate that the transnational is an optic owning the capacity to sharpen our insight into any question or experience related to languages and cultures and, as such, the term is multiply and persistently present. 'Translation' as a key practice and concept of transnational critical thinking is comparably extensive and penetrating and yet often goes unremarked or under-investigated, regarded as a given of global linguistic and cultural practice and as a default in the skill set and the working practice of a linguist. Precisely because translation is fundamental to fathoming how languages and cultures touch one another and interact, there are three essays in *A Handbook* that address translation from different perspectives, challenging readers to recognize the radius of specific knowledge that a focus on translation exposes. Two essays explore 'Stories' in order to prompt diverse consideration of the extent to which the narratives that humans tell, through verbal, visual, aural, and sensory communication between languages and cultures, construct understanding of particular places, times, and experiences. Two essays addressed to 'Me' tell two such stories that invite reflection on how languages and cultures inflect individual, embodied subjectivity in specific settings and encounters.

Recognition of the unique positionality of the active student and researcher is an undergirding principle of *A Handbook*, whether in approaching the collection as an author or a reader or both. The volume aims to encourage readers confidently to bring into their engagement with the essays their own sense of their purposes, curiosities, and anxieties in investigating linguistic and cultural interactions. A reader who approaches the ideas offered in the essays both armed with the knowledge developed through their own intelligence, experience, and feelings and at the same time disarmed by the awareness of not knowing quite how readers or writers of other formations might apprehend the same material is a reader in a powerful position to acquire new understanding and, in doing so, to create new knowledge. Displacing any rigid connection between the materials analysed and a specific language or domain of expertise, the essays ask readers (and authors) persistently to put themselves in someone else's shoes and to find out how it feels when things mis-fit and what can be learned when a part of themselves comes to adapt to and feel like a part of someone or something else. The possibilities opened up by strangeness and discomfort, as well as awareness of the pain and exclusion that they may bring, are what there is to be explored and gained through the conjoined study of languages and cultures, and what *A Handbook* seeks to foster and inspire.

This tentative poise between being at once inside and outside the languages and cultures of others – along with the critical and creative opportunities of analysing the effects of being between – is the position that most who study and teach Modern Languages inhabit. Definitions of the work that is done under that broad disciplinary heading are endlessly problematic: the vitality of the interconnecting fields known as Modern Languages lies in part in their inclusive intellectual capacity to range purposefully into other disciplines and to share reciprocal forms of expertise in order to co-produce new understanding. Essays in this volume, its title, and the title of the entire series use the term 'Modern Languages' as the expedient that it is to denote a disciplinary area and practice that readers recognize and variously identify their own work with, but all uses of the term in the essays equally connote the challenge of defining a discipline that progresses as dynamically and inventively as the languages and cultures that are its object. In this sense, *A Handbook* and the volumes with which it dialogues offer an active contribution to and critical reflection on the ongoing process of making a field of knowledge and expert practice. This is a process that the essays in this volume pause to take critical stock of without envisaging closure and instead aiming to pilot informed and distinctly orientated progression into knowledge futures that the volume and series may contribute to shaping.

Vocabularies of 'other' languages and cultures, 'other' academic disciplines, and 'inside'/'outside' are useful in nominating the position that practised students and researchers in Modern Languages occupy and the specific value of their expertise, but they also whisper of the very boundaries that understanding of languages and cultures reveals often to be artificial, or at least artificially binary. Working with a language and the cultures associated with it becomes almost instantly a practice of identifying patterns and processes largely in terms of their relations with plural languages and cultures, geographically and linguistically both proximate and distant. For this reason, to begin from a transnational perspective in approaching languages and cultures and to apprehend the construction of national languages and cultures within that broad panorama enables an academic practice that speaks coherently to the evidence of how languages and cultures operate and interact across spaces and times. Stepping into another's shoes is not just an act performed by a speaker of one language when speaking in a distinct other language: the combined possibilities and constraints of that act are also the repeated and various lived experience of human subjects across the globe, linguists included.

A further step takes the critical analyst of languages and cultures – or of the 'humanities' – beyond the anthropocentric systems of communication and engagement foregrounded so far in this introduction into forms of co-production of understanding with non-human agents of the planet that humans share. The disposition as well as the expertise common to those who work with Modern Languages – that drive to discover how unfamiliarity or dislocation feels – has long motivated researchers in the broad field to explore the sentience of physical forces and presences in the planetary environment and of non-human animals, and to envision techniques of knowing and communicating in contexts where human reason is displaced or redundant. Likewise, understanding of how cultures work exceeds the canon of cultural artefacts conventionally associated with Modern Languages and extends into histories and geographies of human co-habitations with the non-human, and into stories or speculations of how human and non-human make sense of, or with, one another. Essays in *A Handbook* that speak of soil, coral, seas, animals, climate, plants, and visions of the beyond-human diversely voice this enquiry. Seen in this light, the awareness of borders, risk, damage, and also creative transgression that 'meanness' articulates may inform a kind of intersectional awareness across human and non-human thresholds as well as within an anthropocentric purview of languages and cultures.

It is in mindful recognition of the precarious connection between processes and experiences selected as an object of intellectual enquiry and those same processes and experiences endured in everyday planetary life, whether beneficial or not, that the ethical charge of work in Modern Languages weighs. Here, too, rests its capacity to contribute purposefully to understanding of societal and ecological patterns and challenges such as mobility, inequality of opportunity and access, social injustice, climate injustice, rights, community, identities, and communication. Languages matter and make difference in the lives of individuals, communities, and the non-human environment, so knowing languages and how they operate is an instrument of meaningful participation and intervention in the world, as the essays in *A Handbook* diversely and imaginatively enact.

We extend our thanks to the Arts and Humanities Research Council (AHRC) and specifically its 'Translating Cultures' theme for support of the collaborative research project from which this volume, and the 'Transnational Modern Languages' series, were developed: 'Transnationalizing Modern Languages: Mobility, Identity and Translation in Modern Italian Cultures' (2014–2017). To have open access to this volume was an important principle for us as editors, and in realizing this we are grateful for the financial support from 'Translating Cultures', the University of Bristol and the Institute for Modern Languages Research. We thank also Chloé Johnson at Liverpool

University Press for her positive and expert guidance throughout. Lastly, we are indebted to the external readers of the draft manuscript and to all of our contributors for the critical imagination, expertise, and energy they have channelled into individual essays and into the volume as a shared venture. We have been consistently inspired by their responses to our idea of what this volume could become.

1

# Animal

*Florian Mussgnug*

> *When the last animal disappears, the sun will die out and never rise again.*
>
> Oxana Timofeeva[1]

What is it like to be a bat? When philosopher Thomas Nagel asked this question, more than forty years ago, he wished to draw attention to the subjective character of conscious experience: the unique phenomenon that, for Nagel, is essentially connected with every single human and non-human point of view and that cannot be described in objective, physical terms. We all believe, Nagel remarks, that bats experience the world. And yet, their range of activity and sensory apparatus are so profoundly different from ours that it seems impossible for us to imagine what their subjective experience might be like. For how could we think and feel the world through different senses? 'It will not help to try to imagine that one has webbing on one's arms, which enables one to fly around at dusk and dawn catching insects in one's mouth', writes the philosopher, or 'that one has very poor vision, and perceives the surrounding world by a system of reflected high-frequency sound signals; and that one spends the day hanging upside down by one's feet in an attic'. Even if we were able to imagine this – and Nagel appears doubtful – then we would only be imagining what it is like, for *us*, to behave as a bat behaves: 'To the extent that I could look and behave like a wasp or a bat, without changing

[1] Oxana Timofeeva, 'Animal', in *Posthuman Glossary*, ed. by Rosi Braidotti and Maria Hlavajova (London and New York: Bloomsbury, 2018), pp. 34–36 (p. 36; my emphasis).

my fundamental structure, my experiences would not be anything like the experiences of those animals'.[2]

There is something strangely suggestive about the idea of a distinguished philosopher performing the sensory habits of microchiroptera. Nagel's thought-experiment anticipates the grotesque, humanoid animal figures brought to life in numerous recent works of video and performance art: from Jan Fabre's *A Consilience* (2000), in which specialists at the London Natural History Museum dress as the animals of their research, to the melancholy bear-man in Mark Wallinger's *Sleeper* (2004), and from Marcus Coates's surreal stag-man in *Journey to the Lower World* (2004) to Edwina Ashton's two-minute video *Bat* (2005), in which a costumed human in the guise of the leathery-winged creature obsessively polishes the inside of a cramped, dusty broom cupboard.[3] Such apparent similarities, however, do not point towards a common purpose or shared understanding of the animal other. As cultural critic Ron Broglio observes, contemporary art often stages the relation with the non-human as a contact between radically different worlds: a troubling encounter at the limits of human perception, where 'the friction and opacity of other ways of being' resists full assimilation into human language, but triggers 'a sense of infectious wonder' that becomes the enabling condition for artistic creativity.[4] According to Broglio, creative engagement with non-human animal worlds is ethical, precisely because it transcends our ability to comprehend. 'Absolute knowledge', he writes, 'and full presence [are] denied to the viewer [but] we sense that there is something beneath the surface of the animal', and it is this opaque, incomplete awareness that reminds us that humans and the more-than-human world do not only interact but, more importantly, are co-constitutive.[5] Donna Haraway makes a similar point when she affirms that 'positive knowledge of and with animals might just be possible, knowledge that is positive in quite a radical sense if it is not built on the Great Divides'.[6] Creative explorations of animal phenomenology, in other words, enable new forms of shared knowledge, beyond the familiar scaffolding of anthropocentric humanism. Their open-ended engagement

[2] Thomas Nagel, 'What Is It Like to Be a Bat?', *The Philosophical Review*, 83.4 (1974), 435–50 (p. 439).

[3] Jan Fabre, *A Consilience*, video, 2000; Mark Wallinger, *Sleeper*, Neue Nationalgalerie, Berlin, performance, 14–22 October 2004; Marcus Coates, *Journey to the Lower World*, video, 2004; Edwina Ashton, *Bat*, video, 2005.

[4] Ron Broglio, *Surface Encounters: Thinking with Animals and Art* (Minneapolis and London: University of Minnesota Press, 2011), p. xx and p. xxiii.

[5] Broglio, *Surface Encounters*, p. 18.

[6] Donna J. Haraway, *When Species Meet* (Minneapolis and London: University of Minnesota Press, 2008), p. 21.

with the more-than-human world 'draws us into an endless progression of other questions about specific animals and their lives'.[7]

Nagel's critique of materialist theories of mind, by contrast, treats the interiority of animal experience, from a human point of view, as absolutely unintelligible: 'Our own experience provides the basic material for our imagination, whose range is therefore limited'.[8] Pronouns are revealing in this context. While the first-person singular and plural are used by Nagel to denote humanity, without regard to historical or cultural difference, this sense of shared belonging is never extended to non-human animals. Nagel readily admits that there is some continuity of traits, including psychological traits, among closely related species, but rejects the idea that humanlike mental states may be inferred from humanlike behaviour. Humans regularly refer to non-human animals to exemplify values, experiences, and fantasies, but such seemingly sympathetic representations of the non-human, for Nagel, are merely anthropocentric projections. Indeed, the philosopher remarks, human empathy and sympathy tend to focus on a relatively small group of large, vaguely anthropomorphic mammals: 'I have chosen bats instead of wasps or flounders because if one travels too far down the phylogenetic tree, people gradually shed their faith that there is experience there at all'.[9]

As literary theorist Cary Wolfe has shown, Nagel's critique is directed against the idea of a confidently transparent human language that can fully articulate animal otherness.[10] Non-human consciousness, according to Nagel, eludes every attempt at linguistic mediation, despite the common practice 'of treating cultural representations of animals [...] as screens for the projection of human interests and meanings'.[11] The philosopher's robust critique of anthropocentrism thus relies on a peculiarly anthropocentric contention: for Nagel, there cannot be any symbolic opening to the more-than-human world. The non-human animal is not literally without a language, but its darkness or muteness, for *us*, is absolute. Viewed from an ethical perspective, this 'skeptical terror about the independent existence of other minds', as animal trainer and poet Vicki Hearn puts it, appears to drive a problematic fantasy of essential difference that runs counter to actual experiences of human

[7] Broglio, *Surface Encounters*, p. xxii.

[8] Nagel, 'Bat', p. 439.

[9] Nagel, 'Bat', p. 438.

[10] Cary Wolfe, 'In the Shadow of Wittgenstein's Lion: Language, Ethics, and the Question of the Animal', in *Zoontologies: The Question of the Animal*, ed. by Cary Wolfe (Minneapolis and London: University of Minnesota Press, 2003), pp. 1–58 (p. 9).

[11] Phillip Armstrong, *What Animals Mean in the Fiction of Modernity* (London and New York: Routledge, 2015), p. 2.

contingency and materiality, and to everyday interactions between creatures with vastly different phenomenologies.[12]

Contemporary accounts of animality and humanity have mostly embraced Wolfe's and Hearn's views, and have sought to illuminate the numerous and profound relations between species. The challenge, as Paul Waldau puts it, has been to get beyond human-centredness and to develop multiple focal points, including an enquiry into 'the actual biological, communal, individual, and even personal realities' of non-human species.[13] This attention to shared imaginative and ethical faculties, at the intersection of the human and the non-human, runs directly counter to traditional anthropocentric worldviews, in which the animal is depicted as having limited facilities, measured against every standard in which humans consider themselves superior, and dismissed as inferior to the human, or so foreign as to be untranslatable. Recent studies, by contrast, show that numerous non-human species possess the capabilities deemed necessary for subjectivity: self-consciousness, rational agency, the capacity to learn and transmit language.[14] Consequently, cross-species semiosis has been re-defined, no longer in terms of a more or less complete access to a single (human) ideological and linguistic system, but on the basis of affective patterns that are grounded in a shared pre-linguistic or counter-linguistic sense of belonging. As Michael Cronin explains, our superior scientific understanding of animal lives and cultures – through advances in biology, anthropology, and ethics – has destabilized conventional ideas of the primacy of the human. Communication between species is no longer viewed as an asymmetrical relation that privileges the human, but explored through transdisciplinary metaphors of translation and mediation that have their origin in the comparative humanities.[15]

In this context, Nagel's question, too, has developed a cultural life of its own, and continues to resonate powerfully in the cross-disciplinary framework that links literature, philosophy, the environmental humanities, and the fine arts. Les Murray's poem 'Bat's Ultrasound', for example, makes a subtle effort to give voice to the seemingly inscrutable, winged protagonist of Nagel's enquiry. Bewildering juxtapositions of anthropomorphic and zoomorphic

[12] Vicki Hearn, *Adam's Task: Calling Animals by Name* (New York: Random House, 1987), p. 223.

[13] Paul Waldau, *Animal Studies: An Introduction* (Oxford and New York: Oxford University Press, 2013), p. 4.

[14] See, for example, Paola Cavalieri and Peter Singer (eds), *The Great Ape Project* (New York: St Martin's Press, 1993).

[15] See Michael Cronin, *Eco-Translation: Translation and Ecology in the Age of the Anthropocene* (London and New York: Routledge, 2016).

onomatopoeia work here to erode conceptual boundaries, trigger complex and contradictory longings, and dislodge the reader from their supposedly objective standpoint, as can be seen from this exclamation:

> *ah, eyrie-ire; aero hour, eh?*
> *O'er our ur-area (our era aye*
> *ere your raw row) we air our array*
> *err, yaw, row wry—aura our orrery,*
> *our eerie ü our ray, our arrow.*
>
> *A rare ear, our aery Yahweh.*[16]

A similarly radical, but differently imaginative response to Nagel comes from the Australian novelist Elizabeth Costello: the fictional protagonist of J.M. Coetzee's 1997 Tanner Lectures, *The Lives of Animals*.[17] Written in the form of two linked short stories, this hybrid text narrates Costello's visit to a North American college, where she has been invited to give two public talks on non-human animal life. Foregrounding the tension between philosophical and literary perspectives, Costello proclaims that philosophical anthropocentrism, from a moral standpoint, is simply a failure of the imagination. Human exceptionalism – the belief that humans are essentially different from all other species – is a dogmatic slumber, that makes us oblivious to the demands of biosocial kinship. Against this tendency, Costello evokes the power of a sympathetic, creative imagination, which she believes can fully capture the experiences of different species: 'If I can think my way into the existence of a being who has never existed', she declares, 'then I can think my way into the existence of a bat or a chimpanzee or an oyster, any being with whom I share the substrate of life'.[18] And, in specific response to Thomas Nagel, she proclaims:

> But he is wrong; or at least he is sending us down a false trail. To be a living bat is to be full of being; being fully a bat is like being fully human, which is also to be full of being. Bat being in the first case,

[16] Les Murray, 'Bat's Ultrasound' (1992), in *Collected Poems* (Manchester: Carcanet Press, 1998), p. 368 (my emphasis).

[17] J.M. Coetzee, *The Lives of Animals*, ed. and introduction by Amy Gutman (Princeton: Princeton University Press, 1999). A revised version, without footnotes, appears in *Elizabeth Costello: Eight Lessons* (London: Secker and Warburg, 2003). Subsequent references will be to this version of the text.

[18] Coetzee, *Elizabeth Costello*, p. 80.

human being in the second, maybe; but those are secondary considerations. To be full of being is to live as a body-soul. One name for the experience of full being is joy.[19]

What is it like to be an animal? To make sense of this question, Jacques Derrida surmises, we must think beyond the pseudo-concept of 'the animal', used in the singular, as though all non-human species from the oyster to the chimpanzee constituted a homogenous set to which human beings are radically opposed.[20] 'The animal' in the singular, for Derrida, epitomizes our species' logocentric desire for mastery, which he believes is embraced and taken for granted by Western philosophers from Aristotle to Martin Heidegger. As historian Aaron Gross intimates: 'When the reality of animals becomes "the animal" – that is, a foil and shadow of the human – an opportunity arises, which may or may not be actualized, to forget animals themselves'.[21] For Derrida, this potential 'absenting of animals' – our actual, existing fellow creatures – finds its logical and moral counterpoint in a utopian desire for the absence of the animal, understood as an abstract category. At a lexical level, this utopian longing is marked by Derrida's neologism *animot:* a word that, when spoken in French, recalls the extreme diversity of actual animals (*animaux*) that the abstract category erases, but that also makes us aware, in a typically Derridean shift of signification, that we inevitably depend on the abstract singular (*animal*) that is nothing more, precisely, than a word (*mot*).

Derrida's robust critique of 'carnophallogocentric' Western philosophy echoes profoundly in contemporary human–animal studies, and has inspired an influx of radical voices, across disciplines, and a new idiom centred on companionship and shared vulnerability.[22] Elizabeth Costello's attack on anthropocentrism, in *The Lives of Animals*, is an integral part of this cultural project. As philosopher Cora Diamond has argued, Coetzee's lectures articulate an existential 'woundedness or hauntedness': a painful awareness of the horror of what we do to animals, and an astonishment and incomprehension that this violence should be inflicted on beings who are so capable

[19] Coetzee, *Elizabeth Costello*, pp. 77–78.

[20] Jacques Derrida, *The Animal That Therefore I Am*, trans. by David Wills (New York: Fordham University Press, 2008).

[21] Aaron Gross, *The Question of the Animal and Religion: Theoretical Stakes, Practical Implications* (New York: Columbia University Press, 2015), pp. 187–88.

[22] See, for example, Kelly Oliver, *Animal Lessons: How They Teach Us to be Human* (New York: Columbia University Press, 2009); Cary Wolfe, *Before the Law: Humans and other Animals in a Biopolitical Frame* (Chicago and London: University of Chicago Press, 2013).

of being our companions.[23] Costello, writes philosopher Ian Hacking, 'is shattered by the meat industry, our callow inability to recognize and respect animal lives as lived, our creation of imbecile experiments on them, and our arrogant philosophies about them. She hates our incessant pointing at animals combined with our complete indifference to all but the pets'.[24]

Derrida concurs. The deplorable conditions of non-human animals, writes the French philosopher, are 'all too well known', but they must be hidden from our view, since we could not otherwise endure such immense suffering. The oppressive social order premised on animal suffering is unbearable, since it runs counter to our most basic and innate sense of a meaningful existence: 'the human well-being of man'.[25] Hidden away in laboratories and factory farms, slaughtered at mass disassembly plants, and transformed into sanitized packages of meat, non-human animals have become a focus for reflection in ethics, cultural and literary studies, sociology, anthropology, and economics, because, paradoxically, they have ceased to be visible in the daily experience of most humans. As cultural critic Akira Mizuta Lippit points out, 'modernity can be defined by the disappearance of wildlife from humanity's habitat and by the reappearance of the same in humanity's reflections on itself'.[26]

What is it like to be human? Our answer here depends crucially on the emergent concept of the Anthropocene: the idea that Earth has left its most recent geological epoch, the Holocene, as a consequence of human activity. First proposed by atmospheric scientist Paul Crutzen and ecologist Eugene Stoermer, the Anthropocene has more recently become a staging ground for debates about the future of global capitalism, environmental justice, and the political and cultural effects of population growth, climate change, and biodiversity loss.[27] Planetary approaches reverberate across the arts, humanities, and social sciences, and have emphasized the intersection of social systems with non-human phenomena. Human action impinges directly upon climate patterns, drought zones, glacier flows, species evolution, and so on, which in turn condition and compromise the future of human and non-human life on

[23] Cora Diamond, 'The Difficulty of Reality and the Difficulty of Philosophy', *Partial Answers*, 1.2 (2003), 1–26.

[24] Ian Hacking, 'Deflections', in *Philosophy and Animal Life*, ed. by Stanley Cavell, Cora Diamond et al. (New York: Columbia University Press, 2008), pp. 139–72 (p. 144).

[25] Derrida, *The Animal*, p. 25.

[26] Akira Mizuta Lippit, *Electric Animal: Toward a Rhetoric of Wildlife* (Minneapolis: University of Minnesota Press, 2000), pp. 2–3.

[27] Paul J. Crutzen and Eugene F. Stoermer, 'The Anthropocene', *Global Change Newsletter*, 41 (2000), 17–18.

Earth. As Stacy Alaimo points out, 'the human is always inter-meshed with the more-than-human world'.[28]

In this context, elegiac and melodramatic narratives of animal suffering and extinction foster a nostalgic and pessimistic attitude towards the future, as Ursula Heise has shown.[29] They leave little room for environmental activism or alternative forms of multi-species cohabitation. Eminent conservationists and environmental philosophers have argued that there is little hope, at this stage, to counter the catastrophic consequences of anthropogenic climate change, and that all realistic measures must focus on limiting the pace and extent of environmental devastation. According to Donna Haraway, it is difficult to maintain any hope for the future, or to perpetuate individual or collective efforts to improve the lives of human and non-human others. A 'game-over attitude' appears sadly appropriate and yet, Haraway contends, 'there is a fine line between acknowledging the extent and seriousness of the troubles and succumbing to abstract futurism and its affects of sublime despair and its politics of sublime indifference'.[30] As the shared future of our damaged planet appears increasingly unpredictable, is it time to return to the concept of the animal, with its rich and nuanced history of controversy around essence, vulnerability, and the possibility of encounter? The cultural force of the animal, it has been argued, is only partly located in any specific non-human other, and accrues power and value across multiple figurations. Similarly, in times of growing uncertainty, the planetary future of the human species can only be understood as a process of becoming. What is it like to be us?

Florian Mussgnug is Professor of Comparative Literature and Italian Studies at University College London.

[28] Stacy Alaimo, *Bodily Natures: Science, Environment, and the Material Self* (Bloomington: Indiana University Press, 2010), p. 2.

[29] Ursula K. Heise, *Imagining Extinction: The Cultural Meanings of Endangered Species* (Chicago: University of Chicago Press, 2016).

[30] Donna J. Haraway, *Staying with the Trouble: Making Kin in the Chthulucene* (Durham, NC and London: Duke University Press, 2016), p. 4.

# 2

# Bilingualism

*Claudia Peralta*

> So, if you want to really hurt me, talk badly about my language. Ethnic identity is twin skin to linguistic identity – I am my language. Until I can take pride in my language, I cannot take pride in myself.
>
> Gloria Anzaldúa[1]

## The Political and Moral Dilemma of Bilingualism

Speaking another language besides English in the United States has become a double-edged sword in the education of students. At times the nation has favoured the education of children using their native language. Bilingual education flourished in the nineteenth century especially in places inhabited by German immigrants, as well as in French, Spanish, and Cherokee communities. Many of these early bilingual schools were not bilingual; they were schools in which English was not spoken – English was taught as a subject. Eventually, the first bilingual schools opened their doors before 1800 and they were mostly parochial. In 1839 Ohio became the first state to adopt a bilingual education law, authorizing German–English instruction at parents' request.[2] Louisiana also passed an identical provision for French and English in 1847,

[1] Gloria Anzaldúa, 'How to Tame a Wild Tongue', in *Borderlands/la frontera: The New Mestiza* (San Francisco: Aunt Lute, 1987), pp. 53–64 (p. 59).

[2] I use the term 'parents' to include not only biological parents but also non-biological parents, caregivers, and extended families who are involved in raising a child.

and the New Mexico Territory did so for Spanish and English in 1850. By the end of the nineteenth century, approximately a dozen states had passed similar laws. However, this changed during the First World War era. Fears about the loyalty of non-English speakers in general, but specifically of German Americans, pushed the enactment of laws to 'Americanize' these groups. In 1864 Congress had prohibited Native-American children from being taught in their own languages. By 1920 bilingual education was dismantled throughout the country. The preferred way to instruct students was through English-only instruction.

However, bilingual education resurfaced in the mid-twentieth century because emergent bilinguals[3] – often referred to as English learners – were plunging behind in their academic studies and dropping out of school at alarming rates. In 1967 and 1974 bilingual education was once again implemented. It was recognized on the basis of what seemed to be evident by its very reason for being: the best medium for teaching is its mother tongue. The reaction of many, in the first years of this experiment, was to wait and see. Despite not being convinced by the initiative, some were willing to give it an opportunity to test its potential to reduce inequalities. Others worried that bilingual education might prevent Spanish-speaking students from entering the mainstream of English-speaking American society by creating a cultural divide. Yet another strike at eliminating bilingual education re-emerged in 2002 when Silicon Valley millionaire Ron Unz spearheaded four initiatives to ban bilingual education. California, Arizona, and Massachusetts passed the initiative.

Even though history has shown the repercussion of the linguistic terrorism imposed on Native Americans who had to wait seventy years to have the right to learn their own language, these practices continue to be overtly and subversively imposed in classrooms. Unfortunately, the practice of demanding students to speak only English in the classroom continues to be a common practice among educators. English-only laws, enacted in thirty-two states, make English the official language, banning Spanish and other languages from being spoken in classrooms.[4] In a study I conducted to examine how Latino students[5]

[3] Refers to students whose bilingualism is emerging. In this essay it is used to refer to students who are developing English.

[4] Art Moore, '32 States Make English Official Language', *WND*, <https://www.wnd.com/2018/01/32-states-make-english-official-language/> [accessed 13 May 2021].

[5] Who were either born in Mexico and had immigrated with their families to the United States or were first generation Mexican-Americans. In this essay I will use the term Latino to refer specifically to people of Latin American nationality living in the United States. Latin American refers to countries in South America and North America (including central America and the islands of the Caribbean).

experience education in rural areas in Idaho,[6] as well as in the documentary *Latinos in Treasure Valley, Idaho* (2012),[7] not embracing students' language was a central marker identified to have a devastating impact on their lives in school settings. Many of the students talked about how they arrived at school with their *maletas* (backpacks) filled with treasures, stories, and language experiences, and yet, they were not allowed to use them or to bring them into the schools, into the classroom.[8] Inexplicitly, they were asked to drop them at the school steps because, once inside, English becomes the only official language. The fact that they were proficient in Spanish instead of English guaranteed them a placement below grade level, often a seat in the back of the room, or time in the resource room.[9]

A case in point is the story of Jasmín,[10] who returned from Mexico to the United States to start second grade. She was demoted one grade because she didn't know English. She was literate in Spanish, but this was seen as a deficit instead of an asset. Additionally, for several hours during the day she was pulled into the resource room and, as she revealed, 'out of madness, I forced myself to learn to read [English] quickly'.[11] Another student remembered being asked by her teacher to stop speaking Spanish in the classroom. She agreed but looking back she realizes that she didn't really understand why she couldn't use her home language. A different student recalled: 'I felt frustrated because I didn't understand English and I couldn't answer the teacher. At night I would cry because I didn't want to be in school. I wanted my parents to take me out of school'.[12] These students (as well as many others) were either forbidden to speak their language or relegated to an inferior status in school. Despite the common belief that the United States is a country in which diversity is welcome, languages spoken by minority groups have often been under attack, and regularly relegated to an inferior

[6] Definition of rural areas by the National Center for Education Statistics, *NCES*, <http://nces.ed.gov/pubs2007/ruraled/exhibit_a.asp> [accessed 13 May 2021].

[7] *Latinos in Treasure Valley Idaho*, dir. by Fabio Caramaschi (2012), <http://www.youtube.com/watch?v=9EnNfaJYr4M&feature=youtu.be> [accessed 13 May 2021].

[8] The Merrow Foundation, *Learning Matters: Lost in Translation – Latinos, Schools & Society* (1998), <https://www.youtube.com/watch?v=2qtVWEbtOQY> [accessed 13 May 2021].

[9] This separate remedial classroom is run mostly by paraprofessionals (teacher assistants) who are often not formally trained to work with emergent bilinguals.

[10] The names used for the participants are pseudonyms for the purpose of this essay.

[11] Claudia Peralta, 'Leave Your *maletas* at Home. Education for English Language Learners in Rural Idaho', *The Blue Review* (2014), <https://wayback.archive-it.org/8092/20190724182028/https://thebluereview.org/ell-rural-idaho/> [accessed 13 May 2021].

[12] Peralta, 'Leave Your *maletas* at Home'.

position. This attack is clearly exemplified by the memo written in a Staff News bulletin distributed at a public school:

> When you have 21 languages spoken at one school, there is a lot of ways to swear! We are struggling to manage it. So, for now, we speak ENGLISH at school. Don't ask students to translate for you. If you hear another language, say kindly that we speak English at school. (Email communication, 31 January 2017)

Sadly, policies like this continue to support linguistic hierarchies in which we often perform. We are asking students to drop the language at the door of the school steps, thus becoming someone without a sense of self and without the tools to succeed. The unstated policy of *English only* at the school demonstrates the fear of the other – the unknown – on how it impacts and devastates the educational experiences of emergent bilinguals. What is more, language demands are also placed on parents who are often forced to choose between speaking to their children in their home language or using the language of the dominant social group. In *Hunger of Memory: The Education of Richard Rodriguez*, the author and main protagonist shares his linguistic experience.[13] He began Kindergarten knowing only fifty English words. Because his English was not improving as rapidly as expected, the nuns from the school visited the parents and asked them to speak more English with Richard. Eager to help their son, both of them complied. '*Ahora*, speak to us *en inglés*', they would say.[14] Ultimately, this forced choice causes disconnect between generations of language speakers, and a loss of family ties, traditions, and cultural memory. This is well documented in the study conducted by Ngo[15] with Hmong community leaders on how the exclusionary practices of the schools contribute to the children's Hmong language loss and the ignorance of the refugee experiences and sacrifices of their parents. Yes, Richard Rodriguez became more confident in the English language and he is now a respected writer, but he vividly recounts the profound silence that dominated his childhood. Sadly, this resulted in the erosion of the bond between him and his parents.

The nuns' lack of appreciation for the culture and linguistic wealth that existed in Richard's home continues to be one of the biggest challenges

[13] Richard Rodriguez, *Hunger of Memory: The Education of Richard Rodriguez* (New York: The Dial Press, 1982).

[14] Rodriguez, *Hunger of Memory*, p. 30.

[15] Bic Ngo, 'The Costs of "Living the Dream" for Hmong Immigrants: The Impact of Subtractive Schooling of Family and Community', *Educational Studies*, 53.5 (2016), 450–67. DOI: 10.1080/00131946.2016.1258361

facing educators in the United States. How can we help educators realize the wealth and relevancy that culturally and linguistically diverse families and students bring into the schools? How can we help them understand that the economic, social, and cultural differences are assets and not detriments for the educational success of these students? As educators, we have the power to determine whether students feel included or excluded in our schools and classrooms: 'Teaching about language and power is huge, complex and messy because language policies and colonial practices played out in different ways across the globe'.[16] However, as a bilingual/multi-cultural education professor, answering these questions has led me to design an integrated project extending educators' understanding of learners beyond the wall of the classrooms and into their home communities. As Brazilian educator Paulo Freire stresses in his book *Teachers as Cultural Workers*:

> Educators need to know what happens in the world of the children with whom they work. They need to know the universe of their dreams, the language with which they skilfully defend themselves from the aggressiveness of their world, what they know independently of the school, and how they know it.[17]

The *Child, Community and Context Study* project[18] not only invites educators to visit the homes of the culturally and linguistic diverse learners, but invites them to engage in community walks and encourages them 'being present' when talking to community and family members and the learners, hence affording them the opportunity to understand the wealth of knowledge that exists in communities and homes.[19] The project has four components: (a) Community/Cultural Observations, (b) Focus Children Observation, (c) Informal Chat with Students, and (d) Home Visit. Asking educators to step beyond the classroom

[16] Linda Christensen, 'Uncovering the Legacy of Language and Power', in *Rethinking Bilingual Education. Welcoming Home Languages in the Classroom*, ed. by Elizabeth Barbian, Grace Cornell Gonzales, and Pilar Mejía (Milwaukee: Rethinking Schools, 2017), pp. 98–99.

[17] Paulo Freire, *Teachers as Cultural Workers: Letters to Those Who Dare Teach* (Boulder: Westview Press, 1998), p. 34.

[18] This project is the signature assignment for a graduate class taught to educators who are returning to college to obtain English as a new language endorsement (twenty credits of coursework, which includes a field experience). This endorsement certifies that educators are prepared to work with culturally and linguistic diverse students. Unfortunately, the State of Idaho grants teaching credentials without such preparation.

[19] Tara J. Yosso, 'Whose Culture has Capital? A Critical Race Theory Discussion of Community Cultural Wealth', *Race, Ethnicity and Education*, 8.1 (2005), 69–91.

doors to understand their students is important because it moves efforts from simply a cognitive enterprise to a more embodied understanding. This is consistent with what Perkins describes as educational practices that are 'feet first rather than head first', in that the intent is to 'cultivate practical behaviours along with understanding rather than expecting appropriate behaviours to flow from cerebral understanding'.[20] The project brings educators closer to the reality of the lives of the students. The first component affords educators the possibility to spend time walking and observing the neighbourhood where their students live. They are invited to pay attention to the sights and sounds that surround them, such as the kinds of stores, the children's play spaces, and other aspects of life in the community. Then, they are encouraged to interview members of the community to learn about the main assets, goals, and needs. The second part brings them back into the official space (the school) and posits educators to be mindful while observing students' interactions in the classroom context and outside the classroom. They are urged to pay close attention to the language used by the learners to communicate with teachers, peers, and others when asking questions, volunteering to participate in activities, and when socializing during recess and at the cafeteria. Next, educators engage in conversation with the learners. They are asked to be fully present in the conversation, to pay attention or, as it is frequently referred to, 'bare attention'.[21] This means that attention should not be accompanied by efforts to judge, analyse, ignore, or supress feelings but rather be open to whatever thoughts or feelings emerge, providing the opportunity to step back and understand what is going through their minds.[22] This is especially important because it encourages educators to raise questions about their reactions or actions, giving them an opening to choose how to (re)act, an important ability to master as they visit the home of the learners, which is the final part of the project.

Twenty-eight educators participated in the project, seventy per cent of whom were white[23] and sixty per cent had three or more years of teaching

[20] David Perkins, 'Paradoxes of Peace and the Prospects of Peace Education', in *Peace Education. The Concept, Principles, and Practices Around the World*, ed. by Gabriel Salomon and Baruch Nevo (Mahwah, New Jersey: Lawrence Erlbaum Associates, 2001), pp. 37–54 (p. 52).

[21] Joseph Goldstein, *One Dharma: The Emerging Western Buddhism* (New York: Harper, 2002); Bhante Henepola Gunaratana, *Mindfulness in Plain English* (Somerville: Wisdom Publications, 2011), p. 82.

[22] Jan Kabat-Zinn, 'Mindfulness Meditation', in *Healing and the Mind*, ed. by Bill Moyers (New York: Doubleday, 1996), pp. 115–43.

[23] This percentage mirrors the characteristics of the public-school teachers. In the academic year 2017–2018 about eighty per cent of public-school teachers in the United States were white, nine per cent were Hispanic, seven per cent were Black, two per

experience, the full range being from less than one year to seventeen years. Nine were novice educators with two or fewer years of teaching experience. A third of them spoke a language other than English, and Spanish was the spoken language. Before engaging in the assignment, a baseline survey was administered to evaluate how the project impacted their confidence working with linguistically culturally diverse learners and their families.

Substantial positive changes were shown from the baseline surveys to the post-surveys. At baseline, only eleven per cent of educators expressed confidence in conducting home visits; on the post-survey, a tremendous growth in confidence was shown. Seventy per cent responded that they were now confident, and many shared their commitment to conduct them with all students. A follow-up question was how confident they were in developing two-way communication strategies between families and educators. The pre-survey showed fifteen per cent felt confident and the post-survey showed seventy-eight per cent were now confident. Lastly, when asked how often they encouraged culturally and linguistically diverse students to use their home language in the classroom seventy-one per cent of the educators said sometimes; in the post-survey ninety-three percent foster the use of the learners' language.

When educators were pushed to step out into the unofficial school spaces where the learners inhabit, they were hesitant: 'When I first heard that we were going to be doing home visits, I was filled with a sense of dread. I was intimidated and felt like I would be bothering the families' (Greta, final reflection, 2017). Afterwards they were grateful: 'I am glad that I pushed past my fears and went through the home visits. I will never forget them, and I will make a point of doing more of them in the future' (Greta, final reflection, 2017).

Encouraging educators to go into the homes of the learners and giving them time to explore and assurance that something valuable exists to be found helps increase sensitivity to the openness and mindfulness required: 'we left with knowledge about our students that we would never have been able to learn had we not ventured beyond the walls of our school and into the living rooms of our students' (Greta, final reflection, 2017).

> I discovered that as a teacher it is very simple to assume the unknown, but the reality is not always visible. Oftentimes, we work with our

cent were Asian, and one per cent were of two or more races. American Indian/Alaska Native and those who were Pacific Islander each made up less than one per cent of public-school teachers National Center for Education Statistics (NCES), 2017–2018, *Fast Facts on Teacher Characteristics and Trends,* <https://nces.ed.gov/fastfacts/display.asp?id=28> [accessed 13 May 2021].

> students on a daily basis without understanding what they bring from home. All of our students bring a wealth of knowledge from home that can be integrated into our daily instruction to make concepts relevant to their learning. (Rose, final reflection, 2017)

Educators also understood the importance of building relationships with parents. Several acknowledged that now they understand how much value parents place in education and how willing they are to participate in the school communities. These realizations led them to commit to building closer relationships with all parents and inviting them to be part of the school: 'Parents are more likely to participate in school activities and reach out to teachers when a foundation for a relationship is built' (Teresa, final reflection, 2017).

Encouraging educators to 'be present' when conferring with the learners allowed them to listen to their experiences of discrimination, and the shame felt when speaking their native language (Cortney, final reflection, 2017). These opportunities brought educators to a deeper level of understanding on how to ensure learners feel validated as members of the classroom community (Cortney, final reflection, 2017). An entry by an educator read: 'I want to show them [learners] that they have a voice and they can achieve their dreams and they have a lot to contribute to society, regardless of the sometimes negative view society has of Spanish speaking Americans' (Loraine, final reflection, 2017).

Responding to the linguistic and cultural injustices that characterize the lives of many culturally and linguistically diverse students is an obligation and a critical challenge for educators. Developing potent responses to these challenges takes commitment and time. However, giving educators and learners the opportunity to engage in this project prepares them to identify and name the linguistic inequities present in school and society, confront them, and potentially transform them.

Claudia Peralta is a Professor in the Language, Literacy and Culture Department in the College of Education at Boise State University, researching bilingual education, education of teachers working with multilingual learners, family–school partnerships and refugees.

# 3

# Borders

*Elizabeth Nijdam*

When we think of borders, it is physical lines or boundaries between regions and nations that typically come to mind. According to its entry in the *Oxford English Dictionary*, this definition is essential to its meaning: '[t]he boundary line which separates one country from another, the frontier line'.[1] As such, borders demarcate the beginning of one territory and the end of another, often with political and economic implications. They exist as tangible lines on maps and in the geopolitical sphere. Yet while borders feel physical in their division of people and space, they are in fact imagined demarcations of political power made literal through government enforcement. Borders are therefore just as often arbitrary in their construction as they are ineffective in separating the people and places they seek to divide.

So, while we think of borders as objects that physically separate populations, cultures, and nations, the areas surrounding borders – the border zones – are in fact spaces of flux, flow, and hybridity. Rather than regions of palpable division, they are spaces of interaction and mixing, which produce new and sometimes radical forms of expression at the intersection of people and social practices. International border zones, and specifically the US–Mexico border region, are widely acknowledged as sites of cultural hybridity.[2] In fact, as Howard Campbell observes, instead of essentializing the ethnic and national groups on either side of political borders, research on the US–Mexico border

[1] As quoted by Ila Nicole Sheren, *Portable Borders* (Austin: University of Texas Press, 2015), p. 7.

[2] Howard Campbell, 'Escaping Identity: Border Zones as Places of Evasion and Cultural Reinvention', *Journal of the Royal Anthropological Institute*, 21 (2015), 296–312 (p. 296).

'has emphasized the ways in which linguistic and cultural blending has created unique syntheses of identities that are binary rather than monolingual or monocultural'.[3]

With the emergence of the European Union, the European community similarly expanded with divisions between nations becoming less culturally, linguistically, and economically distinct. For example, by moving towards a single currency and appropriating functions from its member states,[4] the flow of money across the EU's permeable borders continues to increase dramatically.[5] Moreover, with growing reliance on Internet technologies, which erase nearly all political demarcations of territory, media consumption and digital culture similarly transgress borders with the click of a button. Finally, with ongoing political conflict and civil war in many regions of the world, people are also crossing borders in an unprecedented fashion and with increasing frequency. The 'Refugee Crisis' in particular highlights the role of discourses of border crossing in framing the free movement of people. In many ways, while still politically significant, borders have become irrelevant as an effective means of dividing people and culture. Thus, as Héctor Calderón comments, again with particular interest in the US–Mexico border zone, rapidly changing national demographics, international market penetration, transnational media conglomerates and the Internet itself are resulting in continued interaction in cultural and artistic spheres across international borders, rendering the border itself a space of cultural production and meaning-making.[6]

With particular interest in contemporary graphic novels on forced migration, this essay engages discourses in border studies to understand a very different kind of border – the panel border of the comics medium. In particular, my analysis engages theory on borders and border zones as a framework through which to understand panel frames as sites of meaning-making. While still maintaining a relationship to the idea of political borders as essential in this new global genre of contemporary comics and graphic novels, this research sheds light on the interventions this category of graphic narrative makes in discourses on refugee experience. Connecting physical borders between nations with conceptual borders between panels, where both function as boundaries as well as spaces of intersection, this chapter

[3] Campbell, 'Escaping Identity', p. 296.

[4] Joel S. Migdal, 'Mental Maps and Virtual Checkpoints. Struggles to Construct and Maintain State and Social Boundaries', in *Boundaries and Belonging: States and Societies in the Struggle to Shape Identities and Local Practice,* ed. by Joel S. Migdal (Cambridge: Cambridge University Press, 2004), pp. 3–23 (p. 4).

[5] Migdal, 'Mental Maps', p. 4.

[6] Héctor Calderón, 'Introduction', in *Narratives of Greater Mexico,* ed. by Héctor Calderón (Austin: University of Texas Press, 2004), pp. xii–xix (p. xii).

examines how panel borders comment on refugee experience. I argue that comics artists are mobilizing this specific formal characteristic of the comics medium to contend with issues of migration, exile, and displacement difficult to otherwise represent.[7] These cartoonists produce modes of expression that complicate popular understandings of refugee experience in the liminal space between panels. This engagement with border studies theory thus reimagines panel frames as spaces not where the represented moments in time end – though they do that work, too – but as sites in which comics artists continue their work as witnesses to the refugee crisis. Thematizing elements of that experience impossible to represent with the written word or conventional visualization strategies alone within the space of the comics grid, panel borders become sites of meaning-making, much like the political borders they reference. Elevating aesthetic strategies to the role of narrative expression, comics artists writing on the refugee experience mobilize panel borders to add a layer of storytelling that vacillates between the creators' ability to represent a specific experience, emotion, or event and the very inability to represent some forms of violence, trauma, and displacement altogether.

## Comics' Borders in Comics about Borders

Examining borders as sites of meaning-making is also a popular way of examining the formal characteristics of the comics medium. In particular, Scott McCloud theorizes the processes of closure – how the reader constructs the comics narrative – by looking at the role of panel borders and frames in their construction of the gutter.[8] McCloud's canonical text was not the first to be published on the formal qualities of the medium (notably Will Eisner's *Comics and Sequential Art* was published in 1985),[9] but it has become the foremost treatise on theorizing the comics form. Here, McCloud argues that that which is represented within the borders of the panel frame is as essential as that which is not, and it is between the panels – in the gutter – where the reader intellectually stitches together the moments represented to produce the narrative, thereby creating closure and constructing the essential

[7] See Homi Bhabha, *The Location of Culture* (London: Routledge, 1994). Bhabha's theory of cultural hybridity offers one way to read borders as opportunities for the construction of new types of meaning that in fact undermine the binary opposition the border seeks to demarcate. Anthony Pym's scholarship on interculture further highlights the site of interaction between different cultures itself as a site of cultural production: *Negotiating the Frontier: Translators and Intercultures in Hispanic History* (Manchester: St Jerome Publishing, 2000), p. 1.

[8] Scott McCloud, *Understanding Comics* (New York: Kitchen Sink Press, 1993).

[9] Will Eisner, *Comics and Sequential Art* (Tamarac: Poorhouse Press, 1985).

meaning of the text. The panel borders are therefore crucial in the meaning-making process of sequential art.[10]

Even though this is perhaps an essentialist view of meaning-making in comics – after all, as Francesca Lyn observes in her scholarship on female autobiography, closure is not the ultimate goal for some comics artists – the fragmentation afforded by panel frames is as essential to articulating the medium's formal characteristics as it is to its meaning-making.[11] Furthermore, as this chapter argues, the borders of the panels themselves offer a level of potential interpretation that goes all too often overlooked in scholarship.

Since its start in March 2011, the brutal conflict in Syria has become the biggest humanitarian crisis of our time.[12] As little as two months later, Syrian residents were forced to leave their homes, with many of them seeking asylum in refugee camps in Turkey.[13] By December the next year, half a million Syrians had sought refuge in other countries, a number that doubled only four months later, with approximately one million Syrian refugees registered with the United Nations High Commissioner for Refugees (UNHCR) by March of the following year.[14] Now, a decade later, about 5.6 million people have fled the country, with millions more displaced inside Syria itself. Moreover, as of the end of 2019, approximately 79.5 million people have been forcibly displaced worldwide.

Alongside media attention to this humanitarian crisis, media representations of forced migration have likewise proliferated, with comics, webcomics, and graphic novels offering new and creative avenues for thematizing the issues of forced migration. The multi-modal dimension of the comics medium renders it a unique form through which to discuss social justice and human rights issues. With its history of radical politics worldwide and ability to visualize bodies, comics draw attention to issues of representation – as well as to representation itself – in ways unlike other media. Through visualization and spatial and temporal fragmentation, the articulation of human rights issues – as well as our reading experience of them – differs dramatically from their engagement in more traditional texts. Visual cues of ethnicity, gender, class, religion, and ability are not easily flattened into single-issue subjects, making comics fundamentally intersectional, while the history of the form itself asks readers to question

[10] McCloud, *Understanding Comics*, p. 67.

[11] Francesca Lyn, 'Draw Your Demons: Identity, Humor, and Trauma in Autobiographical Comics by Women of Color' (presentation (unpublished), International Comic Arts Forum, Columbia, SC, 14 April 2016).

[12] UNHCR (Office of the United Nations High Commissioner for Refugees), 'Seven Years On: Timeline of the Syria Crisis', 7 March 2018, <https://www.unhcr.org/ph/13427-seven-years-timeline-syria-crisis.html> [accessed 22 March 2021].

[13] UNHCR, 'Seven Years On'.

[14] UNHCR, 'Seven Years On'.

assumptions, stereotypes, and the impact of specific narrative strategies on social justice issues. However, there is also interesting work being done on an aesthetic level that seeks to illuminate issues about refugee experience through the formal characteristics of the medium, specifically at the panel borders. While Charles Hatfield draws attention to the power of layout in the construction of meaning in the comics medium, and with the important exception also of Barbara Postema's work, the narrative capacity of panel borders continues to be an under-researched element of the form.[15]

This chapter therefore looks specifically at the role of panel borders in the supplemental and complementary meaning-making of three comics on forced migration published in 2018, *The Unwanted: Stories of the Syrian Refugees* by Don Brown, *Drawn to Berlin: Comic Workshops in Refugee Shelters and Other Stories from a New Europe* by Ali Fitzgerald, and *Escaping Wars and Waves: Encounters with Syrian Refugees* by Olivier Kugler.[16] The following therefore interrogates what interventions comics artists make through panel borders to comment on both the role of borders in forced migration and the precarious circumstances of refugees. Making several observations on the connection between national borders and panel borders in these comics on border crossings, I propose three avenues for the exploration of their transnational themes. How do these graphic novels engage border studies discourses on a formal level? How do their panel borders comment on the consequences and processes of transgressing national borders? Lastly, if these graphic narratives are about crossing borders and a state of borderlessness in refugee camps, how do panel borders engage this problematic?

Don Brown's *The Unwanted* (2018) depicts moments of hardships and hope in the lives of the refugees he met in three Greek refugee camps. Beginning in March 2011, the graphic narrative is told in the present tense, largely through captions that run along the bottom of the panels. The story recounts the horrors, impossible choices, and occasional triumphs faced by fleeing refugees from the perspective of an unnamed narrator, whose commentary reads distant and neutral but informed. The extensive bibliography at the end of the text further supports the journalistic tone of Brown's graphic novel. Individuals are identified not by name but by their status as

[15] Charles Hatfield, 'An Art of Tensions', in *Alternative Comics: An Emerging Literature* (Jackson: University Press of Mississippi, 2005), pp. 32–67 (p. 48); Barbara Postema, *Narrative Structure in Comics: Making Sense of Fragments* (Rochester, NY: RIT Press, 2013).

[16] Don Brown, *The Unwanted: Stories of the Syrian Refugees* (Boston, MA: HMH, 2018); Ali Fitzgerald, *Drawn to Berlin: Comic Workshops in Refugee Shelters and Other Stories from a New Europe* (Seattle: Fantagraphics, 2018); Olivier Kugler, *Escaping Wars and Waves: Encounters with Syrian Refugees* (Brighton: Myriad, 2018).

refugee, by their role in the family they accompany, or simply by their gender and age. This functions to foreground their status as individuals as well as the universality of their refugee experience simultaneously.

The panel frames in Brown's graphic narrative feature both the consistency of digital reproduction as well as traces of the artist's hand. Drawn in thin black ink, the panel frames appear to be individually created for each separate panel. However, upon closer inspection, the lines – with their minor flaws at their intersection and their overlap – repeat themselves in multiple configurations of panel layout. This renders the hand-drawn impression of the panel frame itself an aesthetic choice – as opposed to a consequence of artistic practice. This tension between hand-drawn and digitally reproduced panel frame, presumably through computational means, underscores the narrative's portrayal of individual yet universal stories.

Furthermore, the panel borders also feature a commentary on violence. As the only element of the graphic narrative to break through the pseudo-hermetically sealed space of the panel frame, the violence encountered by the refugees of Brown's graphic novel literally shatters the borders he so artfully constructs. Bullets fracture the panel edges; bombs explode out of the picture planes; and toxic smoke rises through the panel frames. These violent penetrations send fragments of the panel borders themselves – like shrapnel – into the space beyond the panel's image. Brown thereby mobilizes this formal characteristic of the comics medium to demonstrate the relationship between violence and border transgression with regards to the Syrian conflict: not only did violence in Syria force many of its citizens to begin their journeys across borders in search of safety and freedom; the violence itself was never fully contained within the borders of its nation of origin, with Syrian refugees enduring brutality and loss even outside of Syria's borders. Echoing border studies discourses, Brown demonstrates how some structures transcend borders – culture, social practices and, most poignantly, violence – making a statement about the consequences of civil war penetrating national borders and continuing beyond the region in which it began.

Ali Fitzgerald's *Drawn to Berlin* (2018), on the other hand, takes place exclusively in Germany, where she spent the previous eight years leading drawing classes in a refugee camp in northern Berlin. Addressing both refugee experience and her own role as witness and cartoonist, Fitzgerald recounts the hardships faced by the individuals who survived their harsh journeys from Syria through the images they draw and the stories they tell – from the tragic loss of rafts and violence of tanks to the cautious hopefulness of flowers and the Eiffel Tower.

Much like the irrelevant physicality of the political borders transgressed by these survivors of the Syrian conflict, many of the sequences featured in

*Drawn to Berlin* are interesting for their lack of panel borders. This borderlessness of panels mirrors the uncertainty of her subjects' existence within nationally defined spaces, where the surrounding borders neither protect them, nor define their identity. In fact, borderlessness is in some ways their defining characteristic. Consequently, the imagined homes of Syrian refugees melt into Fitzgerald's present and the refugees' current residence in Berlin. As opposed to separate moments in time, their memories of Syria and their experience of the refugee camp emerge like juxtaposed images occupying the same temporality, with the reader sometimes unable to differentiate where one story or experience ends and a new one begins. The absence or erasure of borders on the comics page thereby interweaves the stories of Berlin and Syria into each other, creating a new hybrid experience – and form of expression – that is simultaneously Syrian and German, as the refugees learn new media (comics and illustration) and incorporate Western references into their remembrance and expression of personal experience.

This melting of time and space into each other has further implications in Fitzgerald's rendering of refugee experience. Fitzgerald's description of the refugee encampment is as a space without a true sense of time: 'People couldn't work or go to school yet. They were caught in a gap between...' Individuals, who once had friends and things to do, recounts Nazir, now only have time.[17] This thematic of time – the excess of it and the constant waiting for its passing (awaiting paperwork to be processed, anticipating a move to another city or camp, etc.) – is an essential element of Fitzgerald's engagement with the subject of refugee experience as well as her aesthetic of rendering it. Without the routine of a normal life, these individuals lose specific and regular sense of the progression of time. Through her absence and erasure of panel borders, which in turn interweaves and expands temporalities sometimes indefinitely, Fitzgerald constructs the same sense of timelessness – the formlessness of days, as Adnan refers to it – on her comics page.[18]

Temporality is an important theme for Olivier Kugler's *Escaping Wars and Waves* (2018) as well, though it manifests through his page layout in opposite terms. Kugler's project spans much of the geography of the refugee crisis, incorporating refugee camps and stories of migrant experience from the Kurdistan region of Iraq, Greece, Germany, England, France, and Switzerland. Also based on many interviews but informed by hundreds of reference photos, Kugler captures the nuance of refugee experience through extensive use of handwritten text and speech balloons, the incorporation of other media images, and the application of bright colours.

[17] Fitzgerald, *Drawn to Berlin*, p. 43.
[18] Fitzgerald, *Drawn to Berlin*, p. 48.

What is most interesting about Kugler's page layout and use of panel borders, however, is that there is no unifying system. Pages emerge as a deluge of colour and text, with no panel frames demarcating space and time whatsoever. In fact, Kugler's figures feature the outlines of limbs and the traces of movement that undermine any normal sense of temporality. Gestures that would have occurred before or after the primary image, which appears on the page in full colour, are rendered in outline, implying movement before or after the main action represented. It is as if he stacks his panels on top of one another, maintaining traces of other moments in time, to complicate the sense of temporarily typically captured by static images. Without the demarcation between panels or their sequentiality, multiple timescapes seem to melt into one another, mirroring the chaos of these individuals' lives in the chaos of the page. Furthermore, as Dominic Umile observes, the thin inked outlines of Kugler's figures in motion also suggest the effect of double-exposed photos.[19] This strategy not only recalls the process of Kugler's comics journalism; it also gestures towards the role of photojournalism in general in constructing a specific kind of image of the refugee crisis – one that is often more invested in the composition of the photographic image and the politics of the Syrian conflict than the individuals experiencing it.

## Conclusion

With the focal point of border studies discourse turning its attention to individuals, practices, and culture, the field has begun the important work of placing human interaction at the fore of its enquiry. Comics and graphic novels on similar subjects do much of the same. By visualizing bodies, graphic narratives on refugee experience put the human back in human rights issues, fostering empathy and understanding for vulnerable populations. And the plethora of human rights organizations supporting the work of comics artists are a testament to this very fact. However, comics also open up new opportunities for the representation of forced migration that moves beyond the potential for the embodied presentation of issues facing vulnerable demographics of people. Looking at the role of panel borders in these stories of national borders and borderlessness is simply one of many avenues for future research on the affordances of the medium in its thematization of refugee experience.

Dr Elizabeth Nijdam is a Lecturer in the Department of Central, Eastern, and Northern European Studies at the University of British Columbia.

[19] Dominic Umile, 'Documenting the Journeys of Syrian Refugees in Comics', *Hyperallergic*, 24 September 2018, <https://hyperallergic.com/461675/olivier-kugler-escaping-wars-and-waves-penn-state/> [accessed 22 March 2021].

# 4

# Cities

*Lorraine Leu*

In March 2018, Rio de Janeiro councilwoman Marielle Franco closed a discussion at the Casa das Pretas, an organization dedicated to empowering black women, with a rousing call to occupy all of the spaces of power from which Brazil's Afro-descendants have been excluded. Franco, a black, queer activist who grew up in one of the city's favelas, advocated for social justice for those sidelined by or sacrificed to successive urban modernization projects. After Franco left the discussion that night she was gunned down in her car. The targeted assassination sought to silence those who challenge longstanding sites of power and dispute the unequal distribution of space and resources in the city. In recent years the coordinated Black Women's Marches in major cities all over Brazil have occupied the streets in order to highlight the oppression and violence they suffer, and to make common cause with women of colour across the diaspora. On the night she died Marielle Franco cited the US Black feminist writer Audre Lorde as a source of inspiration: 'I am not free while any woman is unfree, even when her shackles are very different from my own'.[1]

For those who find national discourses on race, gender, or sexuality to be unproductive for their liberationist agendas, inserting their voices into a dialogue with leading black female voices across the diaspora feeds their political resistance in the modern city. To be visible and occupy public space is an act of defiance in what anthropologist Jaime Alves calls an 'anti-black

[1] Mário Magalhães, 'Marielle e Anderson: O dia em que o Rio, indignado diante da infâmia, deu uma chance à esperança', *The Intercept*, 21 March 2018, <https://theintercept.com/2018/03/21/marielle-e-anderson-o-dia-em-que-o-rio-indignado-diante-da-infamia-deu-uma-chance-a-esperanca/> [accessed 27 March 2021].

city'.[2] Alves uses this term to underline how spatial segregation, mass incarceration, and police killings are fundamental to the reproduction of the urban order in Brazil. The struggle to assert black humanity in the face of national modernizing projects that legitimize anti-blackness highlights poignantly 'the afterlife of slavery' or the 'incomplete project of freedom' in Brazil.[3]

The foundation of cities, as Hernández and Kellett observe, was a fundamental part of the colonizing strategy of the Spanish and Portuguese throughout their new territories in the Americas: 'Cities served as a means for the colonisers to impose their own socio-political and economic structures, thereby establishing themselves in a position of authority. Hence, cities had to be planned in order to materialize such a hierarchical structure'.[4] Peruvian sociologist Aníbal Quijano has underscored how the basis of this hierarchical power structure was race, which outlived the historical period of colonialism to become the globally dominant model of power today.[5] In the spaces that this power structure built in Brazil, argues legal theorist Denise Ferreira da Silva, black bodies occupy a moral and legal no-man's land. Here universality – the notion of fundamental human rights and protections – finds its spatial limits for people whose relationship with the state is based on violence.[6]

We can understand the community of Vila Autódromo in this way, as a neighbourhood relegated to a space outside of legality.[7] In the photograph above, a mother attends to her young child at a plastic pool set up outside their home during a hot Rio de Janeiro summer. The family dwelling appears partially destroyed, and rubble litters the right foreground of the image. The photograph was taken about a year and a half before Rio hosted the Olympic Games. The neighbourhood was located next to the planned site of the Olympic Village and was subjected to a process of ruination led by

[2] Jaime Amparo Alves, *The Anti-Black City: Police Terror and Black Urban Life in Brazil* (Minneapolis: University of Minnesota Press, 2018).

[3] Saidiya Hartman, 'Venus in Two Acts', *small axe*, 12.2 (2008), 1–14 (p. 4); *Lose Your Mother: A Journey along the Atlantic Slave Route* (New York: Farrar, Straus and Giroux, 2007), p. 6.

[4] Felipe Hernández and Peter Kellett, 'Introduction', in *Rethinking the Informal City: Critical Perspectives from Latin America*, ed. by Felipe Hernández et al. (New York: Berghahn Books, 2009), pp. 1–19 (p. 3).

[5] Aníbal Quijano, 'Coloniality of Power, Eurocentrism, and Latin America', *Nepantla: Views from the South*, 1.3 (2000), 533–80 (p. 533).

[6] Denise Ferreira da Silva, 'Towards a Critique of the Socio-logos of Justice: The Analytics of Raciality and the Production of Universality', *Social Identities*, 7.3 (2001), 421–54 (p. 442).

[7] Lorraine Leu, 'Epilogue,' in *Defiant Geographies: Race and Urban Space in 1920s Rio de Janeiro* (Pittsburgh: University of Pittsburgh Press, 2020), pp. 176–88.

Figure 1. Vila Autódromo.
Source: Photo courtesy of Rio On Watch (rioonwatch.org), January 2015 (Catalytic Communities | RioOnWatch).

a partnership of city authorities and major construction companies. One of the arguments used to justify the removal of the community was that it compromised the security of the Olympic Village, thereby criminalizing a community with no established drug trade and very low levels of crime.

Vila Autódromo is located along the Jacarepaguá lagoon in the southwest of the city and residents' oral histories locate its establishment to the 1960s when local fishermen occupied the land. In recent decades, Vila Autódromo went from a peri-urban neighbourhood to becoming part of the rapidly expanding western part of the city. As the city grew, the community became surrounded by luxury condominiums in the upper and middle-class neighborhood of Barra da Tijuca. One hundred and forty families in Vila Autódromo obtained legal title from the State Government of Rio de Janeiro in 1997. The following year, households living on the lagoon's edge were granted a ninety-nine-year legal concession of land use. However, the situation of its residents became extremely precarious with the announcement in 2009 that the adjacent racetrack would be one of the main development sites for the 2016 Olympic Games. Just over a year before the Olympics began, residents had abandoned or been pressured to abandon 590 out of a total of 760 homes in Vila Autódromo. Those who remained complained of 'guerrilla tactics' on the part of the City and the developers to remove them.[8] Cuts to water and electricity services made for exceedingly difficult living conditions. When owners or occupants left, the City moved immediately to demolish their homes and business places, leaving remaining residents surrounded by rubble. As lives and property were reduced to debris, those resisting eviction in Vila Autódromo became witnesses to what seemed like the inevitable 'topocide' or annihilation of their community.[9] However, even as the city sought to destroy the material objects and the memories involved in place making, people also devised various forms of refusal when confronted with the threat of their ruination.

As Katherine McKittrick has observed, black subjects are often imagined as either confined to space – needing to be kept in their 'proper' place, or else as simply un-geographic – incapable of making, transforming, and developing profound affective ties to space.[10] This rendering of black social life was repeatedly articulated in the verbal and visual discourse of municipal publicity material that represented the neighbourhood as uninhabitable and negated the labour of residents who developed the site and made it a community. The image above contests that notion with a poignant affirmation of home. Amidst their decaying surroundings, the family in this photograph has devised a place of relaxation and summer fun for their young child. The intimate, domestic time–space of leisure they have fashioned around the pool disrupts the unrelenting march of the destruction of the neighbourhood. It seems to suspend or hold off the spatial and temporal encroachment of the demolition. This snapshot of family life also has an affective and critical charge that articulates what is at stake for communities of colour that lie in the way of such development projects, as well as their inventiveness in the face of their ruination.

Their refusal to leave recounts another story of the struggle of Afro-descendants to defend their claims to territory. Twentieth-century Afro-descendant mobilizing and resistance are significantly oriented around permanence in space – on the struggle to remain in appropriated spaces.[11] The photograph critiques the displacement of black families and talks back to narratives that construct Afro-descendants as un-geographic. It enacts the

[8] Ruben Berta, 'Apesar de indenizações milionárias, prefeitura não consegue acabar com a Vila Autódromo', *O Globo*, 14 May 2015.

[9] J. Douglas Porteous, *Planned to Death: The Annihilation of a Place Called Howdendyke* (New York: Manchester University Press, 1989), p. 230.

[10] Katherine McKittrick, *Demonic Grounds: Black Women and the Cartographies of Struggle* (Minneapolis: University of Minnesota Press, 2006), pp. x–xi.

[11] Andrelino Campos, *Do quilombo à favela: A produção do espaço criminalizado no Rio de Janeiro* (Rio de Janeiro: Bertrand, 2005), p. 31.

everyday struggle to make and keep a home that underlies histories of black subject making in Brazil. It is a testimony, therefore, to 'defiant black geographies', or persistent black territorializing in the face of violence, surveillance, and control.[12] The image communicates that black experiences of spatiality, as Urban Studies theorist Raquel Rolnik has argued, are not confined solely to experiences of exclusion and the exercise of white dominion.[13]

The moment captured in this photograph celebrates a different kind of black motherhood than that fashioned by national narratives of the *mãe preta* – the black mother of the nation. Gilberto Freyre's foundational work on colonial society in Brazil, *Casa Grande e Senzala* (published in English as *The Masters and the Slaves*), painted an iconic portrait of the *mãe preta* as a house slave who performed domestic tasks and saw to the intimate needs of white family members, suckling their babies and raising their children, as well as being permanently sexually available to the master and his sons.[14] The *mãe preta* is therefore vital to the process of miscegenation, underpinning a national project that idealizes Brazil's history of racial and gender domination.[15] Today white family life still relies heavily on the services of black women for childrearing. In Brazil domestic workers make up 8.1 per cent of the workforce and the majority of them are black women, about sixty-one per cent.[16] In the photograph above the black female body is also re-signified beyond its function to serve white families, countering a powerful visual rhetoric that produces their bodies as 'biological reproducers ... that serve the nationalist goal of whitening'.[17] The image therefore unsettles the 'controlling images' of black womanhood that make poverty and subordination appear as a natural and normal part of everyday life.[18]

[12] Lorraine Leu, 'Deviant Geographies: Black Spaces of Cultural Expression in Early 20th Century Rio de Janeiro', *Latin American and Caribbean Ethnicity Studies*, 9.2 (2014), 177–94; see also *Defiant Geographies*.

[13] Raquel Rolnik, 'Territorios negros nas cidades brasileiras: Etnicidade e cidade em São Paulo e Rio de Janeiro', *Estudos Afro-Asiáticos*, 17 (1989), 29–41, <http:// raquelrolnik.files.wordpress.com/2013/04/territc3b3rios-negros.pdf> [accessed 27 March 2021].

[14] Gilberto Freyre, *The Masters and the Slaves* (New York: Alfred A. Knopf, 1933, 1964).

[15] Kia Lilly Caldwell, *Negras in Brazil: Re-Envisioning Black Women, Citizenship, and the Politics of Identity* (New Brunswick: Rutgers University Press, 2007), pp. 39–40.

[16] Departamento Intersindical de Estatística e Estudos Socioeconómicos (DIEESE), *O emprego doméstico no Brasil*, 2013, <https://www.dieese.org.br/estudosetorial/2013/estPesq68empregoDomestico.pdf> [accessed 27 March 2021].

[17] Caldwell, *Negras in Brazil*, p. 74.

[18] Patricia Hill Collins, *Black Feminist Thought: Knowledge, Consciousness, and the Politics of Empowerment* (New York: Routledge, 2000), p. 68.

This photograph therefore points to the limits of representations of authority and alterity. Here the subject who is ostensibly mute in the image speaks volumes by resisting certain racialized meanings, and by refusing to become an object of the gaze's surveying knowledge. The photograph also frustrates the gaze in that the mother's back is turned to the camera, her child's face is obscured by her body, and it is not possible to clearly discern the expressions on the faces of the men seated around the pool. This too denies the viewer the knowability of the family members as what Poole calls 'image-objects' through which racial difference is imagined, desired, and othered.[19] The subjects' affective engagement with one another and with the space they occupy in the image therefore escapes capture by the gaze. The photograph was taken by a non-governmental organization that advocates for low-income populations in the city, which may account for the respectful distance it establishes between the camera and its subjects. It is as if we have stumbled upon a domestic space – one produced by black family life in the context of constant struggle – upon which we have no right to gaze. This image affords glimpses of experiences of neoliberal Brazil that hint at the reality of inhabiting eliminable racialized spaces. This portrait of maternal love is inseparable from the experience of devastation and dislocation that constitutes black family life that the photograph also represents.

While residents of Vila Autódromo also mobilized collectively in defence of their community in various ways, this photograph reminds us of the many private fashionings of place that obstructed the state's technologies of destruction. The image also contributes to the disputed meanings of the space of Vila Autódromo: land that the developers and the city devalued as unsanitary and squalid, but that had speculative value on the real estate market because of the Olympics, is re-signified in this image as a space of social reproduction for poor families of colour. Such spaces of refusal represent black micro-geographies that challenged the municipality's proposed landscape of development. They demonstrate a resilient capacity for visibilizing Afro-descendant bodies in disputed spaces and disturb the city and the nation's narratives of modernization based on whitening. In the family's determination to stay put, creating a moment of fun amidst the destruction, we see an 'active and ongoing engagement with ruins'[20] that articulated a sense of belonging and entitlement, as well as political resentments that

[19] Deborah Poole, *Vision, Race, and Modernity: A Visual Economy of the Andean Image World* (Princeton: Princeton University Press, 1997), p. 7.

[20] Vyjayanthi Rao, 'The Future in Ruins', in *Imperial Debris: On Ruins and Ruination*, ed. by Ann Laura Stoler (Durham, NC: Duke University Press, 2013), pp. 287–321 (p. 316).

laid bare the technologies of terror of the city government. This photograph articulates the right to stay and communicates a moment that materializes the family's place-making and life-making.

In the end, the City and the developers succeeded in destroying the existing neighbourhood and decimating the community. However, twenty families managed to remain in Vila Autódromo on the condition that the City tear down their houses and build them new ones, which were hurriedly and cheaply constructed in time for the Olympics. Throughout the struggle to remain residents had demonstrated an acute awareness of the power of imagery to contest the City's representation of their community. They used social media for self-representations and to denounce the use of force against them, on one occasion posting images with their faces bruised and bloodied after a confrontation with shock troops of the Municipal Guard gaining a temporary halt to the evictions.[21] Vila Autódromo's few remaining residents and their supporters inaugurated an open-air museum on 18 May 2016 that provided a material, visual counter-narrative to official accounts of modernization and mega-events. The organizers of the Museu das Remoções (Museum of Removals) aimed to chronicle evictions and resistance to them by Vila Autódromo, as well as other communities past and present. Using the rubble from demolished buildings they created seven art installations on an open-air site to memorialize the neighbourhood.[22] The sculptures were built in collaborative workshops in which residents participated alongside architecture students from a local university. In one of them a kitchen chair and a bicycle lie atop a pile of debris – broken concrete slabs and rocks, and the twisted guts of iron and plumbing. In front of it, they tagged a large piece of galvanized iron roofing with the words 'Residents' Association', a key site from which they had organized their protests. Previously, when the struggle to remain was ongoing and the Association building was destroyed, residents had tagged their own houses with those words to demonstrate their defiance.

The installations included photographs and videos, and sought to honour key places and people in the history of the community. One of the former residents honoured in the inaugural display was the *mãe de santo* or priestess Luizinha de Nanã (Heloísa Helena Berto). Dona Heloísa became a prominent advocate and spokesperson for her religion and the community. When she and her family refused to leave their home, which also functioned as a spiritual

[21] Jonathan Watts, 'Forced Evictions in Rio Favela for 2016 Olympics Trigger Violent Clashes', *The Guardian*, 3 June 2015.

[22] Rhona Mackay, 'Vila Autódromo Inaugura Museu das Remoções', *Rio on Watch: Relatos das favelas cariocas*, 24 May 2016, <http://rioonwatch.org.br/?p=19942> [accessed 27 March 2021].

centre for practitioners of *candomblé*, it was enclosed within the construction site of the Olympic Park and cut off from the rest of Vila Autódromo. Visitors were prohibited, and their electricity and water services were suspended, until the house and temple were destroyed on the same day as the Residents' Association building. She reflected that the occupants of the well-off neighbouring area of Barra never accepted having a *candomblé* temple so close by: 'A Barra da Tijuca não iria admitir ouvir os toques dos atabaques e nem ver as pessoas, os negros, vestidos de branco sem ser para servi-los como babá ou como cuidadores'.[23] Her comments point to both the racial nature of de-territorialization and the naturalization of black women's position as subordinate. Although black women frequently lead neighbourhood activist organizations in Brazil, the media has been reluctant to recognize them as political agents.[24] João Vargas asserts that black activism and protest is not legible to the media, the government, and society because of a series of assumptions about who belongs to civil society and can legitimately engage in public spaces and politics.[25] Black urban life therefore seeks to reproduce itself in the face of disavowal and violence. When black subjects make themselves visible as producers of space, as people who have built and expanded the city despite all attempts to exclude them from it, their claims are not understood as legitimate. This is perhaps why despite the pain, trauma, and large-scale protest provoked by the assassination of Marielle Franco, her killers and those who ordered her murder remain at large.

Lorraine Leu is Professor of Latin American Cultural Studies at the University of Texas at Austin and the author of *Defiant Geographies: Race and Urban Space in 1920s Rio de Janeiro* (Pittsburgh: University of Pittsburgh Press, 2020).

[23] Miriane Peregrino, 'Museu das Remoções é inaugurado na Vila Autódromo', *O Cidadão do Bairro Maré*, 26 May 2016, <http://jornalocidadao.net/museu-das-remocoes-e-inaugurado-na-vila-autodromo/> [accessed 27 March 2021]. 'The people of Barra da Tijuca would not stand for the sound of the *atabaque* drums, nor the sight of black people dressed in white unless it was to serve them as nannies or caregivers'.

[24] Keisha-Khan Y Perry, 'Geographies of Power: Black Women Mobilizing Intersectionality in Brazil', *Meridians: Feminism, Race, Transnationalism*, 14.1 (2016), 94–120 (p. 102).

[25] João H. Costa Vargas, 'Black Disidentification: The 2013 Protests, *rolezinhos*, and Racial Antagonism in Post-Lula Brazil', *Critical Sociology*, 42.4–5 (2016), 551–65 (p. 557).

# 5

# Colonization

*Derek Duncan*

On Friday 4 October 1935, the *Scotsman* newspaper's lead headline 'Outbreak of the Italo-Abyssinian War' confirmed Italy's long-anticipated invasion of Ethiopia:

> The war began according to messages from Addis Ababa, with an air bombing attack by the Italians on Adowa – scene of the crushing Italian defeat of 1896 – and Adigrat – the first places of importance beyond the Eritrean frontier.[1]

The report's opening lines capture the geographical, historical, and affective co-ordinates of Italy's colonial endeavour. Eritrea, strategically located on the Red Sea, was established as Italy's first colony in 1890. Attempts to expand into Ethiopia led to humiliation at the Battle of Adowa (Adwa) with the victory of an African army over would-be European colonizers.

Ethiopia, one of the few parts of Africa still free from a direct European colonial presence, remained in Italy's sights until the invasion in 1935, spearheaded by Mussolini's fascist regime. In the interim, Italy also laid claim to the coastal regions of Libya, parts of Somalia, the Greek Dodecanese Islands, as well as Tianjin, a small territorial concession in China. Compared to other European nations, Italian colonization started late and was relatively limited in scope. At the time of the second invasion of Ethiopia, one of the most significant events in world politics in the 1930s, the processes of decolonization had already begun elsewhere. Italy's occupation was brutal and Ethiopian resistance fierce. The Italian Colonial Empire declared in 1936

[1] *Scotsman*, Friday, 4 October 1935, p. 9.

turned out to be short-lived and Italy lost all its colonial possessions in the course of the Second World War. Yet, as Neelam Srivastava has argued, Italy's invasion of Ethiopia galvanized anti-imperial movements across the globe.[2] Its transnational implications continue to be felt.

The *Scotsman*'s lead article was accompanied by a number of shorter pieces that tracked the invasion's ripple effects across the world: the announcement of a forthcoming protest organized by anti-fascist Italian migrants in Argentina as well as reports of civil disturbances in Toulouse and New York directed at resident Italian communities mapped Italy's transnational histories of mobility and settlement.[3] In the latter part of the nineteenth century, Italians had emigrated in large numbers to North and South America as well as across Europe in response to economic underdevelopment in the recently unified state. Plans hatched at about the same time for the occupation of East Africa were underpinned by political anxieties about Italy's subordinate place in Europe at a time of rapid colonial expansion. These plans were also informed by the idea that an Italian territorial presence in Africa might be sustained by providing a better destination for its citizens looking to emigrate.[4] Indeed, settlements of Italians abroad were often referred to as 'colonies', and emigrants and their descendants retained many of the benefits of Italian citizenship. The articles appearing in the *Scotsman* were also of marked interest to the local reader in the 1930s because of the established presence of Italians in Scotland itself.[5]

Characterized by the crossing, breaking, but also the establishment of boundaries and borders, colonization as a practice of occupation and settlement is grounded in political, economic, and social differentials of power, enforced through coercion and violence. This violence is cultural as well as physical. Stuart Hall talks about a 'colonization of the mind' induced by agencies such as the education system that promote and naturalize the

[2] Neelam Srivastava, *Italian Colonialism and Resistances to Empire, 1930–1970* (London: Palgrave MacMillan, 2018). For a detailed account of the bombing raids and subsequent acts of violence see Alberto Sbacchi, 'Poison Gas and Atrocities in the Italo-Ethiopian War', in *Italian Colonialism*, ed. by Ruth Ben-Ghiat and Mia Fuller (New York: Palgrave MacMillan, 2005), pp. 47–56.

[3] Popular opposition to the invasion in Scotland itself intensified hostility to Italians living and working here. See Wendy Ugolini, *Experiencing War as the 'Enemy Other': Italian Scottish Experience in Second World War* (Manchester: Manchester University Press, 2011), pp. 38–39.

[4] Mark Choate, *Emigrant Nation: The Making of Italy Abroad* (Cambridge, MA: Harvard University Press, 2008).

[5] Terri Colpi, *Italians Count in Scotland: The 1933 Census, Recording History* (London: The Saint James Press, 2015).

self-serving values and perspectives that uphold that system of domination.[6] Mary Louise Pratt's influential and flexible concept of the 'contact zone' is an effective way of thinking about how colonization operates through the multiple layers of cultural encounter. She defines these layers as '*social spaces* where disparate cultures meet, clash, and grapple with each other, often in highly asymmetrical relations of domination and subordination – like colonialism, slavery or their aftermaths as they are lived out across the globe today'.[7] The 'contact zone' is where relationships between colonizers and colonized are experienced and negotiated, and their injurious legacies forged. It is a space of unequal social and cultural fusion and of transformation.

Pratt's concept situates the temporal and spatial contours of Italian colonization as an expansive and enduring project. To think about these contours in terms of a transnational 'contact zone', as Srivastava does, brings into play a multiplicity of connections, ensnarled in a common demographic logic or matrix, albeit ostensibly disparate in their location and nature. Colonial expansion and migration are not, however, equivalent vectors of demographic mobility. Yet in this instance, they were, in Pratt's terms, forged through 'highly asymmetrical relations of domination and subordination' in Italy itself and then reiterated abroad.

Until national unification in 1870, Italy itself had been occupied by foreign powers for centuries. The project of national unification was channelled through Vittorio Emanuele, the French-speaking King of Sardinia and Piedmont, who became King of Italy in 1861. Political unification did not translate easily into a politically unified state and Italy's regions remained socially, culturally, and linguistically diverse. Debates about, and perceptions of, the new nation in the late nineteenth century were girded by the belief that economic underdevelopment and endemic poverty in Italy's South constituted its defining problem. The region's perceived intractable cultural and social backwardness was seen by some through the optic of benign concern, but by others through the lens of nineteenth-century ideologies of degeneration and racial hierarchy. Colonization and migration were touted as solutions to, but also seen as symptoms of, its alleged backwardness, while some argued that the Italian South had in effect itself been colonized. This view would be later developed by Antonio Gramsci, the Marxist thinker, whose work on the 'subaltern' position of the South and the violence inflicted on it became very influential in postcolonial studies emanating in particular from India and Latin America.

[6] Stuart Hall with Bill Schwarz, *Familiar Stranger: A Life between Two Islands* (London: Penguin Books, 2017), p. 110.

[7] Mary Louise Pratt, *Imperial Eyes: Travel Writing and Transculturation* (London and New York: Routledge, 1992), p. 6 (my emphasis).

Yet as Rhiannon Welch has persuasively argued, debates on the racial composition and origins of Italy made the question of national identity fraught.[8] The investment in a comprehensive albeit contradictory ideology and experience of economic and cultural entitlement grounded in racial classifications and hierarchies became particularly acute in both the emigrant and colonialist experience. Southern Italians especially in the US were distanced, socially as well as racially, from privileged white Anglo-Saxons on account of their darker skin tone, and the physical proximity of Italians to indigenous people in Africa was a constant source of social and political anxiety. Miscegenation was the feared consequence of the 'contact zone'. To counter this fear, anthropologists had also tried to justify the putative 'whiteness' or cultural superiority of Ethiopia as a positive rationale for colonization. Race was a malleable, imprecise, unstable but very powerful tool.[9]

The uncertainties of racial difference certainly figured in the protests held in New York against the invasion of Ethiopia, which had become an emblem of African liberation and a particularly potent symbol of the pan-African movement in the wake of the victory at Adwa. Harlem and Brooklyn, where the protests against the invasion in 1935 were most intense, had significant Italian as well as African American populations, and protest was directed at local Italian businesses as well as at Fascist Italy itself.[10] There was a high level of support for Mussolini and the invasion among pro-fascist members of the Italian community in the US who raised $500,000 for the imperial cause bringing the conjoined logic of the two types of Italian 'colony' into tight alignment.[11]

These local conflicts are the subject of Claude McKay's satirical novel *Amiable with Big Teeth*.[12] Born in Jamaica, but primarily associated with the

[8] Rhiannon Noel Welch, *Vital Subjects: Race and Biopolitics in Italy* (Liverpool: Liverpool University Press, 2016).

[9] For a varied set of perspectives on the racialization of Italians in the US see *Are Italians White?: How Race is Made in America*, ed. by Jennifer Guglielmo and Salvatore Salerno (New York and London: Routledge, 2003). For a concise summation of the racialization of Italians in the UK and elsewhere see Ugolini, *Experiencing War*, pp. 26–27.

[10] The invasion also prompted hostility to Italians settled in Edinburgh and the boycotting of their businesses. See Ugolini, *Experiencing War*, pp. 38–39.

[11] Donna Gabaccia, *Italy's Many Diasporas* (London and New York: Routledge, 2003), p. 148. For an account of the ways in which the Scots Italians participated in Fascist community organizations including offering support for the campaign in Ethiopia see Ugolini, *Experiencing War*, pp. 55–89.

[12] Claude McKay, *Amiable with Big Teeth: A Novel of the Love Affair between the Communists and the Poor Black Sheep of Harlem* (New York: Penguin Books, 2017).

literary culture of the Harlem Renaissance in the 1920s and 1930s, McKay had lived in Europe and North Africa for a number of years and was deeply involved in global debates on black and proletarian liberation. His Celtic surname is itself the inheritance of Scottish involvement in the transatlantic slave trade and plantation slavery.[13] Set in Harlem, the novel is an ironic commentary on the self-serving fervour of competing political factions:

> The tides of Italy's war in Ethiopia had swept up out of Africa and across the Atlantic to beat against the shores of America and strangely to agitate the unheroic existence of Aframericans. Suddenly the people were stirring with action and churches and lodges and clubs and the street were filled and eloquent with protesting crowds. The burden of the protests was 'Help Ethiopia'. The Aframerican newspapers headlined the news of the conflict.[14]

The author depicts a range of affluent, well-educated, and politically engaged members of Harlem's Black community as well as figures from liberal white circles and a duplicitous representative of Comintern, the Communist International, attempting to win African American support. The novel also acknowledges in passing Italian anti-fascist opposition to the invasion and the Italian migrant contribution to radical politics in the US. The intrigue circulates around Lij Alamaya, an Ethiopian envoy trying to secure support for his nation's cause. Srivastava makes the salient point that 'McKay's imagination is both localized and transnational'.[15] While the novel satirizes the aspirations of the Black middle classes in Harlem, more ambitiously, it sets out '[a]n Afrocentric narrative that attempted to restore both centrality and significance to the Italian invasion of Ethiopia in the development of a black political consciousness'.[16] Her contention that the novel has 'an implied Harlemite reader at its centre' offers a further co-ordinate to Italian colonization's transnational 'contact zone'.[17] Yet the novel simultaneously de-centres the Harlem reader's perspective when it comes to the question of race. The district's African American wealthy elite struggles to move, socially and logistically, across the city, and the novel's primary exploration of race, mobility, and space translates the latest invasion of African territory by a white colonial

[13] See, for example, the essays in *Recovering Scotland's Slavery Past: The Caribbean Connection*, ed. by T.M. Devine (Edinburgh: Edinburgh University Press, 2015).

[14] McKay, *Amiable with Big Teeth*, p. 27.

[15] Srivastava, *Italian Colonialism and Resistances to Empire*, p. 120.

[16] Srivastava, *Italian Colonialism and Resistances to Empire*, p. 122.

[17] Srivastava, *Italian Colonialism and Resistances to Empire*, p. 123.

power into a longer history of domination. Lightness of skin tone makes the city more accessible to some and also in part explains the appeal of the Ethiopian envoy's fair-skin to both black and white Americans. Lij Alamaya, however, objects to approving suggestions he might 'pass' as white. Early in the novel, a newspaper report on the Emperor of Ethiopia's declaration that his country 'was not a "Negro" state [...] and that Ethiopians did not consider themselves kin to the Aframericans' causes consternation amongst his supporters in Harlem.[18] The controversy leads to a discussion of race as a highly localized mode of social categorization. Alamaya explains his nation's identification as an African rather than a 'Negro' state, and as 'Ethiopian' rather than 'Abyssinian'. 'Negro' is a 'European creation', and not a useful term for black self-identification let alone empowerment. 'Ethiopia' is the 'ancient original name', and geographically more expansive than Abyssinia.[19] This discussion illuminates McKay's neologism 'Aframerican' as a critical gesture of self-invention and resistance to the racist logics of white America. Although 'Negro' was then a commonly used term in the US, it appears infrequently in the novel and only in the direct speech of particular characters. Most notably it occurs in a conversation denouncing the simian or 'inhuman' representation of Aframericans in art, a representational practice implying that 'Hitler is right when he says in *Mein Kampf* that Negroes are half apes'.[20] After Italy entered the Second World War, the Scottish press represented Italians as subhuman using identical imagery.[21]

## Postscripts from the 'Transnational Contact Zone'

The abrupt shift of focus to Nazi Germany recalls the transnational 'colonization of the mind' mentioned by Hall through the common lexis of racism. His more general reflections on the term 'postcolonial' as a lens through which to look back at colonization stress that its value depends on how it is able to align complex entanglements of time and space. The postcolonial, he argues, 're-reads "colonisation" as part of an essentially transnational and transcultural, "global" process – and it produces a decentred, diasporic or "global" rewriting of earlier, nation-centred imperial grand narratives'.[22] From

[18] McKay, *Amiable with Big Teeth*, p. 114.

[19] McKay, *Amiable with Big Teeth*, p. 119.

[20] McKay, *Amiable with Big Teeth*, p. 230.

[21] Ugolini, *Experiencing War*, p. 43.

[22] Stuart Hall, 'When was the "Post-colonial"?: Thinking at the Limit', in *The Postcolonial Question: Common Skies: Divided Horizons*, ed. by Iain Chambers and Lidia Curti (London: Routledge, 1996), pp. 242–60 (p. 247).

this perspective, the re-evaluation and re-interpretation of 'colonization' and its aftermaths can never be over nor definitively situated in clear-cut national terms.

The practices of 're-reading' and 'rewriting' raise question of language and agency in the spaces of transnational encounter. Pratt argues, for example, that the management of language was an essential tool for imposing or subverting hierarchies of colonial domination in the 'contact zone'. Through the urbane, multi-lingual figure of Lij Alemaya, McKay's Afrocentric narrative consistently insinuates the difference of an Ethiopian as well as an American perspective into Mussolini's colonial narrative. Conversely, on 30 June 1936, when Haile Selassie, the deposed Ethiopian Emperor, addressed the League of Nations denouncing Italian war crimes, particularly the use of outlawed chemical weapons, in the face of loud heckling by Italian journalists, he chose to deliver his appeal in Amharic, rather than in French or English, the organization's two official languages. Haile Selassie had a high level of competence in both but explained (in French) that he would be able to express himself with greater feeling in Amharic. The *Scotsman* described him as '[a] frail, lonely figure, speaking in a language none of the other delegates understood'.[23] His impassioned address was received in translation and the economic sanctions the League had previously imposed on Italy were lifted.

In her study of the politics and practices of translation of medieval Irish literature into English, Maria Tymoczko draws on the work of anticolonial theorists such as Frantz Fanon, Amilcar Cabral, and Edward Said to argue that throughout the period of colonial occupation, translation and the concomitant suppression of the Irish language constituted a 'tangible, physical oppression'.[24] That said, non-translation can also be used to silence unwelcome voices. Ghirmai Negash, for instance, draws attention to the inaccessibility of global translation markets for work written in African languages. In his discussion of two texts about the early phases of Italian colonization written in Tigrinya, a language shared by Eritrea and parts of Ethiopia,[25] he draws

[23] *Scotsman*, 1 July 1936, p. 13.

[24] Maria Tymoczko, *Translation in a Postcolonial Context: Early Irish Literature in English Translation* (London and New York: Routledge, 1999), p. 19.

[25] Ghirmai Negash, 'Native Intellectuals in the Contact Zone: African Responses to Italian Colonialism in Tigrinya Literature', *Biography*, 32.1 (2009), 74–88. The texts he discusses are Fesseha Giyorgis, *Notizie del viaggio d'un Etiopico dell'Etiopia all Italia. In Vero Tigrai* [translated title] (Rome: Tipografia della Casa Editrice Italiana, 1895) and Ghebreysus Hailu, *The Story of the Conscript* [translated title] (Asmara: Petro Silla Printing Press, 1950). The latter text has since appeared in English translation: Ghebreysus Hailu, *The Conscript: A Novel of Libya's Anticolonial War*, trans. by Ghirmai Negash (Athens, OH: University of Ohio Press, 2013). An English

specifically on Pratt's concept of the 'contact zone', to illuminate the complexities of subject formation under colonial rule. The texts adopt contrasting stances towards Italian colonization, shedding light on the complicities as well as the resistances of the 'contact zone'. The voice of the colonized is not singular. The violence of the invasion and its aftermath has been more recently documented in English and in Italian from the perspective of the Ethiopian diaspora. High-profile writers such as Aida Edemariam, Gabriella Ghermandi, Dinaw Mengestu, Maaza Mengiste, and Abraham Verghese now contest the 'colonization of the mind' as the transnational 'contact zone' dilates into the present of the metropolitan consciousness. Yet, returning to Srivastava's observation on McKay's 'Harlemite reader', is it worth asking what sort of reader these postcolonial texts anticipate? Unlike Haile Selassie, these writers speak in the language of colonization. Their texts habitually contain words in Tigrinya or Ahmaric and sometimes a glossary reminding readers of the reverse linguistic encroachment of the transnational encounter and the cognitive challenges of translation. Processes of translation are not simply matters of linguistic competence, but of cultural co-presence and culturally transformative knowledge production.

Although I am now in Edinburgh writing about events that took place at some distance in both space and time, there are occasions when distances collapse and a single and apparently singular instance allows a critical hypothesis about transnational connectedness to assume material form. The 'contact zones' of colonization stretch wide. In 2001, during a clear out in St John's Scottish Episcopal church in Edinburgh, an Ethiopian Tabot, or consecrated altar piece, was discovered 'in a Victorian leather case at the back of the cupboard'.[26] The Tabot, a colonial possession, had been purloined by a military officer after the Battle of Magdala in 1868 at the time of Britain's own colonial incursion into Ethiopia. The church minister who made the discovery recognized its significance and the Tabot was returned in 2002. The biography of this sacred, obdurate object traces the postcolonial connected contours of de-colonization as a zone of transnational contact traced equally, and only apparently unpredictably, through time and space.

Derek Duncan is Professor of Italian at the University of St Andrews.

translation of the earlier text is also available: Hailu Habtu, 'The Voyage of Däbtära Fesseha Giyorgis to Italy at the end of the 19th Century', *Annales d'Ethiopie*, 16 (2000), 361–68, <https://www.persee.fr/doc/ethio_0066-2127_2000_num_16_1_982> [accessed 24 March 2021].

[26] For details of the discovery and restitution see <http://www.afromet.info/treasure/archives/000030.html> [accessed 15 February 2021].

# 6

# Communities

## *Naomi Wells*

> The benchmark for being admitted into an identity category (as a 'real' or 'authentic' member) is 'having enough' of the features specified for them. This is slippery terrain, because 'enough' is manifestly a judgment, often a compromise, and rarely a black-and-white and well-defined set of criteria.[1]

### Language and Community

When defining communities, we might begin with a list of shared features that identify a community, with language typically figuring highly. Language inarguably has strong ties to community identity, both in the sense of a specific named language treated as either belonging to and/or symbolically representative of a community, and in the sense of shared ways of speaking and overlapping linguistic repertoires that contribute to feelings of communality.

While acknowledging the powerful connection between language and community, we must also recognize that they do not map neatly on to each other. The role of language differs not just between communities, but also between individuals within those communities. In different periods and places, the role of language will shift, at times moving to the foreground as an identity marker to distinguish between those who belong and those who do not, as evidenced in recent years with the proliferation of language

[1] Jan Blommaert and Piia Varis, 'Enoughness, Accent and Light Communities: Essays on Contemporary Identities', *Tilburg Papers in Culture Studies*, 139 (2015), p. 7.

citizenship tests in states across the globe.[2] A single named language can be called upon to create the illusion of unity to a community, demanding that its members ignore the reality of their internally diverse individual linguistic repertoires in the name of a unified and singular community identity.

At the same time, sharing ways of speaking with others can contribute positively to feelings of belonging and a shared sense of identity. With friends and close family, we will often develop shared vocabularies and linguistic features that both result from and can strengthen affective bonds. Being far from one's place of upbringing and suddenly hearing the words or accent connected to that place can provoke feelings of attachment even with strangers previously unknown. This does not mean such attachments are not possible in the absence of overlapping linguistic repertoires, but rather acknowledges that language in many circumstances plays an important role in establishing and sustaining communal relations.

While such bonds can reinforce practices of exclusion, particularly when the focus is on 'native' speakers with racialized connotations,[3] recognizing the role of language in sustaining communal relations can help explain one of the primary motivations for those of us who learn new languages. It is not necessarily that we learn a language to become part of an associated community (by learning Italian we do not straightforwardly 'become Italian'), but rather that learning that language can help us to establish a closer relationship with communities to which we may not feel we entirely belong but certainly develop feelings of attachment beyond a mere 'academic' interest. Nevertheless, as researchers with a special interest in questions of language, we may risk reinforcing its primacy in relation to community identity and neglecting or even delegitimizing other identity markers. In particular, we can fall into the Romantic trap of idealizing isolated enclaves that have 'preserved' more forcefully their language, and consequently, we may be inclined to conclude, their sense of community identity. While not ignoring the role language plays in relation to community identity, this chapter explores this relationship in the context of Valparaíso's Italian community, where language plays a complex and ambiguous role.

[2] See Guus Extra, Massimiliano Spotti, and Piet van Avermaet (eds), *Language Testing, Migration, and Citizenship: Cross-National Perspectives on Integration Regimes* (London: Continuum, 2009).

[3] Alastair Pennycook, *Unexpected Places: Language and Mobility* (Bristol: Multilingual Matters, 2012), pp. 94–97.

## Valparaíso's Italian Community

The Italian presence in Chile has been relatively underexplored, reflecting a preference to study more demographically concentrated communities. Despite the relatively small scale of Italian migration to Chile, in the port city of Valparaíso Italian migration has left a clear mark both in the physical landscape of the city, and in the memories and practices of individuals and groups.

The main period of Italian migration to Valparaíso was from 1880 to 1920,[4] although in later periods many moved on to Santiago or smaller towns. The city still maintains several Italian institutions and associations, arguably the most important of which is the Scuola Italiana, opened in 1941 and attended by many members of the present-day Italian community.[5] The majority of the Italians who came to Valparaíso came from the same region of Italy, Liguria. This has had an important effect in relation to language, as in the late nineteenth century and early twentieth, when most migrated, the majority of Italians spoke not the Italian national language but instead regional language varieties that are often termed 'dialects', but that can be as linguistically distinct from each other as Spanish and Italian.[6] The community is now made up of primarily third- and fourth-generation members, and Pinochet's dictatorship from 1973 to 1990 was a period of heightened isolation from Italy, with the Italian government largely cutting off diplomatic relations with Chile. Although recent years have seen efforts to re-establish stronger links with contemporary Italy, this relative isolation from the Italian peninsula has influenced the development of Italian community identity and belonging in Valparaíso.

This brief contextual information is important in framing the subsequent discussion of what it means to be Italian in Valparaíso. For as Donna Gabaccia establishes, 'migration rarely created a national or united Italian diaspora. But it did create many temporary, and changing, diasporas of peoples with identities and loyalties poorly summed up by the national term, Italian'.[7]

[4] Leonardo Carrera Airola, *Italianos en Chile: Un proceso de inmigración y retorno* (Valparaíso: Ediciones Universitarias de Valparaíso, 2015).

[5] Luigi Follegati, Juan Carlos Jeldes, and Javier Iglesias, 'Una escuela erigida por todos/Una scuola costruita da tutti', in *La herencia italiana en la región de Valparaíso/L'eredità italiana nella regione di Valparaiso*, ed. by Gabriela Castillo Raga (Santiago: Consiglio della Comunità Italiana Regione Valparaiso and Escuela de Diseño Universidad Nacional Andrés Bello, 2011), pp. 178–97.

[6] Martin Maiden, *A Linguistic History of Italian* (London: Longman, 1995), p. 5.

[7] Donna R. Gabaccia, *Italy's Many Diasporas* (London: UCL Press, 2000), p. 6.

Certain practices and features considered to be emblematic of group identity are still recognizable across Italian contexts of migration, such as those connected to food, religion, and, inevitably, language. Nevertheless, the example of the Italian community in Valparaíso highlights distinctions in how these features are displayed, understood, and practiced, and also sheds light on other localized practices that may only be understood as indexing 'Italianness' within this specific context.

## Language, Place, and *Italianidad*

The following discussion draws on a period of fieldwork and a series of interviews with self-identifying Italo-Chileans in Valparaíso. The emphasis in these interviews was on personal narratives as 'a rich source for identity work'.[8] Both at my own prompting and the interest of those interviewed, language remained a key focus of discussion, particularly in the case of Renato, now in his mid-sixties, whose four grandparents all migrated from Italy, primarily from Liguria.

Interestingly, Renato was well-known in the community as one of the few people who still regularly spoke the dialect, typically referred to as Genovese. In the interview, Renato explained that the use of dialect was explicitly discouraged during his time studying at Valparaíso's Italian School, as was also the case across Italy at the time, with dialects generally considered an obstacle to students' progress.[9] Although Renato reported that his mother was told by the teacher not to even use Genovese at home, he and his mother resisted this rejection of Genovese as an unnecessary language.

As well as Renato's proudly polyglot identity, expressed in the interview through his playful use of Italian, Genovese, Spanish, and English, another explanation for his strong desire to maintain Genovese can be found in his affective ties to the language, as illustrated in this extract:

> Y mi madre, mi madre, nos enseñaba. Estaba la tabla para hacer la pasta. Que la tengo en casa y es de mi abuela, la mamá de mi mamá. Está media vieja, pero está, allí está en la cocina. Entonces mi madre, me parece verla, esta es la tabla, mi madre al medio, mi hermano acá a la derecha y yo aquí a la izquierda. Entonces pongan harina, una taza

[8] Mike Baynham, 'Performing Self, Family and Community in Moroccan Narratives of Migration and Settlement', in *Discourse and Identity*, ed. by Anna De Fina, Deborah Schiffrin, and Michael Bamberg (Cambridge: Cambridge University Press, 2006), pp. 376–97 (p. 378).

[9] Tullio De Mauro and Mario Lodi, *Lingua e dialetti* (Roma: Riuniti, 1993).

> de harina. Pongan otra taza de harina. Ábranlo un poquito. Echen una tacita de agua. Después pongan el huevo, vamos aceite. Y allí nos aprovechaba de enseñar un poco la pronunciación.[10]

We see how for Renato the desire to continue speaking Genovese is tied to powerful affective associations of the language with his mother and the home environment. This extract also illustrates the connection between linguistic and other bodily practices: the act of preparing pasta, which is connected to the object of the board for making pasta that Renato has importantly kept in his home as a material possession that carries 'family histories, and multiple, layered stories'.[11] Here we are reminded how people's lived experiences of language take place within specific physical environments that prompt us to adopt certain habits and dispositions associated with a specific society and/or community.[12]

While other members of the community interviewed did not typically continue learning or speaking Genovese, it is important to note that dialect and not Italian was often spoken in the home by grandparents and sometimes also parents. Rather than being the language of the home environment as we often think of heritage or community languages, Italian in reality had more institutional ties, most commonly being associated with the Scuola Italiana. Despite this, Renato still expressed strong affective ties to both the School itself and relatedly the Italian language when I asked him whether such institutions were important:

> O sea, para mí fundamentales. O sea, si no hay Scuola, no es fácil que estudien italiano. O sea, cruzamos la calle y en el cuarto piso dice italiano, ruso, francés, inglés, portugués. Pero no es lo mismo, no es lo mismo tomar un curso rápido y aprender one two three four five,

[10] Renato: 'And my mother, my mother, she taught us. There was the board for making pasta. Which I have at home and it's from my grandmother, my mum's mum. It's very old, but it's there, it's there in the kitchen. And so my mother, I can almost see her, this is the board, my mother in the middle, my brother there on the right and me here on the left. And so add the flour, a cup of flour. Add another cup of flour. Open it up a little. Add a little cup of water. Then add the egg, in goes the oil. And there she used the time to teach us some of the pronunciation'. All extracts have been translated into English by the author.

[11] David Sutton, 'Cooking Skills, The Senses, and Memory: The Fate of Practical Knowledge', in *Food and Culture: A Reader*, ed. by Carole Counihan and Penny Van Esterik (New York: Routledge, 2013), pp. 299–319 (p. 304).

[12] Daniel Miller, *Stuff* (Cambridge: Polity Press, 2010).

que vivir durante doce o trece o catorce años en un ambiente que es la segunda casa. Creo yo.[13]

This and related comments in other interviews illustrate how the Scuola Italiana played an important role for those who attended it as one of the environments in which their sense of belonging to Valparaíso's Italian community was constructed. The description of the Scuola as a second home illustrates Renato's affective ties to it and reveals connections between his sense of being 'at home' both within the school environment and in his use of the Italian language studied there.

Interesting here is how Renato contrasts the experience of learning Italian within Valparaíso's Italian School, a site of shared symbolic importance to the community, to a more 'neutral' language-learning context. Relatedly, during the interview, Renato was keen to understand my own connection to Italy and the Italian language. On outlining aspects of my own biography, in particular having studied the language for a number of years and having lived briefly in Italy, Renato remarked with amusement, 'You're more Italian than me!', drawing attention to potentially competing definitions of what it means to be Italian. In this case treated with amusement, across the interviews my own positioning was a key point of negotiation, and potential tension, concerning what laying claims to an Italian identity might mean. The ironic tone of Renato's comment suggests he was highlighting the contradiction of appearing to display more globally recognized Italian identity markers, most notably linguistic and cultural expertise gained through formal study and a short period living in Italy, while possessing no familial connection and not identifying explicitly with a specific or global Italian community. My biography was thus a reminder of the limitations of relying on specific features, such as knowledge of a specific language, to determine community membership.

In this and other conversations with Renato, he emphasized the importance of other local sites connected to the community, particularly the 'emporios', the stores that were one of the key sites where Italian migrants first worked in Valparaíso.[14] The importance of local sites becomes more salient in the very different case of Victor, again a third-generation Italian although only his paternal grandfather came from Italy. In contrast to most Italian migrants

[13] Renato: I mean, for me essential. I mean, if there isn't Scuola it's not easy for them to study Italian. I mean, we can cross the road and on the fourth floor it says Italian, Russian, French, English, Portuguese. But it isn't the same, it isn't the same to take a quick course and learn one two three four five, as living for twelve or thirteen or fourteen years in an environment which is a second home. That's what I think.

[14] Carrera Airola, *Italianos en Chile*, p. 55.

to Valparaíso, his grandfather came from the Friuli region and Victor himself did not attend the Italian School, nor learn Italian or the Friulian regional language at home, even if both were spoken on occasion by his father and grandfather. He did briefly study Italian as an adult after applying for Italian citizenship, which he did for practical reasons following advice that it could offer him greater protection under Pinochet's dictatorship. This contact with the most institutional form of Italian identity triggered a brief interest in learning Italian, but beyond a very brief course, Victor did not go further in learning or regularly speaking Italian.

While language and more formal Italian organizations in the city were of less interest to Victor, when I asked specifically whether Italian identity in the city was connected to more subtle factors, he explained the significance of everyday habits:

> [...] el hábito que uno tiene, ehm, desde varias cosas. Una es lo que tiene que ver por ejemplo con este tema de los- de los comercios, de los mercados, de los almacenes. Eso. Y eso que tiene que ver al mismo tiempo con los oficios. Eso no es solamente de la colonia italiana en todo caso, pero en algunos- en algunos tiene que ver con la colonia italiana, en otros casos tiene que ver con la colonia árabe, etcétera. Pero que tiene que ver con la gente que tiene ese vínculo, ese aprecio por esa- esa forma digamos y por esa herencia.

He described doing all his shopping in these places with a distinctive way of relating to people, and linked this to questions of family and food:

> Entonces la comida, por ejemplo, eh, y la comida hecha, qué sé yo, yo lo hago aquí. Mi viejo lo hacía también etcétera. Yo hago el pan que consumo, no solamente hago el pan, hago la harina.[15]

Victor's reflections highlight the importance of practices and habits, as well as the exterior environments in which they take place, in relation to what

[15] Victor: [...] the habit one has, ehm, in relation to a number of things. One of them has to do for example with this subject of the- of the shops, the markets, the grocery stores. This. And this at the same time is connected to trade. This is not just for the Italian community in any case, but in some- in some cases it has to do with the Italian community, in others with the Arab community, etcetera. But it is linked to people that have this connection, this appreciation for this- this way, let's say, and for this inheritance. [...] So the food, for example, eh, and the homemade food, whatever, I make it here. My old man did the same too etcetera. I make the bread I eat, I don't just make the bread, I make the flour.

makes us who we are, rather than more static or emblematic identity features. He emphasizes how his sense of Italianness is tied to shared local habits and sites in Valparaíso where language, or at least an identifiably 'Italian' language, does not appear to play a central role. Equally, he emphasizes the role not of specifically 'Italian' ingredients or recipes but rather, again, the bodily practices of cooking from raw ingredients. Victor's sense of Italianness thus rarely points back to an Italian identity and culture as defined within Italy itself. This is seemingly reflected in Victor's ambivalence towards the Italian language, tied for him to a more institutional conception of Italian citizenship and identity.

## Conclusion

The examples of Victor and Renato offer insight into the slipperiness of determining what the benchmarks for claiming an Italian identity might be, highlighting the importance of uncovering local conceptions of what 'having enough' means in relation to much broader identity categories such as 'Italianness'. A strong familial connection to somebody who migrated from the Italian peninsula is most salient for these interviewees, but beyond that the shared emblematic features of the Italian community in Valparaíso are less easily defined. Although the idea of language as a feature of Italianness inevitably still circulates, as illustrated by Victor's brief attempt to learn Italian, at this period in time regular use of Italian or an Italian regional variety is not a notably shared habitual practice and consequently does not appear to constitute an essential feature of what it means to be Italian in Valparaíso. Individual members of the community such as Renato may retain strong affective ties and, relatedly, the habitual practice of using Genovese and Italian, reminding us of the emotional dimension of the lived experience of language.[16] For Victor, however, knowledge of Italian is connected primarily to formal citizenship and national identity as defined from within the Italian peninsula, rather than a locally defined community identity tied to the specific histories and practices of those who originally migrated and their descendants.

In exploring the complex ways in which an emblematic feature of community identity such as language is experienced by individuals within that community, Renato's interview further highlights how language intersects with other features, practices, and the exterior environment. At the

[16] Brigitta Busch, 'Expanding the Notion of the Linguistic Repertoire: On the Concept of *Spracherleben* – The Lived Experience of Language', *Applied Linguistics*, 38 (2015), 340–58.

same time, Victor's reference to other communities with similar practices points to the fluidity of community boundaries and to the challenge, and arguably futility, of attempting to assign specific habits and practices to a single cultural heritage or community. What is of interest then is not the listing of the specific features, habits, and sites themselves, but rather the phrasing and discursiveness through which these elements are combined.[17] While not intended to be generalizable or representative of all communities, or even all members of this specific community, Victor and Renato offer uniquely telling narratives through which to explore this bricolage of places, features, and practices that make up their individual and shared conceptions of Italianness.

Naomi Wells is a Lecturer in Italian and Spanish with Digital Humanities at the Institute of Modern Languages Research, London.

[17] Michel de Certeau, *The Practice of Everyday Life*, trans. by Steven Rendall (Berkeley: University of California Press, 1988), p. xviii.

# 7

# Conflict

*Connor Doak*

The word *conflict* has its origins in the Latin *con* (with) and *fligere* (to beat or strike down), an etymology that points towards one of the paradoxes of conflict. While we normally think of two parties in conflict as utterly opposed to each other – aiming to strike each other down – conflict also brings rival parties together in unexpected ways. One has to know one's enemies, and, when nation is set against nation, transnational knowledge and intercultural skills acquire a premium. Indeed, the history of modern languages as a discipline is intertwined not just with the rise of nationalism, but with international conflict.[1] Interest in a particular language often waxes and wanes in response to shifts in world power: for example, the Cold War period saw increased government investment in Russian Studies, as well as a spike in the number of students learning Russian in the UK and the USA. Some of these learners sought careers in the military, diplomacy, or espionage, while others were fascinated by the language, culture, and people behind the Iron Curtain. Yet the relationship between language and conflict goes beyond intelligence and diplomacy. Conflicts are not conducted solely through physical violence, but through a contest of language, discourse, and narrative. Moreover, if language can be used as a weapon, to divide and conquer, it can also serve as a way to reckon with the evils of war and conflict, and its power may be harnessed in the service of resolution and peace.

*A Handbook* opens with a discussion of how borders are created and enforced, challenged and transgressed. One area where these processes play

[1] For a discussion of the links between language and conflict see *Languages at War: Policies and Practices of Language Contacts in Conflict*, ed. by Hilary Footitt and Michael Kelly (Basingstoke and New York: Palgrave Macmillan, 2012).

out most clearly is in international warfare, where the stakes of conflict are highest. In this chapter, I consider conflict both as a 'coming-together' and a 'tearing-apart', a breaking down of boundaries and an attempt to reaffirm them. In the most literal sense, national borders break down in wartime as the army of one country penetrates another. Battle lines are drawn and redrawn as one side advances and the other retreats, and the map may be altered after a conflict. However, at the human level, wartime also sees boundaries between individuals fractured and reaffirmed, sometimes in unexpected ways. The battlefield can provide an opportunity for meeting the enemy face-to-face, a particularly fraught form of transnational encounter that can be both terrifying, yet also intimate. Gender roles, too, are paradoxically reaffirmed and challenged in times of conflict. War has long been associated with a particular kind of heroic masculinity, but the violence, injuries, and death associated with war also reveal the fragility of masculinity and the hollowness of heroic ideals. And if women were traditionally imagined in wartime texts as the loving, caring wives waiting at home, or as the devoted nurses on the front lines, war has also provided women with an opportunity to engage in roles that challenge the conventions of femininity, both on the battlefield and at home.

Conflict operates at the limits of what language can and cannot express. On the one hand, war furnishes material for a certain kind of story with a predictable plot: a courageous hero overcomes unlikely odds to vanquish an evil enemy. Such tales of heroism can be found across human cultures from ancient epics to contemporary blockbuster films. These narratives have often been used to create a collective memory, shore up patriotism, and forge national identity. Yet the heroic narrative has been adapted, subverted, fractured, and remade over the centuries, showing both its durability and its limitations. Indeed, many writers and artists have moved away from conventional language and forms to depict violence and conflict, creating innovative works that defy generic categorization and experiment with the limits of representation. As military technology has advanced, so writers and artists have responded by finding fresh, experimental ways to convey violence. For example, many poets of the First World War found that the language they inherited to talk about war – one of chivalry, glory, and honour – had little relevance to modern industrial warfare.[2] Some twenty years later, the painter Pablo Picasso employed grotesque surrealism in his famous *Guernica* (1937), a response to aerial bombing in the Spanish Civil War, then a new form of

[2] For a classic account of how the First World War altered literary depictions of conflict in English literature, see Paul Fussell, *The Great War in Modern Memory* (Oxford: Oxford University Press, 1975).

combat. Picasso came to think of art itself as a weapon: '[T]he purpose of painting is not to adorn apartments. It is an instrument of war to attack and defend against the enemy'.[3]

In what follows, I examine the work of two contemporary poets whose experimental depictions of conflict challenge the heroic narrative, complicate our perception of the enemy, question our assumptions about masculinity, and explore the limits of representational language. First, I consider *Dien Cai Dau* (1988) by the African-American poet Yusef Komunyakaa (b. 1947), a collection based on his experiences serving in the Vietnam War (1961–75) as a Combat Correspondent (1969–70) with the Americal Division of the US Army.[4] Komunyakaa's work reimagines the transnational encounter between the Americans and the Vietnamese, showing it as intimate, on the one hand, and mediated by differences of language and culture on the other. As a Black poet and soldier, Komunyakaa places the Vietnam War within a longer history of US race relations, and the history of anti-Black discrimination and marginalization informs his critical perspective on the war.[5] I then turn to Maria Stepanova (b. 1972), a Russian poet whose long poem *War of the Beasts and the Animals* (Voina zverei i zhitovnytkh) (2015) offers a harrowing portrait of the war in Ukraine (2014–present).[6] Stepanova works in a transhistorical, mythological idiom, showing how human beings repeat and rehash the narratives and mistakes of the past. Eschewing conventional, gory representations of violence and death, Stepanova instead evokes the horror of war through a mutilated language and inherited culture of conflict.

The very title of Komunyakaa's book suggests translingual exchange: 'dien cai dau' is Vietnamese for 'crazy', a phrase that Americans picked up during the Vietnam War (1955–75). The use of a Vietnamese phrase in the title suggests an attempt to provide a defamiliarizing perspective on the war.

[3] Picasso in Simone Tery, 'Picasso n'est pas officier dans l'armee Française', *Les Lettres françaises*, 24 March 1945, p. 6.

[4] Yusef Komunyakaa, *Dien Cai Dau* (Middletown, CT: Wesleyan University Press, 1988). Subsequent references to this work appear in parentheses in the main body of the text.

[5] For a fuller reading of Komunyakaa's work, I especially recommend Angela M. Salas, *Flashback through the Heart: The Poetry of Yusef Komunyakaa* (Selsingrove, PA: Susquehanna University Press, 2004).

[6] The poem was first published in Russian in *Zerkalo*, 45 (2015) and is available online at <http://magazines.russ.ru/zerkalo/2015/45/1s.html> [accessed 19 January 2022]. An excellent translation by Sasha Dugdale is available in *Modern Poetry in Translation*, 3 (2017), 183–210. Subsequent references are to the Dugdale translation in parentheses in the text.

Komunyakaa, writing as an American, is all too aware of the haphazard and cruel approach of his own side, justifying the label *dien cau dau.* A case in point is the poem 'The Red Pagoda'. The poet-speaker begins by describing the soldiers' stealth as they skilfully evade Vietnamese snipers en route to their next target, a red pagoda. However, when they reach the pagoda, Komunyakaa offers a defamiliarizing description of himself and his own fellow soldiers arm-in-arm 'like men on some wild | midnight-bound carousal' (10). While the image evokes a strong sense of solidarity, Komunyakaa imagines this male collective not as disciplined soldiers, but as revellers united by some primal energy. If Western literature has often depicted their Asian opponents as unruly or savage, then Komunyakaa reverses the Orientalist gaze here, imagining the American soldiers as wild and uncivilized. On the one hand, the poem suggests a powerful sense of unity among the Americans, with differences of race and status vanishing during their assault on the pagoda, which acts like an initiation rite. On the other hand, the reader is aware that this sense of brotherhood is purchased at the expense of Vietnamese lives and culture. The Americans' sadistic violence and cruelty is underlined in the poem's final image, which sees the exhilarated Americans smash the pagoda 'till it's dried blood' (10).

While 'The Red Pagoda' focuses on relationships among the Americans, 'Starlight Scope Myopia' explores how the Americans see the Vietnamese, highlighting the peculiar dynamics of intimacy and enmity on the battlefield. The poem depicts a group of Americans tracking a band of Viet Cong by night. The poet-speaker watches the Vietnamese through the sights of an M-16 rifle, which makes their bodies appear as white forms illuminated like spectres by the infra-red light. Such visual distortion evokes the peculiarity of the wartime transnational encounter: the Americans are close enough to see the forms of the enemy, yet their gaze is mediated by technology. The Vietnamese do not know they are being watched, and the reader is drawn into the act of voyeurism. Yet, even as the poet-speaker is preparing to shoot, he unexpectedly expresses a desire to protect. Noticing an elderly, bowlegged man among the Viet Cong, he adds 'you feel you could reach out | & take him in your arms' (18). Sunny Yang has argued that this image points the way towards 'a more nurturing form of intimacy that might emerge from the wartime context to transform Afro-Vietnamese relations'.[7] Yet Komunyakaa also highlights the partiality or limitations of the American perspective here. For all the poet-speaker's proximity to the enemy, he cannot reach out to him,

[7] Sunny Yang, 'Expanding the Southscape to the Global South: Remapping History and Afro-Vietnamese Intimacy in Yusef Komunyakaa's *Dien Cai Dau*', *African American Review*, 53.2 (Summer 2020), 79–93 (p. 87).

and he has no way of knowing whether the elderly Vietnamese man would welcome his embrace.

Seeing the Vietnamese soldiers talking, the poet-speaker wonders what their 'ghost talk' (18) is about. Are they discussing women, or 'calling the Americans / *beaucoup dien cai dau*?' (17) Three languages are mixed together here: *beaucoup* (many) is a borrowing that came with French colonial rule, its continued presence in the Vietnamese language a testament to the enduring legacy of another set of transnational encounters and wars. On the one hand, the poet-speaker's attempt to imagine what the Viet Cong soldiers are talking about indicates a sense of empathy. On the other hand, the poem shows the gulf of difference between the two groups. After all, the poet-speaker is putting words in the mouths of the Viet Cong soldiers, which are apparently based on his own heteronormative assumptions (are they talking about women?) and his own perspective as an American (they could be talking about us?). Just as the rifle sights can give only a visually distorted picture of the enemy, so the poet-speaker's attempt to 'rea[d] ghost talk' (18) can be only partially successful. Of course, this point applies to conflict more broadly: while the poem makes room for a transnational, translingual empathy that crosses battlelines, it also hints at the ethical dangers of making assumptions about what the other is thinking.

The ethical ambiguity of the transnational encounter is explored further in 'We Never Know'. In this poem, the poet-speaker approaches to examine the body of an enemy combatant. He picks up and inspects a photograph belonging to the dead man, and turns over the corpse, ostensibly a gesture of charity so he is not lying face down. However, the poem is charged with a sexual energy between the two men. It opens with a phallic image of his and his enemy's two 'white-hot' (35) gun barrels, suggesting the erotics of violence. Paradoxically, the act of killing separates the two men, but also for a transgression of the heteronormative boundaries that would normally divide them. This queer interpretation is given further credence when the poet-speaker approaches the body and picks up the photograph, remarking simply, 'I fell in love' (35). The object of his love – the dead soldier? his girlfriend in the photo? – is purposely left open to interpretation: Yang calls it a 'potentially queer declaration of love'.[8] The poet-speaker's final gesture of turning the dead body upright also suggests a certain affection for the fallen enemy, showing how quickly wartime enmity can transform into love and respect.

Or does it? A different, more uncomfortable reading of 'We Never Know' suggests there is something perverse about the poet-speaker's actions. After all, his intimacy with his enemy is uninvited, possible only after his

[8] Yang, 'Expanding the Southscape', p. 14.

enemy's death. His gaze at the enemy's cherished photograph and the casual declaration of love – whether aimed at the dead soldier or the figure in the photograph – can be interpreted as presumptuous, even violating. One might even argue that the poem itself, which is frequently anthologized and has brought Komunyakaa considerable fame, owes at least part of its success to the death of the unknown Vietnamese combatant depicted therein. Considered in this light, 'We Never Know' offers a more unsettling portrait of transnational relationships during wartime: the fantasy of intimacy with the enemy is fraught with its own power dynamics.

The ethics of writing about war become a key concern in Stepanova's *War of the Beasts and the Animals*. This long poem defies easy summary, as the poet intentionally refuses to supply a unified narrative of conflict, instead creating a pattern of voices and images evoking its horrors. Whereas Komunyakaa begins his poetry on a local level, using the geography of Vietnam and works towards transnational and symbolic connections, Stepanova employs a transhistorical and even mythological idiom from the beginning to describe the war in Ukraine. *War of the Beasts and Animals* provides a rich fabric of allusions extending from Ancient Greece to medieval Russia and the Second World War, and, as the title suggests, to the animal kingdom, as well.

Stepanova's poem thus sews together a transnational and transhistorical patchwork of cultures and societies. However, this tapestry, far from being beautiful to behold, contains violent, bestial images and narratives that have travelled across cultures and remained stubbornly persistent over time. For example, the following lines bring together images from Ancient Greece and Nazi Germany:

> дети на даче играли в богов олимпийских
> после играли в гестапо – да разницы нет
>
> children in the yard play at being Olympian gods
> and then at gestapo interrogation – tbh it's much the same (192)

Here, Stepanova draws a dotted line between Ancient Greek mythology – often hailed as the beginnings of Western civilization – and Nazi Germany – often considered the ultimate expression of evil. Both the heroic narratives of Greek gods and the horror stories of the Gestapo have become part of our children's heritage, and both are reprised endlessly in child's play, without critical reflection. The translator's use of the modern abbreviation 'tbh' (to be honest) in the final line quoted here adds a connection to our own time, and signals a sad sense of inevitability and exhaustion that human beings pass on the narratives of conflict from generation to generation.

In the discussion that followed a reading of the poem in 2017, Stepanova highlighted her belief that even children's culture was saturated in the language and imagery of violence.[9] To this end, her poem frequently combines lyrics of popular songs and even children's rhymes with violent language of war, as in the following examples:

> ехал на ярмарку ухарь
> ямщик во степи замерзал
> [...]
> уходили богомольцы-мукомолы
> ой да на гражданскую войну
>
> This little piggy went to market
> And this little piggy froze to death (186)
> [...]
> hi ho hi ho and off they go
> to civil war (188)

Anglophone readers will almost universally recognize the phrases 'this little piggy' and 'hi ho', but here these childish phrases are wrenched from their usual context, creating a jarring impression of a world that has lost its innocence, and a language that has been mutilated. Such passages pose a particular challenge for Sasha Dugdale, the translator. 'This little piggy' is her rendering of Stepanova's 'ekhal na iarmarku ukhar'' (a go-getter went to the fair), the opening line from a popular Russian poem and song. Dugdale's domesticating approach supplies a cultural equivalent for Anglophone readers unfamiliar with Russian cultural landmarks. Here, we appreciate the importance of the translator as a transnational agent, conveying the work's critique of war and violence to audiences across borders.

Elsewhere, Stepanova evokes the language of the medieval Russian epic *The Lay of Igor's Campaign* (Slovo o polku Igroeve) (*c.*1185), which depicts Prince Igor's failed military campaign against the Cumans, a rival Turkic people. Mimicking its famous opening, Stepanova writes:

> were it not seemly, citizens
> to begin in ancient diction
> to stay silent (191)

[9] Maria Stepanova and David Constantine, 'Launching *Modern Poetry in Translation* "War of the Beasts and the Animals"', The Queen's College, Oxford, 6 November 2017.

не лепо ли, граждане
старыми словесы
начати молчати

Russian readers will recognize key phrases here as lifted from *The Lay*: 'were it not seemly' (ne lepo li) and 'ancient diction' (starymi slovesy). Stepanova keeps the archaic lexis and syntax of Old Russian, which grant the text a quasi-sacred status. However, she intentionally misquotes *The Lay*. Her jarring substitution of 'citizens' (grazhdane) for the ancient 'bratie' (brothers) evokes the modern, and suddenly the reader is confronted not with an ancient epic, but something more akin to a modern politician's speech. This choice not only suggests a historical continuity in how we think about conflict, but also suggests the ways in which contemporary leaders use and misuse historical and fictional narratives for modern ends. Moreover, Stepanova's addition of 'to stay silent' (molchati) provides an unexpected interruption that cuts off the tale. The implication is that the time for this kind of epic poetry that extols military deeds and aestheticizes violence has passed. It would be better to remain silent than to sound again the horns of war.

Throughout the poem, Stepanova is suspicious of the ability of language to convey horrors and mistrustful of the role of the poet in respect to violence. The idea of a narrative interrupted recurs throughout the poem, as in the following lines that convey a rhythmic poem breaking down:

здесь ямбы прыгают, пока четырехстопы,
но спотыкаются о голые глаголы
и падают далёко от европы,
обиженные шкурки кровяня

and here the iambs trip-trap: tetrameters chirrup
but trip up on naked vowels
and fall so far from europe
bleeding pelts, they howl (192)

Unlike contemporary English poetry, much Russian verse still makes use of regular metres and rhyme schemes. Stepanova, however, implies here that the horrors of war have made the sing-song regularity of poetry undesirable, or even impossible. The images of 'naked vowels' hints at the violation and humiliation of war, while 'bleeding pelts' evokes its bestial savagery. The phrase 'so far from europe' perhaps suggests Ukraine's failed ambitions to break away from Russian influence and align itself with Western Europe, or indeed Europe's failure to respond to Russian aggression. The mapping of poetic prosody onto geographical space suggests a critique of the ways in which language and culture are so often used to justify military interventions and incursions across borders.

Stepanova returns to the violent power of language towards the end of her poem:

> это как в замешательстве выплюнешь слово с крючком
>
> а оно уже в деревотеле засело
> или в теле товарища
> в родной
> человекогубе
> вот и нитка запляшет
>
> *рыба рыбу поймала*
>
> like when in a moment's confusion you spit out a barbed word
>
> and it lodges in a treebody
> or the body of a comrade
> or a friendlip
> and the line goes taut
>
> *fish hooks a fish* (210)

Words are 'barbed', like a fishhook, capable of entering another's body, or indeed, of baiting live people. Here, we are reminded of Picasso's idea of art as a weapon that can attack or defend against the enemy. However, whereas Picasso appears optimistic about the potential of art, and Komunyakaa's poetry bears witness to the horrors of Vietnam, words are dangerous in Stepanova's poem, capable of ending friendships, destroying nature, and killing one's comrades.

Just like conflict, language itself can also bring people together or tear them apart. Language and culture are used to construct the stories that supposedly make each nation unique, different from any other, yet language and literature also provide the tools to build transnational connections between nations. Komunyakaa's poetry shows how, paradoxically, conflict emphasizes the differences between peoples and our lack of mutual understanding, while also revealing our common humanity. However, Stepanova's poetry is more unsettling. We often think of language as a phenomenon that differentiates humans from animals, but her poem suggests that human language, literature, and even civilization provide a conduit for a bestial, brutal violence that links us back to the animal world. For Stepanova, the languages, narratives, and cultures that we imbibe from childhood are tarnished and we must begin inventing them all over again.

Connor Doak is Senior Lecturer in Russian
at the University of Bristol.

# 8

# Cosmopolitanism

*Luke Sunderland*

The most immediate connotations of the term 'cosmopolitan' are overwhelmingly positive – openness, mobility, modernity – and the cosmopolitan individual can be thought of as a modern world citizen who can move easily between languages and cultures. Free of national prejudices and limitations, the cosmopolitan is at home anywhere. Yet the term has also been used as an insult.[1] Seen negatively, the cosmopolitan appears rootless, dabbling, parasitic, without commitment to any community or place, lacking loyalty to their own country. Thus, the term has xenophobic, and perhaps more specifically anti-Semitic, connotations, the cosmopolitan being related to stateless or displaced persons, refugees and asylum seekers.

Cosmopolitanism can easily be confused with globalization. Free trade and democracy are often presented as shared, universal values, but actually represent the spread of European liberal, elitist beliefs. Instead, in a tradition that grows out of philosopher Immanuel Kant's concept of the universal *polis* (a city or political community that would include the whole world), cosmopolitanism is sometimes thought of in terms of universal rights and justice. What are we all, as humans, entitled to? The questions of rights to food, water, and safe shelter show how cosmopolitanism can connect with ecological and environment concerns: cosmopolitanism is happening anyway, whether you like it or not, since we are all, as humans, exposed to the same risks and dependent on the same material conditions, making us all part of the same global community. More broadly, 'human rights' to security,

[1] For an example and analysis, see <http://www.politico.com/magazine/story/2017/08/03/the-ugly-history-of-stephen-millers-cosmopolitan-epithet-215454> [accessed 18 June 2017].

liberty, justice, dignity, and cultural and religious expression all transcend national communities. The idea of cultural freedoms clearly makes it difficult to defend the imposition of Western models of modernity on other cultures. Even more problematically, human rights do not sit easily within a world-system where rights are guaranteed by nation-states, which by their very structure encourage peoples to define themselves as separate from the rest of humanity, and to see mobility as negative. Control of immigration and the reassertion of national borders have long been key slogans of electoral campaigns, leading to practices of increased screening and policing. Under this system, we have rights as citizens of a particular state, more than as humans. And, as Seyla Benhabib has argued, the problem with such norms of citizenship is that they affect most keenly those who have no say in determining them: the excluded, asylum seekers, refugees, or stateless persons.[2] Writing in the aftermath of the Holocaust, Hannah Arendt pointed to the problematic lack of a legal sphere above nations:[3] the concept of human rights requires a universal legal idea of the human, but still today human rights are largely guaranteed reciprocal agreements between nations, leaving others outside, unprotected. Cosmopolitanism connects to juridical and moral questions about world law and governance, as well as transnational concerns such as the environment.

Extending this way of thinking, cosmopolitanism can usefully be related to feminism,[4] to anti-racist and anti-slavery movements, and to minority rights. It can be linked to counter-cultures and resistance to a mainstream conservative culture and white male elite hegemony: to be cosmopolitan, on this view, is to accept equality and diversity. Thus, the cosmopolitan question is not just about how different states relate to one another, but about relations within states, especially those that are multi-ethnic. Kwame Anthony Appiah suggests that forms of nationhood could themselves become more multicultural, and that nationhood is not necessarily a problem.[5] Local histories are themselves, he says, the product of movements, since no culture develops in a vacuum. He puts forward the idea of the 'rooted' cosmopolitan, who can pledge allegiance to their country but still remain committed to universal

[2] Seyla Benhabib, 'Another Cosmopolitanism', in *Another Cosmopolitanism*, ed. by Robert Post (Oxford: Oxford University Press, 2006), pp. 11–80 (p. 19).

[3] Hannah Arendt, *The Origins of Totalitarianism* (New York: Harcourt, Brace, 1951).

[4] Mica Nava, 'Cosmopolitan Modernity: Everyday Imaginaries and the Register of Difference', *Theory, Culture & Society*, 19.1–2 (2002), 81–99; Rosi Braidotti, *The Posthuman* (Cambridge: Polity, 2013), pp. 45–50.

[5] Kwame Anthony Appiah, *The Ethics of Identity* (Princeton: Princeton University Press, 2005).

values. Appiah's viewpoint is somewhat optimistic: he does not see patriotism and wider values as incompatible. Homi Bhabha, who is less confident, worries that local, popular forms of heritage might be crushed by spread of an elite cosmopolitan culture.[6] Instead, Bhabha coins the term 'vernacular cosmopolitanism' to image a cosmopolitan who retains their connection to a particular community, while being aware of the need for openness to others. Bhabha also insists that all cultures are mixed, evolving, and hybrid, rather than being eternally fixed entities. Cosmopolitanism in Bhabha's definition, then, means negotiating between cultures, a work of adaptation most often undertaken by the oppressed. We can see today that it is the world's poorest who have to move the most, whether as displaced persons, migrants, or refugees. Thus, Bhabha reminds us that cosmopolitanism should not be seen as the province of the elite.

In another contribution that attacks elitist conceptions of cosmopolitanism, Jacques Derrida critiques French immigration policies in light of the nation's self-identification as a land of openness and tolerance.[7] Noting that immigration into France was actually encouraged for economic reasons, Derrida sees cosmopolitanism in terms of the duties of hospitality: we have an infinite responsibility to welcome those in need, but 'national' concerns will always press for the limitation of rights of residence. Hostility and hospitality are close etymological cousins, Derrida reminds us. For Derrida, the cosmopolitan is a potential enemy, but one we can choose to treat as a friend, making cosmopolitanism a matter of ethics and virtues, rather than rights. We are failing ethically when we build luxury hotels to welcome privileged tourists, but grim camps to house refugees. Derrida thinks we need open spaces beyond state structures for true hospitality to develop, citing the cities of refuge or sanctuary. Clearly, the creation of solidarities beyond borders is something still to come, and cosmopolitanism can be about imagining new worlds: it could, for Derrida, entail 'reflection on the questions of asylum and hospitality – [allowing] a new order of law and a democracy to come to be put to the test'.[8] Like Bhabha, Derrida sees cosmopolitanism as an ongoing project, yet to be achieved or perhaps even envisaged. Julia Kristeva, too, relates cosmopolitanism to the imagination and the psyche, portraying attachment to the (mother)land as childish, and contrasting it to the mature

[6] Homi Bhabha, 'Unsatisfied: Notes on Vernacular Cosmopolitanism', in *Text and Nation: Cross-Disciplinary Essays on Cultural and National Identities*, ed. by Laura Garcia-Morena and Peter C. Pfeifer (London: Camden House, 1996), pp. 191–207.

[7] Jacques Derrida, *On Cosmopolitanism and Forgiveness*, trans. by Mark Dooley and Michael Hughes (London: Routledge, 2001).

[8] Derrida, *On Cosmopolitanism and Forgiveness*, p. 23.

acceptance of the otherness within us all.[9] Our attitude towards strangers is, then, a matter of our relationship to what is most unfamiliar within ourselves. Feelings of dislocation, of not belonging, of not fully being a member of a community can, on this view, have ethical potential, because they open us up to others.

Cosmopolitanism, then, is always affective as well as rational, defined by openness to difference, by respect for other cultures and values, and by the work of adaptation, empathy, and imagination. All these are skills and dispositions that the study of non-Anglophone languages, literatures, and cultures might encourage. The study of narratives has in particular been linked to the development of empathy and the ability to see other people's perspectives.[10] But we must remain vigilant against a narrow or superficial cosmopolitanism: cultures can always be taught and studied along insular, nationalistic, and imperialist lines, and much depends on attitudes and configurations. We can seek expressions of cosmopolitan thinking even in the most nationalized of cultural objects, for example by approaching Shakespeare not as a great Englishman but as a 'global' author who made use of stories and ideas from beyond his own context and who spawned performances, translations, and adaptations – films, novels, works of art – all over the world.[11] In universities, the development of Francophone and Hispanic Studies departments are attempts to get away from the imperial perspectives inscribed in the ideas of 'French' and 'Spanish', which make Europe the centre and relegate African, South American, and other cultures to the status of peripheries. Languages can instead be seen as the common properties of large, transnational groups. The widening of the remit of 'modern languages' departments beyond the teaching of European cultures forms another part of this process. But whichever language you learn, you risk approaching the task in a 'shallow' cosmopolitan way: learning a language for commercial purposes might mean looking solely to those cultures that are already 'open for business' and participating only in a globalized capitalist or consumer culture. In such cases, learning other languages entails nothing more than learning new words for the same old things. Another danger might be an 'Orientalist' approach

[9] Julia Kristeva, *Nations without Nationalism*, trans. by Leon S. Roudiez (New York: Columbia University Press, 1993).

[10] Weik van Mossner, *Cosmopolitan Minds: Literature, Emotion, and the Transnational Imagination* (Austin: University of Texas Press, 2014) gives us a cognitive perspective on the ways literature encourages empathy across national, ethnic and religious boundaries.

[11] This way of thinking about Shakespeare is suggested by Cyrus R.K. Patell, *Cosmopolitanism and the Literary Imagination* (New York: Palgrave MacMillan, 2015).

to other cultures, seeing them as exotic, alluring, dangerous, and exciting but ultimately inferior to Western ways of life.[12] What I would call 'deep' cosmopolitanism depends, instead, on the willingness to see other perspectives, concepts, and identities. Though practices of migration and travel, or repeated contact with other cultures, do not necessarily lead to openness, the cognitive skills of cosmopolitanism can be developed through everyday experience as well as through education. They are not our exclusive or automatic right as scholars of foreign cultures, and we should think of cosmopolitanism as something that needs to be actively practised.

The fluidity and excitement of modern cities, with their mixed cultures, might make them the stereotypical image of cosmopolitan culture, but cosmopolitanism is not just a modern phenomenon. Questions of periodization and canonization are pertinent here. Non-specialists often seize upon texts from my own field of medieval studies as intolerant, citing moments in epic texts where Christians are opposed to 'Saracens', a blanket term for religious others. But medieval texts can be read as showing respect for other cultures and as hoping for common ground. The fourteenth-century Franco-Italian epic known as the *Entrée d'Espagne* has as its hero Roland,[13] best known as the belligerent Frankish hero of the *Song of Roland*, a canonical, perhaps the canonical, medieval French literary work. Like the *Roland*, the *Entrée* narrates a holy war in Spain, but Roland quarrels with his king, Charlemagne, about its conduct. Cast out by Charlemagne, Roland becomes a rebel against the mainstream, imperial culture of crusade, disguising himself as a merchant and travelling across the Mediterranean, where he ingratiates himself with the sultan of Persia thanks to his linguistic abilities – he speaks Greek, Syrian, and Armenian as well as Persian – and to his courtliness and knowledge of good governance. Both Roland's own openness and the hospitality he finds in the East allow for new diasporic identities and connections across cultural lines. Roland admires the Persian culture he finds, and the Persians desire to know more about Frankish chivalry and manners. A counter-culture to holy war emerges here. The exile and the cosmopolitan look the same, reminding us that we often define one kind of movement as positive, and others as negative, without there really being any ethical difference. In the *Entrée*, a hierarchical cultural element remains, however, as the eventual solution comes when the Persians convert to Christianity, which is thus presented as superior, and when Roland returns to fight in Spain. This narrative demonstrates, then, that cosmopolitanism is a 'dialogic psychic

[12] For this concept, see Edward Said, *Orientalism* (London: Routledge, 1978).

[13] *L'Entrée d'Espagne: chanson de geste franco-italienne*, ed. by Antoine Thomas, 2 vols (Paris: SATF, 1913; repr. Florence: Olschki, 2007).

formation',[14] where the mind is pulled in multiple directions by the influences of different cultures. The *Entrée*'s ending suggests a cultural hierarchy, but its meaning is not solely determined by the final state-of-play. The text's other currents suggest more diverse patterns of cultural interaction, exemplifying the way that literary texts can display the conflicting forces at work within and between cultures, thanks to their ability to interweave multiple voices, stories, and trajectories.

The most famous cosmopolitan of the medieval era was probably Marco Polo, member of a family of powerful Venetian merchants. His book is named *The Travels* in the most popular modern editions and presented as a narrative of first contact between Europeans and Asian civilizations.[15] Like the *Entrée*, *The Travels* was written in the hybrid literary language of Franco-Italian, via a collaboration between Marco and the Arthurian romance writer Rustichello of Pisa that took place in a Genoese prison in 1298, just after Marco returned from spending twenty-four years in Asia. Multi-lingual and open-minded, Marco displays 'deep' cosmopolitan attitudes, going far beyond an interest in economic opportunity. He debunks common myths about the existence of monstrous races in Asia and avoids the broad-sweeping geographical labels common in encyclopaedias and world-descriptions of his time – Europe, Africa, Asia – instead documenting in detail the system of kingdoms and provinces that make up the Mongol Empire. He does not see the world in terms of blocs, but rather takes interest in its 'diversity',[16] showing a willingness to incorporate new vocabularies into his thinking. Marco admires the empire he discovers for its sophistication and wealth: its palaces, banquets, ceremonies; its beautiful textiles, spices, and precious stones; its roads, postal networks, and paper money; its variety of customs, crops, and animals. He finds himself 'at home' in Asia, easily shifting identifications. For example, he presents the Buddha as similar to a saint, focusing not on superficial differences but on the hidden common points in the way humans in distant places arrange their cultural, economic, and religious lives.

Unlike modern works, medieval texts are diverse in each of their copies. Different manuscripts of the same work can have, for example, different titles. *The Travels* were better known in the medieval period as *Le Livre du Grand Caam* (The Book of the Great Khan), *Le Livre des merveilles* (The Book of Wonders), or *Le Devisement du monde* (The Description of the

14 Nava, 'Cosmopolitan Modernity', p. 82.

15 *The Travels*, trans. by Robert Latham (London: Penguin, 1958); *The Travels of Marco Polo*, trans. by W. Marsden, revised by T. Wright (New York: Everyman, 2008).

16 On diversity, see Simon Gaunt, *Marco Polo's 'Le Devisement du Monde': Narrative Voice, Language and Diversity* (Cambridge: D.S. Brewer, 2013).

World). Aiming to reshape the way we think about the text, Sharon Kinoshita chose this last title for her recent translation,[17] but none of the medieval titles places the focus on Marco as explorer. *Le Livre du Grand Caam*, in particular, suggests that the real subject is the cosmopolitan Mongolian empire Marco describes:[18] the emperor Qubilai Khan tolerates religious diversity and integrates non-Mongols in powerful positions. The Mongols assimilated 'new' technologies from various peoples, such as the Turkic way of writing known as Uyghur script, and the West Asian textile known as cloth-of-gold, whereas elephants, which the Mongols first obtained via capture from their enemies, were swiftly integrated into public processions. The Mongols often preserved local customs in the provinces they took over, and Qubilai created a genuine cultural fusion, with the 'foreign' intimate at his court, which became a hub of ideas, religions, goods, and people from across Asia. Marco's text describes this medieval world-system, a set of interconnected trade routes. As Janet Abu-Lughod has shown, from 1250 to 1350, travel and communication across Asia were possible thanks to the stability offered by a series of Mongol conquests.[19] Chinese, Islamic, and central Asian materials, skills, and expertise circulated in a world-system where Western Europe was a mere periphery. Marco was accepted in this world because he had the requisite linguistic skills. The prologue says he learned languages and customs quickly, and that he told stories of distant lands and customs that fascinated Qubilai. But he was just one polyglot among many: the translators, officials, diplomats, and merchants of the Mongol court comprised Turks, Chinese, Russians, Persians, and other ethnic groups, and, in fact, the Mongols themselves were a minority. Officials were regularly reposted to different parts of the empire, creating further intercultural contact. There were freedoms of cultural and religious expression. In all this, cosmopolitanism was a work of adaptation undertaken by the imperial power itself. The Mongol court also oversaw vast projects of compiling extensive geographical knowledge from various cultures, and Marco likely drew on the models and information he found there, which supplemented his own eyewitness account.

[17] Marco Polo, *The Description of the World*, trans. by Sharon Kinoshita (Indianapolis: Hackett, 2016).

[18] I draw here on Sharon Kinoshita, 'Reorientations: The Worlding of Marco Polo', in *Cosmopolitanism and the Middle Ages*, ed. by John M. Ganim and Shayne Aaron Legassie (New York: Palgrave MacMillan, 2013), pp. 39–57. María Rosa Menocal details the cosmopolitan culture of medieval Spain: *The Ornament of the World: How Muslims, Jews and Christians Created a Culture of Tolerance in Medieval Spain* (Boston: Little, Brown & Company, 2002).

[19] Janet Abu-Lughod, *Before European Hegemony: The World System A.D. 1250–1350* (Oxford: Oxford University Press, 1989).

His debts to Arab and Chinese cosmographical and encyclopaedic texts can be detected. This further shifts the focus away from the individual European as the cosmopolitan, highlighting a longer tradition of exploration and documentation, and a more collaborative culture of authorship. The violence of Mongolian empire cannot be denied, and indeed Marco narrates struggles between rival provinces. But the empire's violence was not due to its being medieval; indeed, as Bhabha and Derrida point out, the world has not yet seen a completely cosmopolitan space, a fully open realm without inequalities of race and religion.

Cosmopolitanism, then, is not uniquely modern or European, and the Western vantage point has been over-emphasized. We must avoid making cosmopolitanism a neo-colonial privilege, enjoyed by wealthy, globe-trotting tourists, and profit-seeking traders. Marco Polo benefited from extended hospitality in Asia only because he was hospitable to other values, and his own cosmopolitanism was just one of many cosmopolitan practices co-existing in the world before European hegemony. Recognizing the cosmopolitanism at work in the *Description of the World* is also, as we have seen, a question of how we read and frame it: on a Eurocentric reading, the text can be seen as 'about' the cosmopolitanism of the intrepid Westerner – an elite European male – who records his travels in an eyewitness account, or as 'about' the cosmopolitanism of the Mongol empire that the Westerner is privileged to discover and to whose peoples, practices, and texts he is indebted. Both he and they were multi-lingual, and clearly medieval culture realized the importance of multi-lingualism. The study of languages, literatures, and cultures undoubtedly retain this potential for interconnectedness, for stimulating new forms of community, though much depends on what we read and how we read it. Cultures distant in time or space have much to teach us, provided we unmoor ourselves from our comfortable positions of superiority and expose ourselves, with open minds, to other ways of being.

Luke Sunderland is a scholar of medieval Francophone culture and Professor of French at Durham University.

# 9

# Creativity

*Alice Kettle and Tamsin Koumis*

### *Thread Bearing Witness*

Textiles, the use and production of cloth, tell the story of the everyday, of histories and of social and political structures. Textiles speak about lives through their formal qualities, their material substance, and their social context. They transmit the transformative potential of making, the enduring traditional stories, and also carry contemporary relevance. As an artist, my voice is made confident through the medium of stitched textiles. This medium shows how the process of making enables movement back and forth between metaphor as a creative impulse and concrete realization as the work takes shape and that is essential to artistic creation. It also offers a particular narrative voice that can be appropriated to represent the feminine condition. Rozsika Parker's *The Subversive Stitch: Embroidery and the Making of the Feminine* delved into women's creative practice of the domestic crafts.[1] She explored how stitch both marginalized women within the domestic realm and provided a distinct language to escape this entrapment. Needlework affords an enabling space for women, challenging the denigration of their milieu, by using it 'for social or political purpose'[2] and for collective working and creative ends.[3]

[1] Rozsika Parker, *The Subversive Stitch: Embroidery and the Making of the Feminine* (London: IB Tauris, 2010).

[2] Melanie Miller, 'Embroidery and the F-word', in *Hand Stitch Perspectives*, ed. by Alice Kettle and Jane McKeating (London: A&C Black Visual Arts, 2012), pp. 116–31 (p. 119).

[3] Craft and activism are also key areas; see Betsy Greer, *Knitting for Good! A Guide to Creating Personal, Social, and Political Change, Stitch by Stitch* (Boston: Trumpeter

Material knowledge in making is not about being fixed or solid, but about movement, attentiveness, responsiveness, and change. This is the context in which I use stitching and more broadly the creativity of craft, not as a kind of manufacturing of things, but as a common language or way of being that embraces the tradition of women's work. In this essay, I explore how it extends to become a multi-cultural, totally inclusive connecting force, which can affect change.

My focus is on the creative artistic project *Thread Bearing Witness* (2017–2019),[4] which uses thread as a chronicle of shared making and testimony. The project has been a complex and difficult process of learning about, connecting with, and responding to refugees and other individuals seeking asylum. The difficulties are mediated through the absorbent qualities of fabric and their processes, allowing me and those contributing to the project to use textile to present tragedy within the cloth itself and to validate one another's place within a shared material world. It is the first time that I have met or worked with refugees and this work documents a shift from the personal perspective of artist as author to a different, untidy, and unpredictable model of co-creation, with distributed and collective making. Textiles offer a powerful medium through which to explore these themes of cultural heritage, journeys, and displacement. As a domestic practice, textiles can represent home making and home finding, and it is steeped in the history of trade with its associated socio-political and economic use and production.

The link between engaging in a craft activity and active engagement in social issues is explored within the realm of 'Craftivism'. Betsy Greer explains Craftivism: 'it's about making your own creativity a force to be reckoned with'.[5] Through engaging with a craft activity, an individual realizes their ability to manipulate a medium: their power to shape the world around them.

## Textiles and Trade

The migration of textiles and its patterns are bound into our global and local histories as part of a rich cultural exchange. The place of textile in our lives is grounded in the everyday and powerfully evocative. We all possess a version

Books, 2008) and David Gauntlett, *Making is Connecting* (Cambridge: Polity Press, 2011), p. 20.

[4] <www.threadbearingwitness.com> [accessed 7 February 2021]. The exhibition *Thread Bearing Witness* was shown at the Whitworth Gallery, Manchester, UK, 1 September 2018–24 February 2019.

[5] Quoted in Jack Z. Bratich and Heidi M. Brush, 'Fabricating Activism: Craft-Work, Popular Culture, Gender', *Utopian Studies*, 22 (2011), 233–60 (p. 248).

of varied cloths with rich iconography in our homes or in our memory. For example, we are familiar with (even though we may not realize their place of origin) the heavy double-sided damask cloth from Damascus with decorative floral patterns, Paisley Indian shawls, stitched appliqué and beadwork, the Suzani textiles from the Persian tradition with embroidered pomegranates, and the sun and moon discs from Tajikistan, Uzbekistan, and Kazakhstan. The ancient Silk Road and Cotton routes link and leave traces of political, economic, and cultural histories, with trade from Samarkand to the West, to Persia, to China, and to India, forming intersections, threads of connection made through textile. The city of Samarkand (from 200 BC) was a vital meeting point from where iconography and pattern were dispersed and have been adopted, transformed, and represented in new cloths and new Western interpretations of hybrid motifs and forms. The historic migration of Asian and African textile patterns has influenced European designs as a consequence of trade and of the histories of the spheres of socio-political and imperialist influences. The textile historian Philip Sykas suggests that this influence cannot be 'overestimated, nor can the influence of textiles in spreading foreign visual cultures to the other arts'.[6] Patterned cloth is the rich code of place and people, of movement and stability. It is contemporary, relevant, and culturally binding, and indeed textile migrates where people cannot.

## *Thread Bearing Witness*

The current issue of migration is the most pressing challenge of our time. It is impossible to ignore and brings deep questioning of values in relation to equality, power, and vulnerability, and to the social and political structures that impact on notions of justice. *Thread Bearing Witness* connects the migration of textile pattern to the current challenge of migration of refugees and asylum seekers into the European continent. The project concentrates on stitch but draws upon textile as a broad term (including weave, print, and embroidery) with its shared pattern-making character, tangibility, and familiarity.

The pattern of increased movement of people into Europe since the late 1990s and its acute 'crisis'[7] since 2015 represent the disruption and fragmentation of established political infrastructures, in particular outside Europe, and the resistance to displaced people entering Europe. The anti-migration

6 Philip Anthony Sykas, *The Secret Life of Textiles: Six Pattern Book Archives in North West England* (Bolton: Bolton Museum, 2005).

7 We recognise that the use of the term 'crisis' represents a Eurocentric border panic.

lobby was a forceful contribution to the Brexit referendum (23 June 2016) in the UK, epitomizing a kind of nationalistic isolationism.

In 2015 my daughter Tamsin Koumis co-founded the Dunkirk Legal Support Team,[8] an access to rights project in the Dunkirk refugee camp, at a time when migration and xenophobia were reaching a climax in Europe, the consequences of which arguably materialized in Brexit. She has contributed to this piece of writing though it is written through my voice, aside from a few distinct quotes. Koumis wrote: 'After working in the camp in Dunkirk, I felt overwhelmed by the seeming impossibility of change and the enormity of the challenge faced by refugees in Europe'.[9] Koumis became the impetus for me to take responsibility for my own reaction to this human tragedy, and she was the close link between myself and the issues of those seeking asylum and refugees. During the initial stages of the project she acted as a guide to the sector, to its protocols, its language, and to some of the people within it.

Together we went to the Pikpa camp in Lesbos, Greece, which is twelve kilometres across the straits of Euripus to the Turkish mainland.[10] Pikpa, run by Lesbos Solidarity, is a unique and small camp serving the especially vulnerable families who were identified from the other huge local camps as being acutely at risk. Koumis described Pikpa as atypical: 'Pikpa was an experience of optimism and hope, and served to remind me that it could be done – that refugees can be treated with humanity and that a holistic and humanising approach can succeed'.[11] Our aim was to bring creative energy to the camp, part of the overarching focus of the whole project, by stitching and drawing. To be present, to be witnesses, to participate. This approach was burdened with doubts as to the efficacy of mediating horror through decorative means. On the north of the island were banks of life jackets, thousands discarded and washed up on the land. These, with protective silver heat foil blankets, provided much of the source material to cut and rework into banners, bags, streamers, and wall hangings. We decorated the camp, setting up our making-place in its centre. Some came for a few minutes, others day after day, making anything from vegetable bags to decorative hangings and offerings for the artworks made by me. We held the meaning of

[8] <https://wewelcomedthis.wordpress.com/2016/07/25/dunkirk-legal-support-team/>; <https://refugee-rights.eu/>; <https://www.bindmans.com/news/dunkirk-legal-support-team-challenge-home-office-over-forgotten-refugee-chi>; <https://www.facebook.com/DunkirkLegalSupportTeam/> [accessed 9 February 2021].

[9] Personal communication (20 February 2017).

[10] Pikpa was forced to close in 2020. See <https://www.lesvossolidarity.org/en/what-we-do/pikpa-camp> [accessed 19 July 2021].

[11] Personal communication (3 March 2017).

material matter in our hands and in our imaginings. We remade new meaning by mending and reforming cloth as we listened to the news of the bombing by the Syrian government of civilians in eastern Ghouta.

Finding meaning through stitching and making implied 'the generation of meaning'. The anthropologist Tim Ingold describes how materials can foster meaning making: 'many disciplines in the arts and social sciences are currently redirecting their attention to surfaces, and ways of treating them, as primary conditions for the generation of meaning'.[12] Benedict Carpenter takes Ingold's view further to indicate the layering and complexity of 'surface' meaning, 'not in any sense that the surface is thin: meaning is a thick surface, woven between sameness and difference'.[13] *Thread Bearing Witness* draws from this material culture to think about creative identity, which is part of the surface and bound into the making of the textile works. The process and realization of the project has changed and been reformulated, much like the making of a cloth, where the design is established and the materials are selected but the making itself generates the multiple meanings that are secured into each cloth, 'thickly' determined by their reciprocity and relationship.

The project uses pattern to create symbolic monumental textiles populated by imagery from multiple sites and by contributions from individuals, to whom it gives voice. Kathryn Sullivan Kruger talks of 'the mysterious power of fabric', which reproduces symbols and beliefs while acting as a metaphor 'for the creation of something other than a cloth – a story, a plot, a world'.[14] These new textiles are neither local nor culturally specific but represent a mixture of motifs, which serve to chronicle the contemporary migration crisis. The works create new perspectives and configurations of a multicultural, diverse, and unified world where thread bears witness, and textile and pattern are seen as the starting point of change. Life experiences, threats, and conflict seek resolution through textile terms: 'binding people together', 'tying of loose ends', and the making of the 'rich tapestry of life'.

*Thread Bearing Witness* has three primary strands, with satellite activities that feed in and morph in their own ways. Individuals, groups of refugees, and those seeking asylum were invited to contribute to and inform monumental

[12] Tim Ingold, 'Surface Visions', in *Theory, Culture and Society*, 34: 7–8 (2017), pp. 99–108 (p. 99).

[13] Benedict Carpenter, 'Meaning in the Arts: Material and Content in Made Things' (unpublished PhD thesis, Manchester Metropolitan University, 2019), p. 165.

[14] Kathryn Sullivan Kruger, 'Clues and Cloth: Seeking Ourselves', in *The Fabric of Myth*, ed. by Antonia Harrison and James Young (Warwickshire: Compton Verney, 2008), pp. 10–34 (p. 10).

stitched artworks called *Ground, Sea,* and *Sky* (each 3m x 8m) or to make their own works, while a group of more established displaced artists contributed their own work as a collaborative project, under the name *Travelling Heritage Bureau*. Alongside these ran a participatory project called *Stitch A Tree,*[15] which now includes more than 6000 stitched tree contributions from all over the world. Signifying support and collective making, these trees have been stitched together as a vast forest quilt. The creative metaphor and process facilitate discussion of social issues, and how community resilience can be built: 'if we think imaginatively together ... this helps build resilience ... and the creative capacity to deal with great challenges'.[16]

The strands evolved as broad inclusive processes with the metaphorical and physical capacity of stitch to make new, to enrich, and to join together. The method sought to recognize the lived experience of those contributing and with concern for the deep sensitivities, precarities, and individual circumstances. Thus, the completed works are simply the evidence of a much wider project of co-creation. The thread of continuity between these varying perspectives stems from three core elements: human connectivity, textile, and the creativity of people and the resilience of creativity.

## *Ground, Sea,* and *Sky*

The three textile works show three views of three shared universal physical encounters with the world. *Ground* and *Sky* are viewed pictorially as though looking across land and up to skyscape, while *Sea* takes a bird's eye view. *Ground* and *Sky* could not be preconceived, since they are formed through the image tokens, that is, contributed drawings, which couldn't be predicted. I became the pattern maker, choreographing imagery as scattered offerings across a coloured textile surface. *Ground* is intensely filled with a multiplicity of flowers, houses, hearts, people, trees, and patterns, and *Sky* as airy space is the recipient of birds, kites, and planes. The images are surprisingly optimistic, unproblematic, and decorative. There is some reference to conflict, the suggestion of explosive disruption, and the ravages of fire, but

[15] The original idea for the *Stitch a Tree* project came from the Refugee Resilience Collective, who worked with refugee children in the Dunkirk refugee camp, La Linière, in April 2017 and used the 'Tree of Life' – a strength-based narrative therapy tool – to begin conversations with the children about strength and resilience. Gillian Hughes, 'Finding a Voice through "The Tree of Life": A Strength-based Approach to Mental Health for Refugee Children and Families in Schools', *Clinical Child Psychology and Psychiatry*, 19 (2013), 139–53 (p. 150).

[16] David Gauntlett, *Making is Connecting: The Social Meaning of Creativity* (Cambridge: Polity Press, 2011), p. 20.

the randomness of this process reflects the subject itself, a mass of disenfranchised people in movement across the earth. *Ground* forms a new cloth pattern, of asymmetry, multiple and irregular variations that are part of a diverse, multi-cultural environment, and common ground. The view is roughly panoramic, with the sweep of the embroidered surface of persons in motion, of fragments of memory combined with an attachment to a place of origin, sustained tenuously by the prospect of eventual return. Writing about this work, Brandon Taylor suggests that it is 'no matter that we cannot always tell which elements are by Kettle's hand and which are in some sense additions to a one-person conception of the scene'.[17]

*Sea* predates *Ground* and *Sky* and was made through my view as informed through the lens of the media, before the contribution of imagery. It concerns death, disguised in the hue of rich textiles. All three works are based on untidy, disrupted symmetry but that through the repetitious stitching have acquired rhythmic motifs. This could be compared, for example, to the offbeat pattern rhythms in Kuba cloth and to the phrasing of African music, where the rhythmic emphasis shifts back and forth, 'enlivened by offbeat phrasing of accents, by breaking the expected continuum of surface, by staggering and suspending the pattern'.[18] The orchestration of these motifs is one aspect of the wider engagement of the project as a whole, the investment of time and the sustained relationships with those who have participated.

### *Ali*

Among those individuals who took part and to whom we inevitably grew close, was Ali (not his real name), a young unaccompanied minor from Afghanistan, who came into the UK through the work of the Dunkirk Legal Support Team. Ali was well read in Western classics and philosophy, especially Aristotle (about whom he often spoke), the Peripatetic philosophers, and Islamic thinkers such as Avicenna. He had never spoken directly to a woman outside his family, and had left his mother, sister, aunts, and cousins behind in Afghanistan. His father had died in the UK before he could reach him. Ali is extraordinarily gifted, wise, and principled. We worked together, drawing and learning from each other, and we designed a piece of embroidery that his family in Afghanistan made for the project. He also wrote a text on Afghani embroidery,[19] and did

[17] Brandon Taylor, 'Precarious Journeys', in *Thread Bearing Witness*, ed. by Alice Kettle et al. (Alton: The Artists Agency, 2018), pp. 21–43 (p. 35).

[18] Ardis M. Rewerts and Alira Ashvo-Munoz, 'Off-Beat Rhythms: Patterns in Kuba's Textiles', *Journal of Popular Culture*, 32 (1998), 27–38 (p. 30).

[19] <http://threadbearingwitness.com/embroidery-in-afghanistan/> [accessed 10 February 2021].

many drawings that contributed to the larger textile pieces. The embroidery is a flag, a symbol of cultural pride and acts as a love token for the women in his family from whom he is separated. The textile has been able to cross the borders that so definitively separate him from his family.

*Making and Creativity*

The affordances of craft and its relationship with the material world can be 'intimate or outwardly directed – an unfolding engagement that forms an organic link between the self and the surrounding material and social environment'. Craft practice simultaneously promotes more subtle understandings of relational interdependence, empathy, equanimity, humility, and a certain generosity of spirit.[20] In his book *The Craftsman*, Richard Sennett advocates the merging of craft with the world. Sennett suggests that a defining attribute of making is looking outward and beyond instrumental ends, to shape how we converse with one another.

> Both the difficulties and the possibilities of making things well apply to making human relationships. Material challenges like working with resistance are instructive in understanding the resistances people harbour to one another or the uncertain boundaries between people. I have stressed the positive open role routine and practicing play in the work of crafting physical things; so too do people need to practice their relations with one another, learn the skills of anticipation and revision in order to improve these relations.[21]

Sennett talks about craft as a means to make good. 'It is a construct for imaginatively and practically making and remaking place and patterns of living'.[22] Thread and textile with their material capacities are a powerful tool to create and develop dialogue. There has been a shift for me from observer to actively advocating for the plight of refugees with the desire to make a difference. As such the responsibility for artistic voices to transpose the lived experience of others has proved complex and uncomfortable. This has required openness and a willingness to relinquish established methods and

[20] This refers to a longer text by Paul Harper and Alice Kettle, 'Making Leaders/Curating Maker Cultures', presented at the Poetics of Leadership conference, hosted by the Crossfield's Institute, University of Cumbria, 2018, <https://www.crossfieldsinstitute.com/wp-content/uploads/2018/09/Paul-Harper-Alice-Kettle.-Leadership-precis-draft.pdf> [accessed 22 March 2022].

[21] Richard Sennett, *The Craftsman* (London: Penguin, 2008), p. 289.

[22] Quoted in Harper and Kettle, n.p.

to recognize craft as an adaptive process, which fixes, translates, transforms, and moves on. The agency of material and maker encourages a reciprocity and dialogue between place and people, between observation and action, between the singular and the synergistic/pluralistic experience of textiles. It has proved to be a way of listening to material as instrumental in provoking ways of listening to the world and to one another and to operating as sentient, responsible citizens. This utopianism of making is tempered by the specific, practical realities of labour and the context of making. It operates as a way of making good, making more, idealising the future as a place that we want to live in. It follows that the proximal spaces can equally be shaped and reformed.

## Conclusion

The 'making [of] things for ourselves gives us a sense of wonder, agency, and possibilities in the world'.[23] It also helps us to conceptualize ourselves as the protagonists of the change-making. The act of creation can help us to imagine the potential for how we can build the world around us, giving us the tools to shape our own world experience and invest it with meaning.[24] In this sense, through craft, we become aware of our own power.

Bratich and Brush regard craft as 'power (the ability or capacity to act)'.[25] They explain, 'Power here is not equivalent to hierarchy and domination (*potere* in Italian; *pouvoir* in French) but more like capacity or ability (*potenza* and *puissance*)'. They continue: 'Craft fastens the concrete and the abstract into a material symbol. Fabriculture is a materialization of a series of relationships and symbols'.[26] The anger, frustration, and detachment that characterize the feelings of many UK citizens towards the issues faced by refugees and asylum seekers can all be gathered into an action and projected towards a tangible outcome through the stitching process of the *Stitch a Tree* project. Furthermore, craft is an action that can be seen to break down boundaries and binaries, as it 'stitches across common distinctions between old/new, material/immaterial, economic/semiotic, bio/info, and digital/tactile, textual/textured and opens to a new fabric of relations'.[27]

Corbett argues that the power of craft is inherent within its slower pace, that its gentleness is its strength, and that quiet action such as stitching has a

[23] Gauntlett, *Making is Connecting*, p. 9.
[24] Ivan Illich, cited in Gauntlett, *Making is Connecting*, pp. 167–68.
[25] Bratich and Brush, 'Fabricating Activism', p. 246.
[26] Bratich and Brush, 'Fabricating Activism', p. 255.
[27] Bratich and Brush, 'Fabricating Activism', p. 246.

distinct power outside of direct action.[28] She advances the process of making as a means to engage thoughtfully in the issues we are concerned with, to influence and effect change. There is room for what she calls the alternative agency of stitching to influence the outcome of politics.

*Thread Bearing Witness* invites contributions of popular and contemporary imagery as multiple testimonies of migration. These reflect the places that refugees have come from, where they are now, and visualizations of their own futures. In the twisting of thread, and the binding of cultural imperatives, the land is reformed and reimagined as the collective interconnected social world they chose to live within, as a re-assemblage of new futures. This intense period of instability and accelerated global migration forces us to think about how to create order out of disorder. Textile and pattern allow us to think creatively about being human, as we live in the everyday, while also influencing and making the world we want to be within.

Alice Kettle is a contemporary fibre artist and Professor of Textile Arts at Manchester Metropolitan University.
Tamsin Koumis works on social justice and migration projects in the UK and Europe.

[28] Sarah Corbett, *How to be a Craftivist: The Art of Gentle Protest* (London: Unbound, 2017).

10

# Digital

*Thea Pitman and Claire Taylor*

> The vocation of the Net is that of multiplicity and difference. There can never be a single giant Net, a Superhighway with only one style of navigation; the net is contamination and multiculturality par excellence. [...]
> Cyberspatial practices need to contribute to the transformative defence of place and cultural difference (as resistance to the normalizing logic of hierarchies), even as they create novel forms of trans-local interaction and communities.
>
> Arturo Escobar[1]

## The Digital and the Transnational

Scholars have often commented on the imbrications of digital technologies and globalization, with the Internet, in particular, often being seen as helping usher in an era of transnational global capital. Many have pointed out the negative consequences of such a phenomenon: the Internet owes its inception to military intelligence sharing (in the USA), and has subsequently become a key tool of contemporary neoliberal globalization. For example, Manuel Castells's

[1] Arturo Escobar, 'Other Worlds are (Already) Possible: Cyber-Internationalism and Post-Capitalist Cultures', *Textos de la CiberSociedad*, 5 (2005), <http://www.cibersociedad.net/textos/articulo.php?art=18> [last accessible 10 June 2016]. For archived article, see <https://web.archive.org/web/20160610173757/http://www.cibersociedad.net/textos/articulo.php?art=18> [accessed 15 January 2022].

notion of 'informational capitalism' sees the neoliberal, corporatist model of capitalism as facilitated by the structures of flows of information, capital, and symbols enabled by networks. Alternatively, Christian Fuchs defines 'global network capitalism' as the global technological systems and transnational institutions that enable 'global flows of capital, power and ideology that create and permanently re-create a new transnational regime of domination'.[2] This is not to say that digital networked technologies are neoliberal per se; rather that they are frequently used in the service of, and often co-opted by, neoliberal capitalism. Critics of the Internet's potential for spreading neoliberalism the world over have also expressed concern that, from a linguistic and cultural perspective, the result will be the loss of linguistic diversity in the face of global commercial linguas francas, especially English; the flattening/selling-out of cultural/ethnic difference so that it becomes no more than different options available to (Western) consumers; the consolidation of a corporate monoculture of predominantly US origin; and thus the creation of new dynamics of exclusion and appropriation, both real and virtual.[3]

The Internet and other digitally enabled communication technologies are thus of substantial concern for Modern Languages scholars. But while it is certainly the case that the Internet has contributed to a reconfiguring of national boundaries, for example, this does not, of necessity, mean that the Internet *always* has a negative impact in this regard. Other scholars have argued that the Internet offers a significant erasure of the limitations of national/regional boundaries and of centralized power formations through its distributed networks.[4] It thus offers the possibility of a virtual 'commons' with a wealth of opportunities to renegotiate our sense of place and belonging, creating affinity-based rather than place-based networks

[2] Manuel Castells, *End of Millennium* (Oxford: Wiley-Blackwell, 2010), p. 397; Christian Fuchs, *Internet and Society: Social Theory in the Information Age* (New York: Routledge, 2008), p. 113.

[3] John C. Paolillo, 'How Much Multilingualism? Language Diversity on the Internet', *The Multilingual Internet: Language, Culture, and Communication Online*, ed. by Brenda Danet and Susan C. Herring (Oxford: Oxford University Press, 2007), pp. 408–31; Jennifer González, 'The Appended Subject: Race and Identity as Digital Assemblage', in *Race in Cyberspace*, ed. by Beth E. Kolko, Lisa Nakamura, and Gilbert B. Rodman (New York: Routledge, 2000), pp. 27–50; Herbert Schiller, 'The Global Information Highway: Project for an Ungovernable World', in *Reading Digital Culture*, ed. by David Trend (Oxford: Blackwell, 2001), pp. 159–71; and N. Ben Fairweather and Simon Rogerson, 'The Problems of Global Cultural Homogenisation in a Technologically Dependent World', *Journal of Information, Communication and Ethics in Society*, 1.1 (2003), 7–12.

[4] Ronald J. Deibert, *Parchment, Printing, and Hypermedia: Communication in World Order Transformation* (New York: Columbia University Press, 1997).

where not only hegemonic, but also subaltern voices, have the opportunity to represent themselves in a range of different languages, as seen, for example, in the Global Voices Online project.[5] Furthermore, as long as users are aware of the way that the Internet works and how it is governed, there is hope that they can also find effective ways to critique and/or organize protest against neoliberal globalization using the very same technologies used to advance such an agenda in the first place.[6]

One particularly notable example of this use of globalized technologies to contest neoliberal globalization can be seen in the 1994 uprising of the Mexican Ejército Zapatista de Liberación Nacional (EZLN) (Zapatista Army of National Liberation, or the Zapatistas, for short), which took the world by storm. This was not only due to their armed uprising, but also to the way that networked digital technologies were used by supporters, and then by the EZLN itself, to spread information and encourage support for their movement, such that it could not be easily supressed by the Mexican government. It was described at the time as being 'the *first informational guerrilla movement*'.[7] There were electronic mailing lists such as Chiapas95, support websites such as Acción Zapatista and ¡Ya Basta!, then the official websites Enlace Zapatista for communication within Mexico, and Zezta Internacionale for communication with international supporters. The *comunicados* of *de facto* leader Subcomandante Marcos emerged as a creative literary (and now multi-media) genre in their own right. And then there were disruptive acts of digital civil disobedience organized by the Electronic Disturbance Theater and others that gave rise to related artivist forms, such as hacktivism, tactical media, and digital zapatismo. Furthermore, what really caught people's attention was what the Zapatista case showed the world about the potential for local and small-scale social protest movements to have 'viral' global reach through networked digital technologies, and how those technologies could effectively amplify the voices of those who so rarely get heard in traditional media and political fora. We could thus argue that the Zapatistas provide an early example of a highly successful, contestatory form of digitally enabled 'transnationalism from below'.[8]

[5] Dan Bricklin, 'The Cornucopia of the Commons', in *Peer-to-peer: Harnessing the Power of Disruptive Technologies*, ed. by Andy Oram (Cambridge, MA: O'Reilly Media, 2001), pp. 59–66.

[6] Escobar, 'Other Worlds are (Already) Possible'.

[7] Manuel, Castells, *The Information Age: Economy, Society and Culture*, 3 vols (Oxford: Blackwell, 1997), II: *The Power of Identity*, p. 79.

[8] *Transnationalism from Below*, ed. by Michael Peter Smith and Luis Eduardo Guarnizo (New Brunswick, NJ: Transaction, 1998).

Tensions between top-down and bottom-up uses of globalized technologies can be seen in other cases within Latin America. For instance, many governments across the region have been instrumental in promoting the provision and uptake of networked digital technologies through 'digital inclusion' programmes aimed at addressing the emergence of digital divides of access and literacy. These programmes have been intended not so much to 'give voice' to marginalized social groups, as to create consumers and workers for the state's digital economy, embedding both the state and its citizens ever further into the markets of transnational informational capitalism. Indeed, a significant proportion of Internet use across the region corresponds to precisely these vectors: shopping, streaming, service-providing, and so on. Yet, as the Zapatistas so effectively demonstrated, the same technologies can also be used for searching, sharing, and strategizing, and they can therefore be 'appropriated' selectively and critically by socially marginalized and/or politically disenfranchised groups and individuals in order to challenge the status quo, and 'blog back' to their own governments, and to the wider world. Other renowned examples include the long trajectories of Internet use – together with the development of novel forms of 'cultural production' afforded by the advent of more recent audiovisual technologies and social media platforms – by Indigenous activist groups, such as the Asociación de Cabildos Indígenas del Norte del Cauca (Association of Indigenous Councils of Northern Cauca) in South West Colombia and by different Indigenous communities involved in the ethnojournalist project Índios Online in North Eastern Brazil, in order to 'interweave peoples and processes' across the region and beyond.[9] And although the political context, and the consequent accessibility of new technologies, is very different in Cuba, there has nonetheless been a very significant political blogging phenomenon, both on and off the island, since the late 2000s.[10]

These examples of social processes and their resultant cultural production, taken from our own field within Modern Languages – Latin American Cultural Studies – give a sense both of the inextricably intertwined nature of the digital (particularly the networking of digital technologies) and the transnational, and of the changing nature of our work as Modern Linguists as we grapple with the transnational-digital nexus and its results. The complexity of digital phenomena and the 'texts' they generate – from listserv *communiqués*

[9] Thea Pitman, 'Warriors and Weavers: The Poetics and Politics of Indigenous Appropriations of New Media Technologies in Latin America', *Modern Languages Open*, 1 (2018), <http://doi.org/10.3828/mlo.v0i0.207>.

[10] Claire Taylor and Thea Pitman, *Latin American Identity in Online Cultural Production* (New York: Routledge. 2013), Chapter 6.

and websites to blogs, Facebook pages, and Twitter feeds – offer fruitful terrain for the Modern Linguist, particularly one inclined to look beyond the 'text' to the multi-modal dimensions of this cultural production and to the cultural practices involved in its creation and dissemination as well. Indeed, Modern Linguists bring skills that can enhance our understanding of these complex cultural products and practices. Furthermore, it should be noted that while the examples of the digital 'texts' that we have chosen to focus on here relate directly to social phenomena such as protest movements, there is also a vibrant field of born-digital literary and artistic cultural production of variable political charge – electronic literature, net art, online performance art, and so on – that can also provide evidence of the transnationality inherent in its creation and dissemination.[11]

In what follows, we propose to make a case first for why the contributions of Modern Linguists in particular are crucial in the wider fields of Internet studies, new media studies, and/or digital culture studies. We then go on to explore how our work as Modern Linguists changes, and what traditional assumptions we need to challenge or adapt, when we work with networked digital materials that are transnational, transmedial, and/or in constant transformation.

## Modern Languages' Insights in the Digital-Transnational Arena

It is crucially important that Modern Linguists conduct research into the different manifestations of 'digital culture' across the globe, in all their linguistic and cultural diversity, and, in so doing, bring their expertise in particular languages, and particular national and regional contexts, to bear on the object of study. It almost goes without saying that the language skills and deep knowledge of different societies and cultures that Modern Linguists possess are essential for this work to be undertaken, yet there has been a general lack of attention to these issues in the research conducted thus far on digital cultures and cultural production.

All too frequently, digital technologies, their applications and their analyses have been developed in a predominantly anglophone environment. Notwithstanding some landmark volumes that have aimed to contest anglophone models, such as Brenda Danet and Susan C. Herring's *The Multilingual*

[11] Claire Taylor, *Place and Politics in Latin American Digital Culture: Location and Latin American Net Art* (New York: Routledge, 2014); *Poesía y poéticas digitales/electrónicas/tecno/new-media en América Latina: definiciones y exploraciones*, ed. by Luis Correa-Díaz and Scott Weintraub (Bogotá: Universidad Central de Colombia, 2016).

*Internet: Language, Culture and Communication Online* (2007), Gerard Goggin and Mark McLelland's *Internationalizing Internet Studies* (2009), or the Maaya Network's *Net Lang: Towards a Multilingual Cyberspace* (2012), it is the case that digital culture theory is still dominated by the anglophone.[12] What Modern Linguists can thus provide is an attention to cultural and linguistic specificity and heritage that can enhance our understanding of digital cultures. This emphasis includes a questioning of any anglophone assumptions embedded in our approach to digital technologies that actually betray colonialist or otherwise ethnocentric underpinnings (see, for example, early discussions about life 'on the electronic frontier'). Modern Linguists can also illuminate how new digital genres – as varied as hypermedia fiction or hacktivism – do not build exclusively upon an anglophone heritage, but respond to and continue a rich tradition of cultural, literary, artistic, and activist experimentation undertaken by writers, artists, and thinkers working in many different languages and countries. And in these ways, the cultural and linguistic insights that Modern Linguists can contribute are key to ensuring that the study of global digital culture and its transnational networks avoids perpetuating traditional exclusions and divisions.

To give examples from our own research into content creators from Latin America working in a variety of genres, we have explored how their use of digital technologies is both potentially resistant and (resistantly) local – a formulation that of necessity acknowledges the transnationalism of networked digital technologies. In 'Hypertext in Context', Thea Pitman explores the resistant and local dynamics at play in works of hypertext/hypermedia fiction by writers Blas Valdez and Doménico Chiappe.[13] And in *Latin American Identity in Online Cultural Production*, Claire Taylor explores how online practitioners such as Brian Mackern, Belén Gache, and Martha Patricia Niño speak to global movements, *and also* to Latin American-specific cultural and literary traditions and issues.[14] We thus argue for how a Modern-Languages

[12]Brenda Danet and Susan C. Herring (eds), *The Multilingual Internet: Language, Culture and Communication Online* (Oxford: Oxford University Press, 2007); Gerard Goggin and Mark McLelland (eds), *Internationalizing Internet Studies: Beyond the Anglophone Paradigm* (New York and London: Routledge, 2009), and Laurent Vannini and Hervé Le Crosnier (eds) on behalf of the Maaya Network, *Net Lang: Towards a Multilingual Cyberspace* (Caen: C & F Editions, 2012).

[13] Thea Pitman, 'Hypertext in Context: Space and Time in the Hypertext and Hypermedia Fictions of Blas Valdez and Doménico Chiappe', in *Latin American Cyberculture and Cyberliterature*, ed. by Claire Taylor and Thea Pitman (Liverpool: Liverpool University Press, 2007), pp. 227–43.

[14] Claire Taylor and Thea Pitman, *Latin American Identity in Online Cultural Production* (New York: Routledge, 2013), Chapters 1, 3, and 4.

approach can allow us to re-think existing assumptions about digital genres, while at the same time reminding us of the embeddedness of these digital technologies within particular socio-cultural codes.

## The Difference the Digital-Transnational Makes to Modern Languages Research

At the same time as celebrating the difference that Modern Linguists can make to research in the field of digital culture studies, it is also vital that Modern Linguists interrogate the national frameworks within which their work is often conceived – frameworks that may be inadequate to describe the phenomena they are observing and, furthermore, cannot capture the intricate dynamics of the relationships between different languages and cultures as they occur online. For example, in many digital cultural works, production, hosting, and consumption often traverse the boundaries of the nation-state, and in so doing, complicate notions of local, national, or regional identity. This is not to say that local, national, or regional identity cease to exist. Rather, online works often allow us the opportunity to re-think these local, national, and regional affiliations. Building on our own experiences as Modern Languages scholars in which we have had to explore how the implicit nation-state assumptions that conventionally underpin Modern Languages practice need to be re-thought in the light of the opportunities presented by digital technologies for a re-signification of locality, we can offer an enhanced understanding of the digital-as-globalizing debates. In this way, research into digital phenomena that transcend conventional national boundaries can make particularly constructive contributions at a time in which Modern Languages as an interdisciplinary area is interrogating issues underpinning ideas of 'the national' or 'the regional'. We are here referring to the erosion of a shared set of assumptions, including the notion of 'national literature' as reflection of national character, the nation-state as a (relatively) fixed category, or the unity between language and territory. As 'Digital' Modern Linguists, we are ideally placed to explore how cultural identities that transgress nation-state boundaries may be expressed and enabled through digital technologies, and how non-anglophone or plurilingual contexts might provide us with models for understanding the processes of de- and re-territorialization offered by many digital technologies.

An example of this can be seen in the work of US-Nicaraguan artist Ricardo Miranda Zúñiga's *a geography of being: una geografía de ser* (2012), an interactive installation consisting of a video game that narrates the experiences of two young undocumented immigrants in the US, accompanied with sculptures containing an animated display and that provide shortcuts to the video game. The provocative name that the artist gives to these sculptures is 'Undocumented Drones', highlighting both the status of these young men as undocumented and the increasing use of drones by US forces in conflict zones around the globe. Miranda Zúñiga thus makes reference to the geopolitical realities that underpin the waves of migration that his work represents, and re-semanticizes the term 'drone', providing a critique of the use of drones in US national and foreign policy.[15]

Another way in which the study of digital cultural production can contribute to ongoing debates in Modern Languages more broadly is as regards the nature of the 'text'. Modern Linguists working in digital culture have rapidly had to understand that we are no longer just analysing (if ever we were) a text, but that we also need to recognize the intensely multi-modal nature of so much digital cultural production, as well as ensure that we analyse practices, given that flows, re-circulations, and re-postings are just as significant as the 'finished' work itself. Indeed, we can no longer assume that we have the definitive version, or at least a recognizable and retrievable edition, of a work in front of us (in the same way that we might have done with, say, a print novel), and we also need to engage with the inherent ephemerality of digital materials.

Again, this shift fits in a timely fashion with discussions in Modern Languages, in particular the rise in, and increasing sophistication of, cultural studies approaches, and research methods aimed at elucidating the paratext as much as the text, as well as debates regarding the need to recognize the importance of ethnographic methods as a key part of the Modern Linguist's toolkit. Examples of this new kind of Modern Languages approach can be seen in the work of Tori Holmes, which not only demonstrates new ways of understanding the transnational flows of Internet content – demonstrating how blogging in Brazilian favelas functions on a spectrum ranging from hyperlocal to transnational – but has also been crucial in providing new ways of understanding fieldwork in Modern Languages.[16] Arguing that the study of content creation online cannot be achieved solely through approaches developed in literary and

[15] Claire Taylor, 'Serious Gaming: Critiques of Neoliberalism in the Works of Ricardo Miranda Zúñiga', in *Video Games and the Global South*, ed. by Phillip Penix-Tadsen (Pittsburgh: Carnegie Mellon University Press, 2019), pp. 47–60.

[16] Tori Holmes, 'Ethical Dilemmas in Studying Blogging by Favela Residents in Brazil', in *Theorizing Fieldwork in the Humanities: Methods, Reflections, and Approaches to the Global South*, ed. by Shalini Puri and Debra Castillo (New York: Palgrave Macmillan, 2016), pp. 131–49; and 'Linking Internet Texts and Practices: Challenges and Opportunities of Interdisciplinarity in an Ethnographically-Inspired Study of "Local Content"', *Westminster Papers in Communication and Culture*, 9.3 (2013), 121–42.

cultural studies, Holmes's work has illustrated how Modern Languages must learn from multi-sited ethnographical approaches, and that, in so doing, it recognizes the ways in which users move across platforms, and pays attention to both texts *and* practices in the circulation of narratives online.

## Conclusion

As we have argued above, Modern Languages research can and must play a leading role in driving forward digital culture studies, by offering situated approaches, attention to cultural and linguistic diversity, and contesting anglophone paradigms. At the same time, the transnational nature of much digital content creation can be an enabler in current thinking about transnational Modern Languages, as it offers us fruitful new ways of understanding the relationality of local, national, and regional affiliations that go way beyond the conventional boundaries of the nation-state.

Thea Pitman is Professor of Latin American Studies
at the University of Leeds.
Claire Taylor is Gilmour Chair of Spanish and Professor
in Hispanic Studies at the University of Liverpool.

11

# Ecologies

*Sophie Fuggle*

The son of a French prison guard stationed on the archipelago of Poulo Condore during the 1920s, 230 km off the Vietnamese mainland, Paul Miniconi grew up in one of France's lesser-known penal colonies. In contrast to the experiences of the prisoners who nicknamed the island 'hell on earth', Miniconi describes the island as 'un univers luxuriant et exotique où j'ai passé les plus beaux moments de ma jeunesse'.[1] Conveniently framed by a childhood innocence which exculpates him from any responsibility towards the suffering occurring around him, Miniconi offers us a fairly typical dose of colonial romanticism towards what Panivong Norindr has referred to as 'phantasmatic Indochina'.[2] However, the account provides an interesting and somewhat unusual detail about the work overseen by his father. Miniconi recounts watching the convicts mining the island's coral reef. Dynamite followed by crowbars were used to extract the coral, which was then transported inland to be converted into quicklime (*chaux*).[3] As he points out somewhat whimsically, the practice would be frowned upon today for the extensive damage it caused to the island's marine life. While Miniconi omits to mention this, among other things, quicklime was used by the French colonial authorities as a form of torture. Prisoners locked in cells known as tiger cages would have quicklime poured upon them from above. This brief

[1] 'A luxuriant and exotic universe where I spent the best days of my childhood' [My translation]. Frank Sénateur and Paul Miniconi, *Poulo Condore: Le bagne d'Indochine* (Paris: Gobelins, L'école de l'image, 2016), p. 26.

[2] Panivong Norindr, *Phantasmatic Indochina* (Durham, NC: Duke University Press, 1997).

[3] Sénateur and Miniconi, *Poulo Condore*, p. 27.

example serves to emphasize not simply the continuities between colonial exploitation of human and natural resources but the way in which the territory's natural ecology was weaponized against the Vietnamese people.

The archipelago was used by the French as a penal colony for more than a hundred years. Similar to those found in French Guiana and New Caledonia but reserved for Indochinese subjects, both common criminals and political prisoners were housed on the main island, Grand Condore, at various points. During the American War, an airstrip was built, and the island was used as a re-education camp. It is still possible to visit the vestiges of both the French and American cells located just a few hundred metres from the island's main beach.

Following the departure of the French during the 1950s, the archipelago was renamed Côn Đảo. Today, it is considered as a tourist 'hotspot' with significant potential for economic development.[4] At the same time, it has been designated a national park by the Vietnamese government due to its significant marine biodiversity. While marketed to international tourists as a beach resort, most visitors to Côn Đảo are domestic, Vietnamese families keen to make a perhaps once in a lifetime trip to what is considered a key 'source' of present-day Vietnam's peace and prosperity. Many of Vietnam's future leaders, most notably the second President Tôn Đức Thắng, spent time imprisoned on Côn Đảo. Countless others died as a result of the brutal violence of the guards and the insalubrious conditions. The significance of the trip for many Vietnamese visitors becomes apparent as you board the tiny turboprop plane at Tân Sơn Nhất International airport in Ho Chi Minh City. Dressed in traditional Vietnamese *áo dài* together with the promotional caps provided by tour operators, groups pose excitedly for photos next to the plane. Many are carrying large bouquets of flowers. On my first visit, which coincided with Vietnamese Independence Day, I assumed these were for friends and family living on the island. I later came to learn that most of these flowers, together with other offerings, are presented to the grave of Võ Thị Sáu in the island's war cemetery. Võ Thị Sáu was a nineteen-year-old female freedom fighter who was arrested by the French colonial authorities and taken to Poulo Condore in 1952 where she was held briefly before being executed by firing squad.[5] Visits to Côn Đảo might include trips to the beautiful and largely unspoiled beaches, lavish seafood banquets, and guided tours of the former prison buildings yet none of these define Côn Đảo in quite the same

[4] Philip Hayward and Giang Trần Hữu Thùy, 'At the Edge: Heritage and Tourism Development in Vietnam's Con Dao Archipelago', *Journal of Marine and Island Cultures*, 3.2 (December 2014), 113–24.

[5] Nguyễn Đình Thống, *Vo Thi Sau: A Legendary Heroine* (Ho Chi Minh City: Literature and Arts – Culture Publishing House, 2014).

way as Võ Thị Sáu does. Travel to Côn Đảo for many constitutes a pilgrimage culminating in a midnight visit to the cemetery where offerings and prayers are made to the teenage martyr. The rituals observed here challenge Western preconceptions of tropical island tourism. Côn Đảo is not simply a paradise island with a dark past. In contemporary Vietnam, it is a site where the past is called upon to provide renewed hope in a bright future.

In his now classic text *My Cocaine Museum*, the anthropologist Michael Taussig reflects that every treasure island has also, at some point, been used as a prison.[6] Sometimes this dual status occurs across centuries, at others concurrently. While the idea of a 'treasure island' might give rise to images of buried wooden chests full of rubies, emeralds, and gold doubloons, there is also a more contemporary version of the treasure island as a tropical paradise, featuring white sands and palm trees surrounded by turquoise waters. In this rendering, it is the island itself that is reimagined as precious, a hidden gem awaiting discovery by those seeking escape from the vicissitudes of metropolitan living.[7]

In acknowledging the myth of the prison/treasure island and its persistence in tourist imaginaries, literature, and popular culture from Daniel Defoe's *Robinson Crusoe* to TV shows like *Survivor* and *I'm a Celebrity... Get Me Out of Here!*, I want to use a more complex understanding of islands via the notion of ecologies. Ecologies offer a rich critical terminology encouraging us to think about different geographical and cultural spaces beyond reductive binaries. This orientation challenges us to navigate binaries such as nature–culture but also, of equal importance to Modern Languages scholars, those of centre and periphery, metropole and outpost, capital and province, city and hinterland.

Oppositional notions of islands as spaces of confinement and escape are inherently European colonial ideals that posit a distant tropic as a fixed and empty space available to exile and contain. The mass transportation of convicts from France to French Guiana ceased in 1946, almost a century after the UK ended its use of Australia as a penal colony. However, since then islands have never ceased to operate as prisons and penal colonies often used as extra-legal spaces in which to indefinitely detain non-citizens without recourse to due process.[8] The most well-known examples include immigration

[6] Michael Taussig, *My Cocaine Museum* (Chicago: University of Chicago Press, 2004).

[7] On islands as places of escape see David Lowenthal, 'Islands, Lovers and Others', *The Geographical Review*, 97.2 (April 2007), 202–29. On the emergence of the empty beaches as tourist enclaves, see Jean-Didier Urbain, *Sur la plage* (Paris: Payot, 1996).

[8] See, for example, Alison Mountz, 'The Enforcement Archipelago: Detention, Haunting, and Asylum on Islands', *Political Geography*, 30.3 (2011), 118–28.

detention centres like Nauru and Manus Island or extra-territorial prisons like Guantánamo. At the same time, the fantasy of the desert island retreat remains a paradigm of global tourism. Direct flights from Europe to tropical islands in Southeast Asia mean Western tourists can escape to the chosen island refuge of their choice without ever needing to set foot on the mainland. This rendering of islands as on the edge of the world and only consisting of edges is powerfully seductive yet inevitably misses so much.

Islands are both spaces and places saturated with imaginaries projected from elsewhere, often the mainland, but they can be cities and networks of connectedness, culture, and knowledge, as much as they are sites of multitudinous enquiry and experience. Island ecologies that are cultural, linguistic, natural, urban, mixed, commercial, or biological are considered of especial interest to researchers due to the apparently self-contained terrain delimited by a coastline. At the same time, islands exist in complex networks as archipelagos, clusters, chains, and groups, and in relation to the (oft-distant) nation-states to which they are tied politically, culturally, and economically as well as linguistically.

In recent decades, growing recognition of the importance of islands not only as objects of scientific enquiry but as offering new paradigms of knowledge has resulted in the emergence of what Elizabeth McMahon has described as the 'interdisciplinary constellation' of Island Studies.[9] McMahon also notes this still relatively new research focus appears in conjunction with a number of transnational initiatives including, most notably, the International Scientific Council for Island Development (INSULA) of the United Nations Educational, Scientific and Cultural Organization (UNESCO) in 1989 and the launching of two open-access journals, *Island Studies Journal* and *Shima* in the 2000s.

Elizabeth DeLoughrey has emphasized the importance of 'island ecologies' within both ecocriticism and the more recent and expanding field of environmental humanities.[10] Drawing on W.J.T. Mitchell's *Landscape and Power*, DeLoughrey emphasizes how conceptions of nature and the so-called 'natural' world are historical constructs often intended to erase and naturalize

[9] Elizabeth McMahon, *Islands, Identity and the Literary Imagination* (New York: Anthem Press, 2016), p. 4.

[10] Elizabeth DeLoughrey, 'Island Ecologies and Caribbean Literatures', *Tijdschrift voor Economische en Sociale Geografie*, 95.3 (2004), 298–310; Elizabeth DeLoughrey, Jill Didur, and Anthony Carrigan, 'Introduction: A Postcolonial Environmental Humanities', in *Global Ecologies and the Environmental Humanities: Postcolonial Approaches*, ed. by Elizabeth DeLoughrey, Jill Didur, and Anthony Carrigan (New York: Routledge, 2015), pp. 1–32.

the impact of Western colonialism upon different environments along with their human populations.[11] According to DeLoughrey and others, island ecologies also bear witness to the most intensive and thus most visible effects of colonization.[12]

At the centre of DeLoughrey's study of island ecologies is the plantation. The term 'plantationocene' has been proposed by Donna Haraway and others as a means of conceptualizing the far-reaching implications of plantation ecologies as these incorporate the transnational slave trade and other forms of indentured labour and penal servitude together with the mass-deforestation and monocrop cultures that continue to define global food production today.[13] On Côn Đảo it is possible to take a guided tour of the former Sở Rẫy plantation. Now covered in secondary rainforest, the island's convict population was employed in clearing the land for arable farming. What is interesting on Côn Đảo is how the plantation not only represents convict labour within the space of the penal colony but also draws our attention to a continuum between the 'carceral ecology' of the island and that of the colonial rubber plantations largely located in the Central Highlands of Vietnam.[14] In his account of life on the Phú Riềng plantation, *The Red Earth*, Trần Tử Bình describes how workers who protested the harsh treatment, poor pay, and lack of healthcare were frequently criminalized by French plantation owners and their management.[15] In addition to being locked up and brutalized on the plantations, those involved in political resistance could end up, as was the case for Trần, officially imprisoned on Côn Đảo.

The importance of island ecologies also stems from their perpetually threatened existence. Their mythical status along with their frequent omission from maps and atlases makes their real erasure all the easier. For low lying archipelagos around the world, climate disaster and displacement are not something vaguely associated with an abstract future but an everyday lived reality. Islands are often at the greatest risk from rising sea levels, coastal erosion, and destruction of reefs, urban migration, and the replacement of

[11] DeLoughrey, 'Island Ecologies', p. 299; *Landscape and Power*, ed. by W.J.T. Mitchell (Chicago and London: University of Chicago Press, 2002).

[12] DeLoughrey, 'Island Ecologies', p. 299.

[13] Donna Haraway, 'Anthropocene, Capitalocene, Plantationocene, Chthulucene: Making Kin', *Environmental Humanities*, 6 (2015), 159–65.

[14] The term 'carceral ecology' has been used by Ryan Edwards to describe the Ushuaia penal colony in Patagonia. Ryan Edwards, 'From the Depths of Patagonia: The Ushuaia Penal Colony and the Nature of "The End of the World"', *Hispanic American Historical Review*, 94.2 (May 2014), 271–302.

[15] Trần Tử Bình, *The Red Earth: A Vietnamese Memoir of Life on a Colonial Rubber Plantation*, trans. by John Spragens (Athens, OH: Ohio University Press, 2014).

sustainable local industries such as fishing with mass tourism. With these shifts in island ecologies come loss not only of natural habitats but also built and intangible heritage. However, there is also a danger in writing off such spaces as tragically fragile and vulnerable. Reading island ecologies as doomed to extinction from the distant mainland, is to overlook the specific, localized forms of resilience and adaptability developed by islanders.

So, although we might propose a concept of ecologies that is far broader in scope than its oft-assumed association with environmental science, the term must retain or embed questions of sustainability and the ongoing challenges of climate change together with the impact of human activity upon the planet's ecosystems more generally. Hence, the notion of ecology contains within it an implicit ethical imperative to better understand the ways in which our existence and activity are bound up in multifarious material, living, organic systems that are at once vulnerable and resilient, fragile and infinitely resourceful.

Within the growing field of the environmental humanities, 'ecology' is a word that operates simultaneously as a tool for thinking and imagining complex life-worlds and a paradigm of Western scientific knowledge that requires constant deconstruction and deep suspicion. In his detailed account of the ecological history of Vietnam's colonial rubber plantations, Michitake Aso emphasizes the 'entanglements' of scientific knowledge and colonial exploitation.[16] The language we use to think about the environment has high political stakes. Kathryn Yusoff makes a powerful case for challenging the apparent 'neutrality' of terms like 'geology' and the 'Anthropocene'.[17] Such terms, still largely defined by white male scientists from the Global North, allow for a generalizing and abstracting of the human impact upon the planet. The result is to obfuscate the specific violence of white colonialism upon other races and ecosystems via forced migration and labour alongside the radical transformation of landscapes through mining and monocrop plantation culture. In a similar vein, Robert Marzec has emphasized the dominance of discourses of environmental disaster that privilege militarized rather than community responses.[18]

In the context of Vietnam, it is possible to see environmental discourse imposed from without. Anthropologist Christian Culas points out 'that all

[16] Michitake Aso, *Rubber and the Making of Vietnam: An Ecological History, 1897–1975* (Chapel Hill: University of North Carolina Press, 2018).

[17] Kathryn Yusoff, *A Billion Black Anthropocenes or None* (Minneapolis: University of Minnesota Press, 2018).

[18] Robert P. Marzec, *Militarizing the Environment: Climate Change and the Security State* (Minneapolis: University of Minnesota Press, 2015).

the environmental protection projects in Vietnam have been conceived and designed on a Western philosophical and ontological reference'.[19] At the top of the Sở Rẫy plantation, one comes across a couple of ruined buildings from the colonial period. A billboard in Vietnamese and English provides a brief account of the plantation's role in the penal colony. It also informs visitors that in 1997 more than a third of the island's forest was destroyed by tropical Storm Linda. From 2002 to 2004, a reforestation project funded by BP Vietnam (British Petroleum State Oil) took place in a bid to 'recover and maintain' the island's rare plant species.

In exploring the possibility for a Southeast Asian ecology, Guido Sprenger and Kristina Großmann propose the notion of 'plural ecologies' as a means of challenging a 'modern universalist idea of ecology'.[20] These ecologies could, they suggest, effectively combine existing work on political ecology with an anthropology of ontologies. Political ecology is primarily useful in mapping out the hierarchies and exclusions that shape a society or social space. It has been called upon in the context of ecological conflict most notably in relation to resource management and the toxic impacts of certain power structures. However, the primary limitation is a focus on ecology in terms of human politics based upon Western conceptions of ethics, law, and economics. An anthropology of ontologies that the authors stress does not even need to be described in terms of, as I would put it, the somewhat off-putting term 'ontology', explores and deconstructs existing binaries of nature–culture, human–environment, and so on. It is possible to see how this way of thinking might offer a way out of the contemporary paradox that currently frames Côn Đảo in terms of its development potential and endangered biodiversity.

One starting point for resituating island ecologies involves thinking of them first and foremost as spaces of belonging, habitats, and homes. By this I do not mean the abstract, 'suspended promise' of home evoked by McMahon as frequent projection of the world-weary traveller seeking shelter.[21] To define the island as home must incorporate all the banal comforts and everyday challenges this entails.

[19] Christian Culas, 'Nature and Humans in Sino-Vietnamese Conceptions and Practices. Articulations between Asian Vernacular "Analogism" and Western Modern "Naturalism" Ontologies', in *Ecologies in Southeast Asian Literatures: Histories, Myths and Societies*, ed. by Chi Pham, Chitra Sankaran, and Gurpreet Kaur (Wilmington: Vernon Press, 2019), pp. 111–29 (p. 113).

[20] Guido Sprenger and Kristina Großmann, 'Plural Ecologies in Southeast Asia', *Sojourn: Journal of Social Issues in Southeast Asia*, 33.2 (July 2018), ix–xxii.

[21] McMahon, *Islands, Identity and the Literary Imagination*, p. 8.

Travelling with me to Côn Đảo in 2018, photographer and colleague Charles Fox learned that there were five former prisoners still living on the island. They had returned after Independence at the behest of the Vietnamese government keen that the memory of the archipelago as a site of struggle and resistance would be maintained. International journalists reporting on the island's transformation appear uninterested in talking to the survivors, preferring to focus on the eerie juxtaposition of prison buildings located a hundred metres from the island's main beachfront.

The presence of survivors on the island disrupts the binary that represents it as a site of ongoing colonial occupation. It emphasizes the island as a space of perpetual, shifting memory work, a space of care via the creation and maintenance of a local community. It demonstrates how a space associated with violence and suffering can become one of dignity and pride. Photo portraits of the prisoners-turned-islanders formed the focus of an exhibition, *A Poetics of Space: Images of Con Dao*, held at the National Justice Museum, Nottingham in November 2018.[22] Their personal stories, yet to be translated from Vietnamese, both affirm the official national narratives of struggle and victory and describe what we might call an 'ecology of care' that transforms the island into a home. It is this idea of home and not that of the empty pristine white beach as site of exile or escape that should constitute our starting point for thinking afresh about the islands at the centre of our worlds.

Sophie Fuggle is Associate Professor of Postcolonial Studies
and Cultural Heritage at Nottingham Trent University.

[22] Charles Fox, Sophie Fuggle, and Charles Forsdick, *A Poetics of Space: Images of Con Dao* (exhibition catalogue) (London: Pavement Books, 2018).

12

# Ethics

*Rachel Scott*

If ethics is, as defined in *The Cambridge Dictionary of Philosophy*, 'what ends we ought, as fully rational human beings, to choose and pursue and what moral principles should govern our choices and pursuits', then the study of languages and cultures from a transnational perspective raises fundamentally ethical concerns.[1] For while it is the study of communication, undoubtedly, the study of languages is more profoundly concerned with interactions, the movement and evolution of culture and concepts across boundaries of time and place; with the production of knowledge and its interpretation and appropriation; and with the conceptualization and representation of other people and cultures. More than a tool that mediates between us and 'reality', language shapes how we live, how we understand and construct the world, ourselves, and others. We cannot make ethical choices outside of it. The study of languages, furthermore, produces encounters with new voices and perspectives and different ways of being that require us to learn how to read and map the world anew. It therefore brings about a critical understanding of the structural *and historical* dynamics of global relations, exchanges, and power. Indeed, how we study and teach the past is just as important as how we study and teach other languages and cultures. As Anna Akasoy remarks, 'If we practice "politically aware" or "morally involved" forms of scholarship, one lesson to be learned [...] is just how much negotiating the past is part of negotiating the present'.[2]

[1] John Deigh, 'Ethics', in *The Cambridge Dictionary of Philosophy*, ed. by Robert Audi, 2nd ed. (Cambridge: Cambridge University Press, 1999), pp. 284–89 (pp. 284–85).

[2] Anna Akasoy, 'Convivencia and its Discontents: Interfaith Life in Al-Andalus', *International Journal of Middle East Studies*, 42.3 (2010), 489–99 (p. 498).

In this chapter, I address this mix of the poetic, the political, and the ethical with reference to medieval Iberia. A fragmented land of fluid borders where Christianity, Judaism, and Islam co-existed for more than seven hundred years, medieval Iberia provides a particularly productive space for thinking about the ideas raised by this volume. As a transnational space of 'global' movements and dynamic cultural exchange (in a different sense to our own), it exemplifies Mary Louise Pratt's definition of a 'contact zone': a place 'where cultures meet, clash, and grapple with each other'.[3] David Wacks and Antonio Cortijo Ocaña have suggested that medieval Iberia 'responds well to such mixed methodologies and working approaches that reach beyond a single national or classical language or theoretical approach' and that instead make use of 'the ideas of interinfluence, exchange, (bi)culturalism, and (border) crossing'.[4] My focus is a text that illustrates such issues and approaches: a medieval Arabic collection of exemplary fables called *Kalila and Dimna*, which belongs to 'the singularly mobile genre of wisdom literature' – a body of didactic writing that provided moral and practical guidance, often but not always aimed at rulers and their ministers.[5] If any genre could be considered transnational (and transtemporal), it is wisdom literature. This tradition was popular from South and Central Asia through to the Levant, where texts incorporating aphorisms, proverbs, riddles, and exemplary fables abounded in Greek, Syriac, Sanskrit, Persian, and Arabic. These *sapiential* works were continually appropriated and translated, shaped in oral and written form to new and evolving environments; from the East, many subsequently travelled to European vernaculars. *Kalila and Dimna* is no exception. The book derives in part from a Sanskrit text dated roughly to 300 AD called the *Panchatantra*, meaning 'Five Chapters' or 'Five Treatises'. Via a now lost Middle Persian translation (570 AD), the fables came to be translated into Arabic in 750 AD by a convert to Islam called Abdallah Ibn al-Muqaffa, an Abbasid court minister. The work subsequently travelled to al-Andalus, the Muslim-ruled lands of Iberia, from where it was disseminated to Northern and Western Europe. While the first translation into a European vernacular was the Castilian *Calila e Dimna*, commissioned by the future king Alfonso X 'the Learned' (1251), the book did not become more widely known among readers of European vernaculars until the fifteenth and sixteenth centuries, when it

[3] Mary Louise Pratt, 'Arts of the Contact Zone', *Profession* (1991), 33–40 (p. 34).

[4] David Wacks and Antonio Cortijo Ocaña, 'Introduction. Multilingual Medieval Iberia: Between the Tongue and the Pen', *eHumanista*, 14, special edition, 'Multilingual Medieval Iberia: Between the Tongue and the Pen' (2010), i–xii (p. iii).

[5] Louise Marlow, 'Among Kings and Sages: Greek and Indian Wisdom in an Arabic Mirror for Princes', *Arabica*, 60 (2013), 1–57 (p. 2).

was translated from earlier Hebrew and Latin translations (also in thirteenth century) into French, German, Italian, English, Danish, Dutch, and again into Spanish; later waves of translation followed in the seventeenth and eighteenth centuries.

*Kalila*'s transmission mirrors the fluidity of meaning that is intrinsic to its narratorial structure. The book uses a framing technique comprised of a dialogue between a king and his counsellor in which the ruler poses a series of questions or problems to which the minister responds with exemplary stories that provide guidance or resolution. These are then interwoven with yet more fables, with each new story often acting as the frame for yet more tales, many of which are told by animals and feature parallel worlds of men and animals with similar hierarchies, rules, and principles of government – an ancient narrative technique used to explore the nature of truth. They also speak to broader concerns beyond the confines of the court and government, a fact that undoubtedly contributed to the book's popularity. The fables teach how to read other people and their characters and expose the dangers of not being able to recognize the authentic condition of others using both positive and negative examples. Principal topics include friendship and enmity and the consequences of jealously and pride; the consequences of ill-considered action and the need for prudence and measure; and how one should know and act within one's limitations, and be content with one's lot in life.

*Kalila and Dimna*'s themes still speak to modern concerns and ethical problems: the book continues to be engaged with today, particularly in the Arabic-speaking world, where it is taught in schools and has been made into cartoons and short stories for young children. But this is not the only reason why the book is important in the context of the study of languages and cultures. *Kalila and Dimna*'s intercalated structure has important implications for the way in which its ethical themes are interpreted. The lack of one single narrator entails a multiplicity of voices and thus of perspectives; likewise, the clustering of fables within chapters enables different facets of an issue to be illuminated from varying and at times contradictory points of view. This representation of diverse, even contradictory, perspectives gives space to *explore* rather than simply prescribe the 'truth'. The fables show that what is ethically 'correct' is not absolute or fixed; it cannot be applied on a general level in the same way for everyone but rather is contingent upon circumstance, something that later writers would build upon. For instance, Machiavelli in *Il Principe* (1515) claimed 'it is necessary for a prince wishing to hold his own to know how to do wrong, and to make use of it or not according to necessity'.[6]

[6] Niccolò Machiavelli, *The Prince*, trans. by W. K. Marriott (London and Toronto: J. M. Dent; New York: E. P. Dutton, 1931), pp. 121–22.

*Kalila and Dimna* would play an important role in the development of Northern and Western European literature, influencing among others Geoffrey Chaucer, Giovanni Boccaccio, Juan Manuel, and Jean de la Fontaine, whose works – *The Canterbury Tales*, *The Decameron*, *El Conde Lucanor*, and *Fables* respectively – would become foundational in their corresponding national literatures. *Kalila and Dimna*'s reception provides a perspective on ethical conduct that goes beyond a single society to encompass interactions on a transnational axis. As François de Blois writes, the work narrates a remarkable story about 'the history of contacts between civilisations'.[7] It is only in studying *Kalila and Dimna*'s movement between languages and cultures that the ethics of the text fully appear. Tracing its trajectory from East to West opens up questions about what Ben Van Wyke refers to as 'the ethics of cultural encounters that define relationships among the peoples of the world'.[8] Translation, as Van Wyke continues, 'does not merely reproduce ideas and information, but plays an active part in creating culture and civilization'.[9] For me, it is the process by which *Kalila and Dimna* was transmitted and translated that is most interesting, and where it has much to offer the transnational study of languages and cultures.

From its inception, *Kalila and Dimna* was seen as far more than a mere work of moral conduct. The addition of prefaces, dedications, and letters to readers over the centuries provided spaces in which the relationship between different cultures and societies, and the transmission of knowledge and power could be conceptualized. Certain copies of the sixth-century Persian translation, for example, include a preface in which Burzoy, a physician of king Khosrow I Anushirwan and the translator of the book into Persian, voyages to India to find certain mysterious herbs that are believed to be able to revive the dead. The tale is in fact an allegorical account of the work's origins that hinges on a misreading: the 'herbs' represent the wisdom of books whose supposed life-giving properties bring intellectual and spiritual enlightenment to the ignorant. Aside from its commentary on how to read 'correctly', Burzoy's quest touches upon the need to travel beyond the borders of one's own society in order to acquire knowledge hitherto not possessed. In a longer version found in other copies of the Persian translation the acquisition of this very book is explicitly presented as an act of deception:

[7] François De Blois, *Burzōy's Voyage to India and the Origin of the Book of Kalīlah wa Dimnah* (London: Royal Asiatic Society, 1990), p. iii.

[8] Ben Van Wyke, 'Ethics and Translation', in *Handbook of Translation Studies*, vol. 1, ed. by Yves Gambier and Luc van Doorslaer (Amsterdam: John Benjamins, 2010), pp. 111–15 (p. 115).

[9] Van Wyke, 'Ethics and Translation', p. 115.

once in India, Burzoy persuades a local wise man to help him translate it, an act forbidden by the Indian king. Examples of theft and subterfuge can also be seen in other prologues. Ibn al-Muqaffa's introduction to the Arabic includes exemplary stories about robbery in which the objects stolen function allegorically by representing wisdom, which is compared to treasure. Such wealth, it is suggested, has to be guarded and 'spent' wisely, demonstrating the particular kind of ethics conceptualized by Aristotle in the *Nicomachean Ethics*: prudence, or practical wisdom in action.[10] In the version of the Persian preface found in the Old Spanish *Calila e Dimna*, Burzoy orders the books he returns from India with and had translated to be widely disseminated. But, crucially, he keeps 'aquellos que eran más privados en la casa del rey'.[11] Books, asserts Ramsey Wood, 'were immensely rare and valuable, especially if their contents were rumoured to confer competitive political advantage'.[12] *Kalila and Dimna*'s history exemplifies the interweaving of politics and poetics, power and knowledge. Aside from the fact that many of its translators were also diplomats and courtiers, translations are frequently either dedicated or attributed to monarchs: for example, *Calila e Dimna* (1251) to Alfonso X and the *Espejo político y moral* (1654, 1658) to Felipe IV. By the later Middle Ages and Renaissance, the mere possession of *Kalila and Dimna* symbolized political greatness: the motif of treasure once used to represent wisdom generally was now applied specifically to this book, an 'oriental jewel'. The history of *Kalila and Dimna*'s transmission thus foregrounds the hierarchies of power that underlie the act of translation and exemplifies the synthesis of the political, the poetic, and the ethical that characterizes the study of languages and cultures.

Yet, the book has another equally important value for the discipline. Bringing a work of Indian-Persian-Arabic origins into the Modern Languages classroom not only provides a profoundly rich historical perspective on the study of languages, cultures, and their interactions. It offers a case-study in the entanglement of national or regional histories that stresses the interconnectedness of cultures across time and space, destabilizing received

[10] Aristotle, *The Nicomachean Ethics*, trans. by David Ross, ed. by Lesley Brown (Oxford: Oxford University Press, 2009); see in particular the seventh and eighth sections of the sixth book, pp. 108–10.

[11] *Calila e Dimna*, ed. by Juan Manuel Cacho Blecua and María Jesús Lacarra (Madrid: Castalia, 1984), p. 102. The translation into English is 'those that were most highly prized in the king's palace'. *Privado* is a difficult term to translate and encompasses not only a sense of 'private', for example, personal rather than public and 'intimate' but also 'favourite'.

[12] Ramsey Wood, *Kalila and Dimna: Fables of Conflict and Intrigue* (Newport: Medina, 2011), p. 215.

notions of hermetically sealed national cultures and foregrounding instead the *transnational*, the fluidity of cultural production and its evolution. *Kalila and Dimna*'s transmission, says Dagmar Riedel, 'touches on the fundamental question of how to conceive of national and international literary histories if narrative traditions have moved freely'.[13] Its migrations reveal the historical intersections between European vernacular languages and cultures and those of the Middle East, North Africa and South Asia, engaging with questions of nationhood and nationalism, imperialism and colonialism, cultural hybridity and Otherness, and illuminating what Sharon Kinoshita describes as 'the historical layering underpinning cultural production in the "European" Middle Ages'.[14] The book therefore offers an opportunity to broaden and enrich the Modern Languages curriculum. Reading *Kalila and Dimna* alongside canonical works by Juan Manuel, Jean de la Fontaine, and Boccaccio, or similarly ambiguous frame tales such as the *Libro de buen amor* situates European cultural production within a broader transnational context and makes visible the debt owed to languages not traditionally brought into Modern Languages programmes: Arabic and Hebrew, as well as Turkish, Persian, and Sanskrit.

Feedback from students who studied *Kalila and Dimna* as part of their Spanish and Portuguese degree programme demonstrates the impact of including it in a Modern Languages curriculum:

> The dispersion of different adaptations of this collection of stories around Medieval Europe enabled us to rethink our preconceived ideas about European literature as being formed and preserved only by European royalty and nobility and to discover a more inclusive and culturally diverse history than we were originally taught to believe.[15]

A text like *Kalila and Dimna*, with its complex transnational history, encourages us to think critically about the relation between the national and the transnational, the ways we construct our world, and the ways we locate ourselves in it. The students' comments provide a powerful, poignant

[13] Dagmar Riedel, '*Kalila wa Demna* i. Redactions and Circulation', *Encyclopædia Iranica*, XV/4 (2010), pp. 386–95; an updated version is available online at <http://www.iranicaonline.org/articles/kalila-demna-i> [accessed 13 May 2019].

[14] Sharon Kinoshita, 'Translatio/n, Empire, and the Worlding of Medieval Literature: The travels of *Kalila wa Dimna*', *Postcolonial Studies*, 11.4 (2008), 371–85 (p. 372).

[15] The module was 'Global Iberias', a first-year introductory course in the Department of Spanish, Portuguese & Latin American Studies at King's College London. Feedback was given in the 2018/2019 academic year.

reminder of this: 'Studying *Kalila and Dimna*', they said, 'incited and altered our perceptions of European history and learning of its Sanskriti origins proved to be a matter of personal development and even pride to our specific cultures'. As their words demonstrate, including a book that illuminates the impact and influence of non-European cultures in the study of European languages can furthermore promote engagement and identification for those of non-European heritage.

Why does this matter? Like the partitioning of the discipline into 'national' areas, the objects and sources of study that make up Modern Languages are the result of historical and political choices and of particular worldviews. Medieval Iberia has constituted a particularly thorny problem in the shaping of the Spanish concept of 'nation'. From the polemical debate between Américo Castro and Claudio Sánchez Albornoz in the first half of the twentieth century about the debt owed by modern 'Spanish' culture to medieval Iberia's mixed society of Christians, Muslims, and Jews, the Peninsula's past continues to be used as an ideological battleground – see, for example, discussions in volumes published in 2008 and, most recently, 2021.[16] In light of the ongoing politicization of the Middle Ages and the recent grappling with issues of race and diversity within medieval and medievalism studies, it is fundamentally important that *what* and *how* we teach reflects not only the plurality of the past but the contemporary classroom, which is itself increasingly multi-lingual and multi-cultural. Furthermore, recent calls to decolonize university curricula, calls often led by students who do not see themselves in what they study, have foreground the extent to which these are constructed upon hierarchies of power and knowledge, and colonial and Eurocentric narratives of global expansion focused on centres and their peripheries. I suggest, then, that it is our ethical duty as a discipline to respond to these calls by creating programmes that deconstruct such imbalances and biases. *Kalila and Dimna* is one example of how we might respond to the ethical question of what we research and teach, and what moral principles should govern these choices and pursuits, as well as our representation of other languages and cultures.

Dr Rachel Scott is Lecturer in World and Hispanic Literatures at Royal Holloway, University of London.

[16] Américo Castro, *España en su Historia: cristianos, moros y judios* (Buenos Aires: Editorial Losada, 1948); Claudio Sánchez Albornoz, *España, un enigma histórico* (Buenos Aires: Editorial Sudamericana, 1956); Rachel Scott, AbdoolKarim Vakil and Julian Weiss (eds), *Al-Andalus in Motion: Travelling Concepts and Cross-Cultural Concepts* (London: King's College London Medieval Studies, 2021).

# 13

# Event

*Margaret Hills de Zárate*

The event described in this essay took place in Buenos Aires in Argentina while I was undertaking ethnographic research relating to Italian migration. When analysing the fieldwork data, I revisited a constellation of coinciding incidents that had seemed significant and that I referred to in my field notes and research diary at the time as 'events within events; happenings; intermissions and interruptions'.

In the ethnographic literature, incidents such as interruptions (the word that had most immediately occurred to me) may constitute 'key events', in which a particular event or person can be focused on in detail, providing a vignette that serves to illuminate a theme central to the analysis.[1] The term 'key incident'[2] describes 'something that happens during fieldwork that is likely to be revealing for the research' as a whole. Such occurrences in fieldwork have also been described as 'critical incidents' and utilized to initiate researchers' thinking about diverse ways of thinking, doing, theorizing, and valuing.[3]

A review of the broader literature and an excursion into cognitive science underscore that events are understood in terms of the three dimensions of space plus the one dimension of time. The process by which people

[1] Karen O'Reilly, *Key Concepts in Ethnography* (SAGE Publications, 2009) pp. 131–33.

[2] Robert. M. Emerson, 'Working with Key Incidents', in *Qualitative research practice,* ed. by Clive Seale, Giampietro Gobo, Jaber F. Gubrium, and David Silverman, (London: SAGE Publications, 2004), pp. 427–42.

[3] Joan Parker Webster and Theresa Arevgaq John, 'Preserving a Space for Cross-cultural Collaborations: An Account of Insider/Outsider Issues', *Ethnography and Education*, 5 (2010), 175–91.

comprehend a continuous stream of activity and discern meaningful events is an automatic component of human perception known as event segmentation and suggests a definition of an 'event' as a segment of time at a specific place conceived by the observer to have a beginning and an end. However, although event segmentation is a basic perceptual process, identifying an event's boundaries is subject to cultural influences. These influences are reflected in the way people divide their experience into meaningful parts or segments as it occurs and in the types of information people use to determine when these segments begin and end. These 'event boundaries' (which act somewhat like bookends) mark successive events and tend to occur when events change at points within an unfolding activity and observers have difficulty predicting what will happen next, or conversely, link to their prior experiences. Thus, the locus of the effect of culture on segmentation was found to be in the perceiver rather than the perceived.[4]

The results of this research are in keeping with Emerson's observation that 'key incidents' identified as significant by the ethnographer may pass unnoticed or be experienced as totally unremarkable by other observers. His view that such incidents may not 'provide flashes of insight, but rather niggling prods of interest and possibility' resonates with my own experience. As he notes, 'key incidents are not self-explicating but have to be nurtured and mined; often initially opaque and uncertain in meaning and implication. Key incidents provide starting points and push for more empirical inquiry and comparison, not clear-cut analytic claims and propositions'.[5] In other words, they generate further research and allow one to think about different things in relation to one another, generatively, which according to research in cognitive psychology is notoriously difficult with a continuous stream of representations.

Deleuze (for whom an event was a complex, non-linear process) adopts the metaphor of the event as a concert, as he draws together the numerous paths and lives led by artists and audience into the event. He points out that none of these paths disappears in the event or is wholly accounted for by it. When the participants go their own way, they will remember it and act on it differently, and its spatial borders change, depending on how they retell it and observe its repercussions.[6] They may be out of the ordinary, dramatic, exciting, or emotional events but a mundane occurrence may just

[4] Khena M. Swallow and Qi Wang 'Culture Influences How People Divide Continuous Sensory Experience into Events', *PsyArXi*, 27 (2019), 2–14.

[5] Emerson 'Working with Key Incidents', p. 434.

[6] Giles Deleuze, *The Fold: Leibniz and the Baroque* (London: Continuum, 2006), pp. 154–55.

as easily turn out to be a key incident because of how it was perceived by the ethnographer.[7]

However, while these two bodies of research concur concerning the importance of perception, research in event segmentation has been conducted under controlled experimental conditions and has yet to address naturalistic activity in which participants are not merely passive observers of videos but are also actors.[8] In ethnographic research, the ethnographer is an actor who not only observes the life of the subjects studied, but also participates in it. Moreover, there is good reason to think that actors' and observers' representations of an activity differ substantially because the actors and observers involved have access to different aspects of the event. Ethnographers engage, participate, and observe. These actions form part of what constitutes participant observation, which is one of the methods in ethnography, which includes interviews with group members, and an analysis of group documents and objects. Ethnographers are involved in the situations they are researching, but not over-involved, for while they should value an insider's perspective, they must also maintain a critical outsider's perspective.[9] This position is often characterized as 'stepping in and out of context', which involves a sort of distance between self-vis-à-vis the subject of the study, which can be accomplished to some extent through writing.

## Writing Ethnography

Ethnography, quite literally, means writing culture. The ethnographer will keep a research log, a fairly straightforward objective account that serves as a record for the researcher, with sufficient information to verify that the results are valid. Similarly, fieldnotes can be understood as a record of observations made in a particular setting. Although both research logs and fieldnotes can be distinguished from the research diary, the boundaries are often blurred as research is experienced and perceived subjectively. The research diary, however, provides a form through which the interaction of subjective and objective aspects of doing research are acknowledged and brought into a productive relationship. The research diary can be seen as 'a melting pot for all of the different ingredients of a research project including the researcher's

[7] O'Reilly, *Key Concepts in Ethnography*, p. 131.

[8] Lauren L. Richmond and Jeffrey M. Zacks, 'Constructing Experience: Event Models from Perception to Action', *Trends in Cognitive Sciences*, 21.12 (2017), 962–80 (p. 967).

[9] Raymond Madden, *Being Ethnographic: A Guide to the Theory and Practice of Ethnography* (Los Angeles: Sage Publications, 2017), p. 8.

prior experience, observations, readings, ideas and provides a means of capturing the resulting interplay of elements',[10] which will include their reflections regarding their positionality and reflexive notes.

On the one hand, the researcher has to immerse herself in the flow of the research through participation, but on the other, she needs to distance herself to observe. However, what is perceived to be occurring is influenced by the researcher's stance or positionality concerning the social and political context of the study, the community, and the participant group. These factors demand the researcher's self-awareness of their own characteristics, such as gender, beliefs, biases, preferences, theoretical, political, and ideological stances.[11]

Positionality refers to what we know and believe, and reflexivity is about what we do with this knowledge. Reflexivity involves questioning one's own taken-for-granted assumptions. The process of reflexivity constitutes a continual internal dialogue and critical self-evaluation of the researcher's positionality and active acknowledgement and explicit recognition that this position may affect the research process and outcome. The ethnographer's influence on the research and its representation is essential in terms of the ethnographic account's validity and reliability. Thus, reflexivity is an integral part of ensuring the transparency and quality of ethnographic research.

Reflexivity is an ongoing cyclical process from the outset of the study through to data analysis because although an initial idea will inform data collection, the collected data will raise questions about theory, which in turn leads to more data collection, analysis, writing, and the ongoing development of ideas. This inductive 'bottom-up' approach allows theory to emerge from the data itself and includes the researcher's own reflexive account of how her behaviour and reactions affect and are affected by the world she is studying. Research takes place within a social context and reflexivity in contemporary fieldwork is the requirement to think critically about the context and the acts of research and writing that evidences an awareness that ethnography is constructed and acknowledging we are part of the world we study. The ethnography produced is a joint product of the researcher's and the participants' mutual interpretations and negotiation; therefore, these dynamics must be made explicit. This is accomplished by keeping a written record as described above, which ensures the integrity and validity of the study.

[10] Darren Newbury, 'Diaries and Fieldnotes in the Research Process', *Research Issues in Art Design and Media,* Issue 1, The Research Training Initiative, Birmingham Institute of Art and Design, <http://www.utsc.utoronto.ca/~kmacd/IDSC10/Readings/diaries/riadmIssue1.pdf> [accessed 14 February 2021].

[11] Roni Berger, 'Now I See It, Now I Don't: Researcher's Position and Reflexivity in Qualitative Research', *Qualitative Research*, 15.2 (2015), 219–34 (p. 220).

The key incidents I describe here occurred during a festival in Buenos Aires where I was assisted by a colleague who shadowed me and filmed hours of continuous uncut footage, which allowed me to review extensive sequences of visual material. Some of the series of occurrences that struck me as significant in situ were captured on film, but this account has as much to do with thinking about how these might be thought about, as the incidents themselves that form a collage of connected moments. My initial responses were developed throughout an ongoing data analysis, identifying salient themes from the primary data (fieldnotes, film, interviews). This shift in focus here is from 'what' people do to 'why' people do things. It is a move from analysis to interpretation that includes background reading and synthesis of primary and secondary forms of data such as flyers, historical documents, and secondary texts and existing research. As Madden notes, 'the act of writing up causes us to reflect, to alter, to reconsider what we had in mind before we wrote "up"'.[12] The following extract offers a brief outline of this process.

Buenos Aires Celebra Calabria: Día del Inmigrante Calabrés

This event occurs annually at the junction of Avenida de Mayo and Bolivar in front of the Plaza de Mayo, facing the Casa Rosada. It is where Eva Perón, known as Evita (the wife of Juan Perón, the Argentine President (1946–1955)) addressed throngs of Peronists – predominantly low-income, working-class Argentines, known as 'los descamisados'. It is also where the first attempt at the military coup that eventually deposed Perón took place in June 1955. More recently, the Mothers of the Plaza de Mayo have congregated here with signs and pictures of 'los desaparecidos', their children, young people who were arrested, tortured, and 'disappeared' by the Argentine military during the Dirty War (1976–1983). This campaign by the Argentine military junta in power against suspected dissidents and subversives in the National Reorganization Process referred to as 'el Proceso' by the military dictatorship leaders resulted in – according to varying estimates – between 9,000 and 30,000 citizens being 'disappeared' from 1976 to 1983.[13]

On this sunny day in April, the only 'manifestación' is by veterans of the 1982 Falklands War when Argentina invaded the Las Malvinas. Disqualified from receiving a pension on the basis that they were never deployed on the islands, they are camped here in protest against the government's refusal

[12] Madden, *Being Ethnographic*, p. 159.

[13] Carlos E. Cué, 'Dispute Over Official Figures from "Dirty War" Draws Ire in Argentina', <https://english.elpais.com/archive/2016-01-28/> [accessed 17 January 2022].

Figure 1. The Military Band of Los Patricios, Buenos Aires (12 April 2015).

All images are stills taken from footage shot by Carlos Brown and Margaret Hills de Zárate (Buenos Aires, 12 April 2015).

to recognize them as 'continental combatants' and afford them a 'minimal pension'.

Carlos, a colleague, and I are here to film the celebration of the fifth 'Día del Inmigrante Calabrés' in the framework of the 'Buenos Aires Celebra Calabria' cycle, promoted by the Government of the City of Buenos Aires and the National Government. Carlos has his camera mounted on a moving tripod so we can easily move around. It is a festival that includes music, dance, typical food, and costume, involving more than forty Calabrian associations and institutions. A crowd has assembled to commemorate El Día Mundial del Emigrante Calabrés, a project presented by the Lega Donne Calabresi and the Federation of Calabrian Associations in Argentina. This event is part of the six hundredth anniversary of the birth of San Francesco di Paola, patron saint and the first Calabrian emigrant remembered in Italy, and according to the flyer, almost all over the world. A stage is facing Avenida de Mayo, and the area packed with crowds and stalls selling all sorts of Calabrian produce. We arrive as the music and dancing start. Soon the festival is in full swing and then, quite suddenly, it is interrupted.

Someone is singing, but suddenly they are drowned out by a loudspeaker and a declaration from the balcony of the Cabildo, the old seat of the government of Buenos Aires, which once housed the Viceroyalty of the Río de la Plata, now the National Historical Museum of the Revolution of May. It is

Figure 2. Los Patricios leaving the Cabildo, Buenos Aires (12 April 2015).

unclear what is happening. The music grinds to a halt, the crowd drifts towards the edge of an invisible barrier that separates it from what transpires to be another event. The area in front of the Cabildo has filled with soldiers. Carlos has the camera on the tripod and is somewhere behind me as I make my way forwards towards what appears to be a military parade. I ask someone what it is, but he is not sure. Someone else suggests that it is a reenactment of the declaration of independence. A military band in full military regalia begins to play, but there are other soldiers too, and they are wearing combat uniforms.

All attention is turned away from 'El Día del Inmigrante' to this interlude. A proclamation, which I cannot make out, is followed by the military band, a series of marches, a gun salute, and shouts of 'Viva la Patria!' I later discover that this is the change of the Guard of Honour by 'Los Patricios', the main protagonists of the Revolution of May in 1810, which resulted in the Spanish Viceroy's forced resignation. It marks the birth of a local government, the 'Primera Junta', an event that signified the end of colonial rule in Buenos Aires and its hinterland and the beginning of the Argentine War of Independence (1810–1818).

'Los Patricios' march off, and the festival resumes. The performance recommences, and the crowd (many of whom are in full traditional costume) continues its celebration with an outburst of rattling tambourines. A woman dances a *pizzica di Nardò*. The *pizzica* (from 'pizzicare', to bite, pinch, or sting) is a version of the Apulian tarantella danced in Salento, a music and dance genre practised by entire communities. In past times, the *pizzica* was part of a cure in the rite of tarantism: a ritual in which victims, mainly women,

Figure 3. The Dancer of the Pizzica.

who claimed to have been bitten by a spider (tarantula), danced the *pizzica*, sometimes for days, to expel its poison. Made up of fast jumps, steps, and spins that follow the tambourines' insistent rhythm, the pizzica is a dance that leads the dancers to dance without respite until they collapse from exhaustion and the poison expelled. Today, the dancer is jubilant, in bare feet, a white chemise and long petticoat, the undergarments that her great-grandmother would have worn. She is interrupted, but she starts again. This performance and that of the military that preceded it, evoke a liminal space, neither here nor there but somewhere in between, 'linking present and past in the present, and the past in a specific socio-political context',[14] a site of multiple performances of memory.

In Ernesto De Martino's ethnographic study, the practice of tarantism represents a 'culturally conditioned mythical-ritual', and the spider's bite is a symbol of unresolved unconscious conflicts symbolizing a critical episode from the past.[15] The phrase 'crisis of presence' is deployed to refer to the loss of

[14] Luisa M. García-Manso, 'Espacios liminales, fantasmas de la memoria e identidad en el teatro histórico contemporáneo', *Signa. Revista de la Asociación Española de Semiótica*, 27 (2018), 393–417 (p. 395).

[15] Ernesto De Martino, *The Land of Remorse: A Study of Southern Italian Tarantism* (London: Free Association Books, 2005 [1961]).

the sense of self, that exacerbated by the precarity of the *contadino*'s subaltern existence, results in the inability to act on the world and control one's own existence, and ultimately in the individual losing their place in history. In this sense, tarantism represents a means of reintegration that helps individuals overcome the 'crisis of presence' and regain their place in history: in other words, it disciplines psychic conflicts in the unconscious, and reintegrates the victims of the crisis. However, De Martino, a socialist, assumes dynamism rather than homeostasis. In his proposal that crises arise from the atrophy of the dynamic power that ordinarily impels the individual towards the future, he advocated a revision of the ethnological project that focuses on a subaltern people's struggles to make their 'irruption into history'. Therefore, the 'crisis of presence' is only 'a momentary failure and reintegration is not a return to a stable cultural norm, but potentially an exercise in creative, even revolutionary, power akin to the invention of culture'.[16]

This juxtaposition of events and performed identities left me with a sense of unease, which just as Emerson suggests was 'initially opaque and uncertain in meaning and implication'. I finally came to rest on the word 'interruption': a noun that has no consistent definition; variously defined as a break; an abrupt intervention of something foreign; an act of hindrance or obstruction; and a breach of continuity, that links these events. After the event was over, I returned to it through writing as other threads emerged in the data. Among these remain the presence and persistence of the dancer, the interrupted lives of a generation and the long shadow of the disappeared.

Dr Margaret Hills de Zárate is an art psychotherapist and Honorary Senior Lecturer at Queen Margaret University, Edinburgh.

[16] Tobia Farnetti and Charles Stewart, 'Translator's Preface: An Introduction to "Crisis of Presence and Religious Reintegration" by Ernesto de Martino', *HAU: Journal of Ethnographic Theory*, 2.2 (2012), 431–33 (p. 432).

14

# Flow

*Alan O'Leary and Rachel Johnson*

In a strikingly personal passage from a classic text of television studies, Raymond Williams recalls himself 'still dazed from a week on an Atlantic liner' watching a film in (the reader infers) his hotel room in Miami.[1] It is a disorientating experience for the great critic. The crime film set in San Francisco is constantly interrupted, not only by commercial 'breaks' (the scare quotes are Williams's own), but also by extracts from two other films, a romance set in Paris and monster movie in New York, inserted as trailers for later broadcasts. He comments:

> I can still not be sure what I took from that whole *flow*. I believe I registered some incidents as happening in the wrong film, and some characters in the commercials as involved in the film episodes, in what came to seem – for all the occasional bizarre disparities – a single irresponsible *flow* of images and feelings.[2]

'Flow': the word seems innocuous enough, but one feels in Williams's description a nostalgia for the days when an artwork or text could be experienced and analysed in splendid isolation. Though one of the founders of cultural studies, Williams displays a patrician distaste for the mass mediation and commercialization of culture, and 'flow' emerges from his testimony as a powerful but ambivalent trope. The account of his confusion

[1] Raymond Williams, 'Programming: Distribution and Flow', in *Television: Technology and Cultural Form*, ed. by Ederyn Williams (London: Fontana, 1974), pp. 71–111.

[2] Williams, 'Programming', p. 92 (our emphasis).

in Miami lays down an intellectual challenge: how to develop an analytical method equal to the novelty of this experience, so difficult to interpret, of flow?

Many have taken up this challenge, following Williams in using the concept of flow to capture media phenomena that exceed and traverse the single text, the single nation, and, latterly, the single medium. But flow is also one of the key tropes in commentary on modernity and postmodernity, used to characterize the dissolution of social bonds (for good or ill – and usually both), from Karl Marx to Zygmunt Bauman. It is notable in this respect that Williams mentions his transatlantic crossing. This context confirms that his sense of bewilderment before the hotel television is an aspect of modern social experience and emblematic of it, part of a broader shift away from static conceptions not only of artworks but of social relations. Transportation by ocean liner suggests a key feature of modernity, that of migration and mass dislocation, the transnational flow of peoples in search of a better life. Conversely, the fact that Williams's journey seems to have been a form of leisure (a cruise trip, one presumes) itself signals a distinctive aspect of modernity – tourism, or the flow of the few in privileged counterpoint to the forced movement of the abject many.

Nine years after Raymond Williams's foundational essay on television and broadcasting, the trope of flow re-emerges in American philosopher Marshall Berman's account of capitalist modernity as a mode of social organization in which 'all that is solid melts into air' (the phrase is borrowed from Marx and Engels). The idea of the destructive potential of different kinds of fluidity runs through Berman's famous book. If modernity 'pours us all into a maelstrom of perpetual disintegration and renewal, of struggle and contradiction, of ambiguity and anguish',[3] then this dialectic of 'ambiguity and anguish' also marks Berman's own discourse. We find in his ambivalent celebration a continuing anxiety about irrepressible and irresponsible flow that recalls the passage, above, from Williams. Anguish permeates Berman's rhetorical question, 'what happens to all the people who get swept away in those tides?'[4] One answer is that the 'people' turn to the ruling bourgeoisie as the 'Party of Order', the force that promises to arrest the inexorable flow.[5] In vain, of course, because 'social forces are driven in dreadful directions by relentless market imperatives that not even the most powerful bourgeois can control'.[6]

[3] Marshall Berman, *All That Is Solid Melts into Air: The Experience of Modernity* (London: Verso, 1983), p. 15.

[4] Berman, *All That Is Solid*, p. 25.

[5] Berman, *All That Is Solid*, p. 99.

[6] Berman, *All That Is Solid*, p. 99.

Nonetheless, the appeal of the Party of Order is a perennial one, as will be seen in examples below.

In Zygmunt Bauman's famous idea of 'liquid modernity' the trope of flow is transposed from gas to liquid, but it continues to figure the essential experience of our (post)modernity.[7] Liquidity, in Bauman, characterizes some of the most pressing contemporary issues: inequality, migration, colonialism, war, and power as such. Bauman notes that power now flows away from a stable, recognizable centre so that those through whom power operates can escape the local consequences of their actions. The elite flows across borders, its occupation of new places and spaces secured by modern warfare's tidal destruction of obstacles. War itself becomes the pursuit of uncurbed flow, 'not the conquest of a new territory, but crushing the walls which [stop] the flow of new, fluid global powers'.[8] The elite is cosmopolitan, mobile, while the poor are (expected to be) rooted to a particular territory: 'We are witnessing the revenge of nomadism over the principle of territoriality and settlement. In the fluid stage of modernity, the settled majority is ruled by the nomadic and exterritorial elite'.[9] The irony of this vision is that it reverses the picture found in the xenophobic discourse of the wealthy West, in which a settled national majority is typically presented as menaced not by a cosmopolitan elite acting in the voracious interests of transnational capital, but by the 'influx' (from the Latin, 'to flow in') of poorer and/or darker skinned people. As Berman predicted (just as Marx did before him), the threat of this flow (or flood) allows the self-professed defenders of nation and race to present themselves as the 'Party of Order' that will secure social stability and the interests of Bauman's 'settled majority'.

Consider the poster produced by the United Kingdom Independence Party (UKIP) as part of the campaign to secure a vote to leave the European Union in the UK 'Brexit' referendum of June 2016. The 'Breaking Point' poster promotes a xenophobic idea of migration as a menacing flow of bodies. It shows a closely cropped photograph in shallow focus, upon which several captions have been superimposed, representing a queue of people as a winding river flowing towards the camera (the density of the queue is exaggerated by the use of a long lens that has the effect of flattening the space). The context of the Brexit campaign encourages the viewer of the poster to imagine that these people are trying to approach and enter Britain, or have already done so (in fact, the photograph shows people crossing the Croatia–Slovenia border in 2015). The emotive proposition made is that

[7] Zygmunt Bauman, *Liquid Modernity* (Cambridge: Polity Press, 2000).

[8] Bauman, *Liquid Modernity*, p. 12.

[9] Bauman, *Liquid Modernity*, p. 13.

Figure 1. UKIP pro-Brexit poster.
Source: United Kingdom Independence Party (2016).

migration is an overflowing river of 'non-white' men (the in-focus segment of the image shows mainly adult males with Middle Eastern features), which is already threatening to break the 'banks' (the borders) of the UK. This motivates the text in the caption: 'We must break free of the [European Union] and take back control of our [the UK's] borders'. While the populist rhetoric of 'breaking free' is revolutionary in tone, UKIP presents itself as the Party of Order by insisting that the UK must reclaim sovereignty over its borders and, by implication, over its ethnic integrity.

The picturing of migration as a flow that must be resisted on behalf of an endangered white British ethnicity recalls the imagery and content of the notorious address by the politician Enoch Powell to a conservative association in Birmingham in April 1968.[10] The allusion to 'rivers of blood' by which this address has come to be known occurs at the end, but it represents the climactic moment of imagery of inundation that builds through the speech. Powell's theme was the social effects of mass immigration to Britain by people from Commonwealth countries – for which read the formerly colonized nations of the British empire – and his speech was delivered in advance of the passing of a bill designed to make it illegal to refuse housing or work on the grounds of ethnicity. The self-consciously rhetorical speech moves

[10] Enoch Powell, 'Rivers of Blood' also known as 'The Birmingham Speech'. Address to the Conservative Political Centre, Birmingham, 20 April 1968, Transcript, *The Telegraph*, 6 November 2007, <http://www.telegraph.co.uk/comment/3643823/Enoch-Powells-Rivers-of-Blood-speech.html> [accessed 10 March 2021], italics added.

towards its culminating image through recurring reference to excessive flow (variations of the word 'flow' are used six times in 3,000 words). 'We must be mad, literally mad, as a nation to be permitting the annual *inflow* of some 50,000 dependants [of previous migrants]'. Powell's solution is a rational redirection of flow: 'The answers to the simple and rational question [of how to curb immigration] are [...] simple and rational: by stopping, or virtually stopping, further inflow, and by promoting the maximum outflow [that is, 're-emigration']'. The imagery of flow culminates in an allusion to Virgil's *Aeneid*: 'As I look ahead, I am filled with foreboding; like the Roman, I seem to see "the River Tiber foaming with much blood"'.[11] Powell compares himself to 'the Roman' (the poet Virgil) and, implicitly, the UK to imperial Rome (the metonym of the Tiber), imagery that draws on Rome's status as a symbol of Western civilization in order to cast the UK as bastion of civilization under threat of violent inundation.

The invocation of the foaming blood in Powell's speech is ambiguous because it is unclear if Powell is warning about violence (and if so, by whom, and against whom?) or willing it to be. This ambiguity survives in the condensation of the phrase as 'rivers of blood', which evokes a hegemonic (white) popular imagination that simultaneously fears and desires racial conflict, and also suggests racial 'contamination' – copulation and reproduction across ethnicities, the mixing of blood. The river Tiber becomes plural (*rivers* of blood) within the ambivalence of the popular memory of Powell's address, suggesting once again a diffuse and irresistible flow. The persistence of the trope confirms its power to generate anxiety and to stand for the enveloping movement of darker bodies towards a terrified and fascinated white 'us'. As Sara Ahmed has written: 'The emotion of "hate" aligns the particular white body with the bodily form of the community – such an emotion functions to substantiate the threat of invasion and contamination in the dirty bodies of strangers'.[12] Black bodies, contamination, inundation; the 'excreta' that Enoch Powell claims that black children ('wide-grinning piccaninnies') force through an old white lady's letter box;[13] the white social body that UKIP claims needs protection from a wave of black male migrants. Ahmed's riposte is informed by a strategic re-appropriation of flow, an assertion of the inevitability of border crossing. Flow, in Ahmed, describes the essence of the social body; the skin itself is a leaky vessel: 'The skin may open out a moment of undecidability which is at once a rupture or breakage, where the subject risks its interiority,

[11] Powell, 'Rivers of Blood'.

[12] Sara Ahmed, *Strange Encounters: Embodied Others in Post-Coloniality* (Abingdon: Routledge, 2000), p. 39.

[13] Powell, 'Rivers of Blood'.

Figure 2. Protesting crowds in the coda of *The Battle of Algiers*.
Source: Frame grab from Cult Films DVD (2018).

where it meets and leaks into the world at large'.[14] Here, regulated flow seems impossible, and the trope itself is deployed for progressive ends as flow is taken as a mainstay of human experience and social interaction. In the light of these opposed deployments of the trope of flow – one xenophobic and one anti-racist – we might further trace the contours of its ambivalence. If flow has some origin in colonial discourse – notions of the non-white other as a contaminating, fluid mass that must be contained – what does it mean when anti-racist or 'progressive' discourse is structured around the same metaphor?

The film *The Battle of Algiers* is an Algerian/Italian coproduction made to celebrate Algeria's achievement of independence from French colonial rule in 1962.[15] Immensely powerful in its unflinching depiction of oppression and resistance, torture and terrorism, *The Battle of Algiers* is a classic of political cinema, and its anti-colonial message has earned it the status of sacred text in certain left-wing circles. Yet the film's imagery derives in part from the tradition of orientalism developed in the colonial era. As analysed in a great book by Edward Said, 'orientalism' refers to the set of portrayals in Western art, literature, and scholarship that constructed North Africa and the East as inviting physical conquest and occupation.[16] In the section of his book entitled 'Orientalism Now', Said points to flow as an orientalist trope – one that reverses the actual direction of invasion – when he notes 'Western fears of an

[14] Ahmed, *Strange Encounters*, p. 45.
[15] *The Battle of Algiers*, dir. by Gillo Pontecorvo (Casbah Film/Igor Film, 1966).
[16] Edward Said, *Orientalism* (London: Penguin, 2003 [1978]).

Oriental tidal wave'.[17] We find precisely this fear deployed in the anti-colonial *Battle of Algiers*. The metaphor of the wave is found in the exhilarating coda to the film when the Algerian crowds are shown to emerge in their hundreds from the Muslim areas of Algiers, visually and metaphorically to inundate a colonizer unable to resist what has been revealingly dubbed 'the tide of Algerian nationalism'. The film here adopts a perspective employed by the colonialists themselves, in the sense that France understood the Algerian desire for independence as solely to do with the growth of the Muslim population. 'While Algerians endured gross economic and political inequality, French social scientists insisted that *demographic* disparities explained the [Algerian War of Independence, 1954–1962] and that only French-led development could address them'.[18] Political agitation was therefore conceived of as a 'rising tide' or a river overflowing its banks – even, as Connelly (a historian of Algeria) notices, 'by anticolonialists like the director Gillo Pontecorvo. His *The Battle of Algiers* [...] deliberately pictured Algerians as a flooding river sweeping the French before them'.[19] An unsympathetic spectator could perceive the protesting crowds at the close of *The Battle of Algiers* less as a 'people' than as a mere 'population', their number testament to instinctual fecundity rather than political agency. Of course, the deployment of an orientalist trope is consistent with the film's project to address persuasively the old colonizing North on behalf of the new Algerian nation. The use of the metaphorical language of orientalism was a way to ensure that the film could be understood by those whose worldview remained resolutely Eurocentric. The menacing flow of the Algerian popular resistance to French rule is an example of a colonial trope being deployed against itself. Revolutionary power is cast in orientalist terms, all the better to communicate anti-colonial agency, but the ambivalence of the trope generates an ambiguity in the film. Even Edward Said himself, an admirer of *The Battle of Algiers*, worried that the film identified too strongly with the perspective of the colonizer.

*Human Flow* (2017), a film by the artist Ai Weiwei, has been celebrated by critics for its commitment to fostering empathy between audiences and migrants.[20] Shot at the perceived height of the 'refugee crisis' (the film shows that the forced movement of people on a large scale is not such a unique or

[17] Said, *Orientalism*, p. 250.

[18] Matthew Connelly, *A Diplomatic Revolution: Algeria's Fight for Independence and the Origins of the Post-Cold War Era* (Oxford: Oxford University Press, 2002), p. xi [italics in original].

[19] Connelly, *A Diplomatic Revolution*, p. xi.

[20] *Human Flow*, dir. by Ai Weiwei (Altitude Film Entertainment/Amazon Studios, 2017).

Figure 3. A procession of migrants in *Human Flow*.
Source: Frame grab from Altitude Film DVD (2018).

recent phenomenon), *Human Flow* has been most commonly interpreted as a political documentary that seeks to make a direct intervention into debates about migration. However, it may also be read for its ambiguity through the way in which the trope of flow continues to structure the film's narrative and representation of non-European subjects. Notice the marked similarity between some of the imagery in the film, as in the still reproduced here, and the photograph used in the 'Breaking Point' poster. Notice, too, the difference: in the image from *Human Flow*, the viewer's perspective is aligned with that of the migrants. For the film, we are part of the flow, not threatened by it. The film appears to be formed around the notion of a chaotic fluidity deployed, this time, for what might be described as responsible affective ends. Flow gives the form of the film itself, as well as its depiction of migration, 'with the narrative's liquid structure mirroring for the audience all the sensations of uncertainty, of indefinite time, of swirling limbo that refugees experience'.[21] As the film's fluid narrative traverses sixty-three countries and a massive temporal span, it locates the flow of migrants in the larger flow of history, or rather, evolution. The discourse of race is submerged in the acknowledgement of our shared origins as a species when the film depicts the first human (*hominins*) migration two million years ago. In *Human Flow*, fluidity does not appear as a threatening property of the other, but as a characteristic of human

[21] *Human Flow*: Final Press Notes, p. 11, <http://www.magpictures.com/resources/presskits/HumanFlow/HUMANFLOWfinalnotes.dot> [accessed 28 February 2021].

experience per se. As such, it may be seen in relation to Ahmed's project of re-tooling a trope that features so strongly in orientalist discourse. The film remains marked by a twofold ambivalence, however. First, its starting point is the same as that of *The Battle of Algiers*: the colonial and orientalist characterization of non-Europeans as a deluge. Second, it is still addressed, however didactically, to the fearful Eurocentric viewer, even as it aligns that (implicitly white?) viewer with the experience of the migrant or refugee.

As we have seen, flow has been and remains at once a powerful heuristic and ambivalent trope found across a range of discourses. The ambivalence derives from its association with colonialism and the dichotomy of unruly masses and containment/order this association conveys. On the one hand, the 'irresponsible', destructive potential of unregulated flow marks discourses on modernity and migration alike. There is a sense that flow should be restricted to the 'right' people, lest it dissolve social bonds and contaminate privileged ethnicities. This feeling (call it common sense) means that the trope of flow can be deployed, in *The Battle of Algiers*, to hymn the will to freedom of a colonized people, signifying, as it does, a threat to the colonizer. More recently, we might notice a trend towards the self-conscious reclaiming of the trope, in which the negative political connotations of flow are first acknowledged and then diffused by recourse to universalism. *Human Flow* posits flow as a condition, or the condition, of humanity itself. Such attempts might best be understood as *post*-colonial: structured by colonial discourse but attempting to transcend it. Would the metaphor of flow retain its power were our political discourse to be thoroughly *de*-colonized?

Alan O'Leary is Associate Professor of Film and Media in Digital Contexts at Aarhus University.
Rachel Johnson is Lecturer in Film Studies at the University of Leeds.

# 15

# Futures

*Monica Seger*

Sitting down to compose an essay on 'futures', I cannot help but consider my grounding in the present, one that feels rather turbulent worldwide. I write from North America with an eye not only towards Italy, upon which much of my research and teaching focuses, but towards the world as a whole, aware of the inevitably transnational reach of national politics, cultural trends, and even my own daily behaviours. More than anything, when I think of 'futures' in this present era, I think of the very planet on which we live. I am mindful, in particular, of the non-human environment in this epoch that we now call the Anthropocene, 'in which many geologically significant conditions and processes are profoundly altered by human activities'.[1] In 2016, Earth experienced its warmest year on record, with land surface temperatures reaching 1.43 degrees centigrade above the twentieth-century average. The year 2020 came in a very close second. During this same period, unprecedented wildfires have raged out of control in Israel, Portugal, Australia, and the United States, to name just a few locales, while massive earthquakes hit from Ecuador to Indonesia. It is safe to say that the present era holds an uncertain relationship to futures worldwide, especially those related to the well-being of the non-human environment and the creatures in its midst.

So, what does the discipline of Modern Languages have to do with all of this? How does the study of language and culture enter the discourse on changing environmental realities and the future health of beloved landscapes, natural resources, and living beings? To that I respond: how does it not? It is precisely in the study of linguistic and cultural production – and especially, as

[1] Submission on Quaternary Stratigraphy, 'What is the Anthropocene?' <https://quaternary.stratigraphy.org/workinggroups/anthropocene/> [accessed 13 February 2021].

I will argue, of narrative expression – that we find invaluable tools for coping with the present moment and for cultivating responses to possible futures. By examining narrative texts in light of particular linguistic, cultural, and environmental contexts, we have the opportunity to learn about other ways of being in and relating to the world, including the non-human environment. What's more, we are provided space from which to reflect upon our own experiences and behaviours, and to explore paths for new courses of action. When I think of 'futures' in the context of Modern Languages, I think in particular of the Environmental Humanities and the ways in which this ever-growing nexus of scholarly approaches can help us – researchers, students, and the general public alike – to make sense of our most urgent and overwhelming present realities, as well as futures yet to come.

'Environmental Humanities' is a broad umbrella term for an area of research and teaching that comprises 'disciplines such as literature, history, philosophy, film and media, cultural studies, religious studies, cultural geography, and anthropology'.[2] In its breadth, Environmental Humanities aligns particularly well with Modern Languages. The idea of an 'environmental humanities' has circulated since the early 2000s and includes the older subfield of ecocriticism, which is especially pertinent to those of us who study language, culture, and text. In her now-canonical *Ecocriticism Reader* of 1996, Cheryl Glotfelty defines ecocriticism as 'the study of the relationship between literature and the physical environment', an 'earth-centred' approach with a political grounding not unlike feminist and Marxist criticism.[3] Over the past two decades, ecocriticism and Environmental Humanities have broadened to consider a much wider variety of texts and the stories they tell, and to apply a more critical lens towards the role of the human. Almost twenty-five years after Glotfelty, Greg Garrard offers a new take in his disciplinary overview, describing ecocriticism as 'the study of the relationship of the human and the non-human, throughout human history and entailing critical analysis of the term "human" itself', still largely but not exclusively through 'literature, film and other forms of narrative expression'.[4] Other Environmental Humanities scholars seek to de-emphasize the role of the human, particularly through subfields such as Animal Studies or Material Ecocriticism. While the first

[2] The Association for the Study of Literature and Environment, 'Ecocriticism and Environmental Humanities', <https://www.asle.org/explore-our-field/ecocriticism-and-environmental-humanities/> [accessed 13 February 2021].

[3] Cheryl Glotfelty, 'Literary Studies in the Age of Environmental Crisis', in *The Ecocriticism Reader: Landmarks in Literary Ecology*, ed. by Cheryl Glotfelty and Harold Fromm (Athens: The University of Georgia Press, 1996), pp. xv–xxxvi (p. xix).

[4] Greg Garrard, *Ecocriticism*, 2nd edn (New York: Routledge, 2012), p. 12.

examines representations of non-human animals and what they might tell us about the world, the second emphasizes the narrative agency of non-human matter at large. Both approaches seek to trouble the anthropocentricism we generally adopt in the humanities, while exploring what Serenella Iovino, following Nancy Tuana, has called the 'porosity' of the lived world: the enmeshment of all sorts of beings, forms of matter, and stories.[5]

Modern Languages scholars, too, are ever further probing the flows of linguistic and cultural production from one context to another – exploring, for example, what a postcolonial Italian text might share with a Francophone one, as well as how and why they are distinct. Both such movements towards interdisciplinarity, in Environmental Humanities as well as Modern Languages, result in a deeper understanding of the world and its vastly connected networks. Both, too, underline the crucial sense-making function of narrative texts, which allow us to understand past histories just as they provide us with tools for what might yet come – often by way of imagined experience. Although it can remain unarticulated in our academic practices, the process of imagination is so crucial, both to the analysis that we perform as active critical readers looking for clues, and to the experience that we undertake as a receptive audience. As Martha Nussbaum explains, narrative imagination is an essential practice for cultivating humanity, just as it is 'an essential preparation for moral interaction'. She writes: 'habits of empathy and conjecture conduce to a certain type of citizenship and a certain form of community: one that cultivates a sympathetic responsiveness to another's needs, and understands the way circumstances shape those needs, while respecting separateness and privacy'.[6] In allowing audiences to consider diverse circumstances, the process of narrative imagination encourages us to be more thoughtful global citizens, respecting the needs of other living creatures, but also of waterways, ecosystems, and the dynamic material world at large.

Nussbaum's treatment of imagination in the citation above, as well as my own in this essay, does not refer only to fictional narratives, but to all manner of stories and the worlds they contain. Similarly, 'imagination' here does not refer so much to the creative process undertaken by author or artist, as to that undertaken by reader or viewer. More often than not, when we engage with a narrative, we allow ourselves to enter cognitively and emotionally into its storyworld. We find sympathy with particular protagonists, we envision

[5] Serenella Iovino, *Ecocriticism and Italy: Ecology, Resistance and Liberation* (London: Bloomsbury, 2016), pp. 16–20.

[6] Martha Nussbaum, *Cultivating Humanity: A Classical Defense of Reform in Liberal Education* (Cambridge MA: Harvard University Press, 1997), p. 90.

physical environments, and we think about what it may be like to face any number of challenges. In her study of postcolonial econarratology, Erin James contemplates 'the world-creating power of narratives that catalyses an imaginative relocation of readers to a *new, often unfamiliar* world and experience'.[7] By entering through story into cultures, locations, and even languages that may not be primary to us, we have the opportunity to learn a great deal about the world beyond our shores. And as James and others note, this is particularly true regarding the non-human environment. When we trace the 'correlations between such textual [...] worlds, and the physical, extratextual world', we unleash the 'potential of the reading process to foster an awareness and understanding for different environmental imaginations and experiences'.[8] Entry into diverse 'environmental imaginations and experiences,' in particular, allows audiences to expand our awareness of global environments and the effects of human action. At the same time, it allows us to re-evaluate environments and behaviours closer to home, whether through contrast or comparison. The study of other cultures is fundamental for a nuanced worldview, informed understanding of global histories, and thoughtful approach to future actions in an age of increasingly transnational political and social networks. In the same vein, an attention to representations of the non-human environment allows for deeper care and critical reasoning as we assess our relationship to an increasingly endangered planet, learning from pasts and presents (fictional or otherwise) as we contemplate the future.

Anna Tsing writes that 'learning the names of plants is just like learning the names of people you meet; when you know their name, you can get to know them better'.[9] In other words, paying attention to the non-human environment, just as we do to the people in our midst, allows for a deeper knowledge on scales large and small. The beauty of naming, as Tsing writes, or of language and the access it provides to worlds beyond our own, is precisely how I found my way to both Modern Languages and Environmental Humanities. As a young student I had always loved the study of language – the opportunity it provided to produce intriguing new sounds, to embody and explore parts of my identity that I had not previously known, and to learn about other ways of being and framing the world. When I entered university, I took up Italian with the hope that I might be able to study abroad in a few years' time, pushing my own process of ordering the world and knowing it better that much further.

[7] Erin James, *The Storyworld Accord: Econarratology and Postcolonial Narratives* (Lincoln, NE: University of Nebraska Press, 2015), p. xi [italics added].

[8] James, *The Storyworld Accord*, p. xv.

[9] Anna Lowenhaupt Tsing, *Friction: An Ethnography of Global Connection* (Princeton: Princeton University Press, 2005), p. 158.

It was as an exchange student at an Italian university that the process truly came to fruition, as I was more fully immersed in the critical study of Italian arts and letters than ever before. Through courses on topics such as European feminism, the history of the book and, most profoundly, twentieth-century Italian literature, I was able to fully ground my growing knowledge of cultural production within a particular context. This allowed me to explore the ways in which shifting political tides, national identities, and cultural trends had contributed to the development of social movements and artistic traditions within Italy, while also providing the opportunity to think across borders as I traced currents throughout the globe. At the same time, I began to note the presence of the non-human environment in much of the literature I was reading, and the fundamental ways in which it helped to drive a particular narrative or provide insight into the historical moment depicted.

It was from that foundational experience as an undergraduate student that I found my way to my current scholarly pursuits, in which I contemplate the power of creative narrative texts to help us make sense of changing ecosystems, natural disaster, environmental justice, industrial emissions, and more. One category of texts particularly useful in this pursuit is contemporary eco-documentary, a subgenre within 'ecocinema'. Paula Willoquet-Maricondi writes that ecocinema 'overtly strives to inspire personal and political action on the part of viewers, stimulating our thinking so as to bring about concrete changes in the choices we make, daily and in the long run, as individuals and as societies, locally and globally', whether by employing a 'lyrical and contemplative style' or an 'overt activist approach'.[10] The above definition might strike readers as rather narrow: as Cubbitt, Monani, and Rust note, all manner of films can lend themselves to ecocritical analysis and prompt viewers to action, even without an overt environmentalist agenda.[11] Willoquet-Maricondi's definition is particularly apt, however, for a trio of recent Italian eco-documentaries that I mention here in closing, for the way in which they draw viewers into awareness of ongoing environmental crisis and community response in a land we might not otherwise know.[12]

*In viaggio con Cecilia* (Travelling with Cecilia) by Mariangela Barbanente and Cecilia Mangini, *Buongiorno Taranto* (Good Morning, Taranto) by Paolo Pisanelli, and *Non perdono* (Non-Pardon/I Do Not Forgive) by Roberto

[10] Paula Willoquet-Maricondi, *Framing the World: Explorations in Ecocriticism and Film* (Charlottesville: University of Virginia Press, 2010), p. 45.

[11] Sean Cubbit, Salma Monani, and Stephen Rust (eds), *Ecocinema Theory and Practice* (New York: Routledge, 2012).

[12] Monica Seger, *Toxic Matters: Narrating Italy's Dioxin* (Charlottesville: University of Virginia Press, 2022).

Marsella and Grace Zanotto are all set it Taranto, a coastal city in Southern Italy's Puglia region that has been home to the massive Ilva steelworks since 1964.[13] With an annual production capacity of 8,000,000 tonnes, Ilva is the largest steelworks in Europe, as well as the most polluting. It has long been known to emit harmful chemical and mineral by-products well above European Union (EU) limits into the local atmosphere. As a result of these excessive emissions, agricultural practices, including the cultivation of crops and raising of feed animals, have been prohibited within twenty kilometres of the centrally located steelworks; Taranto's once-abundant marine life and related vocations have gone into steep decline; and residents suffer from cancers and other serious illnesses at startlingly elevated rates compared to the national population. Community outcry over the steelworks, which is also the most significant employer in the region, came to a head in 2012 when local groups attempted unsuccessfully to halt its operations due to concerns over health and environment (the national government kept the steelworks open, citing economic factors). Since about that same time, a Tarantine narrative renaissance has blossomed as authors, artists, and filmmakers seek to share the city's story with a vast audience and, indeed, to inspire 'personal and political action on the part of viewers'.

The three films listed above vary widely from one another in terms of style and tone. *In viaggio con Cecilia* follows filmmaker Cecilia Mangini as she returns to Taranto fifty years after having first filmed there, intercutting present-day interviews of Ilva workers with her own archival footage of the steelwork's first years. *Buongiorno Taranto* focuses entirely on contemporary Taranto, favouring protest footage over interviews and featuring the ever-expanding cast of a nomadic and community-based Internet radio programme. *Non perdono* is more experimental than the other titles, containing lyrical sequences featuring a silent cloaked figure moving throughout the city alongside elements of traditional realist documentary, such as first-person interview.

Despite their differences, the three films are closely aligned in a shared drive to explore the spirit of contemporary Taranto, while also imagining what its future might entail. All three visually draw viewers into story-world experience by a process of physical mapping, their cameras tracing Taranto's geographic coordinates by continually moving throughout the city. Additionally, all are heavily dialogue based and marked by a significant

[13] *In viaggio con Cecilia*, dir. by Mariangela Barbanente and Cecilia Mangini (GA&A Productions, 2013); *Buongiorno Taranto*, dir. by Paolo Pisanelli (Big Sur, 2015); *Non perdono*, dir. by Roberto Marsella and Grace Zanotto (Nonperdono, 2016), <https://robertomarsella.com/non-perdono/> [accessed 13 February 2021].

plurivocality – even *In viaggio con Cecilia*, the very title of which indicates a primary human subject. Eschewing authorial scripts and primary narrators, the three films instead choose to feature a wide range of Tarantine voices through talking-head sequences, multi-person interviews, voice-overs, and ambulatory conversations shot as subjects walk Taranto's streets or gather in its squares.

In the context of factory-town Taranto, long dominated visually, economically, and ideologically by the massive steelworks, this common choice to share multiple voices reads as a rejection of a singular dominant narrative. As Marco Armiero writes: 'Narrating means producing counter-narratives, because environmental injustice is not only imposed with tanks and truncheons but also with a narrative that eradicates any possible alternative, that requires an official truth'.[14] By allowing the voices of so many different people to be heard, Barbanente and Mangini, Pisanelli, and Marsella and Zanotto offer viewers a complex set of overlapping counter-narratives, the sum of which suggests that to live amidst Ilva's emissions is as personal as it is collective. At the same time, by regularly showing their various subjects centre-frame, using medium or close-up shots to emphasize facial expressions, they offer a visual reminder of the vast number of individual people effected by Taranto's eco-corporeal crisis.

The beginning of *Buongiorno Taranto* captures this plurality well. After a title sequence that moves from a dynamic underwater shot to an image of thick rust-coloured smoke (visual references to Taranto's former maritime glory and the mineral particles that now escape daily from the steelworks), the camera cuts to shaky footage of a workers' strike. A voice asks, 'Do we think closing a plant cleans up the air? Does a closed Ilva mean clean air?', establishing both the historic moment of the documentary film (2012, a year of unprecedented local protests), as well as its attention to the non-human environment. With this, the camera cuts to a young woman seated in front of a microphone at a makeshift recording booth. 'Good morning, Taranto', she says, taking over the narration of events from the anonymous first speaker. 'Environmental disaster culpability', she declares, explaining the charges just brought against Ilva executives. The camera then cuts back to protest footage, before moving on to a series of brief shots: calm waterfront, blast furnaces, slow-moving fishermen, more protests, and a young mother at home who explains that she must keep her children occupied indoors, as

[14] Marco Armiero, 'An Environmental Historian among Activists: The Political, the Personal, and a Project of Guerrilla Narrative', in *Italy and the Environmental Humanities: Landscapes, Natures, Ecologies*, ed. by Serenella Iovino, Enrico Cesaretti, and Elena Past (Charlottesville: University of Virginia Press, 2018), pp. 163–72 (p. 169).

local playgrounds are contaminated. Fast music begins, the second speaker resumes her broadcast, now listing toxic chemicals, and the camera returns to her microphone ... only to display the face of a new woman, who begins speaking. More shots of city life follow, accompanied by yet another new voice offering what will quickly become a familiar greeting: 'Good morning, Taranto!' Pisanelli's film maintains this same pattern for the next eighty minutes, continually introducing new voices as it visually leads viewers throughout the city, emphasizing steelworks, domestic interiors, and the once active coastline. A catchy refrain, the repeated greeting serves as a diegetic reminder to citizens within the film to wake up to the dire moment in which they live. At the same time, it is an intertextual reference that some viewers might recognize, to the 1987 war film *Good Morning, Vietnam* – a reference, that is, to Taranto as a warzone.

Reflecting the same sort of plurivocality woven throughout *In viaggio con Cecilia* and *Non perdono, Buongiorno Taranto* demonstrates the importance of listening to multiple stories from multiple perspectives so that we may better understand urgent global realities. In this, it contributes to the sort of counter-hegemonic storytelling that Armiero declares crucial to contemporary eco-justice movements, adding depth and intimacy to viewers' understanding of the crisis unfolding in Taranto – a crisis in which questions of employment are at stake, just as the mainstream media reports, but so too are questions of environmental and corporeal health. We can also read these films according to the kind of 'ecopoetics' proposed by Scott Knickerbocker, in which it is a text's form, rather than content, that most reveals the influence of what we have long called simply 'nature'. Doing so, we note that their heavy plurivocality serves an additional function by mirroring the multiplicity of the non-human world, in which so many different organisms, plants, and animals alike manage to live out overlapping stories.[15] Returning to the premise with which the current essay began, it is this attentiveness to the many stories within and beyond the human world that an Environmental Humanities approach offers, as we contemplate our uncertain planetary futures. The crucial work of the scholar, then, is to interpret these stories, connecting one thing with the other so that everything may take on meaning.

Monica Seger is Associate Professor of Italian Studies at William & Mary (Virginia, USA).

[15] Scott Knickerbocker, *Ecopoetics: The Language of Nature, the Nature of Language* (Amherst and Boston: University of Massachusetts Press, 2012).

# 16

# Human

*Jennifer Burns*

What constitutes the human, what may be unique or distinctive about the human, what exceeds the human, and what relationships exist between the human and other forms of planetary life are insistent questions gaining new urgency in the early twenty-first century across disciplines and sectors. The identification of the Anthropocene has urged a consideration of what place humans and their activities have occupied in the physical environment of Earth and its atmosphere, what their geological impacts might have been and continue to be, and what exactly humanity is.[1] Even within what is understood as humankind, there is growing attention to the diversity of experiences of what it is to be human, to the plurality of individual human identities, to the relationship between subjectivity and embodiment, and to the capacity of some humans to act inhumanely. Technologies that enhance or promise to outstrip known human capacities prompt enquiry into how far and with what outcomes the human might extend. The post-human becomes an urgent area of reflection.[2]

These questions challenge researchers in the 'Humanities' to rethink their objects of enquiry and the beneficiaries of the knowledge they produce. In Modern Languages in particular, expertise in how language is formulated, used, and received within and between different language communities may prove an essential competency in calibrating how language contributes to making and un-making the human. The discussion here aims to identify

[1] For a cross-disciplinary introduction to the concept, see Erle C. Ellis, *Anthropocene: A Very Short Introduction* (Oxford: Oxford University Press, 2018).

[2] See Rosi Braidotti, *The Posthuman* (Cambridge: Polity, 2013); Cary Wolfe, *What is Posthumanism?* (Minneapolis: University of Minnesota Press, 2010).

things to look for and reflect upon in studying Modern Languages in order not to know definitively what is the human but to be aware of how humanness is identified and activated in diverse settings.

A novel published in Italian in its definitive form in 1840, *I promessi sposi* (*The Betrothed*), by Alessandro Manzoni, offers a revealing case study.[3] Adopted as the defining Italian novel, constructing a form of the historical novel that would help to shape a sense of national culture in the period leading up to the unification of Italy in 1861, it retains today its centrality in the canon of modern, Italian, national culture. The novel as a literary product equally speaks of intercultural exchange: Manzoni had lived in Paris, was close to bilingual, and remained in dialogue with French writers and thinkers. At a wider level, the novel brought the literary form of the nineteenth-century European and American novel into Italian culture as it was shaping its own modernity. It was translated quickly and has taken its position in a transnational canon as a place marker for a particular configuration of human culture, sociality, and behaviour, in the context especially of 'subaltern' individuals and communities building lives subordinated to the dominant power and having limited capacity to protest.[4] The book thus acquired resonance in distant times and spaces, such as Latin America during the boom of the historical novel.[5] In other words, this 'Italian' novel travels. In its diegesis too, it figures the co-presence of times, places, and cultures, relating in the early nineteenth century events taking place during the early seventeenth-century colonization by Spain of the duchy of Milan, as well as the diverse values and temporalities of rural and urban life.[6]

[3] Alessandro Manzoni, *I promessi sposi* (Milan: Mondadori, 2017); *The Betrothed*, trans. by Bruce Penman (London: Penguin, 1983). Quotations are from the English translation.

[4] Antonio Gramsci's use in the early 1930s of 'subaltern' in his *Prison Notebooks*, ed. and trans. by Joseph Buttigieg, 3 vols (New York: Columbia University Press, 2011) to describe the socially oppressed and disenfranchised has been adopted as a key concept in postcolonial theory, interrogated notably by Gayatri Chakravorty Spivak in her essay, 'Can the Subaltern Speak?' (1988). Original and revised versions of the essay, plus responses from Spivak and others, are included in *Can the Subaltern Speak? Reflections on the History of an Idea*, ed. by Rosalind C. Morris (New York: Columbia University Press, 2010).

[5] Helene Carol Weldt-Basson, 'Introduction', in *Redefining Latin American Historical Fiction: The Impact of Feminism and Postcolonialism*, ed. by Helene Carol Weldt-Basson (New York: Palgrave Macmillan, 2013), pp. 1–46 (p. 2).

[6] See Stephanie Jed, 'Glimpses of Resistance to Spanish (and Austrian) Rule: Reading *I promessi sposi* in a Transnational Frame', *Italian Culture*, 37.1 (2019), 26–46.

The status and significance of Manzoni's novel would seem to be set in stone. Imbued with a Christian faith in Providence combined with liberal civic values, its view of the human privileges the rational, resilient, and compassionate individual, attentive to their own moral and social betterment within a Christian framework, to the prosperity of their community, and to social justice. An omniscient narrator guiding the reader's progress through the narrative cements a certain construction of human authority, vision, and pedagogical care, 'reliable' in its strategic exposure of its own fallibility. Yet, as indicated above, there are undercurrents and counter-flows that suggest other possible perspectives upon the story and other experiences that may inform any one reading and produce diverse meaning. A critical practice homing in on a specific passage can loosen the text from its apparently fixed historical moorings and enable it to speak differently of the human.

The novel is set at the time of the outbreak of bubonic plague in central and northern Italy in about 1630 and the encounter towards the end of the novel of Renzo, one of its protagonists (one of the 'betrothed' of the title), with the devastation caused by the plague in Milan affords opportunities for the author to examine the impact of voracious disease on individual humans and community. This episode foregrounds the human body under attack, forcing the reader to apprehend the body as biological organism, vulnerable to physical corruption irrespective of the behaviour, status, and beliefs of what might conventionally be seen as the 'soul' that occupies it. This is the human exposed and unindividuated as it becomes simply a noxious bulk to be disposed of efficiently: Manzoni describes vividly and brutally the momentary spectacle of heaps of knotted bodies that pass Renzo on horse-drawn carts, heads, arms, and hair spilling from the mass with every jolt.[7] It is an image that for a reader now evokes visual and verbal representations of colonial atrocities, of the Shoah, and of other 'man-made' genocides, all differently accentuating the processes of dehumanization of the individual body intrinsic to any systematic project of population elimination or suppression.

In analysing human behaviours at a time of acute threat to life, Manzoni tracks emotions, the very responses that have in traditional Western philosophy troubled the distinction between human and animal: emotions being identified as the refined, controllable, and speakable manifestation of chaotic physiological reactions.[8] As a reader follows Renzo's discovery

[7] Manzoni, *The Betrothed*, pp. 632–33.

[8] The facility of language has likewise been used in philosophy to distinguish between human and animal. Wittgenstein's influential reflections on 'ordinary' language apparently privilege the human but also open the human–animal threshold to metaphysical enquiry in which other major thinkers have participated. See Matthew

on foot of plague-ridden Milan, they witness a catalogue of responses by human individuals to the experience of bare and degraded life, including fear, greed, suspicion, anger, charity, and love. Sound and smell give Renzo advance intelligence of encounters that might threaten or help him, and he combines these 'animal' instincts with knowledge of social practice to handle each situation effectively. Making sense of Milan during plague through the position of Renzo as a witness-stranger unfamiliar with the topography of the city and with the impacts of the disease, combined with the rationalizing interventions of the narrator, a reader is invited to share in a complex process of intuition that combines the affects ignited by extreme spectacles of human abjection with the intelligence produced by habitual knowledge of social codes. Sense and cognition co-produce understanding in a process that challenges any division of mind from body and collapses sharp distinctions between human and non-human. Manzoni foregrounds the crisis of social hierarchies: upper-class men appear in the streets without hat or cloak, priests without cassocks, men unshaven or with overgrown beards. This is noted as owed partly to fear of contagion (accidental or willed) from contact of bodily extensions with others (p. 636). Highly developed artifices of human authority are thus dismantled by instinctive reaction to human others as threat.

One of a number of encounters in this episode that restores the integrity of the human is Renzo's observation of a mother bringing the corpse of her daughter to be loaded onto a cart for disposal (pp. 638–40). The refinement of language and prose structure in these paragraphs urges the reader to pause and reflect in the same way that the narrative describes Renzo stopping to bear witness. Minute description stresses the point that in this event, those elements of humanity (as understood from the author's Western, Christian point of view) that have elsewhere in this chapter been undermined have been resolutely restored even in the face of loss. The woman herself is described as having troubled but strong bearing and the narrative focalizes her dead daughter, dressed in immaculate white and with neatly styled hair, held upright on her mother's arm. The woman refuses to let one of the corpse collectors take the child from her and instead places the body onto the cart herself, before saying goodbye to the child and stating that she and other family members will join her that same night. Manzoni here elaborates a vision and a feeling of human dignity and sovereignty through a range of elements that signal the distance between the disorderly mass of entangled corpses on the carts or dropped in gutters and the integral personhood that the child represents, looking life-like even in death and being individually

Calarco, *Zoographies: The Question of the Animal from Heidegger to Derrida* (New York: Columbia University Press, 2008).

named by her mother as Cecilia. The mother too is poised, effecting clear verbal and gestural communication with the corpse collector, and calm preparation for her own imminent death and that of another daughter to whom she returns in the house. She performs a collection of feelings and strategic behaviours that the reader is invited to identify as expressing the human in its distinction from other species and in its capacity to transcend the flawed resilience of its biological being.

Gender clearly plays a significant role in this event in which human agency and care appear temporarily to be recuperated by a woman and girl, arresting the vision and behaviours of the men who witness the scene. The scope of this essay does not permit fuller discussion, but the point usefully draws attention to one question core to my reflections on the human. Manzoni's strategies in creating this striking encounter as a centre point of Renzo's journey through Milan would clearly speak to a reader of his times, its references to Catholic Christian values, roles, and iconography, fine-tuned also to the prevalent social questions of the early nineteenth century in Italy, providing a solid framework for interpretation. But what of a reader encountering this passage in English translation in India in the 1930s, or in Spanish translation in Colombia in the 1970s, or in a subtitled film or television adaptation screened in Tunisia in the 1990s? In which frames of reference might these differently situated interpreters locate their responses to this episode and in what ways might it speak to them of the human? The point is not to answer these questions, but to ask them, systematically, of even those works whose hermeneutical range is taken already to have been charted.

Another way of taking books – especially canonical ones – out of place, time, language, and culture is to read them in productive friction against works that appear superficially unrelated. A graphic narrative, *The Arrival*, created by Australian artist Shaun Tan and published in 2006, speaks of and to the human in ways which dialogue interestingly with the insights that Manzoni's novel provides.[9] The story of the migration of an individual man, followed ultimately by his female partner and child, the images and sequences that form the book work both to probe interior human experience and at the same time to dissolve familiar frames of reference in order to open the reader-viewer's mind to the multiple ways in which human (and non-human) activity and resourcefulness may shape how humans live within the planet.

The author makes temporal, geographical, and cultural setting indeterminate in the narrative. The events are somewhat historicized by figuring

[9] Shaun Tan, *The Arrival* (Sydney: Hachette, 2014 [2006]).

the protagonist with the plain suit, hat, and suitcase of iconic images of early twentieth-century migrations and travelling by ship, and also by the tones of the pencil drawings in grey and sepia and the worn, antiquated design of pages and cover. The destination city features no architectural signifiers of known place, and instead combines images of the modern city with deserted landscapes and fantastical scenes of industry. Its inhabitants bear the costume and somatic features of a fusion of global cultures, ancient and modern. Double-page spreads covering the front and back endpapers of the book both display the same grid of sixty portraits of human faces of a diversity of ages, skin tones, genders, and facial and clothing features. For me, the most striking strategy is the absence of language: the narrative is told through images with no captions, obliging the interpreter to decipher the allusive panels of the narrative without the guidance (or interference) of the written word, and also unmooring the story emphatically from nation, culture, and the modern hierarchies of 'global' and 'minority' languages. Language is present alongside other unfamiliar sights of the migration journey as a stranger in the narrative: an undecipherable script of mixed resonances that appears insistently as the traveller navigates his new surroundings and that proves a source of bafflement (and aesthetic fascination) for the protagonist and the reader. In diegesis and form, the book challenges the reader to make sense of human experience while forcefully estranged from arguably the principal human instrument of interpretation, learning, and communication – language – here featuring as a peculiar artefact.

The effect of these disruptions and expansions of the sense-making frameworks the reader may know is to universalize the story of a migration and also to reveal how the individual human is exposed when dislocated from the social and political structures that endow it with meaning (suggesting the obverse effect of the naming of Cecilia in Manzoni's novel). Post-Second World War philosophers from Hannah Arendt to Giorgio Agamben have identified the stateless refugee as the modern figure of what Agamben calls 'bare life': human experience dispossessed of the political agency, legal and social individuation, and state protection that citizenship affords.[10] This notion resonates in a technique used by Tan of multiplication. The repeated ten-by-six grid of uniformly sized portraits in the endpapers offers one example; another is the page that opens Chapter II, where a sequence of nine panels, when read left to right in rows, creates a motion of zooming out from the family photograph that the protagonist gazes at, placed on his suitcase in his cabin on the ship, to the final image of the large ocean liner at sea. The

[10] Giorgio Agamben, *Homo Sacer: Sovereign Power and Bare Life*, trans. by Daniel Heller-Roazen (Stanford: Stanford University Press, 1998).

first three panels offer a view inside the cabin, whereas the next six move gradually outwards, from an external view of the single porthole of his cabin to three, then thirteen, then ultimately forty-five dots of light. The motion of pulling back from the familiar individual to the larger, anonymous human cargo of the vessel emphasizes to the interpreting eye the numbers of human migration – numbers that are almost numbingly familiar to contemporary readers who, in the period since publication of Tan's book, receive frequent tallies of the thousands of humans leaving, arriving, being detained, and dying along global migration routes. Tan's technique of replicating in the sequence of panels a sequential increase in numbers seems to draw attention to this capacity to 'convert' individual human stories into, precisely, numbers. Recalling the heaped corpses on carts in Manzoni's narrative, it signals the capacity of humans to de-individuate others in order to 'manage' both the practical and ethical-emotional demands that they represent.

Non-human creatures in Tan's narrative have individuality, purpose, and agency comparable to those of the human figures. The protagonist discovers in his accommodation in the destination city a creature that combines features of possibly dog, cat, fish, and/or reptile. This becomes his constant companion and also an effective guide and guardian of well-being, leading him to places, demonstrating how things function, and brokering relationships within the unfamiliar signifying systems and social infrastructure of the destination city. Similar non-human animals are figured throughout the novel as the counterparts of other humans within a distinctive sociality that seems to be co-created and sustained by both human and non-human figures.[11] The vision that Tan's images of the migration experience build is one that displaces certainties and, fundamentally, the human reader's confidence in anthropocentric hierarchies of planetary organization and control, or indeed in the notion of 'civilization'. Other animate and inanimate presences on/in Earth are figured as meaningful co-habitants.[12] More importantly, they appear in Tan's narrative emphatically to exceed the characteristics that humans have elaborated to define what is not human and so to gesture towards a post-human polity. If there is a transcendent power in the world Tan draws – a counterpart to divine Providence in the world that Manzoni creates – it is the mysterious dragon-like creatures whose scaly, finned tails

[11] On similar bonds, see Donna J. Haraway, *The Companion Species Manifesto: Dogs, People, and Significant Otherness* (Chicago: Prickly Paradigm, 2003).

[12] Elements of the physical environment have the status of characters. An example is a double-page grid in Chapter II of sixty panels figuring individual cloud formations, individualizing the multiple 'faces' of cloud and suggesting correspondence with the sixty-panel sets of human portraits in the end pages.

loop in the skies above some images of both home and destination and that seem variously to connote protection, care, danger, possibility, and wonder. Their reptilian aspects connect them to the non-human companions featured in the narrative, but these are fleeting inhabitants of the air, uncanny in their unsettling difference from and affiliation with the domestic. Similarly, the protagonist produces a paper bird from under his hat and gives it to his daughter as he departs home, and the motif of flocks of angular, human-crafted birds later appears periodically in the narrative.

The act of using human dexterity and imagination to fashion something clumsily like a non-human creature and to use that item to carry emotional meaning, endowing it with a life of which it appears to take possession, is a cypher of Tan's figuring of the human in this book. In creating images of impossible creatures, indecipherable words and script, preposterous machines and technologies, larger-than-life human(?) figures, and inexplicable enmeshments of cultures, times, and places, he both performs in creative action and narrates the human capacity of creativity. The narrative suggests that the imagining of another life that propels migration, even where this imagining seeks to meet a fundamental need for food, safety, work, or freedom, bespeaks a human (exclusively?) capacity to see beyond and see differently from what is known. In amplifying this urge to create something better into outlandish images of how the world might be other (or is other, once seen from different perspectives), the author-artist exploits and illustrates his own creativity, his interpreter's creativity, and the multiple, everyday stories of human creativity in seeking wonders beyond the known. Shocking as some of these wonders may be – as Tan strikingly demonstrates in nightmarish images of conflict and oppression – they help to fathom the complex emotional life of humans as individuals in constant, exploratory relation with human and non-human subjects and forces. This is work that researchers of languages and cultures – as creative users, interpreters, and analysts of script and stories in various forms – are distinctively equipped to perform, especially when attuned to the difference that language makes as implement of both curious distance from and mindful access to other worlds.

Jennifer Burns is Professor of Italian Studies
at the University of Warwick.

17

# Knowledge

*Charles Burdett*

In an increasingly globalized world where people interact with people from other places, move – whether by choice or necessity – between social frameworks, and live within environments that can be defined as transnational, the creation and circulation of knowledge is called into question. Where is knowledge produced? Who produces knowledge? What cultural and individual values underlie how the world is understood? How do different cultural formations align or diverge in how people and culture are seen? For instance, regarding the preoccupation in recent academic study with how knowledge of the past is created, Astrid Erll has written that a survey of research across a range of disciplines 'reveals an almost ubiquitous curiosity about dynamics which challenge and transcend' any idea of 'self-contained (usually Western) culture'.[1] One of the reasons why the study of the representation of the colonial and postcolonial world, cultural expressions of migration and mobility, or the extensive corpus of travel accounts in all languages is of such importance is precisely because it allows a profound exploration of how knowledge of a given phenomenon is always situated within and across sets of practices, within networks of power and privilege, and how any observer, reader, critic, or spectator is always positioned within changing, overlapping, and continuous cultural formations. This essay touches on a range of instances where knowledge is simultaneously produced and undermined through the complex entanglement of these formations.

In the words of Zygmunt Bauman, 'one thinks of identity whenever one is not sure where one belongs; that is, one is not sure how to place oneself among the evident variety of behavioural styles and patterns' and it is true

[1] Astrid Erll, 'Travelling Memory', *Parallax*, 17.4 (2011), 4–18 (p. 8).

that some of the most basic questions that can be posed of literary or visual representations of transcultural encounters – in whatever form they take place – concern the way in which they present their producer's consciousness, their understanding of self within larger linguistic or cultural configurations.[2] Even non-fictional modes of communication that aspire towards objectivity and purport to do no more than *observe* the everyday flow of reality allow their author to put together a visual or written autobiography of perceptions that, when exposed to analysis, give insights into their attitudes and reactions, placing the author, photographer, or artist within a given time (with all its cultural assumptions) as well as opening up the question of how they experience the sense of their own identity within situations where forces within culture merge or contend with one another.

Central to many works that explore transcultural contact – even those that are less concerned with retaining the impression of objectivity or use fiction as a mode of enquiry – is the investigation into how a sense of self is spatially and temporally relative and how it can be, either suddenly or more progressively, placed under strain or even altered beyond recognition. In his essay, 'A Disturbance of Memory on the Acropolis',[3] Sigmund Freud described the acute sense of disorientation he felt on experiencing the materiality of a monumental site from antiquity that, until his actual visit, had been real to him only through literary and visual representations. His essay is among the most celebrated instances of a disjunction between perception and memory, but one can draw many examples from literature of a character whose sense of subjectivity is dramatically altered by the brief or prolonged immersion in a cultural environment that is initially unfamiliar. One of the key scenes of E.M. Forster's *A Room with a View* (1908) represents a moment when Lucy Honeychurch – one of the main protagonists – suddenly, when walking through the streets of Florence, experiences her sense of self as a young, privileged English woman as constrictive, artificial, and at odds with an identity that is hidden by the conventions of class and gender of Edwardian England.[4] Melania Mazzucco's novel on the experience of Italian emigration to the United States, *Vita* (2003), traces the alteration of the subjectivity of the eponymous heroine as she becomes accustomed to

[2] Zygmunt Bauman, 'From Pilgrim to Tourist or a Short History of Identity', in *Questions of Cultural Identity*, ed. by Stuart Hall and Paul Du Gay (London: Sage, 1996), pp. 18–36.

[3] Sigmund Freud, 'A Disturbance of Memory on the Acropolis', in *On Metapsychology*, trans. by James Strachey, ed. by Angela Richards, The Penguin Freud Library, 11 (London: Penguin Books, 1991), pp. 443–57. First published in 1936.

[4] E. M. Forster, *A Room with a View* (London: Edward Arnold, 1908).

the realities of life in New York at the turn of the twentieth century.[5] In his novel of 1949, *The Sheltering Sky*,[6] Paul Bowles represents the disintegration of the character Kit Moresby's sense of subjecthood when, following the death of her partner and travelling companion, she continues the journey they had begun, travelling deeper into the North African desert and into a space where the co-ordinates in which her life has been led are almost entirely lost. The latter part of the novel indicates that Kit's sense of loss and alienation derives from her intuition of the contingency of the structures on which her understanding of self had been built.

The kind of knowledge that the examination of transcultural situations and experiences creates is one that uncovers the insubstantiality of the very notion of individuality. The theory that what is referred to as the *self* is not an independent entity and that it cannot be separated from the cultural and societal context in which it operates lies at the basis of the philosophical reasoning of a number of highly influential post-structuralist thinkers. Much of the work of Michel Foucault argues, for example, that people, instead of being fully independent, rational subjects, both knowingly and unknowingly occupy 'subject positions' within cultural, social, and economic constructions that are of a vastly larger scale than the individual human.[7] Thus, sensations of independence, choice, and individuality often occur within fairly strict boundaries that are occluded to everyday perception. People do not necessarily decide whether or not to buy into the operation of language and culture; instead, the individual finds that their very structures are operating at an incalculably profound level, even in the way that subjectivity is ordered and understood.

Many of the insights of the work of Foucault are taken further within the field of postcolonial studies and particularly by Edward Said. Much of Said's work, from his seminal *Orientalism* onwards, explores the idea that societies develop inter-connected systems of knowledge of other societies that can be deduced from the ways in which they are represented not only within official documentation but also within the corpus of creative production.[8] The specific argument of *Orientalism* is that Western understanding of the Orient (and the consequent justification of its imposition of imperial rule) drew as much upon constructions of an imaginary space as it did upon more fact-based forms of knowledge. An essential point of more general application

[5] Melania Mazzucco, *Vita* (Milan: Rizzoli, 2003).

[6] Paul Bowles, *The Sheltering Sky* (London: John Lehmann, 1949).

[7] For an introduction to the thought of Foucault, see Lois McNay, *Foucault: A Critical Introduction* (Cambridge: Polity, 1994).

[8] Edward Said, *Orientalism* (London: Penguin, 2003). First published in 1978.

is that there is no unmediated access to other social realities: rather than simply seeing, visiting, and subsequently interpreting an unfamiliar location, anyone who moves between cultures finds themselves enmeshed in the web of concepts, images, and imaginings that form an intrinsic part of how cultures – understood as intertwined sets of practices rather than as discrete entities – view one another. The experience of other cultural formations is, in other words, always mediated by ways of framing. However desirable it might be to believe that a place can be known 'first-hand' and with a freshness of awareness, there is no way of escaping the history of representation of a given place and no way of not repeating elements of how that place has been communicated and imagined.

As Ania Loomba makes clear in her study of colonialism and postcolonialism, one of the questions at the very base of research on the colonial encounter and its manifold legacies is 'the relationship between material and economic processes and human subjectivities'.[9] The importance of analysing cultural representations of the colonial world lies in how it enables an understanding of the intellectual and perceptual categories that were, and in many cases still are, at its base – in other words, an understanding of the structures of colonial knowledge.[10] In whichever form they were framed, representations of the European presence in non-Western cultural contexts indicate the desires and projections that were central to the rhetoric of the time. This is not to say that all cultural production should be seen in one perspective, but, rather, to suggest that the interrogation of works that belong to periods when expansionism was at its height needs, at least in part, to be focused on whether such texts subscribed to and so in part perpetuated the core ideas behind colonialist thinking. An example of the ambiguities that are deeply embedded within characterizations of the colonial world is provided by Joseph Conrad's novella *Heart of Darkness*[11] which – at one level – provides a fierce denunciation of the violence that is intrinsic to imperialist exploitation, while at another level it can be seen, as Chinua Achebe argued in his public lecture (1975) on the text, as complicit in the racism of colonialism by presenting a de-humanizing picture of the African people that it

[9] Ania Loomba, *Colonialism/Postcolonialism*, 3rd edn (London and New York: Routledge, 2015), p. 4. See her discussion of 'Colonial and Postcolonial Identities', Chapter 2, pp. 112–80.

[10] On this question, see Walter Mignolo, *The Darker Side of Western Modernity: Global Futures, Decolonial Options* (Durham, NC and London: Duke University Press, 2011).

[11] Joseph Conrad, *Heart of Darkness* (London: Hodder and Stoughton, 1990). First published in 1899.

represents.[12] Another, less well-known, example is the work of the journalist Ciro Poggiali, who in his diary of the early phases of the Italian invasion of Ethiopia (1935–1936) produced an unparalleled account of its brutality and horror while never questioning Italy's self-appointed imperial mission.[13] In analysing how identity and otherness were or are constructed across a wide variety of texts, it is possible to gain a sense of the complex interplay between complicity and condemnation that defines the position of any artistic or journalistic contributor to formations of knowledge within transnational configurations of power.

The analysis of a wide and highly differentiated array of cultural products may provide clues to the development of the everyday working of colonialism (not only in terms of the relatively recent past and the effects of Western expansionism), but it is important, above all, for what it reveals about the characteristics that were projected onto those subjected to Western, and other, forms of imperialism. It is one means of gaining insight into what Homi Bhabha has defined as the principle of separation and hierarchization, the strategic placing of the dominant with regard to the dominated.[14] The aim of any analysis is to uncover not only the underlying architecture of colonialism, its working both within the material world and within the social imaginary, but as the work of Gayatri Chakravorty Spivak and others has insisted, to discover the voice of those who suffered the imposition of its systems of government.[15] It is, similarly, the purpose of postcolonial criticism to analyse how the forms of knowledge imposed by colonial rule have been challenged and subverted.[16]

Within this frame, the analysis of forms of cultural production can reveal the pervasiveness of the colonial invention of knowledge and serve to direct attention to the provenance of continuing racist and xenophobic attitudes. Research that aims to pursue a decolonial approach goes further in interrogating how systems for generating knowledge are implicated in histories that have facilitated, over extensive periods of time, violence of

[12] Chinua Achebe, 'An Image of Africa: Racism in Conrad's *Heart of Darkness*', in *Hopes and Impediments: Selected Essays 1965–1987* (London: Heinemann, 1988), pp. 1–13.

[13] Ciro Poggiali, *Diario Africa Orientale Italiana* (Milan: Longanesi, 1971).

[14] Homi Bhabha, *The Location of Culture* (London and New York: Routledge, 1994).

[15] Gayatri Chakravorty Spivak, 'Can the Subaltern Speak?', in *Marxism and the Interpretation of Culture*, ed. by Cary Nelson and Lawrence Grossberg (Urbana and Chicago: University of Illinois Press, 1988), pp. 271–313.

[16] For an introduction to the thought of major postcolonial thinkers, see Robert Young, *White Mythologies: Writing History and the West*, 2nd edn (London and New York: Routledge, 2004).

both a material and conceptual kind. In the words of Linda Tuhiwai Smith: 'the ways in which scientific research is implicated in the worst excesses of colonialism remains a powerful remembered history for many of the world's colonized peoples'.[17] The awareness of the extent to which means of pursuing knowledge are imbricated within systems of power with long-standing imperial legacies is one of the most important motivations in seeking to develop ways of knowing that are fully reflective on the nature of their origins, structure, and purpose, that promote a multiplicity of perspectives and speaking positions, and that explore social and cultural phenomena through diverse cultural settings and theoretical frames.

A key practice in addressing questions of knowledge and positionality within transnational environments, is for the observer or reader to interrogate some of the most basic assumptions of the interconnecting systems that make up their own sense of cultural positionality and to identify practices of knowledge-making and the manifold relationships of power that they posit. The purpose is not simply to reflect on separate moments in time and space, but to attempt to gain a heightened perception of how discursive constructions of reality operate across time and space. Such a purpose supports understanding of how the location of people within the workings of a given society depends – to refer to the theoretical approach that has developed from the work of Kimberlé Williams Crenshaw – not upon any one social factor (class, race, religion, sexuality, gender, and so forth) but upon the power of their intersection to create patterns of privilege or discrimination.[18] The consideration of how ways of seeing and knowing integral to the working of individual social constructions come together to reinforce modes of oppression reveals both the complexity of seeking to unravel any relation between past and present and the continuity of compromised ways of knowing.

On the interweaving of temporalities specifically, it is Edward Said's contention in *Culture and Imperialism* that if European involvement overseas is seen not as a series of discrete historical experiences defined largely by separate national cultures, but as a set of 'overlapping territories, intertwined histories', then it becomes easier to identify a 'structure of attitude and reference' that legitimated centuries of colonial appropriation.[19]

[17] Linda Tuhiwai Smith, 'Introduction', in *Decolonizing Methodologies: Research and Indigenous Peoples*, 2nd edn (London: Zed Books, 2012), p. 1.

[18] For a discussion on this body of related theoretical approaches, see Sumi Cho, Kimberlé Williams Crenshaw and Leslie McCall, 'Toward a Field of Intersectionality Studies: Theory, Applications, and Praxis', *Signs*, 38.4 (2013), 785–810.

[19] Edward Said, *Culture and Imperialism* (London: Vintage, 1994), p. 72 and p. xxxvi. First published in 1993.

His work advocates the development of a comparative, or rather a transnational, approach to the representation of imperialism and its consequences, an approach in which the critic or historian reads the conflicting experience of individuals and polities against one another or, to use his term, 'contrapuntally'. In doing so, it becomes easier to appreciate the relativity of the means by which a writer, visual artist, or photographer generates knowledge of a given event or phenomenon. It also becomes easier to appreciate how any cultural producer, whatever their intentions, does not reflect only within the immediate context of their present, but records their perception of macro-historical processes.

Complex questions relating to how knowledge of diverse kinds is accrued and structured lie at the very centre of the canon of postcolonial and migrant literature, from an awareness of the legacies of colonial attitudes and behaviours to how subjectivity is shaped through processes of dialogue and interaction, to how a dialectic between home and elsewhere, familiar and unfamiliar, can occur from an extensive array of viewpoints, to how the pressure of the past impinges on the cognition of the present. To illustrate this point, I conclude with just one example drawn from my own area of expertise, namely the legacy of Italian expansionism in East Africa – a chapter in imperial history that reached its furthest extent with the invasion and occupation of Ethiopia from 1935 to 1941.[20] The novel, *Regina di fiori e di perle* (2007), by the Italo-Ethiopian writer Gabriella Ghermandi, follows the life of Mahlet, in many ways a veiled figuration of the author, as she grows up close to Addis Ababa in the latter part of the twentieth century.[21] The narrative takes its form from the uncovering of past moments from the history of the Italian occupation of Ethiopia. As Mahlet witnesses the persistence of voices from the past, she senses how her own subjectivity is altered and how the world of everyday reality can be disrupted by the unfamiliar, placed in disturbing perspectives, shown in all the contingency of its relation to the past. One of the many implications of the novel is that any enquiry seeking knowledge depends upon the interrogation of the positionality of the subject who enquires. Ghermandi suggests that the story that she tells is also, by metaphorical extension, that of the reader. We might add that one of the principal objectives of seeking to gain an understanding of the ways in which interpretations of reality have

[20] For a recent evocation of the Ethiopian resistance against the Italian occupation, see Maaza Mengiste's novel, *The Shadow King* (Edinburgh: Canongate Books, 2019).

[21] Gabriella Ghermandi, *Regina di fiori e di perle* (Rome: Donzelli, 2007). In English: *Queen of Flowers and Pearls, A Novel*, trans. by Giovanna Bellesia-Contuzzi and Victoria Offredi Poletto (Bloomington: Indiana University Press, 2015).

been and are constructed is to see how we ourselves are positioned in their functioning and, potentially, in their transformation.[22]

Charles Burdett is Professor of Italian and Director of the Institute of Modern Languages Research, School of Advanced Study, University of London.

[22] For a longer discussion of the work of Ghermandi, see Charles Burdett, 'Transnational Time: Reading Post-War Representations of the Italian Presence in East Africa', *Italian Studies*, 73.3 (2018), 274–88.

18

# Language

*Nicola McLelland*

This chapter is about, first, what it means to study *language* transnationally, and second about studying *languages*.

## Studying Language Transnationally

Let's begin by considering what *studying language* means in the sense of how linguistic research questions have evolved within both national and transnational ways of thinking. My examples come from German, but they illustrate developments across other languages, too.

The gradual emergence of a discipline that called itself 'Modern Languages' in nineteenth-century universities coincided with a period of great intellectual energy and innovation in the study of languages. Looking at language of their own day, scholars were particularly interested in dialectology – documenting regional language variation – and in the new science of phonetics to describe the sounds of the spoken language scientifically. Looking into the past, developments in historical-comparative philology (roughly: historical linguistics, trying to explain how today's languages came to be) yielded an understanding of the histories of the major national languages. Scholars identified laws – seemingly akin, in their regularity and universality, to laws in the natural sciences – that explained systematic changes, especially in the sounds of languages, which differentiated related languages from one another and from their 'parent' language. Two well-known examples of such laws are the Germanic Sound Shift and the High German Sound Shift. The first, 'Germanic' sound shift, very roughly 500 BCE, which affected a series of consonants (b, d, g, p, t, k), is one factor separating the Germanic language family from other language groupings within Indo-European. The second, High German shift (very roughly 500 AD) also affected a similar group of consonants, and distinguishes High German – the basis of today's standard German – from the Low German dialects of Germany's north (and also explains the consonant differences between many related English and German words like ten/zehn, pipe/Pfeife, day/Tag, and week/Woche.[1] The discipline of linguistics always had a comparative perspective, then, being 'transnational' in looking beyond a single language. At the same time, the comparative method served to define and delimit the bounds of national languages. The histories of the major European languages were typically written from a teleological perspective. That is, the present-day, unified, national language was viewed as the (more or less triumphant) culmination of centuries of development. It is no coincidence that nineteenth-century Germany saw the founding of the national(ist) project of a comprehensive *German Dictionary*, documenting the German language from the fifteenth century to the present, parallel to the *Oxford English Dictionary* in Britain.[2]

Dialectology and dialect geography, while focused on variation *within* a language, could also sometimes serve a nationalist agenda. Recording regional variants in vocabulary helped document the everyday life of a country's people, including rural lifestyles, already recognized to be disappearing, and which might be evidenced in local topographical names, names of tools used in local agriculture or industry, or other aspects of local culture. Older male rural speakers who had not left their home locale were considered the best informants for documenting a language variety and culture in its notionally 'purest' form, most free from outside influence. Dialect geography, meanwhile, also transcended national boundaries, as German dialectologists and cartographers alike sought to map language borders – which did not necessarily coincide with political ones. Of course, this information could be put to use to nationalist ends, for example to advocate the expansion of the German state to its 'natural' linguistic borders, as in a map commissioned in 1903 by the radical nationalist Pan-German League, which delineated '"German" and "non-German" territory in the most exact and specific terms possible'. Traditional political and geographic boundaries were replaced by the 'intentional yet wandering line of the language frontier'.[3]

[1] See, for example, Sally Johnson and Natalie Braber, *Exploring the German Language*, 2nd edn (Cambridge: Cambridge University Press, 2008), pp. 16–19.

[2] Begun by the Grimm Brothers in the 1830s, the *Deutsches Wörterbuch* was completed only in 1961.

[3] Jason D. Hansen, *Mapping the Germans: Statistical Science, Cartography, and the Visualization of the German Nation, 1848–1914* (Oxford: Oxford University Press, 2015), p. vii.

In the twentieth century, the study of language expanded, from largely historically oriented philological research, into investigating all aspects of human language. Many of the shared 'big questions' for twentieth-century linguists concerned the universal rather than the language-specific. Greenberg identified 'linguistic universals', features of language shared across all or at least large groups of languages; Chomsky postulated a 'Universal Grammar' that encapsulated the limits of what human languages can be like; and applied linguists investigated the processes of language acquisition.[4]

Table 1: German as a national umbrella or roofing language.

| High German standard as a roofing language | | |
|---|---|---|
| Low German (northern) dialects and/or regional colloquial varieties | High German (central and southern) dialects and/or regional colloquial varieties | |
| | Central German dialects and/or regional colloquial varieties | Upper German dialects and/or regional colloquial varieties |

Since the 1960s, sociolinguists have explored the relationship between language use, variation, and change on the one hand, and social factors such as age, gender, education, and social class on the other. They have also been interested in attitudes and ideologies about language, as well as actual language practice. Challenging the nineteenth-century belief in 'the' unified language, sociolinguists have revealed the complicated reality of many language varieties, often described in terms of their deviation from the dominant standard national variety (for example, the 'absence' of certain cases or tenses compared to the standard). A standard language like German is sometimes presented as the 'umbrella' or 'roofing' language, with other varieties grouped 'underneath', including varieties that might not be mutually intelligible with the umbrella standard (see Table 1). This convenient conceptualization also summarizes power relationships and lines of linguistic influence. It also, at least in the case of German, describes a nation state. The roofing language is typically the national language of education, so will tend to influence the regional dialects or

[4] Joseph Greenberg, 'Some Universals of Grammar with Particular Reference to the Order of Meaningful Elements'. In Joseph Greenberg, ed., *Universals of Language*, 73–113 (London: MIT Press, 1963); Noam Chomsky, *Knowledge of Language: Its Nature, Origin and Use* (New York, NY: Praeger, 1986).

urban vernaculars, while other closely related varieties, falling on the other side of a national border, orient towards a different overarching standard (a Low German dialect may converge towards standard Dutch, for example).

Even as the project of codifying and standardizing 'a' national language was still underway in the seventeenth and eighteenth centuries, that ideal was under challenge from transnational pressures, as new language varieties developed in Europe's colonies and, then, former colonies. German's colonial footprint came later, and was smaller, but within Europe, German was, and is, 'owned' by more than one political entity (at least Austria and German-speaking Switzerland).[5] Such so-called *pluricentric* languages have more than one standard, each associated with its own polity.[6] For example, standard Swiss German spelling never uses the <ß> used in German and Austrian German, but always <ss>; aspects of vocabulary and grammar also differ.

Another transnational phenomenon that has shaped language study is the Council of Europe's European Charter for Regional or Minority Languages (ECRML) (1992). It has certainly sharpened awareness of – and encouraged study of – not just national language varieties but also regional, minority, and minoritized languages such as Breton and Low German, within the borders of dominant national languages. In this case, the transnational has drawn attention to the *sub*national.

Transnationalism in linguistics thus means not just looking beyond the borders of the nation, but also at language within borders, including changes that are the result of migration. At first focused on migrants' language acquisition, linguists' work can have repercussions for social justice in how we enable bilingualism and multilingualism, and how we evaluate non-standard language use. Migrant-influenced urban vernaculars were once seen as deficient, incompletely mastered varieties of German, likely to impede their speakers' life chances, but these varieties are now being analysed as sites of linguistic creativity. Study of so-called *Kiezdeutsch* (lit. 'German of the 'hood', originally a derogatory term, but now reclaimed by researchers

[5] For a period of about twenty years up to 1989, there was some discussion of whether the language of the German Democratic Republic and the Federal Republic might develop into two differently codified varieties. See, for example, Patrick Stevenson, *Language and German Disunity. A Sociolinguistic History of East and West in Germany, 1945–2000* (Oxford: Oxford University Press, 2002), pp. 39–41.

[6] See Michael Clyne, *Pluricentric Languages: Differing Norms in Different Nations* (Berlin: de Gruyter, 1992), especially with reference to German; on Spanish, see Darren Paffey, *Language Ideologies and the Globalization of 'Standard' Spanish* (London: Bloomsbury, 2012); on French, Bernhard Pöll, *Le français langue pluricentrique?: études sur la variation diatopique d'une langue standard* (Frankfurt: Lang, 2005).

to refer to multi-ethnic urban youth vernaculars) reveals seemingly ungrammatical utterances as *Ich mach dich Messer* ('I'll knife you', but lit. 'I make you knife'). It can be argued that rather than being 'broken German', this kind of language exploits linguistic possibilities within German in creative ways. The structure has parallels in, say, standard bureaucratic German – so while it is innovative, it need not be viewed negatively, as 'broken' German.[7] Such analyses of migrant and migrant-background language practice are politically and socially significant, to some extent ideological, and may be contested.

Studying language online takes linguists beyond borders, too. Online, participants' location, national identity, and state affiliation are often not identifiable. And the language, especially of younger online users, does not always match the idea of languages as neatly bounded, separate systems, but may mix languages, as in Examples 1 and 2 (from YouTube comments):[8]

1. *Heul jz mal nicht* ***wtf*** *man merkt echt das* [sic] *du unter 13 bist*

   ('Dnt cry now **wtf** you can really tell thatt [*sic*] you are under 13'; the English abbreviation is marked in bold)

The spontaneous and often non-standard language (for example, spelling *das* for the conjunction *dass* in Example 1), and other features like emojis means this 'written' language shares features with spoken language: colloquialisms, false starts, incomplete sentences, and the like. It has challenged assumptions about a tidy distinction between written, well-formed standard language and spoken, informal, less standard language. In its 'conceptual orality' (being written but showing features associated with spoken language) and in its multi-mediality (combining text with images, symbols, and gifs, etc.), such innovative and creative online language transcends all borders.

Example 2 shows how for many language users, non-separation of languages – sometimes called translanguaging – is normal:

2. *Tugay* ***abi*** *mach mal bitte wieder GTA videos* 😁😁😁

   'Tugay [name of YouTuber] **older brother** [polite Turkish term of address for another man of roughly similar age] make GTA [Grand Theft Auto, a popular series of video games] videos again please 😁😁😁'

[7] Heike Wiese, 'Grammatical Innovation in Multiethnic Urban Europe: New Linguistic Practices among Adolescents', *Lingua*, 119 (2009), 782–806.

[8] Collected by Louis Cotgrove, *#GlockeAktiv: Gender and Ethnicity Differences in German-language YouTube Comments* (MA Thesis, University of Nottingham, 2017).

Increased interest in bilingual or multilingual language behaviour has helped displace tacit assumptions that speakers are 'normally' monolingual. The plurilingual repertoires of many speakers are explicitly recognized in the widely used Common European Framework of Reference (CEFR) for language-learning proficiency, updated in 2018 to include specific reference to

> 'Plurilingual and pluricultural competence', recognizing the ability to 'switch from one language or dialect (or variety) to another; express oneself in one language (or dialect, or variety) and understand a person speaking another; call upon the knowledge of a number of languages (or dialects, or varieties) to make sense of a text; bring the whole of one's linguistic equipment into play, experimenting with alternative forms of expression', etc.[9]

## Studying Languages Transnationally

Studying *language* is only one part of studying *languages* at university. So, the rest of this article asks what else belongs in a languages degree, and which languages belong. The term Modern Languages was invented in the nineteenth century to rival the classical languages, Latin and Greek. People lobbying for Modern Languages emphasized that they offered both the intellectual rigours of linguistic study (grammar, language history) and the exploration of ethics and morals that reading the best literature could offer. They offered, thus, the same supposedly excellent preparation for life – life in a particular social class, at least – as the Classics. They had an added advantage, though, offering insights into our nearest neighbours, and the opportunity to communicate with them on equal terms. It was self-evident, as a textbook of German in the early twentieth century put it, that the goal of language teaching was to teach 'what a German of a good average education must know and probably does know; in other words, what falls within the framework of general education'.[10] Matching a cultivated member of the bourgeoisie of the target culture was the ideal, because learners of Modern Languages in schools and university (in England, at least) were themselves all members of a tiny, privileged elite able to access a post-elementary, 'general' liberal education.

The question of what 'really' belongs in Modern Languages study and school and university, was – and remains – a vexed one. In 1918, the Leathes

[9] See the CEFR at <https://www.coe.int/en/web/common-european-framework-reference-languages>, pp. 28–29 [accessed 17 December 2021].

[10] Richard Kron, *Der Kleine Deutsche* (Freiburg im Bresgau: J. Bielefelds Verlag, 1923), p. 3, my translation.

Report on the provision of languages education in England considered how language study could fulfil two aims, compressed into a single sentence. First, it should contribute to pupils' 'liberal education and appreciation of history, literature and civilisation of other countries'. This was already a hugely ambitious goal open to different interpretations, taking Modern Languages – or, as the report preferred to call it, Modern Studies – beyond just studying language and literature, to encompass also 'history' and 'civilization' (itself a word that makes a lot of assumptions!). But in the same breath as all this, Modern Languages should still meet the utilitarian 'interests of commerce and public service', which needed people familiar with other languages and other countries, and able to communicate in their languages.[11]

The Leathes Report asserted that pupils should be 'able to speak the language with accuracy and fluency on particular topics, to read the best authors easily and with pleasure; and to write satisfactory exercises of any simple type' (p. 95, § 90). For those choosing to 'specialize' in a language (that is, at A-level), the focus of attention should be 'chiefly the best authors, but the new as well as the old; besides literature, the continuous story of the people since it began to be a people' (p. 98, §94). At university, Leathes considered the undergraduate degree in Modern and Medieval Languages at Cambridge, his own university, 'a promising and courageous effort to initiate a new era in modern language study' (p. 161, §162). The degree encompassed 'literature, thought and history', 'economic and social conditions', as well as philology (loosely, what we would today call historical linguistics), and left 'considerable latitude' to specialize.

The history of Languages education over the past century is the history of the arguably impossible attempt to do justice to the kind of broad scope outlined by Leathes, and to fulfil both the liberal and utilitarian agendas. Comprehensivization of schooling, beginning in the 1960s, opened up language learning to a far wider social spectrum. Language learning moved increasingly away from the ideal of an elite liberal education, towards meeting practical communicative needs, especially from the 1980s onwards. That development was at odds, however, with how Modern Languages at university were expanding into new and ever wider spheres of interest (just as all university disciplines push at the boundaries and re-define themselves with new knowledge), whose single common feature was perhaps the fact that they did not have as their primary interest the question of practical communication.

[11] Stanley Leathes, *Modern Studies. Being the Report of the Committee on the Position of Modern Languages in the Educational System of Great Britain*, Cmd 9036, 2nd edn (London: HMSO, 1920 [1918]).

That unresolvable tension between competing aims of Modern Languages is often evident when the Modern Languages community makes the case for language learning. As the claim of practical communicative need is undermined by the growing reach of English as a global language, and by the reasonable expectation that technology will soon facilitate much of our basic communication across language barriers, advocates rightly still articulate multiple reasons for valuing language study. An extreme example is the well-intentioned '700 reasons for studying languages'.[12] some of the 700 reasons constitute communal benefits such as social cohesion and economic prosperity; others highlight the benefit to the individual. A recent addition to such lists of individual benefits is evidence of cognitive benefits of bilingualism, even for beginning learners.

A further complication – given finite time and resources – remains the question of which languages to study. In the late nineteenth century and early twentieth, when 'Modern Languages' were first established at universities, that meant French and German. French was, and had been since the Norman conquest in 1066, the first foreign language. In the late eighteenth century, a flowering of German literature and scholarship, combined with the German House of Hanover occupying the British throne from 1714, made German Britain's second foreign language, although Spanish, Dutch, and Italian had all vied for prominence in the sixteenth and seventeenth centuries. The credentials of Spanish – as the language of Spain but also of much of South and Central America – were vigorously advocated from the early twentieth century onwards, but it was only in the late twentieth century that Spanish began to compete with French and German as one of the major European languages in schools, ultimately overtaking German. Besides Spanish, the Leathes Report also recommended that Russian and Italian should be given equal prominence with German in university departments and that non-European languages should not be neglected either – and the century since then did indeed see some growth in all those areas.

Modern Languages in Britain had a Eurocentric limit, or perhaps simply an understandable preference for the near over the more distant. Other languages have most often found a place in separate Schools of 'Oriental and African Studies', 'East Asian Studies' and the like, although that is changing, as Mandarin becomes more established in schools (where in 2018 it overtook German to become the third most popular language at A-level). In some universities, Chinese and other Asian language disciplines are now housed in

[12] See Angela Gallagher-Brett, *700 Reasons for Studying Languages,* 2004, <https://www.llas.ac.uk/sites/default/files/nodes/6063/700_reasons.pdf> [accessed 17 December 2021].

the same unit as European languages. Expanding university language degrees to languages with significant populations of speakers in the UK today – Arabic, Urdu, and others – would give them greater prominence and prestige, but there has not (yet) been evidence of significant demand.

## The Future of Studying Language and Languages

Virtually ever since languages study has had a voice in Britain (at least since the founding of the Modern Language Association in 1892), its advocates have felt they are fighting to justify the subject's existence. Crisis is nothing new; nor are the arguments and the crucial levers of influence. More than a century ago, the Leathes Report devoted considerable space to language teaching methods, appropriate assessment, questions of curriculum time, and organization, and the supply and training of teachers; most of those issues today remain more or less unsatisfactory.

As for the place of *language* in studying languages, we are getting better at including the many kinds of variation of language – transnational, translingual and multi-mode and multi-media language use – even in our 'core' language-learning classes. And in linguistics, as we saw above, looking beyond borders in these ways has led us to see that the exciting research questions are not just at the (perceived) centre of 'standard', 'national' language, but also at the (perceived) peripheries. That is one more tension to add to the many that define the wonderful challenge of studying languages in the twenty-first century.

Nicola McLelland is Professor of German and History of Linguistics at the University of Nottingham.

# 19

# Liveness

*Benedict Schofield*

I'm standing in a gallery, surrounded by thirteen cinema-sized screens. On one, a stockbroker is watching the ever-shifting course of the world financial markets. On another, a figure dressed entirely in white is moving through a series of futuristic-looking spaces. Simultaneously, on different screens, a funeral is taking place, a family dinner is underway, and a news broadcast has just begun. Faced with many choices, I must decide where to turn my attention. Yet even as I try to focus on just one of the screens, I can hear the dialogue from the others, and see them too in my peripheral vision. The installation is called *Manifesto* (2015), a creation of the German artist Julian Rosefeldt, and starring the Australian actress Cate Blanchett. Slowly, I work out that each film is playing on a loop, but no guidance is given on how to watch them – singly, all at once, or in a specific order? Then, at precisely ten-and-a-half minutes into each thirteen-minute cycle, something astonishing happens. The different films fall into synchronicity, the characters turning to face the camera, breaking the fourth wall to directly address me. In a sing-song monotone, the figure nearest to me proclaims:

> No more painters, no more writers, no more musicians, no more sculptors [...] enough of imbecilities, no more anything, nothing, NOTHING, NOTHING, NOTHING.[1]

The effect is extraordinary. My role as the respectful and silent spectator of a work of art is challenged, both because of the uncanny effect of the figure on the screen appearing to acknowledge my presence, and because of what they

[1] Julian Rosefeldt, *Manifesto* (London: Koenig Books, 2016), p. 33.

are saying: in the case above, words from the artistic manifesto of the transnational Dada movement. Founded in Switzerland in 1916 by artists from Germany, Romania, and Austria, but rapidly expanding to include centres in Berlin, Cologne, Hannover, Paris, and New York, the artists of Dada were united by their aim to create art, in the words of poet Hugo Ball, not as 'an end in itself, but [as] an opportunity for the true perception and criticism of the times we live in'.[2] Standing in the gallery, I, too, found myself being asked by the installation to become critically engaged in the world through art, rather than simply remaining a passive admirer of it. Indeed, as critics have noted, much of the power of *Manifesto* lay in its ability to be both a 'filmic re-enactment' of the aims of Dada, but also a 'new supermanifesto' for the role of art in our contemporary world.[3]

There is, however, a problem in my account of *Manifesto.* For, despite my best efforts, the impact of experiencing this installation 'live' is almost impossible to capture on paper. I can try to convince you of its power through my use of descriptive language, and I can leverage academic arguments about its significance. But, on a more fundamental level, to fully understand it (and as we so often say colloquially): 'you really had to be there'. Phrases such as this indeed indicate something crucial about our experience of the world: namely its liveness. Central to everyday parlance in English is a sense that there is a difference between experiencing something 'in the flesh' and experiencing it 'second hand'. We regularly claim that 'seeing is believing'; we have a need to access life 'in real time'; we suffer from *fomo* (the fear of missing out). The idea of liveness thus covers both the desire for immediacy in our experience of things, but also suggests the need for shared collective experiences. It implies the privileging of the live over the recorded, and, on a more abstract level, uncovers somewhat uncomfortable truths about the essentially ephemeral nature of existence, and the challenge of culturally capturing and preserving this ephemerality.

As students of the Modern Languages, we are regularly confronted with issues concerning liveness, perhaps most obviously when we study dramatic texts. Yet when we work on drama, we often begin with methods of close textual analysis. Clearly, though, analysing a script is not the same as analysing a performance, and thus we soon face a conundrum: is the script simply the basis for a performance – and thus of a secondary nature? Or is the script a record of a performance, a means of preserving it for the future?

[2] Hugo Ball, cited in: 'Dada', Museum of Modern Art (MoMA), <https://www.moma.org/learn/moma_learning/themes/dada> [accessed 12 February 2021].

[3] Burcu Dogramaci, 'Sprechen, Spielen, Verwandeln – Manifeste als Metamorphosen', in Julian Rosefeldt, *Manifesto* (London: Koenig Books, 2016), p. 93.

How can we account for performance on the stage in our analyses, which can only ever be represented partially by what we read on the page?

These are not new questions for Performance Studies. Famously, the British director Peter Brook, who has worked primarily in France for the past forty years, argued in 1968: 'I can take any empty space and call it a bare stage. A man walks across this empty space whilst someone else is watching him, and this is all that is needed for an act of theatre to be engaged'.[4] Theatre here is a transnational phenomenon, not indebted to any particular national tradition or space. It is also a form where text recedes into the background, and in its place stands a contract between the act of performance and the act of spectatorship, which together form a theatrical event. For Brook, this theatre is ephemeral because of its spontaneity and immediacy, and thus he argues that it is 'always a self-destructive art'.[5] Practically, Brook acknowledges that productions do ultimately require a structure that allows them to be repeated, and one of these structures is the text or script. But, he laments, 'from the day [a performance] is set something invisible is beginning to die'.[6] Fundamentally, for Brook, we can never capture the liveness of performance, since liveness is predicated on the 'two-way current' between actor and audience.[7]

Philip Auslander calls this stance 'classic liveness', because of its insistence on the simultaneous presence of performer and public.[8] Underpinning classic liveness is thus an emphasis on embodiment, and a rejection of forms of mediation that might interrupt the immediacy of the theatrical experience. Significantly, classic liveness is also a collective experience, since our body is just one among a larger audience to whom we also connect. This combination of connectivity and collectivity has led many scholars in Performance Studies, such as Peggy Phelan, to insist that 'performance cannot be saved, recorded, [or] documented' and that 'once it [is], it becomes something other than performance'.[9] As students of the Modern Languages, we can, of course, view recordings of productions, and often do as part of our studies. But these recordings are precisely what Phelan sees as not being performance. Instead, at best, they might be considered an incomplete archival trace of a performance.

[4] Peter Brook, *The Empty Space* (London: Penguin, 1990), p. 11.

[5] Brook, *The Empty Space*, p. 18.

[6] Brook, *The Empty Space*, p. 18.

[7] Brook, *The Empty Space*, p. 29.

[8] Philip Auslander, *Liveness: Performance in a Mediatized Culture* (London: Routledge, 1999), p. 62.

[9] Peggy Phelan, *Unmarked: The Politics of Performance* (London: Routledge, 1993), p. 46.

The problems created by recording live events are exemplified by what happened when *Manifesto* moved from its original home in the gallery and into the cinema. This was an unusual shift for a work of conceptual art, largely the result of Blanchett's transnational star power, which not only enabled the installation to tour the world, but also led to its cinematic conversion and thus to a genuinely global audience for its German artist. One of the primary challenges in capturing the installation on film was precisely the 'very strong emotional moment' when the various Blanchetts break the fourth wall and directly address the audience.[10] It became clear that this moment of liveness could not be directly replicated in the cinematic version, neither spatially nor temporally, since cinema is primarily a linear form of storytelling, while the gallery space allowed for simultaneity. Ultimately, the moment was reworked as an epilogue to the film, in which all the figures speak, but on just one screen that is split into twelve smaller screens. This signals a significant alteration. In the gallery, we were continually interrupted, every ten-and-a-half minutes, by the Blanchett chorus. In the film, though, it is deferred until the end, and thus becomes a climax to a linear narrative. As a climax, it suggests a fusing of the different artistic manifestos from which the work is created into something coherent, an effect that is politically and aesthetically different from the live-gallery experience, where the manifestos competed for our attention. Filmic mediation of the artwork thus changes the work of art, something Rosefeldt himself stresses: 'It was really, really different. The whole concept had to be broken apart, and we had to forget about what we did for the museum installation'.[11]

This suggests something of an oppositional binary between the live and the recorded, and the performative and the cinematic. Yet precisely these categories are becoming harder to distinguish, not least with the development of simulcasts – that is, the live-screening of a play to cinemas at the same time as it is happening in a theatre. Here, the screening is indeed live in temporal terms, and, as in the theatre, the audience are also sitting together in an auditorium, creating a sense of collectivity. These simulcasts are also often transnational, providing audiences with access to productions that they would usually have no other way of seeing. Nevertheless, a study of a 2017 production of *Titus Andronicus* at the Royal Shakespeare Company

[10] Rosefeldt cited in Soheil Rezayazdi, 'Turning 13 Installation Screens of Cate Blanchett Into One Single-Screen Feature', *Filmmaker Magazine*, <https://filmmakermagazine.com/102408-turning-13-installation-screens-of-cate-blanchett-into-one-single-screen-feature-julian-rosefeldt-on-manifesto/#.WqVgKmacbMI> [accessed 12 February 2021].

[11] Rosefeldt cited in Rezayazdi, 'Turning 13 Installation Screens'.

(RSC), which compared the experiences of theatre-goers with simulcast cinema-goers, suggests that the cinematic mediation of the performance still results in a different result: 'Cinema-goers [...] were more likely to say they found the production moving than theatre-goers, [a result of] how directorial decisions focused the viewer's eye on the detail of actor's expressions [...]. [I]n the theatre, audience members paid more attention to elements of staging, costume, plot, music and choreography, and [...] were more likely to have had a positive, communal experience'.[12]

Despite these differences, Auslander nevertheless urges us to question the 'common assumption that the live event is "real" and that mediatized events are secondary and somehow artificial reproductions of the real'.[13] Indeed, the responses to *Titus* suggest that what changed with the simulcast was not a sense of liveness itself, but a difference in the audience's emotional response, and their sense of the theatricality of the live event. For our purposes as students of the Modern Languages, these debates are important for three reasons. First, they encourage us to recognize that the theatrical text, which appears so tangible on the page, is in fact a source of potential spontaneity, immediacy, and ephemerality; second, it reveals that recordings of performances do not necessarily deliver the direct access to liveness we might at first assume; and, third, it suggests that we should be careful in creating false oppositions between live and recorded forms of art.

Indeed, the existence of a clear oppositional binary between the live and the recorded is further challenged by the increasingly common mediatization of theatrical productions themselves. One prominent figure in this process has been the British director Katie Mitchell. Her German-language production of Henrik Ibsen's *Miss Julie* (2010) consisted of a large cinema screen directly above the stage, with the stage itself composed of a series of enclosed sets. The actors were filmed by a crew on the stage, and the result was projected onto the screen above. The audience could thus choose to watch the film, which was an elegant example of heritage cinema; to watch how the film was being constructed on the stage, or to divide their attention. Through this dramaturgical set-up, Mitchell was playing with the very concept of liveness, ultimately dismantling the binary between the live and the recorded by presenting the audience with both a live stage production and its cinematic simulcast at the same time.

The questions concerning liveness raised so far have perhaps understandably focused primarily on the worlds of theatre, film, and the visual arts.

[12] Fergus Morgan, 'Impact of Stage Violence on Audiences', *Stage*, 26 October 2021, pp. 34–35.

[13] Auslander, *Liveness*, p. 3.

Many of the other forms we study as Modern Linguists, such as the novel, might seem to stand outside of this discussion – after all, reading a novel is primarily a solo experience, and one that we can repeat at will. How might ideas of immediacy, textual mediation, increasing medialization, simultaneity, and collective experience be applied then to genres beyond theatre?

Poetry, of course, has a significant position as both a written and an oral form, and the popularity of the poetry slam is a sign of how it already achieves a form of coexistence between page and performance. The novel, as noted, at first appears to be a more private activity. We might question, though, whether there is not necessarily an element of liveness in the act of reading. For instance, the common notion of 'getting lost in a good book' reveals a transformative power in fiction that is both spatial and temporal (we lose a sense of time as we read; we are transported to other places), which in turn indicates a connection between the written text and reader, which is perhaps an imaginative corollary of the 'two-way current' described by Brook.

Of course, this novelistic 'current' remains distinct from the theatrical, since unlike in Brook's metaphor, the text is not physically alive, and the only body involved is our own. Nevertheless, we could consider the ways in which authors seek to create a sense of literary liveness or immediacy. The French theorist of narratology Gérard Genette,[14] for instance, distinguishes between modes of subsequent, prior, and simultaneous narration, with the latter indicating a scenario in which the narrator tells us their story at the moment it occurs – in other words, live. We might too consider the difference between first- and third-person narrators, or the use of free indirect discourse, as aspects of a literary technique of liveness that aims to produce an effect of immediacy. Tense too, has an important role to play: here we might think of Hilary Mantel's retelling of the rise of Henry VIII through the eyes of Thomas Cromwell in *Wolf Hall* (2009). Despite being one of the most richly mined stories of British history, Mantel's decision to use the present tense for a historical novel both creates a simultaneity of experience between reader and protagonist, and gives the impression that the end of the story is in no way set. Indeed, this is what happens in the theatre in historical drama, as Freddie Rokum has argued: 'The historical figures who are presented on the stage act in their own time "as if" their deeds were being done in the present, while on stage their actions are determined by the fact that they represent historical figures who are appearing again'.[15] It is interesting to note that *Wolf*

[14] See for example Gérard Genette, *Narrative Discourse: An Essay in Method*, trans. by Jane Lewin (Ithaca: Cornell University Press, 1980).

[15] Freddie Rokum, *Performing History: Theatrical Representations of the Past in Contemporary Theatre* (Iowa: University of Iowa Press, 2007), p. 101.

*Hall* became both a successful stage show (RSC, 2013) and a television drama (BBC, 2015). On stage, Mantel's use of the present tense was in essence replicated through the liveness of performance, but on screen this liveness was lost, resulting in a far more traditional re-telling in the format of historical or costume drama.

Our experience of reading can, of course, never fully replicate the collective experience of theatre, or of cinema. Yet there are clearly communities of readers: famously, Benedict Anderson argued that the rise of print culture was central in creating a sense of 'imagined community' among readers, vital for the creation of nations (and, indeed, nationalisms).[16] The phenomenon of world-wide bestsellers also creates transnational communities of readers who then experience fiction collectively. This experience is partly the result of the marketing and simultaneous world-wide release of such works – essentially, flashpoints of liveness in the otherwise individual reading experience. Rebecca Walkowitz has argued that this simultaneity in the global literary market means that these texts – one example she uses is the *Harry Potter* series (1997–2007) – are no longer nationally defined, but already 'start as world literature'.[17] Walkowitz, too, stresses how Anderson's theory of the imagined community links to a transnational simultaneity in reading experience, with the novel able to 'creat[e] the impression of simultaneous reading across space [and] simultaneity among people who never meet'.[18] This notion of collective experience is distinct from that developed in Performance Studies. However, as a broader application of liveness, it encourages us to see the novel as embedded in wider cultural narratives, and a wider cultural industry, which is often transnational.

Considering liveness is thus crucial to our work as students of the Modern Languages, since it moves us beyond any easy understanding of our texts as fixed and static. These texts have lives – on the stage, in galleries, mediated through other forms such as film, and in their transnational circulation – which are not always immediately apparent when we approach them through our primary method of close-reading. This is not to suggest that liveness should displace our focus on the text and its language, but it is to stress that liveness reveals the text in our hands as only one part of much wider cultural

[16] Benedict Anderson, *Imagined Communities: Reflections on the Origins and Spread of Nationalism* (London: Verso, 1983).

[17] Rebecca Walkowitz, *Born Translated: The Contemporary Novel in an Age of World Literature* (New York: Columbia University Press, 2015), p. 2.

[18] Walkowitz, *Born Translated*, p. 26.

processes. This remains most evident in the field of Performance Studies, where the script exists as both origin and record of a performance. Here the category of liveness asks us to think critically about the way that ephemeral forms are archived and recorded in culture, and the difference between those cultural forms and our experience of liveness in communities of spectatorship. When we turn to other forms such as the novel, we inevitably stretch the definitions of liveness as set out in Performance Studies. However, this stretching also encourages us to consider the national and transnational communities of reading that develop around texts, and the narrative strategies used by authors to engender a sense of liveness. In this way, liveness can be applied to all aspects of our work as students of the Modern Languages, demanding that we continuously question what constitutes a live experience, and analyse critically how it is captured culturally.

Benedict Schofield is Reader in German and Co-Director of the Centre for Modern Literature & Culture and the Cultural Competency Institute at King's College London.

20

# Locality

*Marion Demossier*

The year 2017 witnessed the release of the heart-breaking documentary film, *Human Flow*, by the Human Rights activist, poet and artist, Ai Weiwei, son of the revered Chinese poet Ai Qing, favourite of Chairman Mao. That year saw too the presentation of the Turner Prize to Lubaina Himid, a black British contemporary artist and curator, born in the Sultanate of Zanzibar, known for her creative work on the African diaspora. These examples were chosen to illustrate a lecture on globalization I gave recently to postgraduate students. They provided the students with rich material to think about and to understand the cultural texture of our societies as well as to explore transnational lives through creative modes of action and the paradoxes and ambiguities attached to locality and its resonance in a global context. Everybody identifies with, or is identified by, a locality, while mobility has become a commonplace of contemporary societies.[1] Steven Vertovec set out in 1999 an agenda listing reconstructing place and locality as new themes for future research.[2] More recently this agenda has been applied to the field of Modern Languages by cultural theorists developing a 'transnational critical practice reflecting on the ways in which languages, cultures and the people who inhabit them connect and intersect' (introduction to this volume, p. 2).

Locality as an analytical concept has shifted from a national and essentialized notion to a more fluid, contested, and flexible idea, reflecting current debates across the Social Sciences and Humanities. Arjun Appadurai, himself

[1] Ruediger Korff, 'Local Enclosures of Globalisation. The Power of Locality', *Dialectical Anthropology*, 27 (2003), 1–8.

[2] Steven Vertovec, 'Conceiving and Researching Transnationalism', *Ethnic and Racial Studies*, 22.2 (1999), 447–62.

a scholar of South Asian descent occupying a prominent position within the Western academy, has contributed to the development and hybridization of disciplines across the social sciences and humanities. Paradoxically, writing about the production of locality in his seminal book *Modernity at Large*, he was already questioning locality in schemes about cultural flow, arguing for a more enriching approach to the logic of the spatial in the local.[3] For Appadurai, globalization marked a break with the past – with the rise of capitalism – that is identified with the modern not only economically but also culturally and politically. Through migration and the mass consumption of electronic and printed media, imagination constitutes the link between the modern and the global while influencing modern subjects to incorporate the global into their quotidian practices. Both homogenization and heterogenization as assemblages form part of this process.[4] Yet the twenty-first century gives a different flavour to locality, be it in its essentialist expression of belonging and the language of new forms of identification, or in the revolutionary and ambiguous global digital communicative context that students navigate. Locality has thus become an imagined, paradoxical, ambiguous, and contested space.

In this global landscape, migration has challenged the perspective of local as a lived and experienced territory. The anthropologist Daniel Miller, in his recent study of the digital world, argues that social media is more than simple communication – it is also a place where we now live, giving a different depth to the concept of locality.[5] The old idea of the local as an isolated island, village, *quartier*, or tribe is definitely out of date. Engaging critically with locality requires a major rethinking of our disciplinary contexts. The shifting of scholarly attention to the transnational, colonial registers of French history in recent years has likewise helped illuminate the central role of mobility, boundary crossing, transcultural contacts, and commerce in engendering new forms of cultural and place identification. Whalen and Young argue that the French concept (*Heimat* in German, *piccola patria* in Italian, and *patria xica* in Spanish) continues to offer particular insight given the historically

[3] Arjun Appadurai, 'The Production of Locality', in *Modernity at Large. Cultural Dimensions of Globalisation* (Minneapolis and London: University of Minnesota Press, 1996), pp. 178–89.

[4] 'Assemblages' is a term coined by anthropologist Anna Tsing, referring to things emerging from our postmodern condition. See Anna Tsing, *The Mushroom at the End of the World. On the Possibility of Life in Capitalist Ruins* (Princeton: Princeton University Press, 2015).

[5] Daniel Miller et al., *How the World Changed Social Media* (London: UCL Press, 2016).

deep, complex, and often conflicting investment in the distinctiveness of locality and local place.[6] Locality thus remains central to our postmodern condition. The question for Modern Languages is how is locality relevant and productive in terms of theoretical knowledge today? How does the study and teaching of locality provide a useful window to engage reflexively with a contemporary curriculum of Modern Languages and Cultures?

Transnationalism has provided a useful platform to rethink global and area studies in the Humanities, especially following the rise of major paradigms such as postcolonialism, post-feminism, and poststructuralism. Both Modern Languages and Linguistics provide specific expertise and an ambitious and transformative platform to examine, within the framework of transnational studies, how languages and cultures operate and interact across diverse axes of connection. A renewed interest in ethnography is part of this wider reconfiguration of our disciplines.[7]

Starting from French Studies, where the notion of locality has deep resonance and where the nation-state was constructed alongside *la petite patrie*, my own experience of teaching students over the last twenty-five years is rooted in both the ambiguities of belonging as an awkward and ambiguous space and the *regard éloigné* (distanced view) of somebody located outside of her own country. This in-between critical position defines the core of my intellectual engagement as a researcher and a teacher, and is consistent with the tradition of 'French Cultural Studies' embodying the stranger's gaze.[8] As a Modern Languages specialist trained as an anthropologist, it is no accident that I have devoted three decades to the study of identity and to the concept of *terroir*, a very French concept, and that reflexivity has become part of the journey when teaching students of different nationalities.

Students in Modern Languages cultivate similar ambiguities mediating different worlds of meanings, words, and experiences like the anthropologist.[9] They are learners as cultural mediators. Most of my students join Modern Languages at a critical juncture in their life – that of becoming adults and acquiring a sense of being and becoming through the study of others – and

[6] Philip Whalen and Patrick Young, *Place and Locality in Modern France* (London: Bloomsbury Publishing, 2014), p. xiii.

[7] See Naomi Wells et al., 'Ethnography and Modern Languages', *Modern Languages Open*, 1 (2019), 1–16.

[8] Mike Kelly, 'Le regard de l'étranger: What French Cultural Studies Brings to French Cultural History', *French Cultural Studies*, 25.3–4 (2014), 253–61.

[9] Georgia Wall, 'Meaning and Methodology', *Exchanges: The Interdisciplinary Research Journal*, 5.2 (2018), 16–25.

it is this experience that they confront in a wide variety of ways.[10] They start on a journey taking them from language learning to more meaningful experiences of otherness through the close reading of Flaubert or contemporary discussions of ethnicity. Yet their position as students of languages and cultures is reminiscent of that of an anthropologist at the outset of their fieldwork, 'making the familiar exotic and the exotic familiar'. I have always approached my teaching as a reciprocal and interactive experience of ethnographic curiosity and naivety. Why do the French do things like that? What does it mean to be French today? What does *terroir* (as an expression of locality) mean in a French context? How should we translate it? How should we approach locality?

In theoretical terms, the cultural critique of locality has been developed diversely by Stuart Hall (cultural politics), Clifford Geertz (local knowledge), Pierre Bourdieu (cultural capital), and Raymond Williams (structures of feeling).[11] Raymond Williams's work, especially *The Country and the City*, is rooted in his sense of its own humanist and Marxist intellectual positioning and its dominant values explored through literary and historical sources.[12] It explores the ambiguous and contradictory relations between city and country and represents the politics of place as tensions between structures and experiences. Simon During notes now that the field of cultural studies, which has been central to Modern Languages, is much less focused on discrete, filiative, national, or ethnic cultures, or components of such cultures, than it was in its earlier history with work by Raymond Williams and the early Birmingham school.[13]

Etymologically, the term locality was coined as early as the seventeenth century from French *localité* or late Latin *localitas*, from *localis*, 'relating to a place'. It had a special meaning in French political thought as France after 1789 was a unified and uniform entity that relied on a merging of differences: 'local' was seen as the opposite of 'national', a contradiction that could not be glossed over and had to be eliminated.[14] Yet, the twenty-four

[10] Marion Demossier, Lisa Bernasek and Heidi Armbruster, 'Teaching Ethnography as Modern Languages Method: Legacies and Future Practices for Global Citizens', *Language, Culture and Curriculum*, 32.3 (2019), 285–98.

[11] Peter Jackson, 'Mapping Meanings: A Cultural Critique of Locality Studies', *Environment and Planning A: Economy and Space*, 23.2 (1991), 215–28.

[12] Raymond Williams, *The Country and the City* (New York: Oxford University Press, 1973).

[13] Simon During (ed.), *The Cultural Studies Reader*, 2nd edn (London: Routledge, 1999), p. 23.

[14] Thierry Gasnier, 'The Local: One and Divisible', trans. by Richard C. Holbrook, in *Rethinking France – Les lieux de mémoire*, under the direction of Pierre Nora,

provinces listed in Michelet's *Tableau de la France* are presented as insular, self-contained unities, each one imagined by its particular relationship with the soil, the climate, and the kind of person they produce. A perfect illustration is given by *Le tour de France par deux enfants* published in 1877, which has run through more than 400 editions, but still offers a Republican textbook of France's cultural diversity unfolded through kilos of cheese, folkloric idioms, and monuments. Yet a great deal of crossover and competition was simultaneously going on at European level, enabling each nation and region to construct a sense of identity that mattered for their own citizens. Anne-Marie Thiesse's work illustrates the vast cultural fabrication of the nation – and the circulation of the idea of the nation – as well as the crafting of regional literature and culture in its ambiguous and diverse forms.[15] Transnationalism was a reality long before the process of constructing national identities in Europe led to the creation of a 'check-list' forming the basis of all national identities. Regional identities were constructed on the dual relationship between the local and the national: the model of the national as a perfect mosaic of diversity, or the model of the mise en abyme, that is, the local representing the national in miniature. Literature, museums, paintings, and sculptures all contributed to the process of exalting the nation and creating an imagined community.

A useful trope to examine locality and its internal deployment is the French concept of *terroir* – a term almost untranslatable into another language – which has been the subject of a lively and expanding academic debate.[16] The concept illustrates the power of place to define the natural world as *terroir*, seen as a unique environmental and human site linking taste and place in wine and food. *Terroir* is a slippery concept that has long been a staple of French discourse and was given institutional recognition in the form of the 1930s AOC (Appellations d'Origine Contrôlée) (attached to the place of origin) at a crucial period of history when both wine producers and the French State started to define and protect locality against frauds through the regulation of local food and wine production by the producers themselves.[17]

translation directed by David P. Jordan, 4 vols (Chicago: University of Chicago Press, 2001–2010), II (2006), pp. 231–94.

[15] Anne-Marie Thiesse, *La création des identités nationales* (Paris: Éditions du Seuil, 1999).

[16] See Marion Demossier, *Burgundy: A Global Anthropology of Place and Taste* (New York and Oxford: Berghahn, 2018) and more specifically, Amy Trubek, Guy Kolleen and Sarah Bowen, 'Terroir: A French Conversation with a Transnational Future', *Contemporary French and Francophone Studies*, 14.2 (2014), 139–48.

[17] Gilles Laferté, *La Bourgogne et ses vins: image d'origine contrôlée* (Paris: Belin, 2006).

In his recent study, Thomas Parker takes us through the cultural mythology of the natural world developed between the Renaissance and the Revolution and expressed through a wide range of cultural forms from paintings to literature, language, and horticulture.[18] This crafted mythology attached to the power of place (through *terroir*) spanning different centuries and now continents, since it has been widely borrowed and translated in other geographical settings, tells a story of rootedness, time, and space as well as expressions of being and doing in a global setting.

Comparison always brings the additional advantage of stimulating the intellectual and moral imagination enabling the social and cultural worlds to be analysed. In this transnational quest, translating wine cultures and especially the *terroir* story takes different forms and involves different settings, protagonists, plots, contexts, and characters. It is about both conspicuous consumption and the heightened value of 'authenticity' within global capitalism, revealing especially how producers and consumers link cultural production to particular times, social experiences, and places, generating new forms of individual and collective identification. An example from Asian sites of encounter are the wine manga or wine comic books that have played an important role in the circulation of the Burgundy story. First produced in Japan and then translated into different languages and cultural contexts, they offer a window onto the processes at stake when translating wine cultures back and forth. Here, both the original Japanese wine manga and the French translation serve as anthropological lenses to unpack the Burgundy *terroir* story and its translation in different cultural traditions. What remains central to this story is the idiomatic pillar of French wine culture: Burgundy, a plot, a grape, and its producer. Wine manga epitomize Western values of social climbing, democratization, meritocracy, and individualism in a changing context of societal norms where traditional and modern values struggle in an attempt to preserve what may be identified as quintessentially Japanese. While in Japan, popular culture engages with *terroir* as a new story of post-nuclear locality, in New Zealand, Otago wine producers reflect on their place in the world by appropriating central ideas of locality that are attached to Maori culture through Place-Turangawaewae, Care-Kaitiakitanga, and Kinship-Whanaungatanga.

What is interesting for the researcher is to follow these transnational deployments in which new cultural experiences, values, discourses, and encounters are formed, shaped, and negotiated to become part of a process of cultural embodiment. This is far from a straightforward process of translation.

[18] Thomas Parker, *Tasting Terroir: The History of an Idea* (Oakland: University of California Press, 2015).

As Sarah Cappeliez has argued, if the majority of scholarly literature on the transferability of *terroir* to other cultural and national contexts emphasized adaptability, when respondents discuss using these ideas 'on the ground' and in their local specific settings, the meanings of these different common ideas tend to vary, pointing to differences in 'doing' *terroir* in specific places.[19] The transnational perspective – defined as threads and connections that exceed national contexts – reveals the storied reality encapsulating remarkably well what it means to be here and there, or from here and from there, while being global. Stories are central to these processes, but they require also 'thick description' (in the Geertzian sense of the term).[20]

My research as an anthropologist located in a Department of Modern Languages has been defined by first-hand experience and exploration of a particular social and cultural setting, but is also shaped by my *appartenance* (sense of belonging to a community) in the field of Modern Languages. That work has involved a focus on texts, discourses, material culture, performative and other cultural forms, as well as language and modes of expression, but this has also been driven by a focus on the experiences and practices accompanying the object, topic, or theme under scrutiny. I have seen experience as central to my critical enquiry. Malinowski talks of 'foreshadowed problems' driving the research process: if you only focus on words, you miss lots of stuff.[21] Meaning negotiated through more than language, or outside of language and experience, provides a more in-depth approach to the understanding of culture. Ethnography has therefore the power to challenge power and authority and to provide a critical commentary on our modern-postmodern condition.

The study within French culture of locality and *terroir* reveals aspects of the cultural essence of the place while unravelling flux, connections, interactions, and mobility. Long-term ethnographic investigations enable the researcher to embrace and make sense of a certain holism defined as 'the significance of understanding the total social context of the people we are trying to understand'.[22] The concept of *terroir*, both as a malleable and evolutive concept, has enabled us to grasp the fussy, messy, and imperfect

[19] Sarah Cappeliez, 'How Well Does Terroir Travel? Illuminating Cultural Translation Using a Comparative Wine Case Study', *Poetics*, 65 (2017), 24–36 (p. 35).

[20] See Clifford Geertz, *The Interpretation of Cultures: Selected Essays* (New York: Basic Books, 1973).

[21] Bronislaw Malinowski, *Argonauts of the Western Pacific: An Account of Native Enterprise and Adventure in the Archipelagoes of Melanesian New Guinea* (London: Routledge and Kegan Paul, 1922), pp. 8–9.

[22] Alpa Shah, 'Ethnography? Participant Observation, A Potentially Revolutionary Praxis', *Hau: Journal of Ethnographic Theory*, 7.1 (2017), 45–59 (p. 46).

world we study through sticking around and listening, observing, and participating, one awkward step at a time. The *terroir* story has provided the foundations for the construction of an ideology of place as quality-driven, but also humanly contested. This ideology largely rooted in local familial cultures was attached to the perception of working the land as the primary factor in the making of what was defined as quality wines in the context of an economy largely in the hands of the merchants and landowning elites. But it is also about France and its perpetual obsession with place and locality. As Mary Orr has argued, there is a need for awareness of our insider–outsider positions as researchers in Modern Languages, as well as a blend of approaches to mutual interests, to pinpoint the distinctiveness – and potential blind-spots – of what we do in 'French Studies' or in Modern Languages more widely.[23] This allows us to enhance particular and productive applications of knowledge within the field to wider cross-, inter- and intra-cultural work. This remains one of the challenges for Modern Languages today in an ever-changing and challenging environment.

Marion Demossier is a social anthropologist and Professor of French Studies at the University of Southampton.

[23] Mary Orr and Marion Demossier, 'Transnational Terroirs and French Monocultures: The Case for Disciplinary ML Subject Renewal'; presentation at 'Transnational Modern Languages' conference, Italian Cultural Institute, London, 1–3 December 2016.

21

# Me

*Abigail Brundin*

For an essay on 'me', it seems entirely fitting to begin with a personal anecdote. From 2013 to 2017 I was one of three lead researchers on a project, *Domestic Devotions: The Place of Piety in the Italian Renaissance Home, 1400–1600*, based at the University of Cambridge and funded by the European Research Council (ERC). The specific type of funding (a Synergy Grant) was designed to support research that spans disciplines and activates cross-disciplinary collaborations. When we came to define our disciplinary spread for the proposal, we had no problem identifying one of my colleagues as a cultural historian, and the other as an art historian: but what exactly was I? It seemed that the tick boxes provided by the ERC did not easily encompass the kind of contribution I would be making. We spent some time discussing how to describe my disciplinary identity, and in the end settled on 'literary studies'. This seemed like a less than satisfactory outcome: the term felt flabby and unexciting; it lacked the certainty and concreteness of my colleagues' disciplinary titles; it also ignored my specialism in the language of our place of study. What is more, this definition couldn't be appropriated as a scholarly identity, as my colleagues' labels could: I couldn't, or didn't want to be a 'literary student', as they were historians and art historians. What, in fact, was I?

The crisis of confidence provoked by this experience acts as a symbolic starting point for this essay. In carrying out our research for the *Domestic Devotions* project over four years and co-authoring the final book, it was always abundantly clear that my disciplinary perspective *was* different, particular, and valuable as a contribution to our mutual aims.[1] My colleagues

[1] Abigail Brundin, Deborah Howard, and Mary Laven, *The Sacred Home in Renaissance Italy* (Oxford: Oxford University Press, 2018).

easily recognized and appreciated this. What, then, made it so difficult to define? This essay seeks to outline and illustrate a methodology that is commonly used and understood by those of us working on the Renaissance and early modern periods from within the discipline of Modern Languages, and as a result to assert its particularity and value as a contribution to scholarship more broadly. This is not a defensive gesture: I am perfectly convinced that the methodology is valuable. I am also convinced that my position within the overarching discipline of Modern Languages has been of real benefit in affording me the training, the access to models of good practice, and the freedom to carry out my research as I do. What is lacking, seemingly, is the capacity to explain this clearly to others with a disciplinary label that sums it all up, or (the purpose of the current volume), to populate the label we already possess with all the meanings that ought to accrue to it.

My own contribution to the *Domestic Devotions* project focused on tracking the passage of devotional books and other kinds of pious reading matter into homes, and understanding how they were consumed by readers there. This fitted our broad purpose in the project, which was to understand how 'everyday' experiences of religion functioned within the Renaissance household, where devotions of all kinds, from routine prayers to extraordinary miracles, frequently took place and responded to the demands of domestic life.[2] We were interested in homes of all kinds, and particularly in penetrating beyond the elites to more humdrum and 'ordinary' households. Thus, my task included expanding the category of 'reader' to include those who consumed books and text via the loosest kinds of literacy, as well as in oral and aural contexts.[3] The research necessitated a range of approaches, from book history (where were devotional texts of all kinds produced and sold? how far did they travel from their places of production? how did they arrive in people's homes?), to literary analysis of the texts themselves (what did they say and how?), to the history of reading (how were texts used? who used them, where, and when?). This final category of analysis concerns us here, because it included the copy-specific study of the marks that individuals left in their books, as well as the archival records that owners of texts left behind, all of which might alert us to the reception of these texts by their

[2] The other researchers on the team working in 'literary studies' were Marco Faini and Katie Tycz, and their research has deeply informed this article, for which grateful thanks to them both.

[3] On kinds of literacy in the period see Paul Saenger, 'Books of Hours and the Reading Habits of the Later Middle Ages', in *The Culture of Print: Power and the Uses of Print in Early Modern Europe*, ed. by Roger Chartier (Princeton: Princeton University Press, 1989), pp. 141–73.

original consumers. In sum, this was a very broad study that had the most common types of devotional literature at its core (prayer books, rosaries, miracle books, lives of saints, cheap prayer pamphlets, etc.), but sought to open that literature to a variety of frames for analysis that would allow its value and interest to show. This approach seems particularly pressing in the case of devotional literature from the Renaissance period, which has in the past been subjected primarily to analysis that has dismissed it on literary grounds without recognizing its other kinds of value.

A study of Renaissance domestic devotions is a natural place to look for traces left by Renaissance selves as they engaged in pious activities in their homes. Beginning with Augustine's fourth-century *Confessions*, spiritual texts, centred on confession and conversion, have been a rich source for the study of early forms of life writing.[4] The Renaissance period, too, has traditionally been posited as the era of the 'discovery of the individual', beginning with Jacob Burckhardt's enduring formulation.[5] And although Burckhardt's analysis has been modified and rejected in subsequent decades, recent scholars have continued to argue for a 'shift in moral vocabulary' during the Renaissance that was significant in the construction of new notions of individualism.[6] Notably, this shift is not confined by national borders: the development of vernacular genres that offer themselves to an autobiographical reading, as well as to newly reformed religious practices that privileged an intense form of interiority, had an impact on writers across nations, languages, and genres, from Calvin to Montaigne to Erasmus or Thomas More.[7] Thus, the study of Renaissance selves is necessarily interdisciplinary and transnational.

What is notable about spiritual interiority as a framework for considering autobiographical writing is that it need not be defined by gender or status, in the way that most textual production of the Renaissance period was. The famous examples of life writing from the period are all by men, of course (although women wrote increasingly in the confessional Petrarchan mode in sixteenth-century Italy, as well as producing collections of *lettere familiari*).[8]

[4] 'Autobiography', in *The Oxford Companion to Italian Literature*, ed. by Peter Hainsworth and David Robey (Oxford: Oxford University Press, 2002), p. 36.

[5] Jacob Burckhardt, *The Civilization of the Renaissance in Italy*, 3rd edn (London: Phaidon, 1995 [first published in German in 1860]).

[6] John Martin, 'Inventing Sincerity, Refashioning Prudence: The Discovery of the Individual in Renaissance Europe', *The American Historical Review*, 102 (1997), 1309–42.

[7] Books of *ricordanze* and collections of *lettere familiari* are genres that developed in the period with strong autobiographical tendencies.

[8] In Italy, notable autobiographical works include Benvenuto Cellini's *Vita* (composed in the 1550s and 1560s but first published only in 1728), and Leonbattista

Our study of domestic devotions, however, with its deliberately non-elite and non-canonical focus, uncovered autobiographical traces of selves who rarely figure in the mainstream historical record: women, the very old, and the very young, the poor, and barely literate. In the main these were only traces, far from coherent narratives of selfhood and thus requiring careful work of textual translation and reconstruction on the part of the reader. Yet a study of domestic devotions did appear to offer a frame for marginal selves to be glimpsed in new and compelling ways.

## 'Me' in the Margins

A first example shows a woman acting as an engaged, proactive reader who sought to modify her devotional book in strategic and carefully formulated ways in order to draw from it the maximum spiritual profit. At the same time this reader added personal inscriptions and additions that loudly proclaimed the value of her book as a piece of personal property, a marker of selfhood and a maker of networks and connections with other readers, real and imagined. The reader was a nun, Sister Alexia, who carefully recounts the manner in which she came by her book in a detailed inscription: 'Questo libro e de sor Alexia donato da suo barba frate petro mantuano ord[in]is p[re]dicator[um] die 25 septembris 1528'.[9] The book is a copy of the Franciscan *Meditations on the Life of Christ*, in an Italian translation, printed in Venice about fifty years before Alexia received it and bound at the time of printing in brown goatskin over wooden boards, a robust and costly covering to preserve the precious text from one owner to the next.[10] While her ownership inscription is couched in the third person, as is usual in the period, Alexia's statement of personal investment in her text is notably strident, and is further accentuated in two Latin hymns that she has added to the front and back of the book in her educated hand, one a 'Hymn to the holy Virgin' that lists the names of the many women who gave their lives to Christ in perpetual virginity, the other recounting the story of Alexia who joined Saint Ursula on her journey

Alberti's *Vita* (composed in Latin in about 1438 but surviving only in an eighteenth-century transcription). On confessional lyric poetry by women, see some of the examples in Virginia Cox, *Lyric Poetry by Women of the Italian Renaissance* (Baltimore, MD: The Johns Hopkins University Press, 2013). Both Veronica Franco (a courtesan) and Arcangela Tarabotti (a nun) published collections of *lettere familiari* in the period.

9 'This book belongs to Sister Alexia, given by her uncle brother Pietro of Mantua of the Order of Preachers on the 25th September 1528'.

10 *Meditationes vitae Christi* [Venice: Nicolaus Jenson?, c.1478?]: Cambridge University Library, Inc.5.B.3.2[4321].

to martyrdom. Within the text itself, the nun-reader's discreet annotations and marginal notes mark the text at points where she must pay particular attention, as the Franciscan author sets out models for pious behaviour that she seeks to emulate. The work has clearly been studied in its entirety and mined for spiritual value.

Elsewhere in the text, all of a sudden another reader appears, naming herself on the verso of the second leaf: 'Questo libro sia de s[or] teofila guadagna serva de Iesu cristo. Credo in deum'.[11] Teofila's handwriting, of a slightly later date, is considerably more childlike and unsophisticated, as is her blunt declaration of faith. Her presence on the pages of the text is brief but telling. Notably, in the context of a religious institution where, at least theoretically, personal property is sacrificed on entry, two women are very keen to demarcate personal ownership of this book. Alexia goes as far as pointing out its family provenance and connection to her through her uncle, and gestures deliberately at autobiography in her Latin hymns. Teofila's later inscription suggests that Alexia has given her the book as a gift, within the confines of their new, institutional family. Alexia's marks within the text act as a guide, modelling the act of reading for a less well-equipped member of their community. For both women, the reading of the *Meditations on the Life of Christ*, while it is clearly deeply connected with their spiritual vocation within a religious institution, also denotes a private space inscribed by family, property, and identity. The text is preserved, handed down, marked, and altered as it passes through a community of readers, retaining fragments of selves.

It is rare to find such extensive evidence of readers' interactions with Renaissance texts, and even rarer to find a woman reader at work as we do in Sister Alexia's copy of the *Meditations*. More frequently, the traces are less substantial. Sometimes they are humorous, like the naughty boy who practised a crude coat of arms on the inside cover of his Psalter and drew disobedient little faces inside all the 'O's.[12] Sometimes they are painstaking, like the child who carefully copied out the running header in his family's Latin Bible as a way to practice his letter formations.[13] While perhaps not explicitly autobiographical, such childish traces are undoubted markers of selfhood, hinting at selves that are utterly recognizable, children who do not want to say

[11] 'This book belongs to Sister Teofila Guadagna servant of Jesus Christ. I believe in God'.

[12] *Psalterium* [Treviso: Michael Manzolus, *c.*1480]: Cambridge University Library, Inc.5.B.9.2[2047].

[13] *Biblia*, Impressa [...] in felici Venetorum civitate: sumptibus & arte Hieronymi de Paganinis [7 settembre 1497]: Cambridge University Library BSS.120.A97.2.

their prayers or work hard to pass a difficult educational milestone. If these are suggestive moments, however, more concrete traces are also needed.

## 'Me' in the Archives

Other kinds of archival record reveal marginal selves who offer up first-hand testimony. For the *Domestic Devotions* project, trial records were a particularly precious source, often capturing the voices and experiences of the poor and illiterate who, under scrutiny, did their best to describe and defend their religious beliefs and practices. Examples include Isabella, on trial in Pesaro in 1579 'because of a book' ['Isabella, carcerata per un libro'];[14] or Giovanni, called before the authorities in Bassano in 1588 to defend his practice of wearing a prayer sheet next to his body that bore devotional text, images, and symbols.[15] In both cases, the defendants confess that they cannot read the text in question, but have kept it for its talismanic and apotropaic functions. Their illiteracy has left them vulnerable and afraid: as Giovanni exclaims, 'O Dio, che cosa è non saper littere!'[16]

Both the cases of Isabella and Giovanni are typical of this genre of archival document, and alert us to the difficulties of working with trial transcripts. The defendants' accounts of their actions are woolly and unstructured; they omit key details and frequently become confused and inarticulate. Both defendants struggle to speak 'properly' during the trial, forced to adopt a register that is unfamiliar and probably uncomfortable. The language slips and lurches from one paragraph to the next, between the Latin of the questioner, the Italian of the defendant, and the frequent eruptions of ungrammatical and dialectical vocabulary and phraseology. The first-hand testimony of the witness is transcribed by a scribe who adds explanatory marginal notes in Latin, including some of the most troubling kind ('first torture', 'second torture', etc.): these paratexts act as alerts to the increasing unreliability of the narrative voice. Subsequent witnesses recount the same set of events from notably different perspectives: thus the 'facts' in play wobble out of focus, receding behind the cloudy layers of multiple viewpoints. Trial records have long been a key source for historians, but their analysis as literary artefacts nuances and develops our understanding of them in crucial ways.

A final brief example helps to reinforce this point. In the archives of the Santa Casa in Loreto, a long-established and important pilgrimage site in the

[14] Archivio Diocesano di Pesaro, *Iura civilia et criminalia*, fasc. 245; *Liber inquisitionum et condemnationum*, 2, 1579–1581 (Bishop Roberto Sassatelli), fols $41^{v}$–$42^{r}$.

[15] Archivio di Stato di Venezia, Sant'Uffizio, Pezzo 61, fasc. 14, fol. $1^{r}$–$1^{v}$.

[16] 'Oh God, what a thing it is not to know one's letters!'

Marche region of Italy, records of the trial of Lucia Matthei span the years 1577 to 1584.[17] The accusation is familiar: a neighbour claims that Lucia has cast a spell on her. Three material artefacts have been brought to the trial as evidence against her: a length of string, some lumps of dried earth, and a knife. In her defence Lucia claims that she used the items to perform a cure, not a spell, and that it was intended to aid her sick son. Alongside Lucia's own testimony, other voices chime in to reinforce her claim of innocence, including the son himself, his wife, and various neighbours, colleagues, and friends. Other voices insist on 'Lucciaccia's' status as a witch. As the narrative expands and grows more diffuse, the interrogators, in search of clarity, place the defendant on the rack, at which point her testimony changes fundamentally in quality and tone: 'Jesu, S[an]ta maria della vergine, crocifisso Benedetto, santa maria n[ost]ra, crocifisso Salvatore, calatemi, mi manca il fiato, ò Jesu [...] Calatemi giù, che dico quello che saccio [...] Fatemi posar giù, ch'io dirò poi ogni cosa'.[18]

As autobiographical moments in Renaissance documents go, this is a profoundly disturbing one. The narrating 'I' who reaches us down the centuries is terrified and in pain, screaming out in panic. If our search is for a spontaneous communication of selfhood, this must be it: yet the use of torture ultimately leads to a convoluted and erratic trial. In the transcript, which changes hand periodically over the years, Lucia's language becomes ever more fragmented and distorted, and in the latter stages of the trial her voice is almost erased from the transcript. Lucia's trial is an object lesson in the rich possibilities of working with this kind of document as a means to uncover striking autobiographical moments, but also the considerable difficulties of interpretation. Approaching such a text with the tools of translation offered by our specialism in Modern Languages and literary studies allows for a careful account of the gaps, lacks, and slippages in language and narrative, and acts as an important corrective to assumptions about 'truth'.

Abigail Brundin is Professor of Italian at the University of Cambridge, a fellow of St Catharine's College and Director of the British School at Rome.

[17] Archivio Storico Santa Casa di Loreto, Atti Criminali, Processus criminales: 1577–1584: Stregoneria: Luciaccia.

[18] 'Jesus, Holy Mary Virgin, blessed Crucifix, our Holy Mary, crucified Saviour, let me down, I can't breathe, oh Jesus [...] Let me down, I will tell you what I know [...] Let me down and I will tell you everything': Ibid., c. 9v.

22

# Me

*Aurélie Zannier-Wahengo*

Teaching a Foreign Language (FL) abroad brings its share of surprises and involves many adaptations from teachers and learners. European university programmes leading to this profession reasonably cannot expose students to the infinite variety of educational and social realities that teachers of FL will encounter throughout their career. Therefore, programmes remain fairly generic although they generally require students to complete an internship. Understanding a new educational system and culture in a given foreign country is a challenge for most of the teachers of FL. The profession implies a permanent questioning on didactics and requires teachers of FL to confront their teaching practices to the context.

For almost two decades, the learner-centred approach has been considered as a privileged path to teach and learn FLs. It consists in shifting from a teacher-centred concept to place learners at the epicentre of the learning and teaching process. This approach stimulates interactions between teachers and learners and adjusts class activities towards learners' needs. The learner-centred approach is one example among others of a recognized beneficial educational practice that may nevertheless face certain resistance and/or unsuitability in certain cultural contexts.

## Background

Namibia is situated in the north west of South Africa. It gained its independence in 1990. Before that date, the country was ruled by an apartheid-based system built on racial segregation and oppression for non-white citizens. Access to education was one of the means of discrimination separating children on the basis of skin colour.

At independence, Namibia had the delicate task of organizing a new education system towards an education for all. The learner-centred approach was retained as a good measure to support equal education. Yet Namibian educators and government officials were concerned about the risks involved in implementing European concepts into the Namibian cultural context – still healing from the apartheid regime. In 2003, the National Institute for Education Development published a conceptual framework entitled *Learner-centred Education in the Namibian Context*, which intended to clarify the rationale behind the concept chosen for Namibia. In the document, the authors dedicate a section to the comparison between the African and the European environments. They explain:

> There are important differences between the African and the European/American setting, and between African indigenous knowledge systems, which were not sufficiently appreciated previously, and European. African indigenous knowledge systems were seen as inferior. A main principle of learner-centred education is to use the social context of the learner as a resource and to relate learning to the social context. Attention therefore needs to be given to what that context is in general, and for each learner, and to draw upon the implications for the further development of learner-centred education.[1]

French as a Foreign Language (FFL) was introduced in Namibian secondary schools in 1993. The Franco-Namibian cooperation agreed on offering FFL in the disadvantaged schools where learners were less inclined to access international languages. Seven schools, for most situated in the capital city Windhoek, opened FFL as a subject from grade eight to grade twelve. In 1996, the French section at the University of Namibia (UNAM) followed suit. Today, the section counts about 100 students split into two streams; French Studies is offered to learners graduated from secondary school in French, and French as Applied and Business Language for those starting French at UNAM at a beginner level. The first group specializes in French as a major subject for four years before graduating in a Bachelor of Art. The latest are enrolled in French for three years as a minor subject.

According to the French Section lecturers' experience and research, learners of FFL are likely to encounter some obstacles when learning FFL

[1] National Institute for Education Development. *Learner-centred Education in the Namibian Context. A Conceptual Framework* (Windhoek: Namibia, 2003), pp. 17–18. See also Ministry of Education. *The National Curriculum for Basic Education* (Windhoek: NIED, 2010).

in Namibia. First, Namibia is geographically isolated from Francophone countries (the closest in the Southern African Development Community (SADC) being the Democratic Republic of Congo). Moreover, it has a very small French community (about 280 French nationals in 2017) and few French companies are operating in the country. This situation leads to a very limited exposure for students to practice French language outside the classroom and get accustomed to French and Francophone cultures. In addition, African learning culture can sometimes be in contradiction with Western pedagogical theories. In the Namibian framework (2003), authors make clear that valuing systems differences need to be taken into consideration in learner-centred applications. This notion unfolds as follows.

There are significant differences between principles of learner-centred education and conventional African child-centeredness, not least in the issue of questioning given authority. For example, some trends in social constructivism emphasize explicit socially critical theory and practice, whereas criticism in African contexts is an area of life that is carefully regulated according to who is bestowed with the right to be critical, how, and in what situations. Constructivism can be a symptom of the globalization of European ideas, but at the same time can be a powerful tool to construct communal and individual identity as a counterweight to globalization, depending on what values it is founded on. A new understanding of the ideas behind self-reliance could be an important contribution to a value stance in the African context.[2]

They further state that African children 'have a much stronger connection with an identity rooted in their immediate community. You are a person through other people ... They are usually named after someone from an earlier generation, which in some cultures signals that they have inherited that person's spirit and status'.[3]

Aware of the peculiarities of the Namibian environment and its impact on school results, UNAM lecturers try to support learners by offering them tailored methods and materials close to their centres of interests and needs and facilitating their learning language acquisition.

## Namibian Portfolio for Languages: Origins

In 2012, the association of French teachers in Namibia responded to a call for contributions launched by the International Association of French Teachers and submitted a proposal to create an innovative material helping FFL

[2] National Institute for Education Development, *Learner-centred Education in the Namibian Context. A conceptual Framework* (Windhoek: Namibia, 2003), p. 24.

[3] National Institute for Education Development, *Learner-centred Education*, p. 24.

learning in Namibia: *The Namibian Portfolio for Languages* (*NPL*).[4] For a year, five teachers worked on the development of a tool adapted to the needs of Namibian secondary school learners. The main objectives of the project were to promote self-assessment and formative assessment, to give learners a new space to express their singularities in languages and to invite them to reflect on their linguistic and cultural selves.

In 2000, the Council of Europe published the *Common European Framework of Reference for Languages* (*CEFRL*)[5] that laid the foundations for the harmonization of language teaching, learning, and assessing across Europe. One year later, the document was complemented by the *European Language Portfolio* (*ELP*) and its guideline in which the portfolio is defined as to:

> promote plurilingualism, pluriculturalism,
>
> promote learner's autonomy,
>
> be the property of the learner,
>
> value the full range of the learner's language and intercultural competence regardless of whether acquired within or outside formal education,
>
> have both a pedagogic function to guide and support the learner in the progress of language learning and a reporting function to record proficiency in languages,
>
> be based on the Common European Framework of Reference with explicit reference to the common levels of competence,
>
> encourage learner self-assessment and the recording of assessment by teachers, educational authorities and examination bodies,
>
> incorporate a minimum of common features which make it recognizable and comprehensive across Europe,
>
> be one of a series of *ELP* models that the individual learner will process in the course of life-long learning. *ELP* models can cater for

[4] M. Junias-Ameya, S.D. Lumbu, E. Mayumbelo, E. Uises, and A. Zannier, *Namibian Portfolio for Languages* (Windhoek: John Meinert Printing, 2012).

[5] The CEFRL can be accessed in mutliple language versions: <https://www.coe.int/en/web/common-european-framework-reference-languages/level-descriptions> [accessed 31 January 2022].

the needs of learners according to age, learning purpose and context and background.[6]

The *ELP* is divided into three parts: the *Language Passport*, which provides an overview of the individual's proficiency in different languages at a given point in time; the *Language Biography*, which facilitates the learner's involvement in planning, reflecting upon, and assessing his or her learning process and progress; and the *Dossier*, which offers the learner the opportunity to select materials to document and illustrate achievements or experiences recorded in the *Language Biography* or *Passport*.

## Descriptive of the Namibian Portfolio for Languages

In an effort to adapt the *ELP* to the Namibian framework, some contents of the *ELP* have been modified and adapted to the context in terms of curricula, syllabus, and assessment.[7] For instance, the *NPL* does not follow the *CEFRL* levels of competences (which have been replaced by the Namibian syllabi objectives). Moreover, as there is no harmonization between the SADC educational systems, the *NPL* was conceived for Namibia and not as a trans-national tool like the *ELP* is in Europe. Finally, the *NPL* was not introduced as an official examination material but as a complementary assessment tool that could be included in the Continuous Assessment marks. The *NPL* covers the five grades during which learners are learning French. This allows pupils and teachers to visualize and reflect on a consequent cycle of learning progression.

This type of learner-centred pedagogic material is very rarely used on the African continent where alternative assessment is hardly established. African educational systems do generally favour traditional summative assessment. Consequently, *NPL* conceivers provided training for all users

[6] The Council of Europe, *European Language Portfolio (ELP), Principles and Guidelines*, Version 2 (Language Policy Division, 2011), <https://www.coe.int/en/web/portfolio> [accessed 31 January 2022].

[7] For fuller discussions of the *Portfolio* see: S.D. Lumbu and A. Zannier, 'A First Namibian Portfolio for Languages: From Concept to Context', *Journal for Studies in Humanities & Social Sciences*, 1(2) (2012), 69–84; 'The Namibian Portfolio for Languages: A Tool for Formative Assessment in Namibian Secondary Schools', *Journal for Studies in Humanities and Social Sciences*, 5(1) (2016), 156–62; 'Le Portfolio Namibien des Langues: un outil contextualisé pour l'autoévaluation centré sur l'apprenant. Perspective des apprenants des écoles secondaires', *Journal of French Studies in Southern Africa (AFSAA) – University of Kwazulu Natal*, 46 (2016), 82–112.

in an attempt to make them more familiar with the notion of formative assessment. Learners would usually be assessed by teachers and rarely by themselves. On the other hand, the researchers decided to leave the teachers free to organize the implementation and use of the *NPL* in schools (frequency of use, feedback to linguistic progress, guidance on learning strategies). In 2013, the *NPL* was distributed to seven schools and approximately 500 pupils received it in grade eight.

### *Mon identité* – My Identity

In the first chapter, learners have the opportunity to talk about their personality and personal environment (sports, school, living area, family) and their relationship to languages in and outside school.

These sections (see Figures 1, 2, and 3) are a resource for teachers to better appreciate learners' personal life and to adapt their teaching content close to their interests. They also stimulate learners' ability and enthusiasm for languages and draw a map of how, when, and with who they are using them.

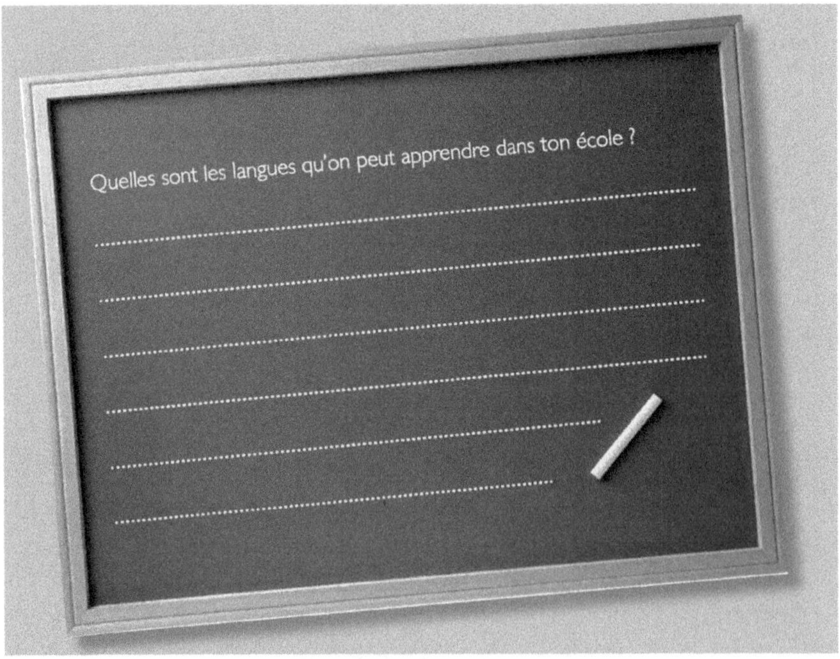


Figure 1. My Identity section.
Source: Namibian Portfolio for Languages, p. 9.

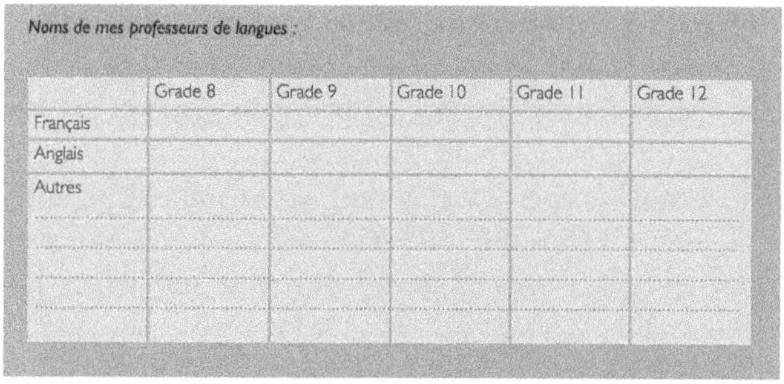

Noms de mes professeurs de langues :

| | Grade 8 | Grade 9 | Grade 10 | Grade 11 | Grade 12 |
|---|---|---|---|---|---|
| Français | | | | | |
| Anglais | | | | | |
| Autres | | | | | |

Figure 2. My Identity section. Source: Namibian Portfolio for Languages, p. 10.

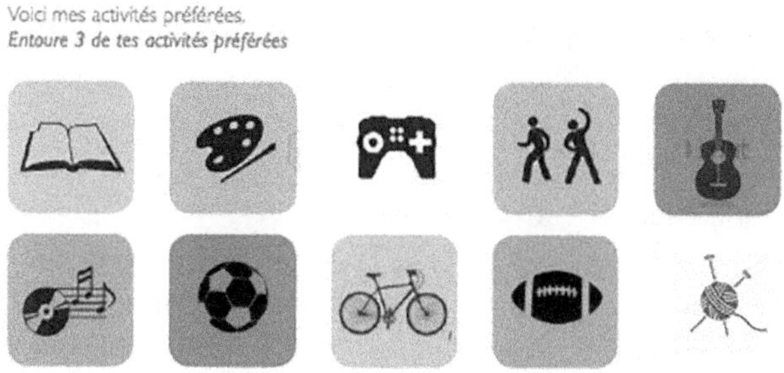


Figure 3. My Identity section. Source: Namibian Portfolio for Languages, p. 10.

## *Mon parcours en langues* – My Linguistic Journey

In this chapter, learners are asked to self-assess themselves according to the prescribed outcomes of the Namibian syllabus for each grade. This assessment is proposed at three different stages during the year. At the end of each grade, teachers comment on the learners' progress and advise them on learning strategies and objectives.

## *Mon dossier* – My File

The last part of the *NPL* offers a space for learners to gather documents linked to languages (productions, official documents, project). There is no specification in the Dossier content. It is a folder in which learners freely express their linguistic journey.

## Namibian Portfolio for Languages: A Tool to Promote Learner's Accountability in the Learning Process

The Namibian Education Ministry does not provide textbooks for learners in FLs; this responsibility rests with the foreign embassies and cooperation missions. When the French language was introduced in Namibian schools, the French government donated textbooks to all learners. Twenty years later, 'one textbook, one learner' is an unfulfilled goal in all subjects. In the case of FFL, learners are still using 1990s textbooks that are kept in the classroom and used by two learners. Therefore, for many learners, the *NPL* was their first learning property. According to research findings, this aspect had a real positive impact on the learner's motivation to learn French and to use the *NPL*. Pupils were proud to own their *NPL*s, and despite teachers' doubts about learners' ability to take care of their material, they proved them wrong: since 2013, very few *NPL*s have been lost or damaged.

The second advantage of the introduction of the *NPL* was to open a dialogue about languages in and outside the classroom. During their training, teachers were strongly encouraged to show the *NPL* to parents, other teachers, and school principals to reflect and share on the learners' singular profiles. This was made possible by the bilingual format of the *NPL* (English/French) and its reader-friendly design.

The 'dialogue' aspect was particularly important in Namibian state schools as class numbers reach up to fifty pupils and the class duration is restricted to forty-five minutes. In these conditions, learners do not have a lot of room to receive individual attention by their teachers. With the *NPL* project, conceivers took the opportunity to try to impulse a new dynamic in the exchanges between teachers and learners. Roles with the *NPL* were redistributed, giving several opportunities to learners to become 'consultants' or 'managers' in their learning experience and thus to share accountability with their teachers.

Research findings proved that the *NPL* drove learners towards more 'autonomy' and 'self-awareness' in their language-learning process. The learner's semi-autonomy was tested through their ability to self-assess themselves. Seventy per cent of the participants declared that the *NPL* developed their understanding of their strengths and weaknesses in FFL. They explained that the *Linguistic Journey* chapter allowed them to 'see their progression in FFL', 'to look back and appreciate their improvements in languages'. Eight-four per cent recognized that the self-assessment gave them more clarity on what was expected from them in FFL. According to them, this aspect had a positive impact on their motivation and self-satisfaction to learn more and improve. Another participant added that he felt 'more committed' to learn once consulting his *NPL*.

On a practical level, the *NPL* has also eased the learners' mobility from schools to schools and once joining the UNAM French Section. The *NPL* offers the traceability of learner's linguistic identity and progress that are precious information for teachers and learners to maximize the learning efficiency in FFL throughout the schooling.

### Namibian Portfolio for Languages: A Tool Enhancing Plurilingual Identity

In the Namibian context, most learners develop competence in languages and cultures outside their educational frame (especially in indigenous languages). The *NPL* helps learners to be conscious of the preciousness of these language particularities. The *NPL* enhances the learner's full range of intercultural and language competences. Learners realize that languages are not only important as part of a curriculum but that they are everyday communication tools for sharing and exchanging in society. In that sense, they also grow better 'citizens' well as open minded on cultural diversities. Enhancing plurilingual identity is also beneficial for non-Namibian learners who sometimes might find it difficult to meld with Namibian learners. For instance, Namibian schools welcome many Angolan nationals who speak Portuguese as their mother tongue (and unfortunately their only language, as most of the Angolan dialects have not been transmitted to younger generations) and are sent by their families to Namibia to improve their skills in English. In that case, the *NPL* is a transnational platform integrating minority groups in the school system and laying foundations for communication and efficient exchanges with neighbouring countries.

From learners' and teachers' perspectives, the opportunity of depicting personal environments (daily life, hobbies, and use of languages in and outside school) engaged pupils in a discussion with themselves and others. A learner even stated that the *NPL* allowed her to 'express herself'.

## Conclusion

Since its enactment, the *NPL* has been a great success story. The project has established a bridge between different actors in the educational chain and tested their flexibility in pedagogical change. At an institutional level, reactions were quite variable: some school principals and heads of department were truly supportive; others surely less. But many language teachers and lecturers demonstrated their interests for the *NPL* and felt motivated to initiate their own portfolios for their subject. Unfortunately, the financial situation of Namibia in the past years obstructed the *NPL* goal to own its status as prescribed material for French. But this important step remains the next move forwards for the *NPL*.

The *NPL* adaptability to the Namibian context in terms of content, design, structure, and practicality was very positive and relevant to its users. In that sense, the *NPL* proved to be a beneficial learner-centred tool conceived at the service of learners first. From the beginning, pupils showed a lot of inquisitiveness and enjoyment with regards the *NPL*. Against all odds, they confidently adapted to the exercise of self-assessment.

The *NPL* is a quality complementary pedagogical resource. It informs teachers on their learners' profiles in FL learning, which facilitates their task to deliver an adapted pedagogy. The Council of Europe reminds us that learners do not accumulate languages side by side; languages constantly interfere with one another, making learners develop their own general communicative skills. Therefore, plurilingualism and pluriculturalism are two crucial dimensions in teaching FLs. In Europe as well as in Africa, it is an opening to individual recognizance and a door to embrace nowadays-multi-ethnic societies. With the *NPL*, learners can express who is their 'me' through an extensive and detailed cartography of their use and progression in languages. They can realize how valuable are the languages they know with or without educational goals. The *NPL* is also an efficient springboard to accept differences and similarities, which fosters open minds and togetherness. Discovering 'me' to understand the 'other'.

Aurélie Zannier-Wahengo is Senior Lecturer in French as a Foreign Language at the University of Namibia.

# 23

# Mimesis

*Ricardo Roque*

The concept according to which Indigenous peoples were seen as if predestined to be civilized, evangelized, educated, assimilated in the model image of Europe guided Western imperialisms from the 1500s. This ideology formed a lexicon of imitation that was part of colonialism and its forms of power in various guises. Yet, simultaneously, European conquerors, administrators, missionaries, and so forth also felt attracted to the imagined otherness of Indigenous people. Sometimes colonial conquest and governance only achieved efficacy by the colonizers actively seeking to adopt, model, or fashion themselves on what were perceived to be Indigenous sociocultural forms. Colonialisms often were not possible without a grip, even if biased and disruptive, on Indigenous worlds; and on several historical occasions mimesis was an important human practice that made colonialisms possible.

Broadly conceived, I pursued this research hypothesis in my work. Through the conceptual lens of parasitism and mimesis, I tried to grasp the entanglements between colonialism, violence, justice, headhunting, and anthropology in the context of the nineteenth- and twentieth-century Western imperialisms. My investigations were set in the late Portuguese colonial empire, which then stretched from Portugal itself to vast territories in Africa and some remnant colonies in Asia – including the eastern side of the island of Timor in Southeast Asia, Portugal's most remote colonial possession. East Timor configured a sometimes extreme but also very revealing case study for my historical ethnographic approach. In this essay, I provide a synthetic excursion through some of my own work on this topic. This is not a roadmap with fixed points and preset destinations. Instead, the reader will find here an open exploratory guide that can be used to undertake independent studies into the complex and productive concept of mimesis.

## Mimesis and Colonialism

Mimesis and colonialism, both as human phenomena and analytical categories, share a long history. Since the Classical Age, the reflection on mimesis as a concept and a practice in human history has fed on a prolific literature and intellectual debate in philosophy, literary theory, psychology, social theory, evolutionary biology, social anthropology, and so on. Nonetheless, only in the last three decades has the 'thematic complex'[1] comprising the terms mimesis, mimicry, and imitation been approached from the perspective of its inscription into colonial processes. Both as a theory and as a practice, mimesis was constitutive of colonial history during the five centuries of European imperial expansionism. It became a relevant mode of relating between Europeans and non-Europeans in colonial encounters – while after decolonization it continued to be constitutive of the transits between Africa, Asia, Europe, America, and Oceania. Anthropological and historical literature on mimesis and colonialism has explored these insights principally within and across three related themes: indigenous resistance and anti-colonialism; the making of identity and alterity in colonial encounters and post-colonial relationships; and, finally, in theories and practices of colonization and cross-imperial relations. As argued extensively elsewhere, one still needs to consider further the significance of crossing the study of mimesis as concept and as praxis (including its companions imitation and mimicry) with the analysis of colonial forms of power, state administration, trade, evangelization, and government.[2] In the following, I summarize this conceptual trajectory drawing principally (though not exclusively) on my own work, linking the study of colonial mimesis to notions of resistance, identity/alterity, and governmentality in the history of empires and colonialism.

[1] Gunter Gebauer and Christoph Wulf, *Mimesis: Culture, Art, Society* (Berkeley: University of California Press, 1995), p. 309.

[2] The present essay re-uses material and summarizes arguments made at greater length elsewhere by the author, especially in Ricardo Roque, 'Mimesis and Colonialism: Emerging Perspectives on a Shared History', *History Compass*, 13.4 (2015), 201–11; 'Mimetic Governmentality and the Administration of Colonial Justice in East Timor, ca. 1860–1910', *Comparative Studies in Society and History*, 51.1 (2015), 67–97; 'Dances with Heads: Parasitic Mimesis and the Government of Savagery in Colonial East Timor', *Social Analysis*, 62.2 (2018), 28–50. See also Patrice Ladwig and Ricardo Roque, 'Introduction: Mimetic Governmentality, Colonialism, and the State', *Social Analysis*, 62.2 (2018), 1–27.

## Mimesis and Resistance

For decades, the theme of indigenous subversion of, or resistance and opposition to, colonialism dominated approaches to colonial mimicry and mimesis. Frantz Fanon's critique of the desire for the imitation of Europe in his concluding remarks of *The Wretched of the Earth* is an early instance of the centrality of the imitation trope in anti-colonial thought and, afterwards, in the academic field of post-colonial studies.[3] Later post-colonial studies also moved beyond negative anti-colonial visions of imitation as a mere tool of European colonial hegemony. The concept of 'colonial mimicry' took one of its most distinctive turns in the work of literary critic Homi Bhabha. In a widely cited article of 1984, Bhabha conceptualized 'colonial mimicry' as an ambivalent process through which colonial authority is distorted, subverted, and resisted.[4] Bhabha's emphasis on subversive mimicry (widely criticized, however, because of its crude textual reductionism) was contemporary to a growing interest from social and cultural anthropology in the counter-hegemonic nature of imitation as a form of 'cultural resistance' to colonialism. In this vein, the concrete indigenous processes and practices through which colonizers could be appropriated and imitated (and thus potentially subverted) have become a fertile area of anthropological study. For instance, in the wake of Jean Rouch's fascinating and controversial ethnographic film *Les Maîtres fous* (The Mad Masters) of 1955, anthropologist Paul Stoller influentially interpreted the West African Hauka movement as a 'horrific comedy', a notion he later re-articulated and expanded as a mode of 'embodied opposition' to colonial power, the mastery of colonial rule through mimesis.[5]

The equation 'mimesis as resistance' thus became a dominant interpretive framework based on two presuppositions: first, that mimesis and mimicry in colonial and post-colonial contexts were principally indigenous (re)actions oriented towards European models, and second, that these (re)actions were meaningful – principally and almost exclusively – in the context of an emancipatory politics of cultural resistance, opposition, and criticism of colonialism. Yet, for what concerns imitation in particular, the resistance framework has been criticized for reinstating the colonizers' Eurocentric anxiety with

[3] Frantz Fanon, *The Wretched of the Earth* (London: Macgibbon and Kee, 1965 [1961]).

[4] Homi Bhabha, 'Of Mimicry and Man: The Ambivalence of Colonial Discourse', *October*, 28.2 (1984), 125–33.

[5] Paul Stoller, 'Horrific Comedy: Cultural Resistance and the Hauka Movement in Niger', *Ethos*, 12.2 (1984), 165–88; Paul Stoller, *Embodying Colonial Memories. Spirit Possession, Power and the Hauka in West Africa* (New York: Routledge, 1995).

indigenous imitations of Europeans – a distress often voiced and formalized by colonial state authorities in the form of surveillance procedures, legal prohibitions, and punitive actions against perceived mockery. These critiques of 'mimesis as resistance' mainly call attention to the broader complexity of cultural meanings behind mimetic ritual performances and other appropriations. Indeed, indigenous copying of Europeans can also be seen as productive and positive modes of incorporation, which are meaningful on relatively autonomous cultural terms, beyond political opposition.[6]

## Mimesis and Identity/Alterity

The wave of critiques of the excesses and limitations of resistance as explanatory framework led to shifts in the study of colonial mimesis, in favour of more nuanced and ethnographically informed readings. It followed a shift from 'mimesis as resistance' to 'mimesis as identity' and it has led to more nuanced and sophisticated interpretations of *indigenous* imitative appropriations of modernity, outsider states, and forms of rule, and colonialism more broadly. In the wake of these critiques, emerging work at the juncture of anthropology and history explored mimesis as a concept that illuminates dynamics of identity and alterity in colonial and post-colonial contexts. As such, mimesis has turned into a key concept in the understanding of the mutual production of Self and Other in colonial encounters, and in an increasingly post-colonial, globalized world. Anthropologist Michael Taussig's works – *Shamanism, Colonialism, and the Wild Man*, and *Mimesis and Alterity* – have been important to this alternative conceptualizing of mimesis within the history of colonialism.[7] Following Walter Benjamin, Taussig described the 'mimetic faculty' as the ability to 'explore difference, yield into and become Other', and he then set forth to reflect on its historical development in the context of colonial contact.[8] Taussig's understanding of colonial mimesis is also associated with the magical mastery of the imagetic powers of alterity. Taussig's viewpoint lays considerable emphasis on Indigenous and European reciprocal processes of representation of otherness and, particularly, savagery, and on their magical efficacy.

[6] See Wilson Trajano Filho, 'Por uma etnografia da resistência: o caso das tabancas de Cabo Verde', Série Antropologia, Universidade de Brasília, 408 (2006), <http://dan.unb.br/images/doc/Serie408empdf.pdf> [accessed 1 March 2021].

[7] Michael Taussig, *Shamanism, Colonialism, and the Wild Man* (Chicago: University of Chicago Press, 1987); Michael Taussig, *Mimesis and Alterity: A Particular History of the Senses* (London: Routledge, 1993).

[8] Taussig, *Mimesis and Alterity*, p. xiii.

His prolific reflections have opened up a broad set of possible analytical directions across the main themes here identified. It has also been productively used in scholarship on resistance and subversive mimicry, on colonial violence, on identity/alterity dynamics in post-colonial contexts, and, also, on colonial government and magic. Taussig's work has been a powerful source of inspiration for developing new insights into the history and anthropology of mimesis and the colonial state.[9] In fact, Taussig's insights on mimesis as a powerful instance of colonial terror and violence reveal that, rather than a practice and a trope that serves the colonized to resist, counter, or disrupt colonial power, mimesis as a European activity could also act productively on the workings of colonialism. It reveals, in sort, that the protagonists of mimetic action were also the colonizers themselves.

## Mimesis and Colonization

As a rule, the above-mentioned approaches to mimesis, resistance, and identity tend to circumscribe the definition of colonial mimesis and mimicry as indigenous actions of reproduction, copying, or representation of European or of other foreign, external, 'models'. However, as Taussig's seminal work indicates, mimesis can be addressed as an important expression of the Europeans' colonizing actions. Conceptual developments on mimesis, identity, and alterity thus can be extended beyond 'native' mimicries to the study of *European* imitative practices in imperial and colonial settings. Imitation and mimesis can configure a faculty of the European colonizer, a meaningful dimension of the praxis of colonization. Europeans in the colonies could be mimetic agents, active subjects of imitative behaviour, rather than just objects of, and models for, indigenous reproduction. Hence from this perspective, colonial mimesis, I propose, concerns the mimetic processes that, in contrast, refer to *Indigenous* Others as a reference for European actions of colonization. For, indigenous societies could become models for colonizing action and for the re-shaping of European identities in a colonial situation. Similarly, they could also become resources for establishing colonial authority and even for the success of a variety of European projects of colonization.

Colonizers were often aware of imitating indigenous worlds as a practical possibility – they could fear its dangers, but they could also manipulate its virtues. They could appropriate and 'internalize' the alterity of indigenous cultures and societies in order to forge their own identities; to strategically

[9] See Patrice Ladwig and Ricardo Roque (eds.), *States of Imitation: Mimetic Governmentality and Colonial Rule* (New York: Berghahn, 2020).

pursue religious conversion; to achieve commercial ends; or with a view to extract some other form of colonizing power. Stories of transcultural Europeans 'going native' – for instance, by adopting polygamous behaviour, non-Christian beliefs, or turning into cannibals or head-hunters – stand as evidence of both the fascination and anxiety that surrounded the mimetic transit into 'other', non-European, cultures. Moreover, imitation as a theoretical framework mattered in understandings of social and intercultural behaviour in the colonies and in wider debates on colonial policy.

European colonial agents could pragmatically look upon local structures and indigenous realities as examples and models for establishing their own peculiar forms of rule – especially, but not exclusively, in backwater settings and where reliance on the local became critical for the very survival of colonial communities. In some instances, the colonial state attempted to administer, control, and integrate its indigenous subjects through mimetic policies of governance. Thus, for instance, drawing on the example of colonial judiciary government in colonial East Timor, I proposed to expand Taussig's point on the magic of colonial mimesis to argue for the notion of 'mimetic governmentality': 'the theories, techniques, and tactics concerned with the "government of others" whose underlying principle of action is the incorporation and reproduction of the perceived otherness of so-called "native" or "primitive" populations, with a view to rule and conduct their existence'.[10] In addition, mimetic theories of government could also implicate a parasitic rationale that, through concrete actions, aimed at abusively extracting power from the perceived alterity of the indigenous world.

The imitation of Europeans by Indigenous people, as noted above, could become a target of state forms of control and regulation. It stands as revealing of the further political significance of imitation that also *European* mimesis of indigenous elements could become the object of control and regulation. Because mimetic practice could threaten the boundaries upon which the difference between Self and Other in colonial relations was ideally to be established, the 'indigenization' of colonizers was often criticized and controlled. Thus, in taking on indigenous customs as model for individual behaviour, or simply in accepting to participate in indigenous social life and rituals, European agents could endanger not just the premises of their identity but, in some instances, also the grounds of the authority of the colonial institutions and national collectives for which they stood.

[10] Roque, 'Mimetic Governmentality', p. 69.

## Naming the Colonial Wild

The point about participation was particularly acute when the agents were representatives of the colonial state and when the 'native' customs under mimetic target were perceived to be especially 'barbaric' or 'savage' – such as the involvement and/or compliance of colonial agents with indigenous headhunting rites, a theme I have analysed extensively in several works in the context of Portuguese colonialism in Timor.[11] For Europeans, in colonial interactions on the ground, savagery was not simply a static property of the Other; it was a dynamic condition of others and of oneself that one ought to manage in practice. Thus 'savagery' – both of others and of oneself – could become the object of a colonial form of mimetic governmentality, in a double sense: as a form of governing others, an art of managing and parasitically exploiting the perceived barbarism of indigenous alterity; and as a form of governing oneself, an art of managing colonial identity in the tropics by fine-tuning difference and resemblance to 'savagery'.

It is revealing that linguistic transactions can also provide evidence of these complex histories. In fact, the mimetic trade of Europeans with the 'savagery' they attributed to others could be discernible in language. Indigenous people could signal the dangers and energies unleashed by this type of European colonial mimesis by nicknaming Europeans as powerful and threatening transgressors: such naming practices could then integrate European imaginaries and mythologies of mimetic 'savagery' as colonial hegemony. I also explored this hypothesis by examining the cross-cultural history of the term *arbiru* as used in Tetum language in colonial East Timor, a former colony of Portugal.[12] East Timorese people used this term as a nickname for a Portuguese colonial officer who actively participated in a number of devastating punitive campaigns in the 1890s. Portuguese colonial accounts understood this usage as the Timorese recognition of European supremacy and supernatural powers. Nevertheless, the colonial viewpoint failed to capture the veiled negative meanings that the Timorese name

[11] Ricardo Roque, *Headhunting and Colonialism: Anthropology and the Circulation of Human Skulls in the Portuguese Empire, 1870–1930* (Basingstoke: Palgrave Macmillan, 2010); 'Dances with Heads'.

[12] Ricardo Roque, 'The Name of the Wild Man: Colonial *Arbiru* in East Timor', in *Swearing and Cursing: Contexts and Practices in a Critical Linguistic Perspective*, ed. by Nico Nassenstein and Anne Storch (Berlin and Boston: De Gruyter, 2020), pp. 209–35. See also Ricardo Roque, 'The Death of the *Arbiru*: Colonial Mythic Praxis and the Apotheosis of Officer Duarte', in *Crossing Histories and Ethnographies: Following Colonial Historicities in Timor-Leste*, ed. by Ricardo Roque and Elizabeth G. Traube (New York: Berghahn, 2019), pp. 92–130.

conveyed. In effect, the term *arbiru* entailed hidden indigenous criticism and the cursing of the colonizers' excessive, threatening, and transgressive actions. It was a linguistic gesture for naming the wild and wicked nature of the colonizers' mimesis of savagery; it was a trace of colonial mimesis inscribed in the transcultural colonial history of languages in this region. Perhaps elsewhere similar linguistic traces of colonial mimesis remain in the global history of colonialisms. How ideas and language formations about mimesis and imitation permeate indigenous constructs and European colonization work; how they themselves could have been born out of particular colonial histories of exchange, violence, and/or governmentality; and how they have entered the visions and praxis of both Indigenous and European agents, needs further research.

Ricardo Roque is a Research Fellow at the Institute of Social Sciences, University of Lisbon, and an Honorary Associate in the Department of History of the University of Sydney.

Acknowledgements

Research work for this essay was funded by FCT, Fundação para a Ciência e Tecnologia, Portugal (grant reference PTDC/HAR-HIS/28577/2017).

24

# Miscegenation

*Jeroen Dewulf*

The term 'miscegenation' is used in reference to the mixing of different racial groups, as derived from the Latin *miscere*, 'to mix' and *genus*, 'kind'. In many Western societies, miscegenation was long considered a form of degeneration, with racial theorists claiming that it weakened certain human and moral qualities, such as physical strength, endurance, honesty, and even fertility. This explains the existence of anti-miscegenation laws in, for instance, colonies of the British Empire, Nazi Germany, and the United States during the era of segregation. Opposition against miscegenation continues to the present day by racist groups advocating white supremacy. Due to this negative connotation, scholars sometimes prefer to use different terms such as 'interracial' or 'interethnic'.

Out of the Second World War and the Holocaust grew a strong awareness about the dangerous consequences of theories advocating racial purity or superiority, which had a positive effect on the general attitude towards miscegenation. In spite of this change in attitude, traditional concepts of racial categorization still remain largely unchallenged. However, the questioning of traditional boundaries in the case of gender and sexual orientation has also begun to affect the debate on racial categorization. A case in point is the discussion that erupted following the decision by the former US President Barack Obama to identify himself as 'Black, African American or Negro' in the 2010 census form. Having a white mother and a black father, he could have made a different choice, such as checking both the 'White' and the 'Black' box or defining himself as 'multi-racial' in the box 'Some Other Race'. Obama's decision to identify himself exclusively as black provoked both satisfaction and disappointment. While groups associated with the Civil Rights Movement tended to greet his decision with joy and interpreted Obama's self-identification as a reflection of solidarity with the nation's traditionally underprivileged black community, organizations advocating a multi-racial America perceived his decision as a lost opportunity.

These mixed reactions reflect a divide between two opposing interpretations of the diversity model: one that celebrates diversity as a rainbow of different racial and ethnic groups, and another that aims at achieving new forms of diversity by blurring racial and ethnic boundaries. The latter challenges the traditional definition of diversity with the argument that it calcifies existing racial classifications and the stereotypes associated with them. Advocates of a multi-racial diversity model often refer to the United Nations' *Declaration on the Elimination of All Forms of Racial Discrimination* (1963), which states that 'any doctrine of racial differentiation or superiority is scientifically false, morally condemnable, socially unjust and dangerous'.[1] They argue that in order to overcome racial discrimination, a strategy that continues to categorize people in ethnic groups or separates them on the basis of their skin colour is not only outdated, but even counterproductive. As such, the Association of MultiEthnic Americans (AMEA) celebrated the introduction of multiple race responses in the 2000 US census as a sign of 'positive awareness of interracial and multicultural identity', a crucial first step 'towards resolving America's profound difficulty with the issues of race and interethnic relations' and the dismantling of 'the mythical notion that race is fixed rather than fluid'.[2]

Such a fluid definition of race is far from consensual, however. Not only does it face opposition by reactionary forces opposed to miscegenation on racial grounds, but also civil rights advocates caution that the disappearance of racial categories could endanger fairness of employment and other affirmative action practices. They warn against a new type of racism, a 'colour-blind racism', and argue that, as long as differences in power and status exist, it continues to be important to assess race and to hold on to racial categorization.[3]

It should also be said that the discussion on miscegenation differs considerably from continent to continent. It is, in this respect, useful to contrast the traditional approach to race and racial mixture in an Anglo-Saxon context

[1] <http://www.un-documents.net/a18r1904.htm> [accessed 21 December 2018].

[2] Carlos A. Fernández, 'Testimony of the Association of MultiEthnic Americans before the Subcommittee on Census, Statistics, and Postal Personnel of the U.S. House of Representatives', in *American Mixed Race: The Culture of Microdiversity*, ed. by Naomi Zack (Lanham: Rowman & Littlefield, 1995), pp. 191–210 (p. 193).

[3] Eduardo Bonilla-Silva, *Race without Racists* (Lanham: Rowman & Littlefield, 2006).

with that in Latin America. This is all the more the case considering that few scholars have had a stronger impact on the development of a multi-racial diversity model than the Mexican writer, philosopher, and politician José Vasconcelos Calderón (1882–1959). To illustrate the complexities, challenges, and pitfalls when building philosophical theories on the basis of miscegenation, I will focus on the case of Vasconcelos and his utopian vision that, by promoting *mestizaje* (the Spanish term for miscegenation), we could solve all problems rooted in racial and ethnic discrimination.

Vasconcelos grew up near the border with the United States at a time when US expansionist aggression against Latin America was at its high point. His political and intellectual career represented a lifelong battle against feelings of Latin American inferiority vis-à-vis the mighty Anglo-Saxon neighbour. Placing himself in the tradition of Simón Bolívar (1783–1830), the 'founding father' of Latin American independence, Vasconcelos strove for Latin American self-awareness. He fiercely rejected suggestions that progress could only be achieved if Latin America were to copy Anglo-Saxon rationalism and advocated a unique Latin American model of modernity. His belief in the power of art and aesthetics to improve Latin American self-confidence reflected itself in his policy as chancellor of the National University of Mexico and Mexican minister of education (1921–1924), when he secured international recognition of Mexican muralist art. Unlike his Cuban contemporary José Martí (1853–1895), who also tried to boost Latin American self-confidence, but perceived race as an old-fashioned issue left behind by modernity, Vasconcelos wanted Latin Americans to become more race-conscious. Contrary to the existing racial theories of his time, however, he believed that the key solution to boost Latin American self-consciousness was miscegenation.

Vasconcelos was well aware of the fact that the white Latin American elite had a long tradition of modelling itself according to Western standards and was, thus, vulnerable to racial theories on the alleged inferiority of non-whites and dangerous consequences of racial mixture. During a trip to Brazil in 1865, for instance, the prominent Swiss-American biologist Louis Agassiz had warned that 'anyone who doubts the evil of this mixture of races, and is inclined, from a mistaken philanthropy, to break down all barriers between them', should come to Brazil. There, Agassiz claimed, they would personally witness 'the deterioration consequent upon an amalgamation of races'.[4] Some Latin American scholars, however, spoke out in favour of *blanqueamiento*, whitewashing through miscegenation. Although they too

[4] Louis Agassiz, *A Journey in Brazil* (Chur, Switzerland: Plata Publishing, 1975 [1896]), p. 293.

carried forward negative stereotypes and subsequent stigmas associated with blacks and Native Americans, they assumed that through a process of miscegenation all 'primitive elements' would slowly but steadily disappear, allowing a general whitening of Latin American society. Brazilian scholar João Batista de Lacerda (1846–1915), for instance, claimed in 1912 that, if only his country would promote miscegenation, Brazil could make its black population disappear entirely by 2012.[5]

Although Vasconcelos's ideas on race built on earlier theories on *blanqueamiento*, they differed in one important point. In an essay called *La raza cósmica* (*The Cosmic Race*) (1925), Vasconcelos no longer looked at miscegenation from a negative or neutral perspective, as an emergency measure to deal with a racial and/or social problem, but rather from an (excessively) positive perspective, as the basis of a higher, superior form of civilization.

In order to understand Vasconcelos's essay, it is important to note that it was written at a time when the ideas of the German philosopher Friedrich Nietzsche (1844–1900) strongly influenced academic scholarship. Similar to that of many other scholars of his time, Vasconcelos's work was influenced by Nietzschean concepts from *The Birth of Tragedy* (1872) and *Thus Spoke Zarathustra* (1885),[6] such as the struggle between primitive/irrational, 'Dionysian', and civilized/rational, 'Apollonian', elements, as well as the announcement of the *Übermensch*, the 'new man' or 'overman', who rejects mediocrity and, by rising above common notions of good and evil, achieves a superior form of life. Of particular importance to Latin American intellectuals like Vasconcelos were Nietzsche's ideas on racial mixture. Nietzsche's opinion on cultural and racial mixture is rather complex, and his use of the word 'race' is confusing. While it mostly refers to a community of people, a *Volk*, or a civilization, Nietzsche sometimes also used the term 'race' in a biological sense. In *Daybreak* (1881), for instance, he described multi-racial people by repeating the type of stereotypes one could find in the racial theories of his time – 'Crossed races always mean at the same time crossed cultures, crossed moralities; they are usually more evil, crueler, more restless'. Yet, according to Nietzsche, out of a disharmonious mixture, a new 'race'

[5] Thomas E. Skidmore, *Black into White: Race and Nationality in Brazilian Thought* (New York: Oxford University Press, 1974), p. 67.

[6] Friedrich Nietzsche, *The Birth of Tragedy and Other Writings*, ed. by Raymond Geuss, trans. by Ronald Speirs (Cambridge: Cambridge University Press, 1999). Friedrich Nietzsche, *Thus Spoke Zarathustra: A Book for All and None*, ed. by Adrian Del Caro and Robert B. Pippin, trans. by Adrian Del Caro (Cambridge: Cambridge University Press, 2006).

could develop, which ended up being superior to the original ones involved in the process of miscegenation. This required, however, a process of purification: 'In the end, however, if the process of purification is successful, all that energy formerly expended in the struggle of the dissonant qualities with one another will stand at the command of the total organism: which is why races that have become pure have always also become stronger and more beautiful'. Nietzsche's reference to purification should, thus, not be misunderstood as a desire to prevent mixture or as an appeal to remove foreign elements in order to preserve purity. Rather, he warned that the positive results of mixture are not automatically present. Mixtures first cause disharmony, which needs to be overcome by 'countless adaptations, absorptions and secretions'. Only after a long process of successful re-harmonization, which he called 'purification', could a superior 'race' originate from mixture. Nietzsche referred to classical Greece as a prime example of such a superior 'race' resulting from miscegenation: 'The Greeks offer us the model of a race and culture that has become pure'. So, when Nietzsche expressed the hope that, one day, a pure European 'race' would come into existence – 'hopefully we shall one day also achieve a pure European race' – this notion of purity should not be misunderstood as a rejection of mixture, but rather as the final result of a process of re-harmonization.[7]

Vasconcelos made an eclectic use of Nietzschean concepts, using some, rejecting others. While Nietzsche's *Übermensch* had remained an abstract notion, Vasconcelos decided to concretize the concept in the shape of the multi-racial man or, as he called it, the 'cosmic race'. Moreover, he added a third, Catholic/Christian, element of love and fraternity to the Nietzschean model in order to soften the latter's aggressiveness. Mixing Nietzschean philosophy with Christian humanism, Vasconcelos constructed a specifically Latin American approach to modernity and cultural identity.

His essay *The Cosmic Race* begins with a list of civilizations in the history of humankind, which he concludes with ancient Greece. Like Nietzsche, Vasconcelos claimed that this 'superior' Greek civilization resulted from a process of cultural and ethnic mixture. From Greece, then, European civilization developed and used its strength to conquer other parts of the world, including the Americas. Borrowing Nietzsche's metaphor of man serving as a bridge leading to the *Übermensch*, he compared the Iberian colonizers in America to 'a bridge', laying the 'moral and material basis for the union of all men into a fifth universal race'. Vasconcelos described the history of Iberian

[7] Friedrich Nietzsche, *Daybreak: Thoughts on the Prejudices of Morality*, ed. by M. Clark and B. Leiter, trans. by R.J. Hollingdale (Cambridge: Cambridge University Press, 1997), p. 149.

colonization of Latin America as a process that began in a Dionysian manner – 'Will is power, blind power running after ambiguous ends ... directed by appetite which uses it for all its whims' – but was later complemented with Apollonian elements – 'Then, reason shines her light, the will is refrained by duty and takes shape into logical thinking' – and will eventually reach its height through the inclusion of a third, Christian-mythical, aesthetic element: 'Logic does not suffice and the will takes on the wings of fantasy. ... It expands into harmony and ascends into the creative mystery of melody ... it becomes passion of beauty'. Once softened by this spiritual, Christian-aesthetic element, he predicted that miscegenation will no longer occur as a physical necessity – as a 'base instinct' – but as the result of curiosity, taste, and love. Society will then no longer be based on norms and rules, but on 'constant inspiration' and will progress 'beyond good and evil' in order to 'live joy grounded on love'. Vasconcelos ended by prophesizing that from Latin America, a new, consciously multi-racial people will spread all over the globe and, with their nomadic impetus, will enable the global advancement towards a superior, 'cosmic' race. This 'cosmic race' will be marked by a superior morality that will overcome all racial prejudices, which ultimately will lead to universal brotherhood.[8]

Later in life, Vasconcelos expressed doubts whether the *mestizo* (mixed-race Latin American) did, in fact, form the basis for a superior society. Deeply disappointed with the social and political reality in Mexico after he failed to become elected as president in 1929, Vasconcelos began to question his own theory. Cynically, he now referred to *mestizos* as the 'comic' instead of 'cosmic' race and, in 1939, even replaced his effusive praise of miscegenation with ideas similar to the white supremacist and anti-Semitic ideology of Nazism.[9]

Despite his own disappointment over the concept, Vasconcelos's essay *The Cosmic Race* had a tremendous influence on major works in Latin American sociology, philosophy, and literature such as Octavio Paz's magnum opus *The Labyrinth of Solitude* (1950).[10] Ironically, the same man who in the final years of his life had sympathized with anti-Semitism even became celebrated by the United Nations Educational, Scientific and Cultural Organization (UNESCO) as the 'father' of a multi-racial diversity model that in the aftermath of the

[8] José Vasconcelos, *The Cosmic Race/La raza cósmica*, ed. and trans. by D.T. Jaén (Baltimore: The Johns Hopkins University Press, 1979), pp. 9, 19, 29–31.

[9] Marilyn G. Millar, *Rise and Fall of the Cosmic Race: The Cult of* Mestizaje *in Latin America* (Austin: University of Texas Press, 2004), p. 44.

[10] Octavio Paz, *The Labyrinth of Solitude; The Other Mexico; Return to the Labyrinth of Solitude; Mexico and the United States; The Philanthropic Ogre*, trans. by Lysander Kemp, Yara Milos, and Rachel Phillips Belash (New York: Grove Press, 1985).

Second World War was perceived as a strategy to combat policies of racial segregation all over the world. Not by accident, the holiday celebrated as Columbus Day in the United States is known in most Latin American countries as Día de la Raza. In the United States, the Latinx advocacy group La Raza was named after Vasconcelos's essay until it adopted a new name, UnidosUS, in 2017.

Starting in the 1960s, however, Vasconcelos's vision presented in *The Cosmic Race* faced increasing criticism. This should not be surprising considering that Vasconcelos's laudatory portrayal of the Iberian colonizers of America was at odds with the new norms and values of post-colonial modernity. His essay became seen by some as a Eurocentric and neo-colonialist theory rather than a model for world peace. They claimed that *The Cosmic Race* continued to affirm the superiority of the (white) Iberian model of civilization, which corresponded to the existing power structure on the Latin American continent since the sixteenth century and, therefore, criticized his essay as the perfect model to legitimize the power structure dominated by the traditional elites. The growing concern for minority rights and the diversity model that grew out of the Civil Rights Movement in the United States also provoked critical questions about Vasconcelos's theory. Considering the fact that white people continue to be vastly overrepresented in positions of political power and economic influence in Latin America, Vasconcelos's model of a multi-racial and colour-blind society came to be seen as a sleep-inducing fairy tale rather than a combative model of revolutionary change. Accordingly, some suggested that Vasconcelos's essay might have contributed more to conservative thought than to progressive ideology in Latin America.[11]

The lack of awareness about the strong impact Nietzsche had on the development of Vasconcelos's diversity concept based on miscegenation might explain why scholars have traditionally displayed a tendency to either assess or criticize the oppressive, elitist nature of his ideas, but not to explain their origin. When taking into consideration the strong Nietzschean influence on his work, it is by no means a coincidence that Vasconcelos's concept clashed with the new norms and values of post-colonial modernity. Not surprisingly, Ilan Stavans concluded that Vasconcelos's ideas in *The Cosmic Race* 'have a Nietzschean echo that suspiciously relates them to the misguided theories on the superiority of the Aryan race advanced by Adolf Hitler in Germany in the 1930s'.[12] In fact, Vasconcelos's theory of the advent of the 'cosmic race' not

[11] Christina A. Sue, *Land of the Cosmic Race: Race Mixture, Racism, and Blackness in Mexico* (Oxford: Oxford University Press, 2013), pp. 15–16.

[12] Ilan Stavans, *José Vasconcelos: The Prophet of Race* (New Brunswick: Rutgers University Press, 2011), p. xii.

only contains parallels with the work of Nietzsche in its conception but also in the diametrically opposing views – a revolutionary model of social change according to some, dangerous conservative backlash according to others – in its reception.

The transcultural analysis of miscegenation that I presented in this article, connecting North and Latin America to German philosophy, shows how complex and challenging reflections on emotionally charged topics of race and racial mixture can be. In a world shaped by globalization, however, where increasing numbers of young people live an international life, it is only natural that attitudes about miscegenation will continue to evolve, which inevitably will force societies to rethink the existing racial categories based on the traditional ethno-racial pentagon (Asian, Hispanic, White, Black, and Native American). Whether the discussion on race will evolve in a similar direction as that on gender and sexuality, where traditional boundaries have become blurred, and fluid rather than static definitions have become the new norm, remains to be seen. What I hopefully was able to make clear in this article, however, is that the concept of miscegenation carries a dark history of racism and that, regardless of which way the discussion on racial mixture moves in the years to come, this history cannot and should not be forgotten.

Jeroen Dewulf is Queen Beatrix Professor in the Department of German and Dutch Studies at the University of California, Berkeley.

# 25

# Multi-lingualism

*Hilary Footitt*

## Challenging Language-silent Disciplines

'International' as a descriptor of academic disciplines – 'International Business', 'International Relations' – has seldom implied any sustained scholarly engagement with the multi-lingualism of international spaces. In this essay, I want to take as an example one particular academic area, International Relations/Development Studies, in order to discuss how Modern Languages research, an engagement with the fact of multi-lingualism, enriches and extends our understanding of the 'international' in this discipline. Much of the material to which I shall be referring is taken from a research project on 'The Listening Zones of NGOs: Languages and Cultural Knowledge in Development Programmes'.[1]

International Relations (IR) has historically had only a slight interest in the presence of diverse languages in its spaces of enquiry. The historic focus of the discipline on the state and the use of force, and the value attached to 'objectivity' through empirical positivism, have left little room for the study of language or individual agents. 'A history of silence has marked the issue of language in IR', argues Fierke. 'There is often a desire on the part of IR scholars to ignore or deny its role [...] the subjects of political analysis are presumed to be mute'.[2]

[1] The Listening Zones of NGOs: Languages and Cultural Knowledge in Development Programmes, <www.reading.ac.uk/modern-languages-and-european-studies/Research/mles-listening-zones-of-ngos.aspx> [accessed 31 January 2022].

[2] Karen Marie Fierke, 'Breaking the Silence: Language and Method in International Relations', in *Language, Agency and Politics*, ed. by François Debrix (New York: Routledge, 2003), pp. 66–86 (p. 67).

NGOs (non-governmental organizations) working in international aid and development are of course operating across national and linguistic borders, 'in, above, and between the traditional "container spaces" of national societies'.[3] But here too, while the role of language mediation may sometimes be mentioned as part of information and data collection, languages are largely absent from the key texts of development.

How can methods drawn from Modern Languages research challenge this language-indifferent sector with the radical relevance of multi-lingualism? A first step in this endeavour, I would argue, involves re-imagining the spaces of international encounter as what Mary Louise Pratt calls 'contact zones': 'the space and time where subjects previously separated by geography and history are co-present, the point at which their trajectories now intersect'.[4] Such a re-imagining shifts attention towards the interactive, the relational, focusing on how Pratt's 'co-presence, interaction, interlocking understandings and practices [...] often within radically asymmetrical relations of power' actually affect the actors involved, how all parties 'on the ground' learn from the intercultural 'contact zones' of intervention. In this sense, international encounters in any discipline are inevitably multi-lingual and transnational. They are sites of hybridity whose borders are uneasy and uncertain, shaped by history, by representations of space, and by the shifting dynamics of relationships on the ground, what Phipps calls 'the mess of human relatedness in languages'.[5]

## Temporality

In International Development, there has been a tendency to adopt a resolutely presentist perspective, seeing history in a short timeframe, largely within the functional needs of a particular development project, normally termed in this case 'evaluation' and 'feedback'. An approach that focuses on the multi-lingualism of the contact zones necessarily engages with what we might describe as the language histories of those who are meeting: 'The past, written into history and recalled as memory, is an essential part of identity, whether individual or organisational. It offers a way of structuring and explaining

[3] Dennis Dijkzeul, 'Transnational Humanitarian NGOs? A Progress Report', in *Rethinking Transnationalism. The Meso-link*, ed. by Ludger Pries (Abingdon: Routledge, 2008), pp. 80–103 (p. 80).

[4] Mary Louise Pratt, *Imperial Eyes. Travel Writing and Transculturation* (Abingdon: Routledge, 2008), p. 8.

[5] Alison Phipps, *Learning the Arts of Linguistic Survival. Languaging, Tourism, Life* (Clevedon: Multilingual Matters, 2007), p. 26.

the values we hold ... history shapes how we think, not just what we think'.[6] International Development NGOs have their own languages history, revealed in public and private archives, and in the personal accounts of staff, and this history establishes the starting points and attitudes that will create the ground of contemporary transnational meetings.

The archives of an international NGO like Oxfam GB tell the story of an organization that always sought to be multi-cultural in the more than forty countries in which it has worked, but that has traditionally placed this imperative within an implicit framework of monolingualism. Historically, the dilemma faced by Oxfam was indeed that of a growing global organization that wanted at the same time to foster narrative plurality and local autonomy: 'We would expect each region to have its own flavour and distinctive configuration of programme/ skills/ size/ spread/etc. However, it is essential to the success of Oxfam's Globalisation project [...] that the staff of every Region feel and behave primarily as part of a larger whole, as part of a global Oxfam, rather than primarily as part of a local Oxfam'.[7] In 1990, the process of consulting Oxfam staff throughout the world on the direction that a globalized and regionalized Oxfam should be taking showed how difficult it actually was for the institution to hear voices that were not anglophone. In the first place, there was a major cultural problem in assuming that Western-derived concepts of strategic planning could be uncritically translated into a variety of different regional contexts. Consultative documents for Oxfam's Strategic Review were not accessible to many of those working with Oxfam worldwide. While some papers had been translated into French and Spanish, others were not: 'many teams did not work in English, and this meant translating the draft plans into English, translating comments on the draft, re-drafting in the original language, working on the document, and then re-translating it'.[8] Given how complex much of the material was, ownership of the translation tended to rest with senior staff whose first language was English.

While consultative staff workshops might claim that Oxfam was a multilingual organization with English as its primary language, the records of the institution make clear that there was in fact no shared idea as to what this implied for Oxfam's working practices across the world. This sort of engagement with historic attitudes to multi-lingualism, mapping the cultural history of dialogue between communities, provides us with a rich

[6] Eleanor Davey and Kim Scriven, 'Humanitarian Aid in the Archives: Introduction', *Disasters*, 39.S2 (2017), 113–28.

[7] Bodleian Library Oxford (hereafter MS Oxfam) PRG 2/1/1 International Division Strategic Plan, 1999–2004.

[8] MS Oxfam PRG 1/13/7, Planning and Evaluation Unit, June 1991.

and nuanced understanding of particular and often unquestioned ways of working that are adopted today. The languages history of Oxfam GB is a highly relevant hinterland establishing the contemporary contact zones of the NGO across the world.

## Spatiality

Reimagining the contact zones of transnational encounter also implies challenging traditional representations of spatiality, above all refusing to accept the nation-state as the necessarily primary unit of analysis, and, with this, the related inference that meetings concern homogeneous and culturally antithetical groups. In Modern Languages research, it is a given that spaces are multi-vocal and that this multi-vocalism radically affects activities and perceptions. In International Relations, the humanitarian/development space has at different times been represented as a third space in which humanitarian agencies can work, a space of vulnerability for affected communities, a space governed by international law, and a politico-military bunkerized space. Modern Languages research, however, would argue that we should re-imagine this development space as multi-lingual and see multi-lingualism as a constitutive component of development relations.

Of course, the English word 'development' itself brings with it a set of preconceptions closely related to a specifically anglophone lexis, *Buzzwords and Fuzzwords*,[9] which seldom have an equivalent in the communities in which NGOs work. In development projects, this vocabulary is often adopted in the form of foreign loan-words, in inverted commas as it were. Assumptions about the power of the English language in aid and development have anyway been widespread, particularly among those government donors who are increasingly major actors in the contact zones. The linkage between the teaching of English and modernization and development is one that has been repeated by British policymakers over the years, despite the fact that there is little evidence that such a link actually exists.[10] For the UK Government, English has tended to be framed as a global language, an international lingua franca, not exclusively associated with a particular country or culture, but

[9] Andrea Cornwall and Deborah Eade, *Deconstructing Development Discourse. Buzzwords and Fuzzwords* (Rugby: Practical Action Publishing with Oxfam GB, 2010), <https://oxfamilibrary.openrepository.com/bitstream/handle/10546/118173/bk-deconstructing-development-buzzwords-010910-en.pdf?sequence=1> [accessed 31 January 2022].

[10] Hywel Coleman, *The English Language in Development* (London: British Council, 2010).

one that crucially represents an admission to a modern, advanced way of life. English is implicitly positioned in development as a means of enabling access to the latest innovations in science and technology, key for communities that seek to transition from predominantly rural economies to a more advanced society. In this development space, multi-lingualism, the existence of other languages, has been traditionally regarded (implicitly as well as explicitly) as an obstacle to progress. In British government donor circles, the development space is marked out by an accepted equivalence between effective aid delivery and monolingualism.

The space of development is, however, one formed by multi-lingualism, and this has major repercussions on the ways in which shared activities take place. Clinton Robinson, in an early examination of language use in rural areas in Africa,[11] argued persuasively that in these contact zones the languages used to discuss development are indeed a key factor in power relations on the ground, particularly in perceiving where development is coming from, and who has ultimate responsibility for it. As Robinson suggests, one of the difficulties in these development relations is actually translating 'development'. In Nugunu, the phrase 'nnúgie gɛɔyɔ' (change of life) was being used, but this was taken by Nugunu speakers to mean 'baptism' or 'spiritual life', and had to be further glossed with 'life of the family, of the village'. Robinson's conclusion was that people who spoke Nugunu in the community in Cameroon in which he worked were overwhelmingly likely to see development as coming from the outside, from white men and Europe, whereas those who spoke French would more easily assign responsibility to local people or to the national government.

This multi-vocal space is thus one in which power relationships are played out linguistically, and in which disparate understandings of the business in hand coexist, often unacknowledged by those ostensibly working on an agreed common endeavour. Imagining spaces as multi-lingual is not an incidental extra, but rather a key factor in mapping diverse assumptions and beginning to engage with the hard task of actually working together.

## Relationality

Modern Languages research is crucially interested in the relations of the transnational, in exchanges and traces, in mutual two-way learning. In this relationality, 'translation' in the sense that Ricoeur uses it, is key to the dynamic, positing a broad ontology of exchange as a paradigm for

[11] Clinton Robinson, *Language Use in Rural Development. An African Perspective* (Berlin and New York: Mouton de Gruyter, 1996).

transnational relations. 'Translation' for Ricoeur is not just a means of communication, but also, and above all, an ethic of exchange, one that replaces any utopic illusion of perfection – as in a 'perfect translation' – with a desire to translate or understand, to engage with the other and, through this engagement, to obtain a broader understanding of oneself. Ricoeur calls this process 'linguistic hospitality': 'Linguistic hospitality [...] is the act of inhabiting the word of the Other paralleled by the act of receiving the word of the Other into one's own home, one's own dwelling'.[12] The notion of translation as an activist performance, situating intercultural openness within a process of mutual exchange, potentially moves our research focus towards a paradigm of conversation, transnational exchange, and narrative plurality, to the ways in which we negotiate 'troubled identifications in order to facilitate cross-cultural communication'.[13] Linguistic hospitality, naming 'foreign others' in their own languages and terms, depends of course on a willingness to cede some measure of control, to accept that there are other ways of being and doing.

The example of Oxfam GB is instructive here. Despite its occasional organizational difficulties, traces of the transnational, of the foreignness of overseas encounters, entered both linguistically and culturally into Oxfam's institutional debates. One of the clearest and most striking examples of this was the alternative language of development spoken in Latin America and Brazil from the 1970s onwards. Oxfam's commitment in Latin America and Brazil at a time of tremendous religious and social ferment, and the lively participation of its Spanish- and Portuguese-speaking representatives, brought a strikingly different foreign development lexicon into the centre of Oxfam's discussions and practices. During this period, Oxfam said it was harmonizing its thinking with progressive Brazilian and Latin American thinkers like Paulo Freire and Gustavo Gutiérrez whose work was then being translated into English. Vocabulary like '*concientización*' in Spanish or '*conscientização*' in Portuguese were widely used in committees and reports. This foreign lexicon was then transferred to Oxfam's activities in other continents, with field directors in Asia being provided with helpful crib sheets: 'In case you are as confused as some of us here have been by some of the ideas coming from Latin America, I am enclosing a copy of a brief and fairly succinct explanation of conscientization ...'[14]

[12] Paul Ricoeur, *On Translation*, trans. by E. Brennan (London: Routledge, 2006), pp. 19–20.

[13] Krista Ratcliffe, *Rhetorical Listening. Identification, Gender, Whiteness* (Carbondale: Southern Illinois Press, 2005), p. 17.

[14] MS Oxfam PRG 2/2/1 Harris to Asian Field Directors, 26 November 1973.

In the case of ex-colonial countries where English was still an official language, it took rather longer for the mutuality of aid relationships to be translated into Oxfam's discussions and decision-making. The process was spurred on by the agency's need to find conduits of aid that were manifestly independent both of local government control, and of overt ex-patriate interference. In Malawi, for example, to avoid dealing with the repressive Hastings Banda government, Oxfam worked with the University of Malawi Centre for Social Research whose academics undertook major projects on their behalf, involving Malawian researchers staying in villages for four months, with a training programme to help assistants explain activities to their communities in Chichewa. This initiative employed local languages as a means of sharing development responsibility: 'a process which enables people to take more control of their lives'.[15] In the wake of these changes, Malawian languages and concepts began to appear within Oxfam institutional documents in the 1990s. Future programme plans noted the range of languages spoken by the majority of Malawians, as opposed to the small number of people who spoke English, and reports on Oxfam activity included quotations in Chichewa – '*Mutu umodzi susenza denga*' (one head cannot carry a roof) – together with discussions of Malawian/Chichewa formulations of leadership.[16]

## Hearing Voices within the Meta Narratives

Modern Languages research can also challenge and subvert some of the broader narratives that are commonly used to frame transnational relationality by allowing the voices of the diverse actors themselves to sound more clearly through their own media – novels, poetry, art, performance, social media, and so on. In the copious literature on development, discussions of transnational meetings have largely been positioned within meta-discourses of postcolonial/subaltern studies that tend to describe development as a hegemonic monolithic enterprise, driven by central control that destroys, rather than respects and learns from, local knowledges and cultures.[17] Despite more recent anthropologically focused attempts to examine the

[15] Roy Trivedy, *Action Research in Southern Malawi*, Oxfam Research Paper (Oxford: Oxfam Publications, 1990), p. vii.

[16] MS Oxfam PRG 3/8/10 Malawi Strategic Plan 1996–99, 26 November 1996, comments 5 March 1998.

[17] Arturo Escobar, 'Anthropologie et développement', *Revue Internationale des Sciences Sociales*, 154 (1997), pp. 539–59; *Discourses of Development: Anthropological Perspectives*, ed. by R. Grillo and L. Stirrat (Oxford: Berg, 1997).

role of individual NGO actors in development relationships,[18] much of this research engages with an analysis of Western/neo-liberal discourses at an institutional level.[19] More recently, however, there has been a move to develop this postcolonial scholarship by theorizing power, 'at the intersections of communicative processes, messages, and structures',[20] as a means of hearing previously silenced voices. This starting point can potentially help us to move debates on transnational relationships beyond monolithic homogeneous postcolonial frameworks towards a greater engagement with the personal experiences of those living through these meetings on the ground, allowing, in Mona Baker's terms, 'for the de-personalized persons of theory [...] to be understood as separate persons [...] with singular sets of characteristics, including but not confined to their political context and/or group identity'.[21]

Juan Javier Rivera Andía, for example, explored how Quechua-speaking highland Peruvians dealing with a transnational mining project in their lands actually represented and characterized their unequal relationships.[22] To do this, he examined the ways in which perceptions of the mining project were expressed through religious and cultural rituals in the community. Rivera's argument is that Quechua understandings of '*pobreza*' (poverty), the label that government and development agencies routinely used to describe this group, are hotly contested by the people themselves. Indigenous rituals, rather than being remnants of a traditional culture, are in fact crucial voices conveying the reactions of their communities to the situation in which they find themselves today. Through folk competitions and religious rituals, Rivera maintains, indigenous voices can be heard that critique and subvert dominant, and apparently consensus, official discourses.

[18] D. Lewis, 'Tidy Concepts, Messy Lives: Defining Tensions in the Domestic and Overseas Careers of UK Non-Governmental Professionals', in *Adventures in Aidland. The Anthropology of Professionals in International Development*, ed. by D. Mosse (New York and Oxford: Berghahn, 2011), pp. 177–97; S. Roth, *The Paradoxes of Aid Work. Passionate Professionals* (London and New York: Routledge, 2017).

[19] Jean-Pierre Olivier de Sardan, *Anthropology and Development. Understanding Contemporary Social Change*, trans. by A. Tidjani Alou (London and New York: Zed Books, 2005).

[20] Mohan Jyoti Dutta, 'A Culture-Centred Approach to Listening: Voices of Social Change', *The International Journal of Listening*, 28.2, (2014), 67–81 (p. 74).

[21] Mona Baker, *Translation and Conflict. A Narrative Account* (London and New York: Routledge, 2006), p. 3.

[22] Juan Javier Rivera Andía, 'Ritual, Folk Competitions, Mining and Stigmatization as "Poor" in Indigenous Northern Peru: A Perspective from Contemporary Quechua-speaking Cañarenses', *Revista de Ciencia Política* (Santiago), 37.3 (2017), 767–86.

## Conclusion

Re-imagining international encounters as multi-lingual, I am arguing, employs some of the unique insights of Modern Languages research, that is:

- the belief that identities are formed over time, that the languages history of groups plays a major role in their present-day relations and activities
- that spaces of encounter are multi-vocal and that this fact of multi-lingualism affects perceptions of 'the other', and conditions activities and relationships
- that relationships involve potential learning and transfers of knowledge, linguistic hospitality, where the ways in which 'the others' name their lives reaches over the borders of our own lives and helps to reshape them
- paying particular attention to the voices of individuals, beyond framings and meta narratives, insisting on listening to these voices in their own terms and within their own media.

Modern Languages research challenges language-silent disciplines to engage with temporality, spatiality, and relationality in wholly different ways and, in so doing, to find their discipline challenged just as our own discipline of Modern Languages has been so productively and uncomfortably challenged over the past few years.

Hilary Footitt is Research Professor in European Studies at the University of Reading.

# 26

# Performance

*Julia Prest*

Performance and Performance Studies are broad fields that encompass a vast array of phenomena, ranging from formal public theatre and improvised street dance to the Olympic Games, selfies, and even, according to some critics, modern terrorist activity.[1] Here I shall focus on theatre in performance. One of the defining characteristics of performance is the emphasis on the spectator or audience. Bennett notes that 'a performance can activate a diversity of responses, but it is the audience which finally ascribes meaning and usefulness to any cultural product'.[2] The 'meaning' of a performance is not fixed; rather it depends on and is partly created by the audience, both as a group and as a set of individuals. Indeed, performance is as much about experience as it is about meaning; performance is experienced by the audience who then ascribe meaning to what they have experienced. Another defining feature of performance is the relatively modest role that is played by the text. France's most famous playwright, Molière (1622–1673), offered some sage advice for individuals reading play texts in the preamble to the published edition of his comedy-ballet, *L'Amour médecin*: 'On sait bien que les comédies ne sont faites que pour être jouées, et je ne conseille de lire celle-ci qu'aux personnes qui ont des yeux pour découvrir, dans la lecture, tout le jeu du théâtre'.[3]

[1] Richard Schechner, *Performance Studies: An Introduction*, 3rd edn (London: Routledge, 2013), pp. 270–80.

[2] Susan Bennett, *Theatre Audiences: A Theory of Production and Reception*, 2nd edn (London: Routledge, 1997), p. 156.

[3] We know that plays are only written to be performed, and I would advise that only people who have the eyes to discern, when reading, the whole art of the theatre, read this one.

Molière's 'tout le jeu du théâtre' can be understood to encompass everything that is included in a performance in addition to the written text, such as the actors' bodies, their movements and gestures, their speech, the stage set, the lighting, the musical score and danced choreography, and the audience response as it unfolds in real time. One of the biggest challenges for students and scholars of performance is that we are often required to produce text-based accounts of non-text-based phenomena. Modern technology has been a boon to contemporary Performance Studies in recent years, making sources such as audiovisual recordings more readily available than ever before. Those of us who work on the pre-modern era must continue to follow Molière's advice in the absence of such materials.

Transnational performance arises – or can arise – when people and works move across perceived national boundaries. Transnational performance as I understand it here is different from other kinds of international performance. The distinction lies with the nature and response to the interaction as two or more cultures come into contact. Many international performances, be they theatrical or social, result in the experience of cultural dissonance (the discomfort felt by the spectator or performer when encountering something alien) or of bemused interest. When this jarring is left hanging, the performance is not transnational; when, on the other hand, the jarring leads to the creation, deliberate or otherwise, of a new kind of performance, this may be described as transnational.

To illustrate this important but admittedly rather slippery distinction, I shall use an example taken from Japanese performance culture in the form of the *kakegoe*, words (often the guild name of the actor) shouted out by well-trained audience members during Kabuki performances. Western visitors to Japan often report that they experience these interventions as unwelcome heckling (interestingly, the *kakegoe* may have their origins in heckling practices that took place during the flower festivals of Middle Japan). Meanwhile, from the performer's perspective, the lack of *kakegoe* when Kabuki troupes go on foreign tours 'can seriously unsettle the performers'.[4] If this unsettling does not produce a creative response, then one might not speak of transnationalism, only of internationalism and cultural dissonance. On the other hand, the fact that the *absence* of *kakegoe* does not unsettle the local audience *outside Japan* suggests that a transnational element may be emerging in the form of a new way of responding to Kabuki, even if it is unintended. For some, this kind of transnationalism threatens the alleged 'purity' of the form; for others who believe that performance – like language – is a living and organic phenomenon in a constant

[4] Robert Cohen, *Theatre*, 5th edn (Mountain View, CA: Mayfield, 2000), p. 175.

state of flux and development, such evolutions are inevitable and often desirable.

## Theatre and Performance in Colonial Saint-Domingue

The remainder of this short essay will be devoted to an examination of theatrical performance in the former French slave colony of Saint-Domingue (present-day Haiti) in the late eighteenth century. While transnational Saint-Dominguan performances will be celebrated up to a point, this is in no way intended to justify the fact that they all reflect a broadly colonial viewpoint.

The public theatres in Saint-Domingue were set up to bring a bit of France to displaced citizens living in their country's most lucrative colony. Announcements in the press detailing upcoming performances in, particularly, the towns of Port-au-Prince and Cap-Français (now Cap-Haïtien) sometimes liken them to earlier performances in France's major cities, especially Paris and Bordeaux. As dozens of plays, opéras-comiques, and opéras-ballets were transported across the Atlantic for performance in the colonial Caribbean, one can certainly speak of a *transatlantic* tradition of French theatre, but its status as transnational needs some unpicking. Theatre in Saint-Domingue was aimed principally at a French audience and Saint-Domingue was a French colony, so one might argue that we are dealing with something that presented itself as a *national* theatre tradition. However, a number of factors would suggest otherwise, the most important of which being the process of theatre production, the composition of the theatre audience, and the emergence of local theatrical forms.

## Theatre Production and 'National' Status

As we have seen, theatre productions in Saint-Domingue often claimed to be like theatre productions in metropolitan France, but often the only element that was physically transported from one side of the Atlantic to the other was the text of a play or the libretto and score of an opera. If and when the theatre text arrived safely in Saint-Domingue, this was only one element in the process of creating a new performance. The remaining elements had to be built up using local resources. While those did sometimes include the occasional actor visiting from France, or even costumes and stage properties from France, the majority of the materials of the production (the stage sets, the lighting, the costumes, the stage itself, the playhouse, the people who built the playhouse, and so forth) were local. More importantly, the process of putting together the production was entirely local even if it sometimes drew on the occasional memory of an individual who had attended the theatre in

France. In short, the work was rehearsed, developed, performed, and received in Saint-Domingue: it was both global and local or, to use an anachronistic term, glocal.

This putting together of the many elements of a theatre performance using a combination of French sources and local resources chimes with Vertovec's account of 'syncretism, creolization, bricolage, cultural translation and hybridity' and with Rosenau's 'distant proximities'.[5] More specifically, the process of theatre production drew on the works and talents of metropolitan French and Creole (Creole in this context meaning local or Caribbean) individuals, including free people of colour, as well as, occasionally, in the theatre orchestra, the enslaved population.

While the metropolitan and Creole French were citizens within the nation state of France, their geographical distance from the seat of that nation set them apart. And, of course, it was widely understood that individuals born in metropolitan France were more French than French Creoles (and that Creoles who had visited France were more French than those who had not). A sense of one's belonging to a nation thus varied from one group to another and from one individual to another. It is perhaps useful here to think in terms of 'theatrical citizenship', which, according to McKinnie, 'has often been conceived in more communitarian ways, either in contradistinction from the national state, or in opposition to it'.[6] While, as will be seen below, the theatre community in Saint-Domingue perpetuated social division and was not as communitarian as McKinnie's model, this separation of formal nationhood from a sense of theatrical belonging remains useful.

## The Theatre Audience and Social Status

Although theatre began in Saint-Domingue as a white, colonial activity, performed by and for French people nostalgic for life in the metropole, the increasingly business-like nature of the public theatre combined with the expanding numbers of free people of colour in the colony (many of whom were wealthy land and slave-owners) led to the admittance to the playhouse of a small number of non-white, not fully French audience members. With the admittance of the free people of colour came segregation on the basis of

[5] For an exposition of these theoretical points in this volume, see Bond, 'Stories', pp. 280–81.

[6] Michael McKinnie, 'Performing the Civic Transnational: Cultural Production, Governance and Citizenship in Contemporary London', in *Performance and the City*, ed. by D.J. Hopkins, Shelley Orr and Kim Solga (London: Palgrave, 2009), pp. 110–27 (123).

racial ancestry. There was no designated area for enslaved people, but they accompanied their masters to the playhouse and may have stayed for some performances. Although segregation by ticket price is a familiar feature of the traditional playhouse to this day, the racialized approach to segregation in France's Caribbean colonies sets its performance context apart from that of metropolitan France in some significant ways.

Some manuscript documents from 1780 arguing in favour of the founding of a new playhouse in Saint-Pierre in the French Caribbean colony of Martinique offer further insights into the social performance dimension of attending the theatre. The 'Mémoire Concernant l'Etablissement d'un Spectacle à St-Pierre de la Martinique' (1780), tells of 'les avantages sans nombre qui résultent du spectacle' (the innumerable advantages that spring from the theatre) and specifically of the effect of theatre on social behaviour (*les mœurs*). While it is acknowledged that the previous theatre in Saint-Pierre had been badly run, the authors of the document insist on its positive, visible effects on the local population. They claim that island-born whites, who had been subject to the much-feared phenomenon of degeneration 'y ont puisé tout à coup de l'énergie, le gout et l'ardeur de s'instruire, tellement que plusieurs aujourd'hui se distinguent avec avantage parmi leurs concitoyens' (promptly found in the theatre the energy, inclination and drive to better themselves, so much so that many among them are seen today to outshine their fellow citizens). As for the free people of colour in the theatre audience, the authors claim that they have lost 'la barbarie de leur origine, se policent et prennent des mœurs' (their original barbarity, police themselves and behave better). They even predict, rather hyperbolically, that with the help of the theatre, in a few years' time the only difference between those people born on the island and those born in metropolitan France will be the climate. In Martinique as in Saint-Domingue, there was, then, a sense that the theatre audience went to the playhouse to learn how to perform their roles as full French citizens. Theatrical citizenship could, it is suggested, lead to national citizenship. While this idea attempts to shift theatre in Saint-Domingue back towards a would-be national tradition, the very fact that the audience's Frenchness is in question owing to the risk of degeneration in the stifling heat of the Caribbean supports my contention that this was a form of transnational theatre.

## New Theatrical Forms

Further evidence of the transnational lies in the creation and performance of a small number of new theatrical works that draw on local influences. Extant examples are rare, but two will serve to illustrate this phenomenon here: first, an anonymous three-act comedy in French called *Les Veuves créoles*

(The Creole Widows) and, second, a Creole-language parody inspired by Rousseau's *Devin du village* (The Village Soothsayer). We understand that *Les Veuves créoles* (published in Paris in 1768) was performed in Saint-Domingue in 1769 and 1779. The play writes itself into the French comic tradition in terms of its techniques, structure, and so on, but also provides a distinctly Creole dimension thanks to its colonial setting and message.[7] Set in Saint-Pierre in Martinique, the play includes references to local trading practices and other customs, it features enslaved characters, and while it satirizes the foibles of Creole society, the ultimate message of the play features the triumph of that society over the metropolitan imposter. One line of Gallicized Creole is included when one of the protagonists addresses her domestic slave at a moment of supposed crisis (II, 8). Spectators at the performances of *Les Veuves créoles* in Saint-Domingue will not, then, have been transported to France or had their social behaviour improved by their exposure to metropolitan French culture. This Creole hybrid features characters of European and African descent behaving in ways that drew on the daily lives of the theatre audience. The anonymous author of the play evidently hoped to succeed in his would-be transnational enterprise, for he included a series of explanatory footnotes in the published text aimed at reducing any jarring incomprehension in his metropolitan readership and potential audience. Although there is no evidence of *Les Veuves créoles* having ever been performed in metropolitan France, the play went on sale in Paris and descriptions of its content were provided in several metropolitan publications: the *Mercure de France*, *L'Année littéraire*, and the *Journal encyclopédique*. All three reviewers acknowledged the theatrical, and specifically, comic potential of the text in performance, but only one displayed a potentially transnational response when advising his readership to be ready sometimes for different codes of behaviour.[8]

The most popular local work to be performed in Saint-Domingue was by a man called Clément. His one-act musical comedy, *Jeannot et Thérèse*, is described in the local press as a Creole-language parody of Rousseau's *Devin du village* but is in fact a reworking of a patois parody of *Le Devin du village*, called *Les amours de Bastien et Bastienne* (The Loves of Bastien and Bastienne).[9] The work is set in Saint-Domingue and features black characters.

[7] *Les Veuves créoles, comédie*, ed. by Julia Prest (Cambridge: MHRA, 2017), pp. 1–25.

[8] See *Les Veuves créoles, comédie*, ed. by Julia Prest (Cambridge: MHRA, 2017), pp. 4–5.

[9] Bernard Camier and Marie-Christine Hazaël-Massieux, '*Jeannot et Thérèse*: un opéra comique en créole au milieu du XVIIIe siècle', *Revue de la société haitienne d'histoire de géographie*, 215 (2003), 135–66 (p. 138). Camier's new edition of the work, including its musical scores, will be published in 2022.

Performances of *Jeannot et Thérèse* raise a number of ethical issues that are borne of the work's transnational status and that are of interest to the student or scholar: these include its cheerful depiction of slave life and the performance (with one known exception) of black roles by white performers, sometimes with darkened skin, before a non-representative and segregated audience. On the one hand, the creation of *Jeannot et Thérèse* is to be celebrated because it offers a direct alternative to the French national tradition in the form of a rare and early example of a sustained piece performed in the Creole language (interestingly, the stage directions are in French), and because it constitutes a new, hybrid form of theatrical performance depicting local life; on the other hand, *Jeannot et Thérèse,* for all its transnationality does nothing to address the more flagrant inequities of the society it depicts.

But what was the effect of *Jeannot et Thérèse* on its audience? In the absence of any recorded audience responses, we are obliged to fall back on informed guesswork. Here it is perhaps instructive to consider the one recorded instance of a performer of colour taking a lead role in a performance of *Jeannot et Thérèse* (or *Les Amours de Mirebalais* as it was referred to in this instance). The Saint-Dominguan newspaper *Les Affiches américaines* informs its readers of an upcoming performance in the town of Saint-Marc of a 'parodie nègre' (black parody) of *Le Devin du village* featuring 'la Demoiselle Lise' as Thérèse.[10] Lise was one of only two named actor-performers of colour who are known to have performed in the public theatre. The other was her more famous half-sister, Minette. Their mother was of mixed European and African ancestry, while their fathers were European, and they were probably pale skinned. Nonetheless, the Saint-Dominguan audience would have recognized Lise as an exception to the tradition of white actors that otherwise dominated the public stage. While Minette never performed anything other than roles assumed (by default) to be white, Lise performed one role that was understood to be black. Her performance as Thérèse, then, was an exception among exceptions. We know that white performers sometimes wore skin-darkening make-up when performing *Thérèse et Jeannot,* but no mention is made of this in the case of Lise. How were these roles performed and what effect did Lise's appearance in a black role have alongside an otherwise white cast? It is impossible to know, but it seems inconceivable that no audience member on 6 February 1786 noticed that Lise's performance was different.

A transnational approach to performance is a useful one as many performances are by their very nature transnational. The transnational, in comparison with the international, can also be a useful yardstick by which

[10] *Affiches américaines*, 28 January 1786.

to measure the effects of the movement of performance across perceived national contexts and global spaces. Furthermore, a transnational approach can be useful more generally as a means of bringing some healthy scepticism towards our overreliance on and sometimes casual use of categories, national and otherwise. Returning to the tradition of Kabuki theatre, one of its most celebrated features is its use of an all-male cast and the particular skill of the *onnagata* (male actors specializing in female roles). Yet, in its early days, Kabuki featured female actors, who were then banned from the stage for reasons of supposed (im)morality. Just as the international performance of Kabuki and other forms of theatre has the potential to evolve along transnational lines, so also does a transnational approach to the study of the form have the capacity to remind the researcher that nothing is fixed, especially in performance.

Julia Prest is Professor of French and Caribbean Studies at the University of St Andrews.

27

# Postcolonial

*Charles Forsdick*

Discerning a disciplinary identity underpinning Modern Languages and creating links between its constituent parts was, for a long time, a largely intuitive process. Language acquisition to a high level was clearly part of the definition, with 'native speaker' competence – in both written and spoken forms – an often-unrealistic benchmark. The role of other aspects of the curriculum in defining any underpinning, subject-specific philosophy remained, however, unspoken.

The undergraduate programme I began to study in the late 1980s was characterized by an undeniably broad chronological range and a commitment to philological rigour, but these emphases were on the whole regulated by geographical limitations and a rigid sense of national canonicity. Literary history was privileged to the detriment of any spatial diversification. Five centuries of French colonial expansionism emerged only on occasion, not least in study of Rabelais's parody of the travelogue as it was practiced among his contemporaries or in engagement with Montaigne's searingly critical 'Des Cannibales', but the persistence of what has subsequently been dubbed 'French global' – a transnational, diasporic Frenchness, evident in the most canonical of works – was largely ignored.[1]

I could barely imagine, as a result, the growing prominence at the time of wider literary production of the area now increasingly known as the Francosphere. Translingual writing in French was already showing signs of buoyancy in the 1990s, with authors who had migrated to French, such as Vassilis Alexakis and Andreï Makine (of Greek and Russian origins,

[1] Christie McDonald and Susan Rubin Suleiman (eds), *French Global: A New Approach to Literary History* (New York: Columbia University Press, 2010).

respectively), receiving growing attention through French prize culture. This was also the decade in which the importance of a new generation of so-called 'Francophone' writers – the *Créolistes* in the French Caribbean, Assia Djebar in Algeria, Sony Labou Tansi in sub-Saharan Africa – was widely recognized. Shifts in public perception were increasingly apparent, and although the language of postcolonialism would be actively resisted in France (where it is still a subject of controversy), it was clear that the methodological nationalism on which French studies had long been constructed – with its overly hexagonal emphases and assumptions – would increasingly be subject to a robust postcolonialization.

Before becoming an undergraduate, I had worked as an *assistant à temps partiel* in Brittany, a posting that happened to coincide with the waning of Breton nationalist activism. Exposed to a critique of French republican universalism from this 'peripheral' region as it underwent rapid change, and working in an environment that – despite France's rhetoric of ethnolinguistic nationalism – was militantly bilingual and internationalist, I had already been exposed to new ways of exploring Frenchness: these moved between the subnational and the transnational, decoupling national identity from any overreliance on national culture, and introducing me to the notion of internal colonialism. It was in that context that I discovered the work of the traveller, poet, and essayist Victor Segalen (1878–1919), but I had to wait until my doctoral studies to explore his writings in earnest. Through Segalen, I discovered both the 'Francophone' and the 'postcolonial', and then began to understand the implications of bringing these two intersecting terms together. Such a manoeuvre is perhaps not an immediately obvious one: an early twentieth-century naval doctor and post-symbolist poet, Segalen was an agent of empire who relied on his colonial privilege for access to the locations that would allow him to elaborate his distinctive and increasingly influential 'aesthetics of diversity'. His engagement with Polynesian and Chinese culture led, nevertheless, to an unprecedented experimentation in cross-cultural production. *Les Immémoriaux*, a 1907 novel recounting the 'fatal impact' of European civilization on Tahitian culture, attempts to recount this process from an indigenous perspective. It is written in a hybridized French that prefigures the new forms of writing that emerged later in the century in Francophone writing. *Stèles*, a poetry collection from 1912 inspired by Chinese funerary monuments, juxtaposes Chinese characters with French text. It transforms the page of French poetry into a translation zone, evidence of a new bilingual poetics that subverts both languages, challenging any sense that French literature is monolingually stable and reliant on a single mode of expression.

Through works such as these, Segalen engaged with the exoticism of his contemporaries, but pushed this in new directions, not reflecting the domesticated difference evident in much colonial literature but gesturing instead towards a more radical sense of alterity. Edward Said – in *Orientalism* as well as *Culture and Imperialism* – absorbed Segalen in lists of his exoticist contemporaries (including writers such as Pierre Loti), but I was drawn instead to alternative readings by Francophone postcolonial authors, most notably the Martinican Édouard Glissant and Moroccan Abdelkebir Khatibi. These axes of influence proved to be both cross-cultural and postcolonial: they exemplify the disruptive potential of transnational and translingual readings in the reassessment of metropolitan texts; at the same time, they reveal the richness of a French-language corpus that draws on work from the wider Francosphere. For me, Segalen triggered approaches that were both postcolonial and postcolonializing.[2] These permitted me actively to prize open a familiar field of reference to include new material while suggesting – often in creative counterflows, casting new light on France itself – that new understandings and methods were required adequately to analyse this expanded field.

The encounter of postcolonial studies with Modern Languages was very nearly a missed disciplinary rendezvous as the emergence of the former was, counterintuitively given its (heavily Francophone) intellectual origins, largely Anglocentric. Postcolonial studies developed primarily in Departments of English Literature in the Anglophone academy, where attention to 'Commonwealth' writing gave way in the 1980s to the study of texts in English increasingly recognized as 'postcolonial'. An early critic of this tendency, Harish Trivedi, made a case for a postcolonialism that did not only 'have ears for English'.[3] While this specific observation focused on the need for an openness to indigenous languages, it implied at the same time the importance of reflecting on the postcolonial in linguistically sensitive terms. It suggested also the importance of understanding the role of specific

[2] Ato Quayson coined the term 'postcolonializing' to question understandings of the 'postcolonial' that privilege what he calls 'chronological supersession'. See *Postcolonialism: Theory, Practice or Process?* (Oxford: Blackwell, 2000). Such an approach provides justification of one of the persistent aspects of the postcolonial project, that is, 'drawing on a notion of the centrality of colonialism for understanding the formation of the contemporary world' (p. 10). Quayson's objective is not to designate certain situations or phenomena as somehow existing in binary terms before or after empire, that is, as essentially 'colonial' or 'postcolonial', but instead to 'suggest creative ways of viewing a variety of cultural, political, social and chronological realities both in the West and elsewhere via a postcolonial prism of interpretation' (p. 21).

[3] Harish Trivedi, 'The Postcolonial or the Transcolonial? Location and Language', *Interventions*, 1.2 (1999), 269–72 (p. 272).

languages in processes of colonial domination, in the emergence of decolonization, and in the forms of neo-colonialism and postcoloniality that have persisted in its aftermath.

Such an approach, in which Modern Languages has gone on to play a key role, implies a radical diversification of the assumptions underpinning postcolonial studies, and a notable shift away from single historical paradigms – such as the British Empire in the Indian subcontinent and its afterlives – that tended to influence the emergence of the field. Engagement with, for example, Francophone postcoloniality brings with it a series of alternative models of de/colonization, relating not least to Haiti, whose Revolution and War of Independence provide a very different historical texture to accounts of the end of empire (that often tend to limit the process to the second half of the twentieth century). An openness to alternative postcolonial histories also expands the canon of postcolonial texts, adding major but largely ignored early works such as the Baron de Vastey's *Système colonial dévoilé* (1814),[4] a text that anticipates by more than a century the anti-colonial thought of Aimé Césaire, Frantz Fanon, and others.

The Anglocentric emphases of early postcolonial studies is surprising given the comparative dimensions of much early work in the field. Often given foundational status, Edward Said's *Orientalism* ranges transnationally across language traditions and draws extensively, for instance, on the work of nineteenth-century French Romanticists (such as Châteaubriand, Lamartine, or Nerval) or on later French-Algerian writers (such as Camus). Moreover, key early critics (Said again, but also notably Gayatri Spivak) were translators in their own right, revealing the complex cross-cultural dynamics underpinning the emergence of postcolonial criticism. Such approaches – made possible not least by the active engagement of Modern Languages with the area – reveal the ways in which postcolonial studies is best understood as a field of study born transnationally and in translation, that is, the result of the transatlantic (and translingual) crossing of texts by anti-colonial thinkers such as Césaire and Fanon as well as works by poststructuralists such as Jacques Derrida and Michel Foucault. Translated into English and reinterpreted across North American campuses, these French and Francophone roots were largely eclipsed or even rendered invisible, with the result that when postcolonial studies was, with a certain time lag, translated back to France, it was dismissed then as another instance of 'French theory', with its relevance as a means of analysing history, society, and cultural production in the Francosphere initially denied. It is only in recent years, with the work

[4] For the English translation, see Baron de Vastey, *The Colonial System Unveiled*, trans. and ed. by Chris Bongie (Liverpool: Liverpool University Press, 2014).

of pioneering critics such as Achille Mbembe and Pap Ndiaye, that this resistance has subsided and that France itself has been studied alongside its cultural production through a postcolonial prism.

The emergence in Modern Languages at about the turn of the millennium of a specifically Francophone postcolonial studies was, therefore, an attempt to address the monolingualism of postcolonial studies while at the same time suggesting that French studies itself needed to move beyond its exclusively national parameters. This postcolonial project was, as a result, associated with a geographically transnational effort to extend the purview of a particular subfield of Modern Languages in order to embrace the historical and cultural complexity of the wider Francosphere. (Parallel developments have emerged in other subfields, inevitably with different emphases according to the relative place of colonialism in national history and culture, as in German and Italian studies, or the dynamics associating former colonizing and colonized countries, a major factor in Hispanic and Latin American studies.) On the one hand, there was a need for French studies to address seriously the extent to which, while the Francophone world had developed in ways very different from its Anglophone, Hispanophone, Italophone, Lusophone, and other equivalents, there was a wider Francosphere beyond France that urgently required study. By the late twentieth century, the literary and cultural production of this area had achieved such prominence that to be immune to it was to ignore what it meant to study languages and cultures in a postcolonial and globalized context – a context defined not least by heightened transnational connections. On the other hand, this postcolonial turn implied a major shift in the relationship to France as the traditional object of study in French studies: not only was this nation-state understood as part of (and not necessarily central to) a wider transnational field of enquiry in which it was increasingly relativized and even – to borrow Dipesh Chakrabarty's term – 'provincialized';[5] but also, attention to the postcolonial led to a diversification of understandings of France itself, seen as increasingly hybridized as a result of migration in the aftermath of empire, with its literature, culture, society, and politics subject to significant changes as a result.

The emergence of what Laurent Dubois dubbed a 'république métissée' (hybridized republic) – questioning the inclusiveness of *liberté, égalité, fraternité* on which the modern French state was founded – provoked also a reassessment of pre-revolutionary understandings of Frenchness.[6] This is

[5] Dipesh Chakrabarty, *Provincializing Europe: Postcolonial Thought and Historical Difference* (Princeton: Princeton University Press, 2007).

[6] Laurent Dubois, '*La République métisée*: Citizenship, Colonialism, and the Borders of French history', *Cultural Studies*, 14.1 (2000), 15–34.

a tendency evident in the *French Global* project, a collection of essays (now, importantly, translated into French) that understand French culture in an actively transnational frame. The persistent unpopularity of such approaches in France itself was made clear in the field of historiography, when Patrick Boucheron's *Histoire mondiale de la France* triggered controversy as it was seen to underline (and by extension undermine) the historiographic nationalism of many narratives of the French past.[7] The reassessment that such works propose is part of a wider process of (largely unfinished) decolonization that – as Sartre noted in the 1950s – was as necessary in France as it was in Algeria and other parts of the French colonial empire. Such decolonization extends beyond the analysis of history and society. This has major implications for the study of culture too, challenging the strict policing in France of the boundaries of national literature (with the result that the study of 'Francophone' literature was relegated to the field of *littérature comparée*). The postcolonialization of French studies has led not only to a prizing open of the field of reference, and to a collapse of the artificial 'French'/'Francophone' distinction (a dichotomy challenged also by the 2007 world-literature in French manifesto),[8] but also to an acknowledgement that the postcolonial refuses to obey the geography of centre and periphery according to which the colonial world was regulated. At the intersection of Modern Languages and postcolonial studies is recognition of the existence of black culture, history, and identity at the heart of European nation-states, of the importance of phenomena such as hybrid Afropean cultural production, and of the need to see world literatures as fundamentally entangled with stories of migration, both past and present.

In such critical manoeuvres around the boundaries and assumptions of a disciplinary field, respect for the distinctiveness of keywords is essential. While the 'postcolonial' implies connections that are transnational, and while the 'transnational' impacts on configurations that are firmly postcolonial, the two terms are far from synonymous. In retrospect, the development of Francophone postcolonial studies, by failing to acknowledge that its transnational reach might extend beyond the Francosphere, risked collapsing back into the monolingualism to whose limitations it sought to respond. The intersection of the transnational and the postcolonial is a reminder that colonial histories are entangled, and that postcolonial memories are multi-directional (study of the interplay between Francophone postcoloniality and discussions

[7] Patrick Boucheron (ed.), *Histoire mondiale de la France* (Paris: Seuil, 2017).

[8] 'Manifeste pour une littérature-monde en français', *Le Monde des Livres*, 15 March 2007. English translation by Daniel Simon: *World Literature Today*, March–April (2009), 54–56.

of decoloniality emerging from Latin America is, for instance, likely to prove increasingly fruitful). This means that an attention to transcolonial detail can yield connections eclipsed by the division of fields of study in national units defined by single languages. Key to such an approach is an attention to mobility, and this is an area in which Modern Languages has contributed considerably to understanding the convergences and divergences of the transnational and the postcolonial.

In Modern Languages, travel writing has emerged as one of the genres in which these intersections of the transnational and postcolonial are most effectively explored. The boundaries of the form have been policed to such an extent historically that the presence of postcolonial voices in the genre has remained, until recently, rare.[9] So-called 'migrant' literature is increasingly recognized as the location at which contemporary postcolonial journeys are inscribed, and questions about human rights and the afterlives of empire increasingly explored. Francophone postcolonial studies has permitted the direction of attention, however, to a wider corpus of texts that might be seen as postcolonial travel writing.[10] Key to such material is the work of the Ivoirian author Bernard Dadié. It is with reference to his travelogue *Un nègre à Paris* (1959) that I will conclude, by way of illustrating the interconnections of the postcolonial and transnational. Dadié's text recounts the journey to Paris of his loosely (auto)fictionalized narrator Tanhoe Bertin. It was the first in a trio of travel narratives by Dadié, with two later works serving as narratives of journeys to the USA (*Patron de New York* (1964)) and Italy (*La Ville où nul ne meurt* (1968)).[11] *Un nègre à Paris* presents France itself as a destination in its own right for African travellers, with its inhabitants, the French, cast as the indigenous population or 'travellees'. Dadié's satire describes the protagonist's journey from his home to Dakar to Paris, exploring the discrepancy between an imagined France (constructed through colonial education and wider colonial culture) and the reality of the place his protagonist discovers. His account demonstrates the gap between the African traveller's self-perception (and belief that travel bestows an equal status) and the ways in which he is perceived. This manoeuvre not only satirizes the ethnocentrism and solipsism of the conventional French

[9] See Aedin Ní Loingsigh, *Postcolonial Eyes: Intercontinental Travel in Francophone African Literature* (Liverpool: Liverpool University Press, 2009).

[10] See Robert Clark (ed.), *Cambridge Companion to Postcolonial Travel Writing* (Cambridge: Cambridge University Press, 2017).

[11] Bernard Dadié, *Un nègre à Paris* (Paris: Présence africaine, 1959); *Patron de New York* (Paris: Présence africaine, 1964); and *La Ville où nul ne meurt* (Paris: Présence africaine, 1968).

travelogue to Africa, but also allows a series of *faux naïf* reflections on contemporary France itself.

Unpinning the narrator's ethnographic observations is an awareness of the work's context: published in 1959, *Un nègre à Paris* is dated July–August 1956, and so is to be situated squarely in the context of French sub-Saharan African decolonization. The travelogue deploys the devices of transnational travel as both a critique of the assumptions and prejudices on which colonialism was based, and also as a means of reflecting on the relationships that might emerge between France and Africa in a postcolonial frame.

Central to this shift is the status of Dadié's protagonist as tourist, free to travel where he pleases (although often still subject to a persistent white gaze). In this capacity, from the exoticizing perspective of reverse ethnography, he provides a precocious postcolonial account of the successes and failures of French history and culture, gesturing towards the challenges inherent in new forms of postcolonial mobility, and in the development of political and social relationships in the shadow of the colonial past. Dadié's text is part of a long tradition of narratives of the 'journey-in', exoticizing and even provincializing France itself. It consciously adopts the dynamics of the reverse gaze, deployed in numerous French travel narratives since Montesquieu's *Lettres persanes* (1721). It renews, however, such tropes to provide a visceral response to its context that captures the pain and anxiety of a country, France, still to acknowledge its own postcolonial status. As such, it anticipates many of the questions now evident at the intersection of Modern Languages, the transnational, and the postcolonial.

Charles Forsdick is James Barrow Professor of French at the University of Liverpool.

# 28

# Premodernities

*Sharon Kinoshita*

Shortly after his arrival (*c.*1274) at the court of the great Mongol ruler Qubilai Khan, Marco Polo, then aged about twenty, quickly learned four languages and their scripts; so we learn from the Prologue to his *The Description of the World* (*Le Devisement du monde*), composed some two decades later.[1] Tantalizingly, except for 'Tartar' (Mongolian), we are not told which languages these were. Even allowing for some exaggeration, this mention of the young man's linguistic prowess illustrates how much multi-lingualism, if not exactly routine, was highly prized across the medieval world. To call this phenomenon 'transnational' would be anachronistic, for this world – a patchwork of empires, khanates, kingdoms, sultanates, duchies, city-states, and more – precedes the advent of nations, not to speak of 'national languages', by many centuries. In fact, the linguistic geography of medieval Eurasia was highly complex: a blend of cosmopolitan scriptural languages, local and regional vernaculars and dialects, literary *koines*, and lingua francas. Recovering this multi-lingual mix is a challenge – limited, even in the case of literate cultures, by accidents of the survival of textual evidence, not to speak of the strictly oral circulation of many dialects and vernaculars. This essay takes Marco Polo's *The Description of the World* as a guide to exploring the messy linguistic geography of high medieval Eurasia. In the second part, we examine ways in which this sometimes surprising linguistic pluralism is both reflected in, and shaped by, literary texts and their circulation.

[1] Marco Polo, *The Description of the World*, trans. by Sharon Kinoshita (Indianapolis: Hackett, 2016), p. 10.

## I.

Marco Polo's *The Description of the World* – better known in modern English translation as 'The Travels' – was composed at the midpoint of the remarkable century when the empires produced by the Mongol conquests enabled the circulation of people, commodities, and ideas on an unprecedented scale. Written in 1298 in a collaboration between the Venetian merchant and an Arthurian romance writer named Rustichello of Pisa, the *Description* maps a world of great linguistic complexity. Let's begin with the text itself, composed neither in Latin (still Western Europe's predominant language of literacy for learned and official discourses) nor in 'Italian' (as the origins of our two co-authors might lead us to presume) but in the variant of Old French that modern scholars call 'Franco-Italian' (or, recently, 'the French of Italy'). In this generation before Dante's *Divine Comedy* elevated his Tuscan dialect to the status of a written language, French (a literary language since the mid-twelfth century) was the vehicle of choice for Italians wishing to work in the vernacular: in chronicles (like Martin da Canal's *History of Venice*), encyclopedias (like Brunetto Latini's *Book of Treasure*), romances (like Rustichello's own *Méliadus*), or epics (like the many *chansons de geste* copied or composed at northern Italian courts).

But let's return to the four languages Marco so quickly mastered. Soon after his arrival, Rustichello reports, he 'learned the Tartars' customs, languages, and writing so well that it was a marvel' (10) – 'Tartar' being the name routinely but inaccurately used for the Mongols throughout the *Description* and other Western European texts. Within Qubilai's vast empire, Mongolian was an obvious choice. On a previous journey through Asia, Marco's father and uncle had become 'well acquainted with the language of the Tartars' (5), and Marco sprinkles Mongol names for their customs and practices throughout the *Description*: *Quecitain* (80) for the Great Khan's imperial guard, *bularguci* (83) for the Mongols' lost-and-found officer, *ianb* (89) for stations in their famed long-distance postal service. The script Marco learned is less uncertain. In 1255, the Franciscan William of Rubruck, returning from a mission to the Mongols, brings the French king Louis IX a letter from the Great Khan Möngke in the Mongol language, in the script borrowed from the Uighurs (Turkic speakers who had previously adopted and adapted their writing system from Syriac). In 1269, however, Qubilai commissioned a Tibetan lama named 'Phags-pa to develop a script that could be used for all the languages of his empire. Despite the Great Khan's mandate, 'Phags-pa never caught on in replacing either Chinese characters or the Uighur script. But given the timing of his arrival and his closeness to the Great Khan, might Marco have learned his Mongolian in the 'Phags-pa script?

Given the vast territory and variety of peoples they ruled, the Mongols' empire was multi-lingual of necessity and by design. Under Möngke (Qubilai's predecessor as Great Khan), senior ministers, themselves mostly Mongols, relied on an army of scribes handling records in Chinese, Tibetan, Uighur, Tangut, and Persian as well as Mongolian. Decades later, in 1345, inscriptions on a gateway north of Beijing praised the piety of the last Mongol emperor in Sanskrit, Chinese, Mongolian, Uighur, Tibetan, and Tangut.[2] Meanwhile, the Mongols, as foreign speakers of Chinese, encouraged writing in the colloquial rather than the classical language – explaining the emergence of a flourishing theatrical tradition in the vernacular. And merchants like Marco Polo would have routinely encountered paper money inscribed in Chinese both in traditional characters and in 'Phags-pa, and, in the markets, official weights with inscriptions in Chinese, Mongolian, and Persian.[3]

Such multi-lingualism was typical of empires and polities that ruled subjects speaking different languages and often of different religions. In the medieval Mediterranean, court chanceries housed administrators literate in multiple languages. In twelfth-century Sicily, the Norman King Roger II kept tax and boundary records in Arabic.[4] In the 1190s, even as the power of Arabophone administrators was declining, the chronicler Peter of Eboli described the capital city of Palermo as 'richly endowed with three tongues', evoking the ancient trope of a trilingual Sicily whose languages were Latin, Greek, and Punic; the copiously illuminated manuscript of his *Liber ad honorem Augusti sive de rebus Siculis* (*Book in Honor of Augustus or The Affairs of Sicily*) depicts pairs of notaries, distinguished by their dress and facial hair as 'Greci', 'Saraceni', and 'Latini'.[5] In twelfth- and thirteenth-century Anatolia, the Seljuk sultans of Rum, themselves ethnically Turkish, adopted Persian and Arabic for internal administration, Greek for external correspondence with Christian powers, and Persian as its literary language.[6] Rulers sometimes made

[2] Toghon Temür was Qubilai's great-great-great grandson. Herbert Franke and Denis Twitchett, 'Introduction', in *The Cambridge History of China*, ed. by Herbert Franke and Denis Twitchett, vol. 6 (Cambridge: Cambridge University Press, 1994), pp. 1–42 (p. 35).

[3] Franke and Twitchett, 'Introduction', *The Cambridge History of China*, p. 36.

[4] This vestige of Sicily's time under Muslim rule provided Roger a convenient way of circumscribing the power of his Latinate nobility. Joshua C. Birk, *Norman Kings of Sicily and the Rise of Anti-Islamic Critique: Baptized Sultans* (Cham: Palgrave Macmillan, 2016), pp. 162–63.

[5] Birk, *Norman Kings of Sicily*, p. 276.

[6] Elizabeth Zachariadou, 'Records of the Turkish Anatolian States, c. 1250–1330', in *Pragmatic Literacy, East and West, 1200–1330*, ed. by Richard Britnell (Woodbridge: Boydell, 1997), pp. 199–205.

a show of their multi-lingualism. Emperor Frederick II, grandson of Roger II and successor to the Norman kings of Sicily whom nineteenth-century historian Michele Amari called 'baptized sultans',[7] understood Arabic and enjoyed sending philosophical queries to foreign scholars.[8] Rashid al-Din, the court historian of Mongol-ruled Persia, credited the Ilkhan Ghazan with a knowledge of 'Arabic, Persian, Hindi, Kashmiri, Tibetan, Chinese, Frankish, and a smattering of other languages' along with his native Mongolian.[9]

The languages spoken by local populations, as opposed to rulers and chancery officials, are harder to ascertain. An early thirteenth-century copy of the laws and customs of London written in French describes the multi-lingualism of post-Conquest Britain:

> Now you should know that in Britain, which is now called England, there were five languages and I will tell you what they are: Breton and English and Scottish, Pictish and Latin – now there is the sixth that is called Norman and French – which were known by many people through the teaching of old texts.[10]

In twelfth-century Palermo, the babel of peoples and languages on the ground far exceeded what we have already seen of the Norman kings' multi-lingual administration:

> Arabic was of course used by the Muslim population, but also by a sizeable Jewish minority [...] As for Greek, it was employed in court and city alike as the language of culture by a composite Christian milieu, no doubt effecting a synthesis between autochthonous (Sicilian) elements [of various kinds and] an Arabo-Christian immigration [including] a Syrian elite following the Melkite rite and already characterized in the East by a Graeco-Arabic cultural and liturgical bilingualism.[11]

[7] Cited in Birk, *Norman Kings of Sicily*, p. 2.

[8] David Abulafia, *Frederick II, A Medieval Emperor* (Oxford: Oxford University Press, 1992), p. 252.

[9] Thomas Allsen, 'The Rasûlid Hexaglot in its Eurasian Cultural Context', in *The King's Dictionary. The Rasûlid Hexaglot: Fourteenth Century Vocabularies in Arabic, Persian, Turkic, Greek, Armenian and Mongol*, ed. by Peter B. Golden (Leiden: Brill, 2000), pp. 25–48 (p. 29). Ghazan was Qubilai Khan's great-great-nephew.

[10] The description of England, from which the passage about its 'five languages' comes, was translated and adapted from Henry of Huntingdon's *Historia Anglorum*, adding the 'sixth' language – 'Norman and French': Claudio Lagomarsini, 'The Prose *Description of England*', *Medium Aevum*, 80.2 (2011), 325–35.

[11] Benoît Grévin, 'Linguistic Cultures and Textual Production in Palermo', in *A*

What about the multi-lingualism of individuals? In his unfinished Latin treatise *De vulgari eloquentia* (*c.*1303–1305), Dante distinguishes the vernacular language – 'that which we learn without any formal instruction, by imitating our nurses' – from 'another kind of language, at one remove from us, which the Romans called *gramatica*'.[12] This latter, which Dante deems 'artificial' because it requires formal instruction, characterizes cosmopolitan languages:

> [L]anguages of high culture and bureaucracy [...] governed by strict, institutionalized laws of grammar [...] self-consciously designed to resist historical change [...] The person who studies and learns a cosmopolitan language leaves the intimate, homely topography of the mother tongue to enter into a much wider and much more populous world.[13]

Across premodern Eurasia, *literati* were bilingual: schooled in an 'artificial' language of formal instruction (Latin, Arabic, Hebrew, Greek, Sanskrit, classical Chinese) alongside a vernacular in which they spoke and occasionally wrote – like the Italian cultivated by Dante, followed by Petrarch and Boccaccio.[14] Others even wrote across cosmopolitan languages, like the twelfth-century Jewish polymath Moses ben Maimon (Maimonides), who wrote in both Arabic and Hebrew. Furthermore, minority religious communities sometimes used the scripts associated with their sacred languages to transcribe the majoritarian languages that served as their everyday vernaculars: Judeo-Arabic (Arabic written in Hebrew script) or *aljamiado* (Iberian romance vernaculars written in Arabic script), alongside a spate of languages written in Hebrew script: Judeo-Spanish (Sephardic or Ladino), Judeo-French, Judeo-Greek, Judeo-Persian, Judeo-Italian, Judeo-Occitan, Judeo-Portuguese, Judeo-Syriac, Judeo-Turkish, and of course Yiddish. Such combinations, which seem like puzzling curiosities today, reflected business as usual in the multilingual, multi-confessional communities that proliferated in the Middle Ages.

*Companion to Medieval Palermo*, ed. by Annliese Nef (Leiden: Brill, 2013), pp. 413–36 (p. 418).

12 Dante Alighieri, *De Vulgari Eloquentia*, trans. by Steven Botterill (Cambridge: Cambridge University Press, 1996), p. 3.

13 Karla Mallette, 'The Metropolis and its Languages', in *Cosmopolitanism and the Middle Ages*, ed. by John Ganim and Shayne Legassie (New York: Palgrave Macmillan, 2013), pp. 21–37 (p. 21). Mallette's understanding of 'cosmopolitan' follows that of Sheldon Pollock.

14 Compare the gendered diglossia in Heian Japan, where men wrote in Classical Chinese while women used a phonetic syllabary to write in vernacular Japanese, as in Lady Murasaki's *Tale of Genji* or Sei Shonagon's *Pillow Book*.

While Marco Polo undoubtedly served Qubilai as part of the corps of foreigners whom the Mongols employed as functionaries, his family were merchants first and foremost. Two documents richly illustrate the multi-lingualism of fourteenth-century commercial networks. The Codex Cumanicus (*c.*1330–1340), a compilation of texts named for the Cumans (also called Qipchaq, a Turkic-speaking confederation that dominated the Western Eurasian steppes before the Mongol conquests) includes an 'Interpreter's Book', a trilingual glossary in vulgar Latin, Cuman, and Persian assembled in the 1290s by Genoese merchants in the Crimea (Cuman and Persian, as linguae francae in the khanate of the Golden Horde and from Anatolia to India, respectively, are good candidates for two of Marco's four languages). The Rasulid Hexaglot is an early fourteenth-century wordlist in six languages – Arab, Persian, Turkic, Greek, Armenian, and Mongol – likely assembled in the Ilkhanid (Mongol-Persian) capital Tabriz.[15] It survives today in a manuscript copied *c.*1370 under al-Malik al-Afdal, the Rasulid sultan of Aden (the Arabian port at the southern entrance to the Red Sea, a centre for the Indian Ocean trade).[16] While the Codex Cumanicus and the Rasulid Hexaglot are certainly exceptional documents, their choice of languages and vocabularies offers us a glimpse of the complex mosaic of languages informing the commercial world of medieval West Asia.

## Multi-lingualism and Literature

The multi-lingualism of the premodern world inevitably shaped literary production. Authors sometimes highlight their own linguistic skills. In the prologue of her *lai* (short verse narrative) 'Laüstic', set on the border between Normandy and Brittany, Marie de France evokes the multi-lingualism of the Angevin empire:

> Une aventure vus dirai
> Dunt li bretun firent un lai.
> *Laüstic* ad nun, ceo m'est avis—
> Si l'apelent en lur païs;
> Ceo est "russinol" en franceis
> E "nihtegale" en dreit engleis.[17]

[15] Benoît Grévin, *Le parchemin des cieux* (Paris: Seuil, 2012), p. 252.

[16] The same codex also contains an Arabic-Ethiopian lexicon: Grévin, *Le parchemin des cieux*, pp. 352–53 (p. 353).

[17] 'I shall tell you an adventure / of which the Bretons made a lai. / Its name is *Laüstic*, I believe – / so they call it in their country; / that is "rossignol" in French /

At about the same time, the troubadour Raimbaut de Vaqueiras constructed his lyric 'debate' poem 'Domna, tant vos ai preiada' (*c.*1190) in alternating stanzas in Provençal, in his own voice, and in Genoese (among the earliest written attestations of that language), spoken by the lady he is trying to seduce.[18] Rejecting his advances, she exclaims that she values his Provençal speech 'less than a Genoese coin' and understands him no better than she would a German or Sardinian or Berber.[19] In his best-known poem, 'Eras quan vey verdeyar', Raimbaut pushes this multi-lingualism to new heights. Since his lady has turned against him, the poet explains, he will produce *discordance* in words, sounds and languages (lenguatges).[20] The resulting *descort* is a tour-de-force featuring successive stanzas in Provençal, Italian, Old French, Gascon, and Galician-Portuguese – once again, some of the earliest written examples of those languages.[21]

In the premodern world, with its predisposition towards multi-lingualism, translation – the transmission and adaptation of texts across languages and cultures – was a privileged form of cultural production. Latin Europe thematized this process in the topos of *translatio studii*, a version of the discourse of Western Civilization asserting the transmission of learning and textual culture from Greece to Rome to medieval France or Germany. Such transmissions were facilitated across 'scriptworlds' – the linguistic communities that shared the same script, as in the case of Persian, Arabic, and Turkish.[22] More striking, and counterintuitive, are examples where literary texts, tropes, or forms mixed or crossed languages, scripts, and religions. Best-known are examples from medieval Islamic Iberia (al-Andalus): the *muwashshah*, a lyric poem in classical Arabic with its closing verses (*kharja*) in vernacular Spanish transcribed in Arabic script, and the Hebrew lyrics that developed in emulation of the Arabic, also with closing verses in vernacular Romance. Then there's the way *al-gharīb*, the Arabic word for stranger, became a loanword and cultural concept to ponder notions of foreignness, estrangement, and exile in the work of writers as varied as Judah Halevi, the great Hebrew poet of al-Andalus, in his *Book of Refutation and Indication Concerning the*

and "nightingale" in proper English'. *The Lais of Marie de France*, ed. and trans. Claire M. Waters (Peterborough, ON: Broadview, 2018) (ll. 1–6). Marie, the earliest known woman author in French, wrote in England under Henry II (r. 1154–1189).

[18] *The Poems of the Troubadour Raimbaut de Vaqueiras*, ed. and trans. Joseph Linskill (The Hague: Mouton, 1964), pp. 98–107.

[19] *The Poems of the Troubadour Raimbaut de Vaqueiras*, ll. 71, 73–76.

[20] *The Poems of the Troubadour Raimbaut de Vaqueiras*, (lenguatges, l. 8).

[21] *The Poems of the Troubadour Raimbaut de Vaqueiras*, pp. 191–98.

[22] David Damrosch, 'Scriptworlds: Writing Systems and the Formation of World Literature', *MLQ*, 68.2 (2007), 195–219.

*Lowly Faith*, composed in Arabic; the Anatolian Sufi poets Jalāl al-Dīn Rūmī (writing in Persian) and Yūnus Emre (writing in Turkish); and Mkrtich' Naghash, the fifteenth-century Armenian Christian bishop and poet writing in Middle Armenian – 'a literary language [...] replete with loanwords from Arabic, Persian, and Turkish'.[23]

Finally, there are the multi-lingual characters *within* literary texts. In Rudolf von Ems's early thirteenth-century Middle High German romance *Der Guote Gêrhart*, a Moroccan prince, finding a German merchant who does not understand his 'heathen' tongue, asks if he knows French; he does, and the two are able to converse in that language.[24] In several of the tales from Giovanni Boccaccio's *Decameron* (c.1350) set in the Mediterranean, protagonists speak foreign languages or learn them readily: a Genoese merchant's spurned wife who turns up, cross-dressed, in Alexandria quickly becomes fluent enough to be appointed the sultan's markets inspector; two star-crossed lovers from Lipari (near Sicily) each ends up in Tunisia – Gostanza in a house of female handiworkers whose language she learns in very short order; and the Saracen sultan Saladin, wishing to inspect Christians' preparations for the Third Crusade, travels incognito to Italy. Since he, his companions, and servants 'tutti sapevan latino, per che molto bene intendevano e erano intesi'.[25] Lest we think these examples to be fictional exaggerations, there is the case of the Sicilian king Charles of Anjou (r. 1266–1285), who ordered surveillance at his ports for fear of polyglot Muslim assassins arriving aboard Genoese merchant vessels disguised as Franciscans![26]

Such are the complexities of the linguistic geography of the global Middle Ages.

Sharon Kinoshita is Professor of Literature at the University of California, Santa Cruz specializing in medieval French, Mediterranean Studies, and the Global Middle Ages.

[23] Michael Pifer, 'The Age of the *Gharīb*: Strangers in the Medieval Mediterranean', in *An Armenian Mediterranean*, ed. by Kathryn Babayan and Michael Pifer (Cham: Palgrave Macmillan, 2018), pp. 13–37 (p. 32).

[24] William Crooke, '*Der guote Gêrhart*: The Power of Mobility in the Medieval Mediterranean', *postmedieval*, 4 (2013), 163–76 (pp. 167–68).

[25] 'all knew Italian, and therefore understood [their host] well and were well understood'. Tale 10.9, Giovanni Boccaccio, *Decameron*, ed. by Vittore Branca, vol. 2 (Turin: Einaudi, 1992), p. 1209. The other tales are 2.9 and 5.2.

[26] Grévin, *Le parchemin des cieux*, p. 87.

# 29

# Routes

*Peter Campbell and Krešimir Vuković*

The waters of the Mediterranean may be the greatest museum of Antiquity. Scattered across the seafloor are shipwrecks from every time period. Cargos of wine, oil, and fish were transported in clay amphoras, which are found stacked in the sands or spilling down submarine cliffs in waterfalls of ceramics. There are also other items: lamps, cooking pots, anchors, and fragments of everyday life. These objects tell human stories, which archaeologists carefully tease out of the material record. It is sometimes possible to identify the ship's previous ports of call, their home port, or their intended destination. Since the first shipwreck discoveries by early divers, a database of Mediterranean shipwrecks has slowly been built and recreated the paths that the ships navigated.[1] It reveals a 'globalized' ancient Mediterranean that spread cargo, languages, religions, war, and ideas. The efflorescence of ship-borne connectivity was possible through the creation and sharing of *routes.*

How does one navigate space to get from one place to another? Generally, one can follow a prescribed route or blaze a new one. But what is a route, precisely? The etymology of *route* comes from the thirteenth-century Old French term *rute* meaning road, way, or path, which itself derives from the Latin *via rupta* meaning a broken path or way.[2] The term 'route' denotes a prescribed or customary path that people or animals travel. This is also the source of *routine*, which is a behavioural path or course of action.

An unknown author in the fourth century BC began writing down distances and names of sailing destinations in the Mediterranean. The project would

[1] A.J. Parker, *Ancient Shipwrecks of the Mediterranean and the Roman Provinces* (Oxford: BAR Intern. 580 Archeopress, 1992).

[2] Oxford English Dictionary (Oxford: Oxford University Press, 2010), s.v. route.

Figure 1. A fourth-century AD shipwreck discovered in Albania, lying on the seafloor in its original shape and transporting North African amphoras filled with fish sauce.
Source: Albanian Center for Marine Research/Elaine Ferritto.

continue for centuries as the text was copied, changed, and updated until the present surviving text, which dates to the first century AD.[3] Known as the *Stadiasmus Maris Magni,* this *periplus,* or a sailing guide, lists placename, distance, and a description.[4] The combination of distance and visual cues allowed the mariners to plan and follow a route. For example, in one part of the guide we find:

> From Alexandria to Chersonesos, a harbor, 2 stades. From Chersonesos to Dysmai, a harbor for merchant ships not exceeding a thousand units of cargo, 7 [stades]. From Dysmai to Plinthine, an open roadstead, harborless, 90 stades. From Plinthine to Taposiris, the city is harborless, with a sanctuary of Osiris, 7 stades. From Taposiris to Chimo, a town, with rocky shoals visible, 7 stades.[5]

[3] Arnaud Pascal, *Les Routes de la navigation antique* (Paris: Editions Errance, 2005).
[4] Karl Müller, *Geographi Græci Minores* (Paris: Ambrosio Firmin Didot, 1855).
[5] Müller, *Geographi Græci Minores*, p. 481.

[ Ἀπὸ Σύρου εἰς Ἄνδρον σταδίους ρν' ].

Ἀπὸ Ἄνδρου εἰς λιμένα Γαυρίου σταδίους π'.

Ἀπὸ Γαυρίου ἐπὶ [ τὸ Παιώνιον ] ἀκρωτήριον σταδίους ν'.

Ἀπὸ τοῦ ἀκρωτηρίου εἰς [ Γεραιστὸν ] ἔγγιστα ἄκρας σταδίους υν'.

Ἀπὸ τῆς Γεραιστοῦ εἰς Κάρυστον σταδίους ρκ'.

Ἐκ Καρύστου εἰς Πεταλίας σταδίους ρ'.

284. Ἐπάνειμι πάλιν ἐπὶ τὰ ἐκ Δήλου διαστήματα πρὸς νήσους τάσδε·

Ἐκ Δήλου εἰς Θήραν στάδιοι τν'.

Ἐκ Δήλου ἐπὶ τὴν Ἀμοργίαν ( εἰς τὴν Μινώαν ) στάδιοι χν'.

Ἐκ Δήλου εἰς Ἀνάφην στάδιοι ρ'.

Ἐκ Δήλου εἰς Ἴον στάδιοι χν'.

Ἐκ Δήλου εἰς τὰς Κορσίας στάδιοι χν'.

Ἐκ Δήλου εἰς Κίμωλον στάδιοι ω'.

Ἐκ Δήλου εἰς Σίφνον στάδιοι χμ'.

Ἐκ Δήλου εἰς Κύθνον στάδιοι τν'.

Ἐκ Δήλου εἰς Τῆνον στάδιοι τν'.

Ἐκ Δήλου εἰς Νάξον στάδιοι τν'.

Ἐκ Δήλου ἐπὶ τὴν Δόνουσαν στάδιοι τκ'.

Ἐκ Δήλου εἰς Πάτμον στάδιοι ων'.

Ἐκ Δήλου ἐπὶ τὸν Μελάντειον σκόπελον στάδιοι ρπ'.

*A Syro ad Andrum insulam stadia* 150 ].

Ab Andro *extrema* ad Gaurium portum stadia 80.

A Gaurio ad [ *Pæonium* ] *Andri* promontorium stadia 50.

Ab eo promontorio ad [ *Geræstum* ] proxime promontorium stadia 150 (ν).

A Geræsto ad Carystum stadia 120.

A Carysto ad Petalias insulas stadia 100.

284. Revertor rursus ad distantias quæ e Delo sunt ad insulas hasce :

A Delo ad Theram stadia 550 ( φν' ).

A Delo ad Amorgiam ( sc. ad Minoam urbem ) stadia 650.

A Delo ad Anaphen stadia 700 ( ψ' ).

A Delo ad Ium 450 ( υ' ).

A Delo ad Corsias stadia 750 ( ψν' ).

A Delo ad Cimolum stadia 800 ( 500? ).

A Delo ad Siphnum stadia 340 ( τμ' ).

A Delo ad Cythnum stadia 350 ( 450? ).

A Delo ad Tenum stadia 150 ( ρν' ).

A Delo ad Naxum stadia 150 ( ρν' ).

A Delo ad Donusam stadia 320.

A Delo ad Patmum stadia 850.

A Delo ad Melantium scopulum stadia 180.

Figure 2. The Greek (left) and Latin (right) versions of the *Stadiasmus Maris Magni* giving accounts of locations and distances in the Aegean Sea. Source: Müller, *Geographi Graci Minores*, p. 499.

This is information enough to create a mental map of the Mediterranean. Mariners knew how fast their vessels travelled and they calculated how far they would travel in a half day or day. The description in *periploi* allowed them to predict the days at sea ahead of them.

As cultural historians, we use archaeology and historical texts, as well as contemporary ethnographic information, to understand how people conceive of and negotiate spaces – including ancient spaces that no longer exist. Whether these are enduring places like Rome's ancient marble foundations or more mutable spaces like the sea, it is the previously 'broken path' encoded as mental maps that allowed geography to be shared.

## Traditional Navigation: (Re)conceptualizing Geography

There are exceptional cases where ancient footprints are preserved and allow us to follow people's path directly.[6] However, aside from these rare cases, it is necessary to reconstruct routes through texts or the archaeological record. There are several ancient texts that give accounts of navigational routes, while the archaeological record includes cities or settlements, shrines, and shipwrecks. Paths themselves may be marked with road markers, stone cairns, or blazed trees – marks cut into the bark and the origin of the term 'trail blazing' – and trail trees, which are purposefully bent to indicate a route.[7]

The most common means for navigating space is the sharing of mental maps. This is done through a process of embedding meaning in the physical landscape, creating an itinerary of visual cues.[8] This may include estimates of travel time or distances, called *reckoning*, such as in the *Stadiasmus*. Features commonly embedded with meaning include prominent mountains, water sources, and islands, but could also include built structures like church spires or lighthouses. Toponyms like 'Mount Everest' or 'Pennsylvania Avenue' are a common way to embed meaning that can be shared with others.

## Itineraries, *Periploi*, and Maps

Three types of texts survive from Antiquity that give insight into the ancient conception of routes. An *itinerary* is an account of a journey, listing nodes along the route taken. The term comes from the Latin *iter, itineris*, which means journey. Ancient itineraries were accounts of, or plans for, journeys, but they could be re-used later. *Periegesis* were a form of travel guide (for example, Pausanias who wrote a famous travel guide of ancient Greece). *Periploi* were mariners' navigation guides (for example, *Stadiasmus*). *Periploi* contained information for mariners, including built structures such as cities

[6] Gordon Roberts, Silvia Gonzalez, and David Huddart, 'Intertidal Holocene Footprints and Their Archaeological Significance', *Antiquity*, 70 (1990), 647–51.

[7] Dennis Downes, *Native American Trail Marker Trees: Marking Paths through the Wilderness* (Chicago: Chicago's Books Press, 2011).

[8] Manel Calvo, David Javaloyas, Daniel Albero, Jaume Garcia-Rosselló, and Victor Guerrero, 'The Ways People Move: Mobility and Seascapes in the Balearic Islands during the Late Bronze Age (*c*.1400–850/800 BC)', *World Archaeology*, 43.3 (2011), 345–63. See also Timmy Gambin, 'Maritime Activity and the Divine – an Overview of Religious Expression by Mediterranean Seafarers, Fishermen and Travelers', in *Ships, Saints and Sealore: Cultural Heritage and Ethnography of the Mediterranean and the Red Sea*, ed. by D.A. Agius, T. Gambin, and A. Trakadas (Oxford: Archeopress, 2014), pp. 3–12.

and harbours, natural features such as rivers and headlands, and resources like water and winds. Brian Campbell argues that *periploi* convey routes in a visual sense, as their narrative includes phrases such as 'to arrive at' and 'to find'.[9]

There are also maps such as the Peutinger Table, the most complete extant Roman map. The thirteenth-century AD parchment is a copy of a fourth-century AD map; however, the fourth-century version is thought to build on a first-century AD original.[10] Pompeii, destroyed in 79 AD, is included on the map, while Constantinople and Antioch are given prominence, which indicates fourth-century additions. The Peutinger map looks odd compared to modern maps because it is not meant to reflect an accurate depiction of geography, but routes. The map is designed around the roads and the nodes within the roads, as opposed to the geographical space. Similarly, later maps have exaggerated coastal features, which aided mariners with visual markers.

## Religious Routes

Routes are important to religious experience and the way believers engage with the divine in many traditions. Catholic Christianity celebrates certain days of the year – called *festivals* – where worship takes the form of a solemn procession in which believers carry a holy object around a particular area or to/from a sacred site. Figure 3 depicts the route pilgrims took to visit Rome's seven basilicas for the Holy Year of 1575. In Orthodox Christianity, priests and deacons perform a procession – called 'the entrance' – inside the church during the divine liturgy.[11]

Routes are a feature of pilgrimages, which are journeys to sacred sites. There are many such sites but most popular in the Abrahamic religions of Christianity, Judaism, and Islam is the city of Jerusalem, which is very significant in the history of these traditions. In Islam, the annual pilgrimage to the holy city of Mecca is called the Hajj. It is one of the five holy pillars of Islam and all adult Muslims who can afford it must perform the Hajj at least once in their life. During the Hajj, pilgrims circle the Kabah mosque seven times in an anticlockwise direction.[12]

[9] Brian Campbell, *Rivers and the Power of Ancient Rome* (Chapel Hill: University of North Carolina Press, 2012), p. 51.

[10] O.A.W. Dilke, *Greek and Roman Maps* (London: Thames and Hudson, 1985), p. 238.

[11] I.J. Hapgood, *Service Book of the Holy Orthodox-Catholic Apostolic Church* (Englewood: Antiochian Orthodox Christian Archdiocese, 1922), p. 83.

[12] Karen Armstrong, *Islam: A Short History* (New York: Modern Library, 2002), pp. 10–12.

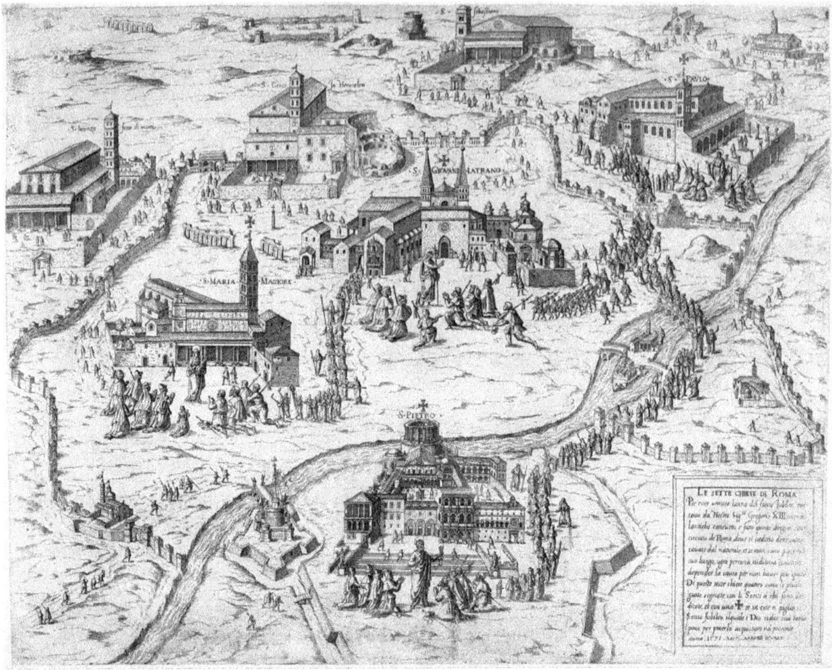


Figure 3. A map of Rome showing the pilgrimage route for the Holy Year of 1575, which visited the city's seven basilicas.
Source: Antonio Lafreri. Credit: Metropolitan Museum, Rogers Fund, Transferred from the Library, 1941.

In ancient Rome, processions played a key role in defining sacred space. Lustration was a form of ritual in which the participants went around an area in an anticlockwise direction in order to purify it and invoke divine blessing. Lustrations took many forms and were a part of everyday life throughout the Roman Empire. Ancient texts talked about lustrations of armies, navies, fields, cattle, city quarters, and the people during a census.[13] The most famous Roman procession was the *triumph* in which a victorious general rode a chariot through the city, followed by his troops. This was unusual, as the army was normally not allowed inside Rome. The troops displayed trophies and spoils of war.[14] The celebration took the form of a procession and culminated with a sacrifice to the god Jupiter.

[13] Krešimir Vuković, 'The Topography of the Lupercalia', *The Papers of the British School at Rome*, 86 (2018), 37–60 (pp. 50–57).

[14] M.L. Popkin, *The Architecture of the Roman Triumph* (Cambridge: Cambridge University Press, 2016), pp. 6–11.

## Irregular Routes

Religious routes are examples of paths with restricted access, in this case available only to religious practitioners. What happens when The Route – the standard or normative route – is unavailable to certain individuals? Within every culture there are power inequalities and social hierarchies that privilege certain knowledge and spaces for some and exclude others. As a result, there are routes unavailable to certain groups. These people are forced to take new, illegal routes. The result is dangerous and, at times, deadly.

The shipwrecks in the opening paragraph describe the author's archaeological discovery of fifty-three wreck sites in Fournoi, Greece.[15] While divers work on the seafloor, Syrian refugees navigate the waters above. They seek to reach Europe via the nearby island of Samos, while Turkish warships attempt to interdict their small vessels. Archaeology provides a perspective from the *longue durée*. We found amphoras, ceramic jugs that served as barrels in Antiquity, transporting wine, olive oil, and fish products, while at night we dined on those same goods. The artefacts tell a story of an arterial route connecting Egypt, the Levant, and Syria to Cyprus, the Aegean, and Black Sea in every time period. Sometimes the flow of people and goods goes in one direction; sometimes it goes in the other. However, the flow of people continues along this previously broken path.

Those who have the usual route closed to them must resort to irregular routes. This includes refugees, who must travel through war, social divisions, or economically depressed areas to reach a border. Once at the border, they may face a politicized route of entry, as many countries do not wish to admit large numbers of refugees, leading to irregular routes.

Routes are negotiated through cultural factors, including politics. The route between Mexico and the United States is different for a US citizen than it is for a Central American refugee. This is particularly evident through a policy known as Prevention Through Deterrence, or PTD.[16] First articulated by the United States in 1993, it was designed to block straightforward passage from Mexico into the United States, leaving only hazardous routes available to those seeking refuge. The policy argued that if the route was dangerous enough then individuals would not attempt to travel it, thereby preventing immigration. A version of this approach was adopted by the European Union to counteract refugees from Syria and North Africa. The number of sea journeys, as well

[15] Peter B. Campbell and George Koutsouflakis, 'Shipwreck Capital of the Aegean: The Fournoi Underwater Survey', *INA Quarterly*, 44.3/4 (2018), 9–15.

[16] Jason De León, *The Land of Open Graves: Living and Dying on the Migrant Trail* (Oakland: University of California Press, 2015), pp. 4–5.

Figure 4. A ship used by refugees that was run ashore in Greece with a Turkish naval vessel patrolling the channel in the background. Source: David Ang.

as a major increase in deaths, increased as a result of agreements between Turkey-EU and North Africa-EU closing land routes and forcing refugees to undertake sea routes.[17] Twenty-five years of data demonstrates PTD does not prevent crossings, but instead results in trauma and death.[18] The same result is evident with Mediterranean refugees following 2012.[19]

Just as travellers and mariners share itineraries, *periploi*, and maps, refugees and smugglers share information about irregular routes. Known as migration-specific capital, it is the sharing of secret routes.[20] Sadly, it is not always effective. Despite the fact that only 1 per cent of refugees travel by sea, 58 per cent of reported refugee deaths occur along sea routes.[21] These routes have come to symbolize the current flow of displaced people and contemporary power dynamics.

[17] UNODC, *Global Study on Smuggling of Migrants* (New York: United Nations, 2018), p. 6.

[18] Jason De León, 'Undocumented Migration, Use Wear, and the Materiality of Habitual Suffering in the Sonoran Desert', *Journal of Material Culture*, 18.4 (2013), 321–45.

[19] UNODC, *Global Study on Smuggling of Migrants*, pp. 6–7.

[20] De León, 'Undocumented Migration', pp. 321–45; A. Singer and D. Massey, 'The Social Process of Undocumented Border Crossing among Mexican Migrants', *International Migration Review*, 32.3 (1998), 561–92.

[21] UNODC, *Global Study on Smuggling of Migrants*, pp. 6–9.

## Exploiting Routes

Where there is an established orthodoxy, there are people who break it. In terms of cargo routes, this deviance takes the form of smugglers and pirates. Smugglers transport resources that are in demand but cannot travel along established routes either due to taxes on items like cigarettes or alcohol or prohibition such as the immigration of certain people. Smugglers create new, small-scale routes circumventing the established route. Antiquities, stolen from archaeological sites, museums, or collections, are one such product. They are smuggled from source countries to market countries through 'fluid networks'. These are ad hoc routes that are constantly changing to fit the geographical and social landscape.[22] As a corrupt border guard is replaced, the network changes to take advantage of another permeable border, shifting the route. These fluid routes result in millions of criminal profits from illicit antiquities trade.

Pirates and wreckers, on the other hand, exploit established routes. Knowing a route location allows brigands and highway men to lie in wait and spring a trap on unsuspecting travellers. Merchant traffic draw pirates, congregating at straits where ships were forced into constricted space such as the Fournoi Islands.[23] Edward Daniel Clarke described the experience of sailing through the pirate-infested strait of Fournoi in the nineteenth century:

> [O]ur Captain busied in appointing an extraordinary watch for the night, as a precaution against the pirates, who swarm in these seas... They lurk about the Isle of *Fourni*, in great numbers... After they have plundered a ship, and murdered the crew, they bore a hole through her bottom, sink her, and take to their boats again.[24]

The chances of coming upon a ship in the open ocean is miniscule, but within restricted spaces like straits pirates can take prizes because established navigational routes guarantee large amounts of traffic.

[22] Peter B. Campbell, 'The Illicit Antiquities Trade as a Transnational Criminal Network: Characterizing and Anticipating Trafficking of Cultural Heritage', *International Journal of Cultural Property*, 20.2 (2013), 113–53.

[23] Henry A. Ormerod, *Piracy in the Ancient World* (Baltimore: The Johns Hopkins University Press, 1997).

[24] Edward Daniel Clarke, *Travels in Various Countries of Europe, Asia and Africa: Part The Second Greece, Egypt and the Holy Land* (London: T. Cadell and W. Davies, 1813), p. 245.

Wreckers take advantage of dangerous waters or cause passing ships to sink.[25] They congregate along shipping routes and place false lights to confuse passing vessels, causing them to crash. The wreckers then strip the ship of anything they can reach. The odd shipwreck may benefit a local coastal community, but it is unpredictable. Entire communities of wreckers developed in key areas along navigation routes, being sustained annually through wrecked vessels.

## Conclusion

Routes are a means of conceptualizing and sharing spatial information composed of not only geographical data, but also reflecting hazards, politics, deviant behaviour, and other cultural information. A route for one person may be non-negotiable for another based on these factors. Routes have connected people for centuries and, even with satellite positioning and digital maps, people continue to rely on the previously 'broken path'.

Dr Peter Campbell is a maritime archaeologist and Lecturer in Cultural Heritage Under Threat at Cranfield University.
Dr Krešimir Vuković is a classicist and Alexander von Humboldt Research Fellow at Ludwig Maximilian University of Munich.

[25] Bella Bathurst, *The Wreckers: A Story of Killing Seas, False Lights and Plundered Ships* (New York: Harper, 2006).

# 30

# Sexualities

*Elliot Evans*

Early 1990s Abidjan: the third most populous French-speaking city in the world and the cosmopolitan economic centre of Ivory Coast (Côte d'Ivoire). In the Adjamé district, Mathurin and Ferdinand walk together, both wearing red shirts tucked into belted jeans. Mathurin's arm rests on Ferdinand's waist as they walk together side by side through public gardens, those around paying no attention at all, even despite the film crew following the couple. Speaking in French,[1] Ferdinand explains:

> *woubis* have great radar. They know exactly where to find each other. Whether in Europe, America ... or here in Adjamé. Ghettos or not, *woubis* always manage to have their hideouts. They're like bats, they live hidden. They move in groups, like birds nesting in the trees. They gather bit by bit, and you don't see them until suddenly the tree is teeming with them. That's *woubis* for you.[2]

*Woubi-can* is a secret, coded language spoken by the *branchés* of Ivory Coast – *branchés* being another coded word 'encompassing several categories of same-sex desire and practice'.[3] The term is derived from the French 'brancher'

[1] Since protagonists in the film speak multiple languages (generally French or Dioula), I will cite only the English subtitles here.

[2] *Woubi Chéri*, dir. by Philip Brooks and Laurent Bocahut (California Newsreel, 1998).

[3] Matthew Thomann, 'HIV Vulnerability and the Erasure of Sexual and Gender Diversity in Abidjan, Côte d'Ivoire', *Global Public Health*, 11.7–8 (2016), 994–1009 (p. 994).

Figure 1. Ferdinand and Mathurin walk together in *Woubi Chéri*, dir. by Philip Brooks and Laurent Bocahut. California Newsreel, 1998.

meaning 'to be plugged in', connected, hip.[4] As the charismatic leader of L'association des travestis de Côte d'Ivoire (Travesti Association of Cote d'Ivoire), Barbara, explains:

> [W]e have our own dictionary, our own way of talking. So, for example, when we say *woubi*, *woubis* are boys who play the role of the woman, who aren't necessarily *travesti*, who remain boys and who love men. Me, I am a *travesti*, it's special. Well, they call me *woubi* too because despite everything, I am a boy but I behave like a woman. And then there are the *yossis*. They are boys who sleep with women, *travestis*, and homosexuals. They are boys who keep their role. They play the role of the boy. They are the ones who behave like boys. They are the husbands of the *woubis*.[5]

[4] Thomann, 'HIV Vulnerability', p. 999.

[5] Matthew Thomann and Robbie Corey-Boulet, 'Violence, Exclusion and Resilience among Ivoirian Travestis', *Critical African Studies*, 9.1 (2017), 106–23 (p. 112).

There are further terms – *controus* are those who oppose this *branché* community, sometimes violently. *Toussou bakari* means a woman (*toussou*) who loves women. Other expressions allow members of this community to discreetly discuss sexual preferences, acts, and compatibility.[6]

Barbara, Mathurin, and Ferdinand all appear in the documentary *Woubi Chéri* (Darling Woubi) (1998) by Philip Brooks and Laurent Bocahut. The film's numerous protagonists speak in both French and Dioula (or Dyula; Jula), a language spoken by millions across the West African countries of Ivory Coast, Burkina Faso, and Mali. The film documents the lives of this *branché* community, with protagonists explaining their identities and relationships, their hopes, and day-to-day realities. Ultimately, *Woubi Chéri* culminates in a colourful *djémé* – a traditional feast – held by Barbara and L'association des travestis de Côte d'Ivoire in the Bingerville suburb of Abidjan.

While sexuality is often considered to be a private affair – something of personal rather than public concern – nation states have in fact carefully and fiercely regulated sexual practices and identities for centuries. Consider various legislation in numerous countries outlawing sodomy; state support for monogamous heterosexual unions through the institution of marriage; incentives for giving birth to children (as under the Third Reich, for instance); or laws restricting sex work. Michel Foucault has argued that nation states have regulated sexuality through disciplinary power: examining it through scientific investigation; governing it through legislation and institutions. Such disciplinary institutions include prisons and hospitals, schools and asylums: consider, as one example, the Salpêtrière institution in Paris, which operated from the mid-seventeenth century and was used to confine and observe female sex workers, 'hysterics', and other sexual deviants.[7]

Foucault's focus on power as it manifests through governance by the nation state is, however, no longer sufficient to consider sexualities as they manifest today: contemporary sexualities map out the complex web of transnational, global forces at play around us under globalized (or *almost* globalized) late capitalism. These forces include multi-national organizations; non-governmental organizations (NGOs); pharmaceutical companies; digital and communication technologies; social media and mass media. As George Chauncey and Elizabeth Povinelli argue, research into sexuality has turned to 'the effect of the increasingly transnational mobility of people, media, commodities, discourses, and capital on local, regional, and national modes

[6] Thomann and Corey-Boulet, 'Violence, Exclusion and Resilience', p. 109.

[7] Michel Foucault, *The History of Sexuality: An Introduction* (New York: Pantheon, 1978).

of sexual desire, embodiment, and subjectivity'.[8] Recent studies of globalization are not principally concerned with 'the fact of a set of global economic, political, and social connections' so much as with 'their scale, intensity, and density in post-Fordist capitalism and [...] their effect on the social practices, identities, and imaginaries of people throughout the world'.[9] The intensity of these global connections is such that it affects all of our sexual identities and practices: sexualities in the UK in 2020 are shaped variously by global apps such as Tinder, Hinge, and Grindr; multi-national pharmaceuticals producing Viagra, contraceptive devices, and pregnancy tests; and – at the time of writing – a global pandemic (Covid-19) shaping each of our attitudes towards intimacy.

But the 'global' is not neutral – not everyone benefits (or benefits equally) from this increasingly transnational hyper-connectedness. What dominates is the 'First World', the 'West', the 'Global North': often, in effect, former colonizers. Indeed, as Dennis Altman writes: 'in a sense, globalization is capitalist imperialism writ large [...] What was once accomplished by gunships and conquest is now achieved by shopping malls and cable television'.[10]

To return to the protagonists of *Woubi Chéri*, how have Ivorian sexualities been shaped by national and global forces? Events within the country have certainly played a large role in shaping Ivorian sexualities, and not only those within the *branché* community. Formerly colonized by France, Ivory Coast won independence in 1960 and enjoyed a highly successful economy for the next twenty years. Some have linked this economic success to the country's relatively liberal views on sexuality during the 1970s.[11] Conversely, civil conflict in 2010–2011 following the disputed presidential election fought between Laurent Gbagbo and Alassane Ouattara led to increased violence against *travestis* at the hands of the Forces Républicaines de Côte d'Ivoire (FRCI), who had been established as the new national army when Ouattara eventually took power.[12]

And yet, these 'national' events cannot be explained in a vacuum, but only from a more global perspective – indeed, they are inextricable from the country's relation with and to other nations; from the ongoing legacy of

[8] George Chauncey and Elizabeth A. Povinelli, 'Thinking Sexuality Transnationally: An Introduction', *GLQ*, 5.4 (1999), 439–50 (p. 439).

[9] Povinelli and Chauncey, 'Thinking Sexuality Transnationally', p. 440.

[10] Dennis Altman, 'Rupture or Continuity? The Internationalization of Gay Identities', in *Postcolonial, Queer: Theoretical Intersections*, ed. by John C. Hawley (Albany: State University of New York Press, 2001), pp. 19–42 (p. 31).

[11] Claudine Vidal, 'Guerre des sexes à Abidjan: Masculin, feminine, CFA', *Cahiers d'études africaines*, 17.65 (1977), 121–53.

[12] Thomann and Corey-Boulet, 'Violence, Exclusion and Resilience'.

French colonization and efforts of decolonization; to the country's location within a globalized world economy. Reinterpreting the examples above along these lines, first, Ivory Coast's economic success in the 1970s was due to a continued relationship with France (and also with the US) that many have described as neo-colonial, even while President Houphouët-Boigny ostensibly established an independent nation.[13] Second, the increased violence against *travestis* on the part of the FRCI led to greater support for these individuals from NGOs operating within Ivory Coast. These organizations had formerly focused on sexual minorities alone, and had even been hostile to gender minorities, including *woubis*. Their change of direction may be explained in relation to global forces, and some have argued that it is at least partly motivated by 'an increasing interest in transgender issues on the part of international donors'.[14]

John C. Hawley notes that 'there is a long tradition of multiple sexualities in Africa, but it is a tradition that has been violently interrupted by Western colonialism'.[15] While homosexuality is often decried as a foreign, Western imposition – as 'un-African' – by some political leaders in Africa,[16] laws criminalizing homosexuality in African countries are very often colonial legacies. Laws against homosexuality in countries colonized by Britain such as Kenya, Zimbabwe, Uganda, and Ghana (just to cite a few examples from the African continent) are built upon laws against 'unnatural acts' imported by Britain to its former colonies from the mid-nineteenth century onwards. While France decriminalized homosexuality before it colonized West Africa, and therefore did not import any such law, the colonial legacy remains a factor in West African relations with Western NGOs. Indeed, Matthew Farmer has argued that transnational NGOs negotiate the 'colonial baggage' of working in formerly colonized nations.[17]

Sexualities are not innate or inbuilt. Our various sexual identities are not simply expressions of variations in biology (our genetic code; our hormonal or chromosomal makeup). They are, rather, just as much formed *by* and

[13] Abou Bamba, *African Miracle, African Mirage: Transnational Politics and the Paradox of Modernization in Ivory Coast* (Athens, OH: Ohio University Press, 2016).

[14] Thomann and Corey-Boulet, 'Violence, Exclusion and Resilience', p. 106.

[15] John C. Hawley, 'In Transition: Self-expression in Recent African LGBTIQ Narratives', *Journal of the African Literature Association*, 11.1 (2017), 120–34 (p. 120).

[16] See, for example, Thérèse Migraine-George, 'Beyond the "Internalist" vs. "Externalist" Debate: The Local–Global Identities of African Homosexuals in Two Films, *Woubi Chéri* and *Dakan*', *Journal of African Cultural Studies*, 16.1 (2003), 45–56.

[17] Matthew Farmer, *Transnational LGBT Activism and UK-Based NGOs: Colonialism and Power* (London: Palgrave Macmillan, 2020).

*through* culture: laws governing what is socially acceptable; the references we have available to us in media representations; and, crucially, the language we have available to describe and make sense of ourselves. María Lugones argues that the related concepts of sexuality and gender are not only inseparable from colonialism, but in fact can be understood as a colonial invention. Colonizers used gender and sexuality as a tool of subjugation in the imperial project: 'colonialism did not impose precolonial, European gender arrangements on the colonized. It imposed a new gender system that created very different arrangements for colonized males and females than for white bourgeois colonizers'.[18] Gender and sexuality are thus a 'mode of organization of relations of production, property relations, of cosmologies and ways of knowing', and, as such, 'heterosexuality, capitalism, and racial classification are impossible to understand apart from each other'.[19]

Altman has theorized the potential existence of a global gay identity, and as Migraine-George notes, 'the protagonists of *Woubi Chéri*, who live in the highly urbanized and cosmopolitan context of Abidjan, refer to a global gay community with which they (at least partly) identify'.[20] Yet, as the *woubi-can* language outlined by Barbara above shows, the Western model of lesbian, gay, bisexual, transgender, intersex, or queer-questioning (LGBTIQ) identities simply does not map onto many local contexts. Language is key to shaping our sexual identities. The assumption that Western terms and models of sexuality are universal, and will therefore fit everywhere, is a form of linguistic imperialism. The *imposition* of these Western terms (through the work of NGOs or public health discourse) amounts to cultural colonization.

To offer an example of this from the Ivorian context, Thomann describes the way in which human immunodeficiency virus (HIV) prevention programmes in Abidjan funded by large transnational NGOs have the effect of erasing local identity terms and gender diversity in favour of the supposedly 'neutral' term preferred in public health discourse: MSM (an acronym used to refer to men who sleep with men).[21] Clearly the *branché* identities Barbara outlines above encompass something more complex than MSM – not all *branchés* are men for a start, and even among men there are very different gendered positions ranging from *woubi* to *yossi*. And yet Thomann describes the way in which local organizations' funding is dependent on them 'recruiting' more and more 'MSM into intervention programming, data which they can then

[18] María Lugones, 'Heterosexualism and the Colonial/Modern Gender System', *Hypatia*, 22.1 (2007), 186–209 (p. 186).

[19] Lugones, 'Heterosexualism and the Colonial/Modern Gender System', pp. 186–87.

[20] Migraine-George, 'Beyond the "Internalist" vs. "Externalist" Debate', p. 50.

[21] Thomann, 'HIV Vulnerability'.

use to prove a "return" on donor investments'.[22] While some Ivorians have 'internalised and reappropriated' the MSM category, actually identifying *as* an 'MSM', Thomann argues that 'it remains a deeply normative category', and one that is enforced by US-based funding. The particular organization Thomann writes of is Heartland Alliance International, whose global arm is 'a nearly $82 million Chicago-based NGO'. Heartland funds HIV prevention programmes in Abidjan, including those delivered by *Alternative* (Alternative) and *Arc-en-Ciel* (Rainbow).[23]

In this way, wealthy 'global' NGOs based in the West are shaping the sexual language and identities of West Africans. The amount of money involved in these public health interventions have led to Thomann and others describing them as an industry, one that 'shapes new forms of sociality among sexual and gender minorities'.[24] As one worker at *Alternative* in Abidjan says: 'in Africa, we [*branchés*] have become a bit like AIDS. We're an industry. Meaning that most people are taking more care of what is going back in their pockets than the lives of *branchés*. Organizations care about *branchés* insofar as they can fill their pockets'.[25]

By focusing on the example of Ivorian sexualities, I in no way mean to suggest that only peripheral or non-Western sexualities are constructed through the web of transnational structures and systems. While the nature of globalization means that wealthier countries (as well as organizations based in those countries) have a greater material and cultural influence globally – consider the global dominance of English as *lingua franca*, for instance – sexual identities within Western countries, the global North, or former colonial powers are just as constructed.

To offer a specific example from the UK, Jamie Hakim argues that the emergence of 'chemsex' (extended sex parties organized, generally by gay men, through hook-up apps and fuelled by drugs such as Gamma Hydroxybutyrate (GHB) and crystal methamphetamine) in the UK is inseparable from the societal condition of neoliberalism.[26] Such parties offer a release from the competitive individualism of neoliberal capitalism, and are also influenced by global capital flooding areas of London such as Vauxhall, the gentrification of which has led to the closure of resident gay clubs and sex venues, pushing the community to private domestic space. Hakim notes that the flow of global

[22] Thomann, 'HIV Vulnerability', p. 998.

[23] Thomann, 'HIV Vulnerability', pp. 997–98.

[24] Thomann, 'HIV Vulnerability', p. 1004.

[25] Thomann, 'HIV Vulnerability', p. 1005.

[26] Jamie Hakim, 'The Rise of Chemsex: Queering Collective Intimacy in Neoliberal London', *Cultural Studies*, 32 (2018), 249–75.

capital to London, and the many migrants brought with it, has also led to a rise in chemsex parties due to new arrivals seeking to make bonds and alleviate loneliness.[27] Oliver Davis builds on Hakim's work to demonstrate how the representation of chemsex by global media platforms (VICE Media, specifically, which boasts shareholders including the Walt Disney Company and 21st Century Fox) has shaped its governance in the UK.[28]

More broadly, Edward Said's *Orientalism* argued that the Western idea of the 'Orient' was a fantasy tied to imperialism.[29] Joseph Massad, following Said, has argued that the West has positioned the 'Orient' as its sexual 'other'.[30] In previous centuries, it defined itself in opposition to the 'sexual licentiousness' of Islam, with France justifying its invasion of Egypt in 1798 as a *mission civilisatrice* (civilizing mission), and with many (including notable literary figures including André Gide and Oscar Wilde) viewing North Africa as a playground for experimenting sexual tourists from Western countries. More recently, the West has defined itself as a liberal 'saviour' in opposition to Islam's supposed sexual repression, again justifying military intervention on such grounds.[31] The very idea of 'Frenchness' – not to mention the nation-state of France itself – does not and could not exist in isolation from its former colonies and legacy of imperialism, its current overseas territories and its relation to other colonial and postcolonial structures.[32] Any possibility of a collective French sexual identity would be equally inseparable from any of these realties.

Describing the ways in which sexualities are formed and produced by transnational factors as I have done throughout this article should not be taken as a denial of the agency of sexual subjects. As well as being shaped

27 Hakim, 'The Rise of Chemsex', p. 267.

28 Oliver Davis, 'Prison Everywhere? The Imbrication of Coercive and Pastoral Governance in the Regulation of "Chemsex" and New Psychoactive Substances', in *Prohibitions and Psychoactive Substances in History, Culture and Theory*, ed. by Susannah Wilson (London: Routledge, 2019), pp. 209–34 (p. 219).

29 Edward Said, *Orientalism* (New York: Vintage, 1979).

30 Joseph A. Massad, *Desiring Arabs* (Chicago and London: University of Chicago Press, 2007).

31 Gayatri C. Spivak, 'Righting Wrongs', *South Atlantic Quarterly*, 103 (2004), 523–81.

32 For an exploration of one literary construction of French sexual identity defined in opposition to racialized 'others' (including Arab 'repression'), see my analysis of *La Vie sexuelle de Catherine M*: Elliot Evans, '*Liberté sexuelle*: Pleasure and Identity in Catherine Millet's *La Vie sexuelle de Catherine M.* (2001)', in *Plaisirs de femmes: Women, Pleasure and Transgression in French Literature and Culture*, ed. by Carrie Tarr, Elliot Evans, and Maggie Allison (Oxford: Peter Lang, 2019), pp. 123–38.

by global forces, the protagonists of *Woubi Chéri* are certainly their own agents. While their sexual practices and identities may be formed through transnational forces, they not only show resistance to dominant narratives, but bend them to fit their needs. These protagonists create space for themselves in the world: through community by subverting the traditional *djémé* to render it a celebration of gender and sexual diversity; through the language of *woubi-can*, using French and Dioula to create words that are not only hidden to mainstream society, but creatively express and fashion their own realities and identities.[33] Barbara in particular is portrayed in the film as a force to be reckoned with. Reflecting on her experience, she shows an agility that manages to side-step many of the forces that would constrain her, telling the filmmakers: 'you have to be creative, live life like an artist'. As well as elucidating the global forces that shape our realities, research in the field of sexualities must also offer a way forward by highlighting these areas of creative resistance.

Elliot Evans is co-organiser of *Critical Sexology* and a lecturer in sexuality and gender at the University of Birmingham.

[33] Matthew Durkin, 'Laurent Bocahut and Philip Brooks, directors. *Woubi chéri*. 1998. 62 minutes. French. Côte d'Ivoire. California Newsreel. $24.95', *African Studies Review*, 60.2 (2017), 286–87 (p. 287).

# 31

# Sound

*Cara Levey*

> Como los nazis, les va a pasar, adonde vayan les iremos a buscar.[1]
>
> Song frequently heard at *escraches* in Argentina.

Buenos Aires, a warm sunny day in November 2007, before the stifling summer takes hold. Metres away from the famous Obelisk that dominates the downtown skyline, a noisy crowd has convened at the intersection of Lavalle and Diagonal Norte, two arterial thoroughfares that bisect the Argentine capital. The sound of voices singing and chanting is accompanied by drumming from the *murga*, a band of street musicians.[2] As the cacophony increases in volume and intensity, the unsuspecting passers-by might be forgiven for mistaking this gathering for a carnival celebration or the *previa* (build-up) to a local football derby. To those who listen more carefully, they may be able to make out the stark warning delivered: 'wherever you go, we will find you'. This is an *escrache,* a noisy form of protest that has been deployed since the mid-1990s by H.I.J.O.S (Hijos por la Identidad y la Justicia contral el Olvido y el Silencio), the group that brings together the children of victims of the 1976–1983 dictatorship.[3] The word *escrache* is derived from

[1] 'Just like the Nazis, it will happen to you, wherever you go, we will find you'. Translation, and all those that follow, are the author's.

[2] Diana Taylor, *The Archive and the Repertoire: Performing Cultural Memory in the Americas* (Durham, NC and London: Duke University Press, 2003), p. 182.

[3] The collective H.I.J.O.S (Sons and Daughters for Identity and Justice against Forgetting and Silence) was founded in the mid-1990s by the (by then, grown-up)

the Rioplatense word for 'expose' or 'uncover', alluding to the way in which participants 'out' perpetrators accused of human rights violations and ensure that society will not forget such crimes.

Back to November 2007. Although the building where the protesters congregate may seem unremarkable, it is the office of Oscar Hermelo, a lesser-known civilian accomplice of the military Junta. Other songs inform those in the vicinity that he worked in the Escuela Superior de Mecánica de la Armada (ESMA) (the Navy Mechanics School), the most notorious of the approximately 500 dictatorship-era clandestine detention centres, where about 5000 of those forcibly disappeared by the state were taken. The majority of these *desaparecidos* were never seen again. At the time of the *escrache*, like many perpetrators, Hermelo had evaded prison and continued to work as a federal lawyer, maintaining the regime's wall of silence.[4] However, in spite of the obstacles to putting the accused on trial, the *escraches* have noisily interrupted institutional silence and dramatically torn off the cloak of anonymity enjoyed by so many perpetrators, unveiling their crimes, and, crucially, their faces, to wider society.

Following roughly the same format, and realized in the wake of a concerted publicity drive, participants assemble at a pre-determined location and march to a perpetrator's home or workplace. After several hours, the voices and drumming fall silent and participants disband; the only material trace a few abandoned flyers and fading graffiti on the pavement outside. This fleeting, yet vociferous, interruption into everyday life is illustrative of the role of sound in shaping the environments that we inhabit, as well as in challenging the troubling legacy of state repression.

The study of sound has garnered increasing interest from scholars in the last few years, expanding significantly to include anthropological, historical, and cultural studies approaches. Writing in 2004, Pinch and Bijsterveld defined Sound Studies as 'an emerging interdisciplinary area that studies the material production and consumption of music, sound, noise, and silence and how these have changed throughout history and within different societies'.[5] Less than a decade later, the duo made the case for Sound Studies, not as an

children of mainly those who were disappeared or murdered by state security forces. There are branches throughout the country and also elsewhere in Latin America and in Europe.

[4] Francesca Lessa and Cara Levey, 'From Blanket Impunity to Judicial Opening(s): H.I.J.O.S and Memory Making in Post-Dictatorship Argentina (2005–2012)', *Latin American Perspectives*, 42.3 (2015), 207–25.

[5] Trevor Pinch and Karin Bijsterveld, 'Sound Studies: New Technologies and Music', *Social Studies of Science*, 34.5 (2004), 635–48 (p. 636).

interdisciplinary field straddling various areas of study, but as a more established discipline in its own right.[6] Indeed, scholars from outside musicology and composition have sought to conceptualize sound's relationship with surrounding environments, both locally and transnationally. Sound does not only affect *how* we live, but has much to tell us, as speakers, listeners, scholars, and learners of modern languages, about different societies.

A pioneer of the connection between sound, culture, and environment R. Murray Schafer adopted a holistic approach to the sonic environment to advocate for the 'soundscape'.[7] Within the soundscape's cacophony of sounds is what Bernie Krause has dubbed 'anthropophony':[8] noise created by humans (as opposed to nature) either intentionally or non-intentionally. The *escrache* is comprised of anthropophonic sounds that can be categorized, as Krause does, as distinctly human-generated: physiological (grunting, talking, or, in the case of the *escrache,* shouting, singing, and chanting), electromechanical, controlled sound (music, theatre, etc.) and incidental (footsteps, rustling, etc.). The *escrache* is the result of a blend of intentional and unintentional sounds, part of a constellation of noise within the soundscape.

As analysis of the *escrache* elucidates, sound profoundly effects not only the immediate vicinity in which it emerges, but can reverberate beyond. H.I.J.O.S and their supporters seek to alter our perception of the neighbourhood *and* construct an alternative (almost utopian) vision of Argentina's authoritarian past and post-authoritarian present, one in which all perpetrators will be held to account. The *escrache* should be framed within the recent global interest in sound employed as a means to change. The ongoing project 'Protest and Politics' attempts to capture not only what protest looks like, but how it sounds, resulting in a database that maps protests of different volumes. It is no surprise that two of the audio tracks included in this cartography of cacophony are from Argentina. Both are reminiscent of the *escrache,* featuring drumming and chanting but were convened in response to environmental issues.[9] Furthermore, another two of the examples featured are highly influenced by Argentine and South American demonstrations: the pot-banging – *cacerolazos* – that became iconic during the dying days

[6] *The Oxford Handbook of Sound Studies,* ed. by Trevor Pinch and Karin Bijsterveld (Oxford: Oxford University Press, 2012).

[7] R. Murray Schafer, *The Soundscape: Our Sonic Environment and the Tuning of the World* (Rochester, VT: Destiny Books, 1993).

[8] Bernie Krause, 'Anatomy of the Soundscape: Evolving Perspectives', *Journal of Audio-Engineering Society,* 56.1/2 (2008), 73–80 (p. 73).

[9] The project is the work of Stuart Fowkes, a sound artist from Oxford, who claims that it is the first project to globally map sound: Protest and Politics, <https://citiesandmemory.com/protest/> [accessed 10 January 2021].

of the Pinochet regime in Chile and in the 2001 financial crisis in Argentina have been taken up in Iceland to critique austerity measures; iterations of *Que se vayan todos* (They must all go), the cry that filled Argentina's streets in rejection of successive ineffective governments in the early 2000s, have reached Greece to articulate similar frustrations.[10] Sound is not only invoked to challenge the powers that be, but sonic protest has travelled transnationally, evolving as it encounters different histories and geographies.

To understand the evolution of the *escrache,* and noise therein as a foundational element, we briefly revisit its inception. As noted, post-dictatorship Argentina was characterized by impunity, enshrined in laws passed in the 1980s that restricted criminal prosecution to a small number of perpetrators.[11] By the early 1990s, silence had been firmly established with regard to past crimes. In the aftermath of impunity laws, Kaiser asserts that Argentines lived in a 'cultural scenario of impunity', described as 'society's apparent adaptation, conscious or unconscious, to the reality that torturers, assassins, and "disappearers" have a place within streets, restaurants, coffee shops, television screens, magazines, holiday resorts, official ceremonies, and even significant public office'.[12] This undoubtedly had both symbolic and tangible effects on the post-dictatorship city. Indeed, it was not uncommon for victims of the dictatorship to encounter perpetrators in the streets of Buenos Aires. Carlos Pisoni, a member of H.I.J.O.S, has described feeling compelled to take part in the *escrache* when he identified the man who tortured his father in a bar.[13] The prevailing sense of cultural impunity was underpinned by silences around the crimes of those sharing urban space with the victims, survivors, and relatives and the overwhelmingly muted public discussion about this recent past.

In this sense, the *escrache* took its cue then from the *lack* of justice and silence from the perpetrators and broader society. The first *escrache* was launched by H.I.J.O.S in December 1996 against Jorge Luis Magnacco,

[10] Ezequiel Adamovksy, 'Afterword', in *Argentina since the 2001 Crisis: Recovering the Past, Reclaiming the Future,* ed. by Cara Levey, Daniel Ozarow, and Christopher Wylde (New York: Palgrave, 2014), pp. 233–38 (p. 38).

[11] Following a long process of judicial challenges at domestic and international level, Congress finally repealed the Laws of Due Obedience and Full Stop in 2005, paving the way for legal challenges to impunity.

[12] Susana Kaiser, 'Escraches: Demonstrations, Communication and Political Memory in Post-Dictatorial Argentina', *Media, Culture and Society,* 24.4 (2002), 499–516, (pp. 501–2).

[13] Francisco Peregil, '"Comencé a escrachar al encontrarme en un bar al torturador de mi padre"', *El País,* 13 April 2013, <https://elpais.com/politica/2013/04/12/actualidad/1365788868_011504.html> [accessed 21 January 2021].

an obstetrician implicated in the clandestine births of babies who were kidnapped and illegally 'adopted'. He still worked as a doctor in a Buenos Aires hospital and was protected by the ongoing impunity laws.[14] As the Buenos Aires branch of H.I.J.O.S explains: 'en aquella época era imposible aplicar justicia. Estos genocidas vivían con total impunidad, ocupaban puestos de responsabilidad en la sociedad'.[15]

During the late 1990s, the *escrache* would revolutionize human rights protest, not only in Argentina but reverberating beyond to neighbouring Chile and Uruguay, and later to Spain.[16] With the coming of age of a new generation of activists, sound was generated to challenge official amnesty and amnesia. The sound of the *escrache* is closely connected to its raison d'être: the need to shatter this silence and to reject reconciliation with the perpetrators, to prevent them from going about their everyday lives in the city unnoticed. In this sense, the noisy nature of the *escrache* broke rank with other long-standing sites of human rights protest, such as the more subdued *rondas* of the mothers seeking information about their disappeared children in the iconic Plaza de Mayo.

Furthermore, central to the success of the *escrache* is not only its visibility, but its audibility, which inhibits those who might encounter it from simply walking on by. Liz Greene, however, contends that noise – understood as a series of sounds – might be hidden or ignored. This is a particular risk with protest that unfolds in noisy urban environments, where it is in danger of being drowned out by traffic or background noise within the complex soundscape. As Greene continues, noise tends to be considered less meaningful than sound, yet if we listen carefully, it can acquire significance.[17] Indeed, the *escrache* shows us that the divisions between noise and sound are more blurred than we might initially think, but that within the cacophony of voices, music, and background noise, there is a clear message.

Through amending the lyrics to well-known songs or melodies, sound serves to challenge silence and impunity. As signalled by the lyrics that announced this chapter, the *escraches* issue a direct warning to any perpetrator

[14] Victoria Ginzberg, 'Diez años de H.I.J.O.S', *Página 12,* 17 April 2005, <https://www.pagina12.com.ar/diario/elpais/1-49866-2005-04-17.html> [accessed 21 January 2021].

[15] 'During that period, justice proved impossible. Those guilty of genocide enjoyed absolute impunity, and held positions of responsibility in our society', in Peregil, '"Comencé a escrachar"'.

[16] Ginzberg, 'Diez años de H.I.J.O.S'.

[17] Liz Greene, 'From Noise: Blurring the Boundaries of the Soundtrack', in *The Palgrave Handbook of Sound Design and Music in Screen Media: Integrated Soundtracks*, ed. by Liz Greene and Danijela Kulezic-Wilson (New York: Palgrave, 2016), pp. 17–32 (pp. 21–22).

or accomplice wishing to live a quiet life: they will be hunted down like the Nazi war criminals, such as Mengele and Eichmann, who had fled abroad. The *escrache* mirrors this search by attempting to identify perpetrators living in anonymity with a view to bringing them to justice in the future. Lyrics are also tailored to each target of the *escrache*. For Hermelo '[...] te vinimos a escrachar [...] para que todos se enteren [...] y dejes de ser fiscal'.[18] Another referenced his shady involvement in the appropriation of the disappeared's belongings, this time to 'Cuando yo me muera' by Uruguayan singer Rubén Rada. Sound provides an element of unexpectedness as passers-by may recognize the melody but not lyrics; the familiarity and repetition elicit participation from those in the vicinity. It is when members of society take part, be that by singing, chanting, or applauding, that the *escrache* is fully realized, that it comes into being.[19] The symbolic 'street' justice meted out here is not dependent on future intervention from the authorities, but is both more immediate and attainable in the here and now. This attempt to make the streets a prison for the perpetrator is accompanied by concrete measures to challenge impunity, usually the submission of a file to the judiciary, to ensure that the case does not fall on deaf ears. This is of paramount importance. Kate Lacey's work has been instrumental in shifting academic debates away from noisemaking as a political act, to considering the question of who *listens*. She urges us to remember that 'any intervention in the public sphere is undertaken in the hope, faith or expectation that there is a public out there, ready to listen and engage', in other words, that participants find resonance with a wider audience and prevent sound being lost forever,[20] in the case of the *escrache*, bringing debates about democracy and justice out of hiding, changing public perceptions and putting pressure on the authorities.[21]

The commotion created by the *escrache* temporarily interrupts the everyday, yet, when the noisy protagonists have disbanded and the everyday neighbourhood hubbub, what remains? As an 'ephemeral' site of condemnation and commemoration, the *escrache* has a unique relationship to space and time.[22] The aim is to 'leave a mark on the place so that once we leave, in

[18] 'we came to "escrachar" you [...] so that everyone knows [...] and you won't be a lawyer anymore'.

[19] Interview with 'Jorge', former member of HIJOS capital, Buenos Aires, March 2008. Name changed at interviewee's request.

[20] Kate Lacey, 'Listening Overlooked: An Audit of Listening as a Category in the Public Sphere', *Javnost – The Public*, 18.4 (2011), 5–20, (p. 11).

[21] Temma Kaplan, *Taking Back the Streets: Women, Youth, and Direct Democracy* (Berkeley, Los Angeles, London: University of California Press, 2003), p. 3.

[22] Cara Levey, *Fragile Memory, Shifting Impunity: Commemoration and Contestation in Post-Dictatorship Argentina and Uruguay* (Oxford: Peter Lang, 2016).

Figure 1. A *murga* at the *escrache* of Oscar Hermelo, downtown Buenos Aires, 28 November 2007.
Author's image.

the days that follow people still wonder what happened there'.[23] In this way, the *escrache* discourages complacency and obsolescence, by converting the passive listener into active voice. The fleeting intervention is part of a larger process that makes making condemnation and commemoration a truly participatory activity by altering citizens' and neighbours' perception of the surrounding area long after the protesters have fallen silent.

Landmark judicial shifts, and a shift in the federal government's stance towards addressing the past in the 2000s, brought *escraches* to an impasse. They continued for a few years after the overturn of impunity laws in 2005, but went rather quiet after 2008 in response to the increasing opportunities for justice. However, just because it was out of sight and earshot, did not mean it had disappeared entirely. H.I.J.O.S were resolute in their view that the *escrache* 'will always return, because there are many criminals who remain unpunished'.[24] And return it did. In May 2015, an *escrache* was convened

[23] Interview with 'Francisco' of H.I.J.O.S Capital, quoted in Lessa and Levey, 'From Blanket Impunity to Judicial Opening(s)'.

[24] H.I.J.O.S 'Escrache: Memoria en Acción', *Página 12*, 19 February 2011, <https://www.pagina12.com.ar/diario/elpais/1-162640-2011-02-19.html> [accessed 11 January 2021].

against two prominent businessmen: Vicente Massot, owner of the daily newspaper *La Nueva Provincia* in Bahía Blanca, and Carlos Blaquier, former president of the agricultural corporation, Ledesma. Both were implicated in the disappearance and murder of their workers. Proceedings against these two individuals had stalled on the grounds of lack of evidence, a not unfamiliar scenario in spite of the more favourable judicial panorama since 2005. The *escrache* was redeployed as part of a wider societal and judicial attempt to identify and highlight the role of these *genocidas civiles* (civilian mass murderers) in repression. In this sense, while there is significantly more debate about past crimes, there are still unanswered questions about the authors of these crimes. These gaps, and the ongoing stalling and hampering of trials, are precisely what the *escrache* seeks to call out. Meanwhile, the digital age has ushered in new technologies capable of capturing and circulating sound,[25] which has implications for the reverberation of the *escrache* transnationally. As I have argued elsewhere,[26] social media outlets such as YouTube and Facebook have played an important 'beyond-site' role; official and unofficial recordings of the *escrache* are shared online, holding out exciting possibilities to engage with new and diverse listening publics beyond the specific geographies and temporalities of the *escrache*.

Cara Levey is a lecturer in Latin American Studies working on memory, human rights and dictatorship at University College Cork, Ireland.

25 Pinch and Bijsterveld, *Oxford Handbook of Sound Studies*, p. 5.

26 Cara Levey, 'Archiving the Repertoire, Performing the Archive: Virtual Iterations of Second-Generation Activism in Post-Dictatorship Argentina', in *Social Movements, Cultural Memory and Digital Media: Mobilising Mediated Remembrance*, ed. by. Samuel Merrill, Emily Keightley, and Priska Daphi (New York: Palgrave, 2020), pp. 199–223.

32

# Stories

*Emma Bond*

No nation now but the imagination[1]

Jacques Derrida's famous 1966 lecture 'Structure, Sign and Play in the Discourse of the Human Sciences' is perhaps best known for signalling the arrival of post-structuralist thought in the United States.[2] But if we are to pick apart and reassemble key moments in the essay, it can actually be used to formulate an enticingly dynamic manifesto for how to read stories in a transnational frame. Derrida's premise (much simplified) is that structures of knowledge and culture have, in the past, been assumed to function outward from a pre-established centre, or 'locus'. This centre anchors the structure in question, organizing and delineating it, but it also stagnates any potential for creative play or innovation. Instead, Derrida asks us to follow the deconstructionist methods of Nietzsche, Freud, and Heidegger: turning away from the centre and replacing it with a kind of 'nonlocus', or non-centre that allows for processes of substitution, transformation, and re-assemblage to take place. In this way, a space will be created for a mapping of 'freeplay' that privileges the relations between the signs that make up the structure.

This process of relational decentring becomes even more relevant when Derrida applies it to the human sciences. He takes as his example ethnology,

[1] Derek Walcott, 'The Schooner *Flight*', in *The Star-Apple Kingdom* (New York: Farrar Straus & Giroux, 1979), pp. 3–20 (p. 8).

[2] Jacques Derrida, 'Structure, Sign and Play in the Discourse of the Human Sciences', in *Writing and Difference*, trans. by Alan Bass (London: Routledge, 2001), pp. 351–70.

which emerged as a science just as European culture itself was being 'dislocated, driven from its locus, and forced to stop considering itself as the culture of reference'.[3] And this is where his argument might suggest how to engage the transnational as a narrative methodology, something I will illustrate here by placing Ubah Cristina Ali Farah's 2014 novel *Il comandante del fiume* into dialogue with the multi-media artwork of Maud Sulter (1960–2008). By privileging this ethnological impulse to look beyond old imperial centres of knowledge in order to bring new networks of cultural diversity into relational contact, I want to dislodge the transnational from its usual cultural associations with an author's biography or the contents of a book, and instead see where we can identify it in stories as a stylistic or technical choice, or even as a methodological tool of analysis.

When seen in this way, cultural production that we term 'transnational' cannot simply be conflated with other labels such as 'multi-cultural', 'global', or 'world', which rely on transactional practices of circulation and commerce.[4] Rather, the transnational has specific intentions to negotiate systems of time and space through that same sense of relational linkage or exchange described above, of 'multiple ties and interactions linking people or institutions across the borders of nation-states'.[5] In terms of style, the transnational embodies a similar association with play through its 'fluidity of constructed styles and practices: syncretism, creolization, bricolage, cultural translation and hybridity'.[6] It is this practice of construction by addition and association that lies at the heart of the transnational story, and is equally identifiable in Derrida's discourse on the ethnological method of 'bricolage' in 'Structure, Sign and Play'. Derrida is here discussing the work of anthropologist Claude Lévi-Strauss, who defines the 'bricoleur' as someone who uses 'the means *at hand*', that is:

> The instruments he finds at his disposition around him, those which are already there, which had not been especially conceived with an eye to the operation for which they are to be used and to which one tries by trial and error to adapt them, not hesitating to change them whenever it appears necessary, or to try several of them at once, even if their form and their origin are heterogeneous – and so forth.[7]

[3] Derrida, 'Structure, Sign and Play', p. 356.

[4] Maria Koundoura, *Transnational Culture, Transnational Identity: The Politics and Ethics of Global Culture Exchange* (London: I.B. Tauris, 2012), p. 5.

[5] Steven Vertovec, *Transnationalism* (London: Routledge, 2009), p. 3.

[6] Vertovec, *Transnationalism*, p. 7.

[7] Derrida, 'Structure, Sign and Play', p. 360.

The term 'at hand' takes on a critical importance here, since it specifically implies a range of bodily acts of selection. Hands that choose, cut, and paste enact playful manual juxtapositions and re-assemblage that rely on the dynamic interplay between the here and now of corporeal organs of perception and tactility, yet that can also access materials (within reach) that originate from or simply reference other times and spaces. This emphasis on the body as placed in a local setting is characteristic of transnational storytelling, in which the local and the global are inevitably entwined.[8] Transnational narratives span 'distant proximities',[9] in which the global works precisely by means of linking up a series of particularities. Transnational methods can therefore be identified in stories that feature interactions of bodies and material (texts), narrative interactions that allow – crucially – for the creation of *new* meaning from existing parts.

Such transnational practices of cultural bricolage thus stage relations of proximity and distance that lead us back to Derrida's insistence on the relationality of signs. For equally, the abandonment of the centre, as a presupposed, original, absolute value, is also essential for an understanding of contemporary human diaspora and mobility. As Vertovec states, diasporic consciousness is 'marked by dual or multiple identifications' and an individual 'awareness of de-centred attachments, connections elsewhere, multi-locality'.[10] It is during such processes, as we will see through analysing examples of both written and visual narratives, that the imaginary can actively *re*-create, in a transnational fashion.

*Il comandante del fiume* is Ali Farah's second novel and tells the story of Yabar, a troubled Roman teenager of Somali heritage. It is narrated from a first-person perspective that nonetheless muddles any sense of strict temporal linearity and combines an Italian language narrative with Somali and English insertions to form a complex series of flashbacks, memories, and myth-building. This characteristic of folding together composite elements is not, however, confined to the structural or linguistic composition of the story. The element of bricolage becomes absolutely fundamental to Yabar's remapping of his own composite identity through the recuperation of social and cultural signs, symbols, myths, and memories. In a literal sense, this process begins with the play sessions he recalls from his childhood:

[8] Ulf Hannerz, *Transnational Connections: Culture, People, Places* (London: Routledge, 1996), p. 27.

[9] James Rosenau, *Distant Proximities: Dynamics beyond Globalization* (Princeton: Princeton University Press, 2003).

[10] Vertovec, *Transnationalism*, p. 5.

> Nei giorni di pioggia [...] ci sbizzarrivamo con tempere, colla, cartoncini, conchiglie, foglie secche, insomma *tutto quello che ci trovavamo per le mani in quel momento.* [...] Non ero bravo a riprodurre le figure esattamente com'erano [...] a me piaceva dipingere le scene mentre accadevano: battaglie navali, astronavi nello spazio, un esercito di formiche, tutto succedeva mentre lo armeggiavo con il pennello.[11]

Yabar perfectly reproduces the bricolage activity of using found objects (at hand) to create fantasy scenarios that rely equally on imaginative or creative re-assemblage. Yet such practices become a fundamental element not only in his desire to recuperate lost memories connected to his Somali origins, but also constitute an attempt to literally reinsert himself (as a Black Italian) into the popular national cultural identity, one that seems to reject him at every turn. As an example, he recounts how he and his mother attempt to reproduce a Will Smith doll, the first cultural symbol he has encountered that physically resembles him. His mother Zahra locates a generic male doll that the two proceed to dismember together and re-create in the image of the African American actor.

> Mia madre mi aiutò a segare la testa del pupazzetto, che incollammo con il Super Attak al corpo nudo di un guerriero muscolosissimo, dopodiché lo colorai con un pennarello marrone indelebile, in modo che avesse la pelle dello stesso colore del mio eroe. Mamma si mise a cucire un intero set di abiti per Willie. [...] L'ultimo vestito che ricordo fu quello da soldato. In quell'occasione usammo la iuta di una confezione di riso thailandese e il quadratino di cuoio dell'etichetta.[12]

The feelings of attachment to the miniature model engendered by this trans-nationalizing bricolage allow Yabar to achieve a sense of mastery through

[11] Ubah Cristina Ali Farah, *Il comandante del fiume* (Rome: 66thand2nd, 2014), p. 39 (my emphasis): 'On rainy days, we would let our fantasy run riot with colours, glue, card, shells, dried leaves, basically *anything that we could lay our hands on in that moment.* [...] I wasn't very good at reproducing figures exactly, but I preferred drawing scenes while they were happening: naval battles, spaceships in orbit, an army of ants, it all happened while I was holding my paintbrush'.

[12] Ali Farah, *Il comandante del fiume*, pp. 85–86: 'My mother helped me to saw off the head of the doll, which we glued onto the nude body of the super-muscly warrior with Super Attak, after which I colored it in with a permanent brown marker, so that its skin was the same color as my hero's. Mum started sewing a set of clothes for Willie. [...] The last outfit I remember was the soldier. On that occasion we used the jute from a box of Thai rice and a small square of leather from the label'.

active play, as well as to experience positive aesthetic emotion. As Lévi-Strauss explains, this pleasure is drawn precisely from the small-scale dimensions of such an object, whereby the virtue of reduction means that the concept represented by the object 'can be grasped, assessed, and apprehended at a glance'.[13] Through such bricolage artistry, therefore, Yabar successfully achieves a certain self-knowledge (of the transnational whole of his identity rather than composite parts of his mixed heritage), for 'in it and through it, a person is made into a subject'.[14]

But most importantly for the narrative action itself, this kind of transnational bricolage also characterizes the decomposition and subjective *re*-composition of Yabar's relationship with his father, who has disappeared following his involvement in the violence of the Somali civil war. Yabar can't remember clearly what his father looks like since his mother has removed all traces of him from the house, but he manages to find some photos of them together in a box where as a child he would keep 'monete del mondo, conchiglie, cartoline e altre piccole cose'.[15] In this box are four images of Yabar and his father taken in a photo booth on the one visit he paid his son at the boarding school he is temporarily placed into soon after their arrival in Rome.

> Nelle immagini si vedono due facce sempre tagliate, un uomo e un bambino i nostri visi non erano mai completi, allora ho preso le forbici per separare la sua faccia dalla mia e un cartoncino su cui attaccare i pezzi. Mi ero messo in testa che dovevo comporre le nostre facce, per vederlo di nuovo, ma i pezzi non combaciavano tra loro e così il risultato appariva mostruoso, un occhio più grande, la bocca sul collo, la fronte troppo bassa.[16]

The shattering of his family unit by inter-clan fighting and resultant diasporic movement is thus re-enacted by Yabar in his collage work in a way that may not allow for an easy recuperation of his past heritage or his father figure, but

[13] Claude Lévi-Strauss, *The Savage Mind* (London: Weidenfeld and Nicolson, 1972), p. 23.

[14] Lévi-Strauss, *The Savage Mind*, p. 23.

[15] Ali Farah, *Il comandante del fiume*, p. 134: 'coins, shells, postcards and other little things'.

[16] Ali Farah, *Il comandante del fiume*, p. 135: 'In the images you can see two faces that are always cut off, a man and a child [...] Our faces weren't ever complete, so I took some scissors in order to separate his from mine and a bit of card that I could stick the pieces onto. I'd got it into my head that I needed to recompose our faces to see him again, but the pieces didn't fit together properly and the result was monstrous, one eye bigger than the other, the mouth on the neck, the forehead too low'.

that crucially does allow for another display of mastery through re-presentation. Moreover, Rome itself provides a wider canvas for other positive bricoleur acts, as witnessed in Yabar's encounter with a fantastically adorned homeless woman, the composite migrant community of the other riverside characters, and in the Tiber itself as a repository of local and global riches, representative of multiple timespaces:[17]

> Si dice che nel letto del Tevere siano custoditi tesori fantastici, perle preziose, lance di lanzichenecchi, pistole garibaldine, statue di marmo bianco e antichi candelabri. Naturalmente ci sono anche altre cose nelle profondità del fiume, carcasse, relitti, carogne, e quando vengono a galla bisogna rimuoverle perché possono accumularsi sotto i ponti e ostacolare il flusso.[18]

These presences below the river waters not only conjoin the ancient Somali myth of the book's title to the Tiber of Yabar's contemporary physical location, but also recall the salvage diving of Derek Walcott's 'Schooner *Flight*', where the sea is imagined as a fish broth, 'so choke with the dead', that only the colonial subject can know the 'pain of history words contain'.[19]

Within the narrative context it is up to Yabar to negotiate such identity treasures and burdens, and this transnational conflict is – as above – mapped out through the context of creative linguistic bricolage. The colonial presence of Italian hovers in composite words ('isbaghetti') voiced by a Somali migrant Yabar encounters in London, and back in Rome, he corrects the Italianized pronunciation of his friend Libaan's name from a double back to a single 'b'.[20] Libaan cannot speak his mother's language, Somali, and engages Yabar to act as a composite, by proxy mouthpiece for their communication. This constitutes a *physical* journey of recuperation for Yabar, too:

> (V)edo le parole in fila dentro la testa, le sento e le vedo tutte, scalciano e prendono forma come noci, e io spingo con la fronte e con

[17] Jon May and Nigel Thrift, eds., *Timespace: Geographies of Temporality* (New York: Routledge, 2001).

[18] Ali Farah, *Il comandante del fiume*, p. 134: 'people say that the bed of the Tiber guards fantastic treasures, precious pearls, medieval lances, pistols from the time of Garibaldi, white marble statues and antique candelabras. Of course there are other things at the bottom of the river too, carcasses, wreckages, corpses, which need to be removed when they come up to the surface because otherwise they accumulate under the bridges and can block the flow of the water'.

[19] Walcott, 'The Schooner *Flight*', p. 7, p. 12.

[20] Ali Farah, *Il comandante del fiume*, p. 121.

> gli occhi per farle passare. Le parole sono dure, mi tagliano la testa [...] sento una fitta tra gli occhi e riprendo fiato. Ma anche così il dolore non smette, allora ricomincio a spingere con forza ed ecco che sento le parole venirmi alla gola e tocco la loro forma con la lingua.[21]

The retrospective action set of the bricoleur can be identified in this representation of temporal and linguistic (re)-birth, a bricoleur who turns back to an existing set of knowledge or objects in order to set up the means for a dialogue.[22] It thus functions as an acknowledgement that knowledge can be useful because it is known,[23] and because it allows for a successful fusion of past and present, here and there:

> La voce della madre arriva a tutti e due e le nostre voci le arrivano insieme. Sento le parole tutte intere nella bocca, era tanto tempo che non le sentivo, e quelle parole sono le parole del figlio e sono anche le mie, io e Libaan diciamo insieme 'hooyo', mamma, e 'waa aniga', sono io.[24]

In an episode such as this, 'discourse and syntax supply indispensable means of supplementing deficiencies of vocabulary',[25] permitting translational relationships that are determined by particular histories. Movements of play are 'permitted by the lack or absence of a center or origin', and Yabar's collated mediation thus succeeds in facilitating a transnational 'movement of supplementarity' throughout the narrative.[26]

In *Il comandante del fiume*, it is language that ultimately affords a successful suturing of elements of the past and the elsewhere into the transnational 'freeplay' of the contemporary moment of the text. In a different

[21] Ali Farah, *Il comandante del fiume*, p. 126: 'I see the words lined up in my head, I feel them and see them all, they take shape like nuts, and I push with my forehead and my eyes to get them out. The words are hard, they cut my head [...] I feel a pain between my eyes and take a deep breath. But even then the pain doesn't stop, so I try pushing again, harder, and now I feel the words coming to my throat and touch their form with my tongue'.

[22] Lévi-Strauss, *The Savage Mind*, p. 20.

[23] Lévi-Strauss, *The Savage Mind*, p. 9.

[24] Ali Farah, p. 126: 'His mother's voice reaches us both, and our voices reach her together. I feel the words whole in my mouth, it was such a long time since I'd felt them, and those words are the words of her son, and mine too, me and Libaan say together "hooyo", Mum, and "waa aniga", it's me'.

[25] Lévi-Strauss, *The Savage Mind*, p. 1.

[26] Derrida, 'Structure, Sign and Play', p. 365.

example of transnational bricolage, visual artist and poet Maud Sulter recasts diverse political and historical fields through a dynamic interplay between image, word, and sound. In her own words: 'Language is powerful. And the application of language itself is a site of power'.[27] Sulter's use of language allows her to collage together portmanteau, dialect, and vernacular forms that speak of transnational mobility and play in order to subvert the power dynamics usually embedded in hegemonic discourses. Once inserted into her visual art, 'words and images disturb, abrade, supplement and entrap each other' to create a new mode of transnational storytelling.[28] The technique of photomontage and text–image relations that Sulter employs in collections such as *SYRCAS* (1993) fold and bend both time and space. Juxtaposing Welsh and German elements in the title, it is presented as the imaginary collage work of a fictitious Afro-German child named Helga, who collates images in order to weave together lost stories and visuals into a narrative of unorthodox, dynamic history. As the accompanying poem, 'Blood Money (Remix)', states: 'She was good with things metal, like scalpels / and scissors, and made pretty pictures / to hang on the walls of their pretty home'.[29] The static status of the stylized Alpine landscapes in the background is disrupted by the collaged overlapping of anonymized artefacts from Africa, which in turn neutralizes both as *non-loci* and asks us as viewers to '(re)adjust our vision'.[30] The 'disjointedness of the assemblies' draws attention not only to the 'dislocation of these artworks, often forcibly removed by war, stealth and theft',[31] but also works towards 'recovering, analyzing and making visible the historical presence of black people in Europe'.[32] This radical re-situating of African subjects within German history is here overlaid with the gaps and absences caused by their persecution in the interwar period and beyond. Sulter uses this collage method to warn against the dangers of easy racial categorizations in the face of the 'dazzling' variety of encounters and fluidity of categories that makes up the transnational reality of contemporary Europe.[33]

[27] Maud Sulter, *Passion* (London: Altitude Editions, 2015), p. 9.

[28] Sulter, *Passion*, p. 9.

[29] Sulter, *Passion*, p. 71.

[30] Eve Rosenhaft and Robbie Aitken, 'Introduction', in *Africa in Europe: Studies in Transnational Practice in the Long Twentieth Century*, ed. by E. Rosenhaft and R. Aitken (Liverpool: Liverpool University Press, 2013), pp. 1–16 (p. 5).

[31] Deborah Cherry, 'The Ghost Begins by Coming Back: Revenants and Returns in Maud Sulter's Photography', in *Maud Sulter: Syrcas* (London: Autograph ABP, 2016).

[32] Rosenhaft and Aitken, 'Introduction', *Africa in Europe*, p. 5.

[33] Patricia Clavin, 'Defining Transnationalism', *Contemporary European History*, 14.4 (2005), 421–39 (p. 423).

Figure 1. Maud Sulter, *Noir et blanc: Un* (1993).


In both Sulter's visual and poetic collages and the textual bricolage enacted in Ali Farah's *Il comandante del fiume*, signs gain meaning from their interplay with other signs. Such transnational play is revealed in the disruption of presence through the alternative presence of absence, and works to command both. The aesthetic pleasure produced by this rupture creates a sensual line of communication between past and present cultural production and its future users.[34] In the words of Michel de Certeau, 'what the map cuts up, the story cuts across',[35] and, as we have seen, this transnational story of bricolage necessarily spans different forms and media. This richness does not mean hiding the violence of the cutting and ripping actions of global history,[36] but rather points to the possibility of exploiting the 'openness' of the transnational in the supplementary creation of new composite elements, 'patterns in which they serve alternatively as ends or means'.[37]

Emma Bond is Reader in Italian and Comparative Literature at the University of St Andrews.

[34] Lévi-Strauss, *The Savage Mind*, p. 27.

[35] Michel de Certeau, *The Practice of Everyday Life*, trans. by Steven Rendall (Berkeley: University of California Press, 1984), p. 129.

[36] bell hooks, *Black Looks* (Boston: South End Press, 1992), p. 4.

[37] Lévi-Strauss, *The Savage Mind*, p. 33.

33

# Stories

*Julian Preece*

Stories have always travelled through time and space, have been transmitted down generations and have crossed oceans, land masses and human-made obstacles such as state borders or barriers erected by language. Seafarers, for instance, return home with tales. They can be of their own experiences, such as those related in Homer's *Odyssey*, a founding work of Western literature but also nothing less than a compendium of shared myths and legends, or by Odysseus's equally intrepid Arab counterpart Sinbad, whose sometimes similar experiences are related in the collection of international stories we know as *The 1001 Nights*. Travellers also relay tales that they have heard in the places they have visited – adapting, translating, and domesticating them as they go. In a classic essay entitled 'The Story-Teller', written in 1936, the philosopher Walter Benjamin introduces two story-telling archetypes. As well as the traveller there is the person who stays at home. Benjamin writes:

> 'When someone goes on a trip, he has something to tell about', goes the German saying, and people imagine the storyteller as someone who has come from afar. But they enjoy no less listening to the man who has stayed at home, making an honest living, and who knows the local tales and traditions. If one wants to picture these two groups through their archaic representatives, one is embodied in the resident tiller of the soil, and the other in the trading seaman.[1]

[1] Walter Benjamin, 'The Story-Teller: Reflections on the Work of Nikolai Leskov', *Illuminations*, ed. and with an introduction by Hannah Arendt, trans. by Harry Zohn (London: Fontana, 1973), pp. 83–110 (p. 85).

The 'resident tiller of the soil' thus becomes an expert on the tales of the land where he has lived all his life, but if this stay-at-home storyteller has not travelled him- or herself it is still likely that the stories themselves have done so. Until the Romantic era, when poets and academics started first to transcribe and then to invent their own versions, folk- and fairy-tales were anonymous and attached to traditions rather than authors. They were thought to have emanated from the collective spirit if not from the very soil. Like Aesop, Homer is unlikely to have been an individual.

Narrative ethnographers such as the Brothers Grimm in Germany romanticized this native storyteller as an elderly peasant who was close to the land. In *Germany. A Winter's Tale* (1844) their contemporary Heinrich Heine claims that he heard fairy tales from his wet-nurse while she suckled him as a baby. Famed for his irony, the German-Jewish poet is gently mocking the idea that children should be weaned on their ethnic folklore. It is a neat proposition but stories are unlikely to stay constricted to one place for long. Like human beings, they mix and mingle, inter-marry and cross-fertilize. Benjamin saw his two storytellers as interdependent, adding: 'The actual extension of the realm of story-telling in its full historical breadth is inconceivable without the most intimate interpenetration of these two archaic types'.[2] The Brothers Grimm were embarked on a nativist project at a time their country, which would not become a nation state for another sixty years, was largely under French occupation. They disguised the origins of some of the fairy tales in their famous collection of *Kinder- und Hausmärchen* (Children's and Household Tales) (first published in 1812): many are translations from written French or Italian sources. Such was the force of the Grimms' versions, however, which were promptly re-exported in translation into other European languages, that stories such as 'Rotkäppchen' ('Le Petit Chaperon rouge' / 'Little Red Riding Hood') would be known henceforth as 'Grimm's fairy tales'. Bizarrely, they were often considered distinctly Teutonic, especially when it came to their depiction of violence that, in fact, was often more marked in earlier non-German versions.

These opening remarks bring us too face to face with the question of power relations between national or linguistic groups. Such relations are never based on equality. An articulate traveller returning to her home community may easily find an audience ready to listen to accounts of her exploits or versions of stories she has heard on her travels, which she could easily have assimilated into her own experience and then claim as her own. The pressure exerted by such an audience can be so great that the traveller elaborates and embroiders, as the Greek Herodotus is thought to have done

[2] Benjamin, 'The Story-Teller', p. 85.

when it came to describing the hippopotamus that he pretended to have seen on his voyage up the Nile. His fifth-century BC *Histories* count as the first example of travel writing and are full of what today we would class stereotypes and exoticisms.

The current dominance of English enables one of the greatest purveyors of border-crossing stories of the last one hundred years, the Anglophone film industry also known as 'Hollywood', not only to attract the best talent from across the world but also to re-export stories originally drawn from outside in anglicized and thus usually homogenized formats. In the twentieth century Disney versions of fairy tales, often conservative in their representation of relations between the sexes, as well as sentimental, became the best known. Translators operating in the literary adaptation business are inclined either to revert to stereotypes or to eradicate traces of the foreign source in the quest for popularity. The latter procedure is known as 'domestication'. The translation theorist David Bellos has called this tendency 'translating up'; in contrast, when the movement is in the other direction, from a powerful to a less powerful language, the foreign elements are less likely to be disguised.[3] The result is that the transnational nature of much cultural production is more or less hidden and unacknowledged.

A more intriguing example of 'translating up' is provided by *The 1001 Nights*, which contains stories from Persian, Egyptian, and Indian sources, making it an intrinsically transnational narrative phenomenon. Yet the formats in which this classic collection of anonymous tales set in or around the Middle East usually circulates in the West is to some degree the creation of the French scholar and translator Antoine Galland (1646–1715), the originator of a trend that came to be known as *Orientalism*. *The 1001 Nights* depict the oriental world through Western eyes, achieving greater significance in the lands of their purported origin once the collection was re-exported to the languages of its sources.[4] This is an example of 'translating back', which always takes place both in a transnational context and within the power dynamic of 'up' and 'down' defined by Bellos. Another is provided by the nineteenth-century German ethnographer Gert Frobenius who collected the stories contained in *Der schwarze Dekameron: Belege und Aktenstücke über Liebe, Witz und Heldentum in Innerafrika* (1910)

[3] David Bellos, *Is that a Fish in Your Ear? Translation and the Meaning of Everything* (London and New York: Penguin, 2011).

[4] Madeleine Dobie, 'Translation in the Contact Zone: Antoine Galland's *Mille et une nuits: contes arabes*', in *The Arabian Nights in Historical Context between East and West*, ed. by Saree Makdisi and Felicity Nussbaum (Oxford: Oxford University Press, 2008), pp. 25–49.

(The Black Decameron: Evidence and Documents about Sex, Jokes and Heroism in the Interior of Africa) at the height of European colonialism. Yet Frobenius was an important reference point for black writers in the negritude movement in the 1950s and 1960s. A different example is the American writer Ernest Hemingway's posthumously published memoir, *A Moveable Feast. Sketches of the Author's Life in Paris in the Twenties* (1964) translated into French by Marc Saporta that same year as *Paris est une fête*. It became a best-seller in France fifty years after first publication in the wake of the terrorist attacks on entertainment venues committed in Paris on 13 November 2015. The Parisian way of life filtered through the literary consciousness of a Nobel Laureate from Western culture's hegemonic centre gave contemporary inhabitants of the city a sense of self-validation.

Two of the most Arabian popular tales from *The 1001 Nights*, *Aladdin* and *Ali Baba*, are likely to have been French inventions. *The 1001 Nights* might be best characterized as a mixture of tales told by Benjamin's two archetypes. According to Marina Warner, they 'present a polyvocal anthology of world myths, fables and fairy tales. But the book is also a masterwork of Arabic literature, distinctively arranged and told'.[5]

Stories take different shapes and fulfil various functions. Parables, such as those told by Jesus in the New Testament, are stories that impart wisdom, teaching their listeners how to live the right life; fables, such as those collected by Aesop, are stories that teach a more localized moral lesson. Aesopian Fables are populated by talking animals, each of which represents a particular characteristic, who between them contribute to the communication of a simple moral. The idea appears to be all but universal, as such stories exist in many cultures and can be translated easily. Stories can subvert the status quo by poking fun at authority, as demonstrated by the episodic novel and masterpiece of Czech literature, Jaroslav Hašek's *The Good Soldier Svejk and his Fortunes in the Great War* (1921–1923). Stories can also be deployed as propaganda, which makes them, as a form, politically neutral; deeds such as betraying one's parents to the state in support of the revolution can be presented as heroic in a story.[6] Stories can be read 'for the plot', which satisfies a desire for closure by finding out what happens, or they can make people either laugh or gasp in horror. Bertolt Brecht, the originator of the term 'epic theatre' for a type of drama that tells

[5] Marina Warner, 'Introduction: Shahrazad's Way', in *Stranger Magic: Charmed States and the Arabian Nights*, e-book, n.p. (45.8/1394) (originally published London: Vintage, 2012).

[6] See Catriona Kelly, *Comrade Pavlik: The Rise and Fall of a Soviet Boy Hero* (London: Granta, 2005).

stories, believed that in literature, as in life, it was not what happened that should provoke our interest but how it happened. Narrative perspective is all-important because stories take radically different shapes according to who is telling them. Brecht wrote for the world and his plays are sourced across the globe.

According to the French psycho-analyst Boris Cyrulnik each individual needs a positive story of him- or herself in order to retain good mental health.[7] Trauma Theory has taught us in recent years that horrific events, whether experienced first- or second-hand, disrupt fundamentally our ability for narration. Whether we can tell any kind of story about ourselves becomes a touchstone of our humanity. Nations as 'imagined communities' coalesce around narratives too, which makes it all the more remarkable that stories themselves cross national borders so easily. The deeds of King Arthur and his knights were recorded in the mid-twelfth century in Latin by Geoffrey of Monmouth, spawning verse epics in French, German (initially largely translations from French), and English. Perceval / Parzifal, Gawain, Lancelot, Guinevere, and the rest became emblematic heroes for all three nations. As Welshman, the 'original' Arthur would have identified with none. Stories can focus on what Elias Canetti, writing in the immediate aftermath of the Holocaust and National Socialism, terms 'national crowd symbols'. Canetti chooses the sea for England, the forest for Germany, and the Revolution for France, adding: 'A modern nation's consciousness of itself and its behaviour in war depends largely on its recognition of the national crowd symbol'.[8] Today most European states continue to define themselves with reference to the Second World War, which ended more than seventy-five years ago. Thus, Germany accepts responsibility for the crimes of the Nazis and officially repudiates the ideologies that contributed to them, seeking a supra-national European identity. Britain and Russia, in contrast, look back proudly on their brave anti-Nazi defiance, thus setting their own national story against a possibly rival transnational alternative. It is notable that the European Union has failed to inspire a narrative about itself with which European citizens can identify.

Stories are often based on real events. The Great Flood, for example, is related in three ancient works, in the Book of Genesis (in Hebrew), in the Epic of Gilgamesh (in Akkadian), and by the Roman poet Ovid in *Metamorphoses*

[7] Boris Cyrulnik, *Talking of Love. How to Overcome Trauma and Remake your Life Story*, trans. by David Macey (Harmondsworth: Penguin, 2009).

[8] Benedict Anderson, *Imagined Communities: Reflections on the Origins and Spread of Nationalism* (London: Verso, 1983, revised 1991 and 2006); Elias Canetti, *Crowds and Power*, trans. by Carol Stewart (Harmondsworth: Penguin, 1973), p. 206.

(in Latin). In each story there is never-ending rain and intrepid survivors in a boat. The narrative of Noah following divine instructions by selecting animal pairs to escape God's anger and the concluding rainbow covenant between the Almighty and humanity are present only in the version related in the Bible, however. Comparison shows us that the Bible author has fashioned his material, which he imported and domesticated, to illustrate a moral fable about sin, punishment, and reconciliation.

Folk- and fairy-tales, in contrast, can hardly be inspired by real deeds or individuals but there can be little question when they derive from the same source or belong to the same family. Tales of giant-slaying, such as 'Jack and the Beanstalk', 'Odysseus and the Cyclops', or 'David and Goliath', exist in dozens of different languages. The folklorists Stith Thompson and Antii Arne found they were able to classify tales from across the world according to plot types, motifs, and central characters.[9]

Until the invention of writing, stories must have travelled exclusively by word of mouth. But it was not until the epoch of mass literacy beginning in the mid-nineteenth century that print became the principal medium of transmission. Print can facilitate complication, fragmentation, and narrative sophistication such as meta-fiction at the expense of repetition, rhyme, and formulae, which are easier for the teller to recall. Modernist short narratives in a collection such as *The Dubliners* (1914) by James Joyce cannot be easily memorized and do not moreover draw on archetypes in the way that oral storytellers do. According to the Palestinian critic Edward Said, however, complex ideas in the print era are transferred on essentially similar routes to stories.[10] In the twentieth century print was joined by cinema, radio, and television. Digital broadcasting platforms such as Netflix have revolutionized how viewers access content, but the demand for epic stories in the form of long-running series such as *Babylon Berlin*, *The Bureau*, or *The Sopranos* or in audio through podcasts continues.

Stories travel in different ways in the digital age, but the principle of travel has remained constant. Taking 'the fall of the Berlin Wall', which began on the evening of 9 November 1989, as her example, Julia Sonnevend argues that what she calls 'iconic events' that shape the international news are formed with five 'narrative dimensions': foundation, mythologization, condensation,

[9] Stith Thompson, *Motif-Index of Folk-Literature. A Classification of Narrative Elements in Folk-tales, Ballads, Myths etc*, 6 vols (Bloomington, IN: Haminassa, 1932–36).

[10] Edward Said, 'Travelling Theory', in *The World, the Text and the Critic* (Cambridge, MA: Harvard University Press, 1983), pp. 226–47.

counter-narrative, and remediation.[11] It is only once all five are in place that a story gains traction and assumes a shape in international consciousness. Government spin doctors and public relations specialists call this gaining control of the narrative, which they understand as a framework for what amount to motifs in a breaking story.

Like jokes, rumours are stories that can travel with remarkable rapidity. Travelling stories are not necessarily a force for good. Again, however, it seems likely that 'fake news' has always been so, as suggested by the contemporary proverb: 'A lie can be half-way round the world before the truth has got its boots on'. The so-called 'blood libel' legend according to which Jews need the blood of a Christian child to bake un-leavened bread, which was needed in religious rituals, has been traced to England in 1144, from where it spread to Germany the following century, Spain, where it was used to justify the expulsion of the Jews in 1492, and from there to Italy and Poland up to the twentieth century.[12] The legend itself remains depressingly constant in each case, however different the local contexts over eight centuries appear to be on the surface.

National literatures tend to be founded on imported stories in the shape of translations, which merge into adaptations and re-makes. Thus, the English Chaucer in *The Canterbury Tales* (1387–1400) imitates the Tuscan Boccaccio in *The Decameron* (1353) and the German *Sturm und Drang* (*c.*1770–1786) was inspired by Shakespeare. Modern Europeans first measured themselves against the classical Greek and Roman authors, borrowing and adapting ideas and formats. Shakespeare never dramatized an original story; he re-wrote existing material, setting his plays across locations in a semi-imaginary Europe. His contemporary, the first great European novelist Miguel de Cervantes, credits an Arab author by the name of Cide Hamete Benengeli as the chronicler of the adventures of Don Quixote and his squire Sancho Panza. *Don Quixote* (1605/1615) is the prose classic of the Spanish Golden Age about a brave-hearted nobleman whose mind has been turned by reading too many chivalrous romances, which makes it a story about a man who believed he was a character in a story. It was published more than one hundred years after the expulsion or enforced conversion of Spain's Jewish and Muslim population yet is a product of this multi-lingual and intercultural mingling. In other words, it is both a transnational but also a pre-national work, intrinsically post-modern in its meta-fictional conceits and archaic in its reliance on narrative.

11 Julia Sonnevend, *Stories without Borders: The Berlin Wall and the Making of a Global Iconic Event* (Oxford: Oxford University Press, 2016).

12 See *Urban Legends. A Collection of International Tall Tales and Terrors* ed. by Gillian Bennett and Paul Smith (Westport, CT: Greenwood Press, 2007), pp. 243–45.

Translated into other languages, it inspired the development of the novel in other languages, including English, French, and German.[13]

Julian Preece is a cultural historian and Professor of German at Swansea University.

[13] Ben Hutchinson argues that this shows him 'speaking spoof to power', *Comparative Literature. A Very Short Introduction* (Oxford: Oxford University Press, 2018), p. 43.

# 34

# Translation

*Lucas Nunes Vieira*

Many Modern Languages students experience translation as an instrument for testing or appraising linguistic performance. In a language-learning context, target-language renderings may be classed as effective or ineffective according to specific criteria that often – though not exclusively or necessarily – measure students' knowledge of the source language or their command of the target language. This type of analysis or assessment is usually based on translation as a textual product. Another way of conceptualizing translation is to see it as a process. Empirical studies in translation have been increasingly interested in how the process of translating is influenced by a wide range of factors including the translator, the commissioner (if applicable), different cultural and socio-economic contexts, and, importantly for this chapter, the tools that may help to bring the translation into being.

Technological tools are nowadays central to the study of translation. This is in large part due to the radical ways in which machine translation systems like Google Translate can change not only translation processes and products, but also what society expects of translations and of their role in communication. In the language industry, machine translation is used by professional translators as a tool that can speed up their work. Machine translation systems can also be a first port of call for 'everyday' translation needs of casual users, which has wider implications for how information is assimilated and disseminated across languages.

The study of translation and technology is therefore essentially diverse. It is not strictly focused on the linguistic relationship between source and target texts. It is not necessarily focused on specific languages, countries, cultures, or textual genres either. Rather, studying translation from the perspective of technology often means trying to examine concepts, patterns, and procedures across these factors. This chapter draws on previous empirical research to provide a brief introduction to uses and implications of machine translation for language professionals and non-linguists. The chapter first reviews how machine translation can influence translators' work and how the professional use of this technology is often modulated by complex socio-economic issues. It then looks at how the use of machine translation by non-linguists can present challenges as well as solutions to information accessibility and multi-lingual communication. The chapter ends with a brief discussion of the increasingly important role of cognitively and sociologically oriented approaches to the study of machine translation.

## Machine Translation as a Professional Translation Tool

Machine translation has in some contexts made it possible for translators to post-edit and incorporate automatically generated suggestions into their translations. The process of editing machine-produced translations is almost as old as machine translation itself,[1] but post-editing of machine translation as a structured professional activity is a slightly more recent phenomenon.[2] Post-editing is often motivated by a high demand for large volumes of multi-lingual, time-sensitive texts. Consider the software or user manuals that come with mobile phones or laptop computers, for instance. All these products contain a high textual volume, including instructions, troubleshooting guides, terms, conditions of use, and other customer support content. A fast turnaround in the translation and localization of this content allows these products to be released faster in different parts of the world, so in a commercial sense machine translation may present time- and cost-saving opportunities. A central question, however, is the extent to which machine suggestions can indeed be of assistance to translators. When machine translation is used by translators as a professional tool, this question revolves around two important yet complex concepts: translation effort and translation quality.

Effort is a key aspect of machine translation use in that the more effort involved in fixing or incorporating machine suggestions into a human-produced text the less worthwhile this practice is deemed to be for

[1] Yehoshua Bar-Hillel, 'The Present State of Research on Mechanical Translation', *American Documentation*, 2 (1951), 229–37 (p. 230).

[2] See Lucas Nunes Vieira, 'Post-Editing of Machine Translation', in *The Routledge Handbook of Translation and Technology*, ed. by Minako O'Hagan (London: Routledge, 2019), pp. 319–35.

professional translators. Effort in this case is usually formulated as a triad consisting of temporal, technical, and cognitive effort.[3] Temporal effort is the time translators spend working on the translation. Cognitive and technical effort are, respectively, the mental effort that goes into making decisions and the physical or mechanical effort involved in operations such as typing. This effort triad has been extensively studied in translation process research[4] with evidence of how using machine translation as a source of assistance can reduce all types of effort relative to drafting the translation from scratch.[5]

Examining machine translation's usefulness can be methodologically challenging, however. While temporal effort is relatively straightforward to measure, cognitive effort has no standard unit of measurement such as seconds or minutes. Yet cognitive effort is considered a core component of the overall concept of translation effort.[6] It accounts for the distinction between a task that is just laborious and one that is cognitively demanding. This has sparked a series of studies that investigate the concept and estimation of cognitive effort in translation. Among the parameters normally used as proxies for effort in this context are eye movements recorded with eye trackers and pauses in typing captured with key-logging software. The rationale for using these methods is largely grounded in experimental psychology research where eye fixations on a text while reading are assumed to be a sign of mental processing.[7] The assumption regarding pauses is similar. They are regarded as part of the mental processing that precedes the act of producing a given segment of text.[8] These assumptions prompted researchers to use the count and length of typing pauses and of eye fixations to approximate cognitive effort in translation. Research tools that incorporate key-loggers[9]

[3] Hans P. Krings, *Repairing Texts: Empirical Investigations of Machine Translation Post-Editing Processes* (Kent, OH: Kent State University Press, 2001), pp. 178–79.

[4] *New Directions in Empirical Translation Process Research: Exploring the CRITT TPR-DB*, ed. by. Michael Carl, Srinivas Bangalore, and Moritz Schaeffer (Cham: Springer, 2016).

[5] Antonio Toral, Martijn Wieling, and Andy Way, 'Post-editing Effort of a Novel with Statistical and Neural Machine Translation', *Frontiers in Digital Humanities*, 5 (2018), <https://doi.org/10.3389/fdigh.2018.00009> [accessed 16 February 2021].

[6] Krings, *Repairing Texts*, p. 179.

[7] Marcel A. Just and Patricia A. Carpenter, 'A Theory of Reading: From Eye Fixation to Comprehension', *Psychological Review*, 87 (1980), 329–54 (pp. 330–31).

[8] Joost Schilperoord, *It's About Time: Temporal Aspects of Cognitive Processes in Text Production* (Amsterdam: Rodopi, 1996), pp. 8–9.

[9] Wilker Aziz, Sheila Castilho, and Lucia Specia, 'PET: A Tool for Post-Editing and Assessing Machine Translation', in *Proceedings of LREC 2012, Eighth International*

and/or eye trackers[10] have been specifically designed to investigate cognitive translation processes based on these methodologies.

If the goal in estimating effort is to examine the usefulness of machine translation as a tool for translators, translation quality should also be considered. For one thing, the quality of the machine suggestions is known to be directly influenced by the source and target languages[11] as well as the lexical and syntactic complexity of the text being translated.[12] The impact of language technologies on the translation process, therefore, needs to be evaluated across texts, languages, and domains. In addition, time savings in the translation process are only meaningful if they do not have a detrimental effect on the resulting translations. In terms of effort, experiments have supported the time-saving powers of machine suggestions for several language pairs, including English to Korean, Japanese, Chinese, and French.[13] Experiments of this nature are often based on technical texts, but more recently machine translation research has also ventured into literary translation.[14] In terms of the quality of the final translations, results are less abundant, but in this respect too there is evidence that supports the use of machine translation as a tool in human translation.[15]

Notwithstanding these results, several caveats should be noted. The history of machine translation is marked by overstatements of what the

*Conference on Language Resources and Evaluation,* ed. by Nicoletta Calzolari, Khalid Choukri, Thierry Declerck, Mehmet Uğur Doğan, Bente Maegaard, Joseph Mariani, Jan Odijk, and Stelios Piperidis (Istanbul: European Language Resources Association, 2012), pp. 3982–87.

10 Michael Carl, 'Translog-II: A Program for Recording User Activity Data for Empirical Reading and Writing Research', in *Proceedings of LREC 2012,* pp. 4108–112.

11 Melvin Johnson, Mike Schuster, Quoc V. Le, Maxim Krikun, Yonghui Wu, Zhifeng Chen, Nikhil Thorat, Fernanda Viégas, Martin Wattenberg, Greg Corrado, Macduff Hughes, and Jeffrey Dean, 'Google's Multilingual Neural Machine Translation System: Enabling Zero-Shot Translation', *Transactions of the Association for Computational Linguistics,* 5 (2017), 339–51.

12 Spence Green, Jeffrey Heer, and Christopher D. Manning, 'The Efficacy of Human Post-Editing for Language Translation', in *CHI '13: Proceedings of the SIGCHI Conference on Human Factors in Computing Systems* (New York: Association for Computing Machinery, 2013), pp. 439–48.

13 Ventsislav Zhechev, 'Analysing the Post-editing of Machine Translation at Autodesk', in *Post-editing of Machine Translation: Processes and Applications,* ed. by Sharon O'Brien, Laura Winther Balling, Michael Carl, Michel Simard, and Lucia Specia (Newcastle: Cambridge Scholars Publishing, 2014), pp. 2–24.

14 Toral, Wieling, and Way, 'Post-editing Effort of a Novel'.

15 Green, Heer, and Manning, 'The Efficacy of Human Post-Editing'.

technology can do.[16] A recent example involves an experiment conducted by researchers at Microsoft, who made the bold claim that a new machine translation system they had developed was on a par with human translation in terms of quality.[17] Their system was based on a variant of a new methodology referred to as neural machine translation.[18] While this method brought about significant improvements, an independent re-analysis of Microsoft's data showed their parity claim to be unfounded.[19] Among other problems, the texts that acted as human reference translations in Microsoft's experiment – the 'gold standard' to which the machine translations were being compared – had serious grammatical errors, which set a low bar for the assessment of the machine translations.[20]

Microsoft's study and its rebuttal are noteworthy for how they bring the complexity of translation quality to light. This study shows how human translations are not necessarily synonymous with high-quality translations. Quality is in fact more than just semantic accuracy and linguistic correctness. In professional contexts, translation quality is a multi-faceted concept that depends, among other things, on the purpose and nature of the text, on the needs and expectations of the text consumers, and on the context in which the translation will be used. While comparing human and machine translation may serve a purpose in some contexts, framing this comparison as a contest of humans versus machines is therefore often unhelpful. This type of framing risks presupposing simplistic notions of

[16] John Hutchins, 'Machine Translation: A Concise History', *Journal of Translation Studies*, 13 (2010), 29–70.

[17] Hany Hassan, Anthony Aue, Chang Chen, Vishal Chowdhary, Jonathan Clark, Christian Federmann, Xuedong Huang, Marcin Junczys-Dowmunt, William Lewis, Mu Li, Shujie Liu, Tie-Yan Liu, Renqian Luo, Arul Menezes, Tao Qin, Frank Seide, Xu Tan, Fei Tian, Lijun Wu, Shuangzhi Wu, Yingce Xia, Dongdong Zhang, Zhirui Zhang, and Ming Zhou, 'Achieving Human Parity on Automatic Chinese to English News Translation', *arXiv preprint*, arXiv:1803.05567 (2018), <https://arxiv.org/abs/1803.05567> [accessed 17 February 2021].

[18] Dzmitry Bahdanau, Kyunghyun Cho, and Yoshua Bengio, 'Neural Machine Translation by Jointly Learning to Align and Translate', *arXiv preprint*, arXiv:1409.0473 (2015), <https://arxiv.org/abs/1409.0473> [accessed 17 February 2021].

[19] Antonio Toral, Sheila Castilho, Ke Hu, and Andy Way, 'Attaining the Unattainable? Reassessing Claims of Human Parity in Neural Machine Translation', in *Proceedings of the Third Conference on Machine Translation (WMT)*, ed. By Ondřej Bojar, Rajen Chatterjee, Christian Federmann, Mark Fishel, Yvette Graham, Barry Haddow, Matthias Huck, Antonio Jimeno Yepes, Philipp Koehn, Christof Monz, Matteo Negri, Aurélie Névéol, Mariana Neves, Matt Post, Lucia Specia, Marco Turchi, and Karin Verspoor (Brussels: Association for Computational Linguistics, 2018), pp. 113–23.

[20] Toral et al., 'Attaining the Unattainable?'

quality. It also ignores the fact that human and machine translation in most cases are not mutually exclusive but rather complementary.[21]

Another important aspect of machine translation as a professional tool is the socio-economic context in which the technology is deployed. Previous research on translators' attitudes to machine translation has shown that translators can often be critical not strictly of machine translation itself, but of the business practices that surround its use.[22] Specifically, translators may be asked to accept discounted pay rates per word because of expectations that machine translation will allow them to deliver more words in less time.[23] If, in these cases, the machine suggestions are not as useful as predicted, conflict can arise due to unrealistic expectations of what translators should deliver and of the extent to which the technology can assist them. While at first glance this may seem like a pragmatic transactional issue, overstatements of machine translation's capabilities might skew industry-wide expectations of translation productivity. This in turn risks installing a logic of efficiency at all costs, which can influence perceptions of the value of translations and of translators' work. Importantly, tecno-deterministic discourses[24] that separate technology from its human-made social context can – advertently or inadvertently – promote machine translation as the conveniently 'non-human' party to blame for the low standards and poor work conditions to which some translators may be subjected. The debate on machine translation as a professional tool cannot, therefore, examine just time savings or issues of translation quality. The structure of the economy, 'precarization' of labour,[25] and the pressures of globalized markets should also be accounted for in this debate.

## The Challenges and Opportunities of Machine Translation as a Tool for Non-linguists

In addition to how machine translation can change professional translation, more broadly it can also profoundly influence 'everyday' communication.

[21] Maite Aragonés Lumeras and Andy Way, 'On the Complementarity between Human Translators and Machine Translation', *Hermes*, 56 (2017), 21–42.

[22] Lucas Nunes Vieira, 'Automation Anxiety and Translators', *Translation Studies*, 13 (2020), 1–21.

[23] Nunes Vieira, 'Automation Anxiety and Translators'.

[24] See Maeve Olohan, 'Technology, Translation and Society: A Constructivist, Critical Theory Approach', *Target*, 29 (2017), 264–83.

[25] Joss Moorkens, 'Under Pressure: Translation in Times of Austerity', *Perspectives*, 25 (2017), 464–77.

Google Translate alone is used to translate trillions of words every year.[26] In some cases, a circumstantial lack of more suitable alternatives might see this technology make its way into high-stakes settings such as courts and hospitals.[27] The use of machine translation in high-stakes contexts often represents a conundrum in that the technology can facilitate language accessibility while in return posing considerable risks. In the US, an asylum applicant who had been a victim of serious racial violence had her testimony called into question after using Google Translate to complete a form, for instance.[28] Since the act of translating texts online usually involves sharing the content with the machine translation provider, the mere use of the technology can have serious consequences. If a couple uses Google Translate to communicate this could, for example, preclude them from claiming spousal privilege if they are legally requested to disclose the conversation, a possibility that has been considered in case law even if not actively pursued.[29]

Machine translation therefore has wide-ranging societal implications. Importantly for Modern Languages, this technology might change perceptions of language-learning practices and purposes. Empirical Education research has looked at the potential for machine translation to act as a substitute for 'English as a lingua franca'. In one such study,[30] speakers of English as an additional language wrote essays in their native languages – specifically, Chinese and Malay – and machine-translated the essays into English before submitting them. The researchers checked to see if the machine-translated essays were equivalent to work written originally in English by students whose level of English was just about enough to grant them a place at an English-speaking university. Although results were mixed, the authors' assessment was that the machine-translated essays were not consistently or

[26] James Kuczmarski, 'A New Look for Google Translate on the Web', <https://www.blog.google/products/translate/new-look-google-translate-web/> [accessed 17 February 2021].

[27] Lucas Nunes Vieira, Minako O'Hagan, and Carol O'Sullivan, 'Understanding the Societal Impacts of Machine Translation: A Critical Review of the Literature on Medical and Legal Use Cases', *Information Communication and Society*, <https://doi.org/10.1080/1369118X.2020.1776370> [accessed 17 February 2021].

[28] Jeanette L. Schroeder, 'The Vulnerability of Asylum Adjudications to Subconscious Cultural Biases: Demanding American Narrative Norms', *Boston University Law Review*, 97 (2017), 315–48 (p. 320).

[29] US v. Pugh, 162 F. Supp. 3d 97 – Dist. Court, ED New York 2016, <https://scholar.google.com/scholar_case?case=10165936483680238055> [accessed 17 February 2021].

[30] Michael Groves and Klaus Mundt, 'Friend or Foe? Google Translate in Language for Academic Purposes', *English for Specific Purposes*, 37 (2015), 112–21, <https://doi.org/10.1016/j.esp.2014.09.001> [accessed 21 December 2021].

unequivocally inferior grammatically to the essays drafted in English,[31] which shows how machine translation might influence the international status of English in the academic community.

While the public use of machine translation is a matter for ongoing research, this technology raises several important issues that linguists should negotiate and critically analyse. How does it affect cross-cultural understanding? How might it affect political discourse? How might its availability on social media affect the trustworthiness of information shared online? Given machine translation's ease of use and wide availability, these questions have far-reaching ramifications. They also call for a knowledge and understanding of translation that Modern Languages students are well placed to provide.

## Conclusion

By presenting a brief overview of translation as a process and the ways in which this process might be influenced by machine translation technology, this chapter hopefully raised awareness of ongoing issues that can profoundly influence translation as a practice and discipline. Examining these issues often means analysing translations not necessarily just from the perspective of a specific original author, a translator, or their respective languages. It means analysing translations also from a broader point of view that considers multiple translation processes and their wider consequences for how information is consumed, disseminated, and processed. Looking at translation in this way may take the shape of attempts to advance and generalize knowledge of how translation takes place, or it may take the shape of theoretically informed discussions of issues including how translation technology affects professional translators and the world of work, how it might change perceptions of language and attitudes to language learning, and how it might influence language policy. As language technologies become increasingly available and widespread, questions of this nature go to the heart of cross-cultural understanding and communication, and therefore, I would argue, to the heart of Modern Languages.

Lucas Nunes Vieira is Senior Lecturer in
Translation Studies at the University of Bristol.

[31] Groves and Mundt, 'Friend or Foe', p. 118.

35

# Translation

*Loredana Polezzi*

> È un po' come la storia del calabrone, che essendo molto pesante, e avendo eliche molto leggere, dice, da un punto di vista tecnico, di non poter volare. E naturalmente vola lo stesso.
>
> Paolo Fabbri[1]

## The Problem with Perfect Translation

In an essay reflecting on the nature of translation, the semiotician Paolo Fabbri compared translators to bumblebees, able to fly in spite of their weight and the weakness of their wings. He also described them as spies, double agents, and apostates: traditionally despicable figures whom he instead presented as admirable or even heroic. Evoking secret agents and improbably flying insects, Fabbri played with two common and related assumptions about translation and translators: first, their untrustworthiness, frequently associated with the Italian saying *traduttore traditore* (translator traitor), and, second, the paradoxical idea of translation as a pervasive, unavoidable, and yet impossible activity. If we believe that translation is impossible, then both its process and its products can only be forms of betrayal: manipulations or falsifications of the originals they replace. The agents carrying out that

[1] 'It's a bit like the story of the bumblebee who, given its weight and its very light thrusters, says that technically speaking it cannot fly. Yet, naturally, it flies all the same'. Paolo Fabbri, 'L'intraducilbilità da una fede all'altra', in *Elogio di Babele* (Rome: Meltemi, 2000), pp. 81–98 (p. 86); the translation is mine.

practice – translators and interpreters – are therefore traitors, consciously or unconsciously distorting the original and only providing the recipients of their work with an inferior copy.

These views depend on a further series of assumptions about translation, language, and, ultimately, culture as well as about cultural products. They rest on the belief that cultures and languages are self-contained and incommensurable, characterized by ways of seeing and speaking about the world that are so distinctive they are, in fact, untranslatable. Similarly, texts – especially though not exclusively texts considered particularly valuable and representative of a culture, such as religious or literary works – are seen as unique and stable, both in terms of content and form. Often, their authenticity and originality are associated with notions of authorship, as the product of an individual voice (sometimes more than one), and therefore linked to the value and authority attached to subjectivity.

An aura of perfection and permanence hangs over this image of translation. An original text is seen as somehow perfectly enshrined in its finished, fixed format. The translator's task is to capture that unique combination of content and form, transferring it to a different yet equivalent text that exists in a different place and, frequently, time. The etymological roots of the word 'translation' and of related ones in many European languages (*traduction/traduccion/traduzione*) reinforce this message, with the Latin words *traductio* and *translatio* both referring to transfer and transportation (and the Italian *traslazione* even indicating the relocation of sacred relics). Yet if texts, cultures, and languages are marked by an irreducible difference, there can be no perfect equivalence. A perfect translation becomes impossible, and translators find themselves in an epistemological bind, expected to be faithful to their source text, but by definition unable to satisfy that requirement.

The question of faithfulness and equivalence makes perfect translation impossible and, in turn, raises ethical issues. Faced with multiple demands, who should translators be loyal to: authors, readers, or perhaps publishers and other clients who pay their wages? Should translators prioritize being faithful to the source text or producing a satisfactory target text for its users?[2] This notion of perfect translation has further ethical implications. Christiane Nord noted that while fidelity is an intertextual relationship, loyalty is an

[2] This dilemma was famously captured in seventeenth-century France in the sexist image of *les belles infidèles*: like women, the explanation went, translations could be ugly and faithful or beautiful and unfaithful. For a critique of this imagery, see Sherry Simon, *Gender in Translation: Cultural Identity and the Politics of Transmission* (London and New York: Routledge, 1996), pp. 10–11.

interpersonal one.[3] All interpersonal relationships involve some degree of subjectivity, as does translation: whether reading written texts or listening to speech, a translator or an interpreter is carrying out a hermeneutic process – a process of interpretation. In doing so, they bring their own knowledge, experiences, and worldviews to the decoding and recoding of a message. Yet translators (and interpreters) unlike authors (or speakers) are expected to be objective rather than subjective, with professional codes often requiring them to adhere to principles of neutrality and impartiality. Besides the tensions between source and target texts, or those between authors on the one hand and commissioners or readers of translations on the other, translators also have to deal with the impossible task of being at once subjective and objective, personal and impersonal.

Unsurprisingly, given the contradictions inherent in this model, translation is often portrayed as both impossible and undesirable. Starting from the premises outlined above, it becomes at most a necessary evil, unavoidable because the human condition does not allow access to all information in its original form (that, nevertheless, in the absence of perfect translation, always takes priority in terms of value, authenticity, and truthfulness). This negative view is inscribed in established cultural imagery as well as commercial and educational practices. The myth of Babel is a foundational narrative of the Judeo-Christian tradition, presenting the multiplicity of languages as the burden of human sin, while associating the pre-Babelian condition with a desirable state of monolingualism. The dream of a universal language regularly resurfaces across time, as exemplified by today's myth of English as a lingua franca. The same is true of the myth of instantaneous translation, whether in the form of the Pentecostal gift of languages, an alien 'Babel fish' placed in one's ear,[4] or (once again 'perfect') machine translation. In economic terms, the low value attributed to translation is reflected in the reluctance to invest in its processes and its agents, and in the frequent over-estimation of its cost. Economic considerations are often cited to support the imposition of single national languages, shoring up nationalist ideologies through utilitarian, instrumental arguments in favour of monolingualism. In the realm of education, translation has acquired equally negative connotations, as a prescriptive and ineffectual language-learning technique or a second-grade way of accessing 'foreign' cultural products.

It is not surprising, then, that translators should be looked at with suspicion or mistrust. Yet Paolo Fabbri and his provocatively contradictory images

[3] Christiane Nord, 'Loyalty Revisited: Bible Translation as a Case in Point', *The Translator*, 7.2 (2001), 185–202.

[4] See Douglas Adams, *The Hitchhiker's Guide to the Galaxy* (London: Pan Books, 1979).

– praising traitors, watching bumblebees fly – invite us to challenge assumptions and look at how translation happens all the time and frequently becomes a creative engine, a form of positive 'contagion' disregarding perfection to produce new, original meaning.[5] Translators discover and create meaning as they translate, enriching cultures in the process. If they are traitors, Fabbri says, what they betray is the false belief that individual languages and cultures are closed, self-contained systems.[6]

## The Translational Fabric of Social Life

What happens if we follow Fabbri's advice and look at the evidence that emerges from practices of translation, aiming to reassess its notion, scope, and role? Redefining translation changes ways of thinking about linguistic and cultural processes and about the production, circulation, and reception of cultural products. It also poses questions about difference and how to approach it – raising issues about the professional ethics of translators and about the ethical foundations of human activity, our interaction with social and natural environments.

By abandoning the notion of perfect translation with its corollaries of faithfulness, equivalence, and substitution, the map can be re-drawn starting from different premises and using incrementally broader notions of translation. In its narrowest sense, the term refers to the transposition of a written source text from one language to another, what Roman Jakobson described as 'interlingual translation or translation proper'.[7] Jakobson, however, widened the range of phenomena referred to as translation, including intralingual forms of re-writing (within the same language) as well as intersemiotic transpositions (across different media). These additional categories highlight the complex layering of communication: no language is ever a homogeneous, monolithic whole, hence the need to translate across its variants (geographic, historic, social); and verbal language is only one aspect of human communication, often intersecting with other semiotic systems and codes.

In the late twentieth century, the 'cultural turn' in translation studies stressed the importance of culture to any discussion of translation, marking a shift towards a descriptive approach and an emphasis on the reception of translation. This target-oriented model moves away from idealized notions and

[5] Fabbri, *Elogio di Babele*, p. 82.

[6] Fabbri, *Elogio di Babele*, pp. 87–88.

[7] Roman Jakobson, 'On Linguistic Aspects of Translation', in *On translation*, ed. by Reuben A. Brower (Cambridge, MA, Harvard University Press, 1959), pp. 232–39 (p. 233).

prescriptive approaches, historicizing translation and stressing its crucial role in cultural exchange, in the creation and dissemination of knowledge, or in the formation, mediation, and re-mediation of memory. Homi Bhabha described the process of cultural translation as 'how newness enters the world', while memory scholar Aleida Assmann noted that, while 'in its narrow sense, the problem of translation is the preservation of meaning; in a wider sense, the potential of translation is the generation of meaning. It is precisely in these constant shifts of transferal and displacement that meaning is generated'.[8]

This broader understanding of translation has been paralleled by developments in sociolinguistics, multilingualism, reception, gender, and postcolonial studies, which have all contributed to questioning established hierarchies of values. Understood as a vital mechanism of cultural transmission and component of intertextuality, translation is always already present, even in what we call 'an original'. Shattering notions of originality and authenticity calls into question the idea of translation as inherently secondary and derivative, while rewriting, adaptation, and post-translation are acknowledged as creative processes. Similarly, feminist and postcolonial scholars have claimed the right of translators to take an explicit ethical position eschewing the traditional demand for neutrality and allowing them, instead, to declare their own positionality and agency. Postcolonial studies have also stressed the multidirectional nature of translation, which does not move only from centre to periphery, but follows much more intricate itineraries that encompass local forms of transculturation as well as the appropriation or hybridization of indigenous knowledge as it travels towards colonial centres of power. The decolonization of translation studies also provides an effective critique of the dominant metaphors in the field – such as transfer, transportation, or bridging – highlighting the different imagery of other languages and traditions. Forms of activist translation are animated by similarly strong ethical impulses and aim to empower individuals and groups engaged in the production and dissemination of knowledge through official and unofficial routes, including contemporary resistance movements and transnational climate change protest networks. These forms of translation and their agents engage in practices that encompass Jakobson's three types (interlingual, intralingual, intersemiotic), but also fluid processes of linguistic mobility,

[8] Homi Bhabha, 'How Newness Enters the World: Postmodern Space, Postcolonial Times, and the Trials of Cultural Translation', in *The Location of Culture* (London and New York: Routledge, 1994), pp. 212–35; Aleida Assmann, 'Translation as Transformation', in *Zwischen den Kulturen. Theorie und Praxis des interkulturellen Dialogs*, ed. by Carola Hilfrich-Kunjappu and Stéphane Mosès (Tübingen: Max Niemeyer, 1997), pp. 21–33 (p. 21).

including multiple acts of self-translation (with repeated movements between two or more languages) and translanguaging (where speakers access what are described as different languages, treating them like an integrated repertoire). Translingual authors who decide – through personal choice, exile, migration, colonial education, or a number of other motives – to write in an adopted language offer a primary example of these practices, deeply embedded in the translational fabric of our lives.

This complex map shows translation to be much more than a dichotomous system opposing source text and target text, source language and target language, source culture and target culture. Instead, translation is a complex network of multilingual and multimodal practices, constitutive of our experience of the world and continuously contributing to the dissemination and the creation of meaning, information, and culture. In this broad sense, translation, still rooted in textual and linguistic systems, is best understood as a continuum of practices allowing movement between those systems, ensuring their fluidity, porousness, and dynamism. As a continuum of practices, translation is a process that does not stop once a target text has been completed: rather than being a static bridge between two shores, translation acts like a ping pong ball, which can bounce off in different directions, producing unexpected effects within the target culture and, sometimes, bouncing back towards the source culture (for instance, by modifying the perception of a text in its place of origin, as is often the case when translated authors receive prestigious awards like a Nobel Prize). Additionally, the notion of a continuum highlights the inadequacy of traditional models of translation that weld it to abstract concepts of subjectivity. Instead, it foregrounds how the practice of translation is both embodied and anchored in diversity, locally unique and collaborative in nature: translators do not work in splendid isolation, but are part of networks of agents, including editors, publishers, graphic designers, or local informants and co-translators.

Thinking about translation as a complex network of productive practices allows a reassessment of its relationship with difference and its ethical implications. In the absence of a rigid source text–target text model, translation is no longer a process based on erasure and (imperfect) substitution. Rather, as a form of co-presence and a guarantor of narrative continuity, translation traces the links connecting us to our past and future stories, to the way in which we, our communities and our cultures have come to be what we are. By following the meandering, fragmented, and frequently traumatic routes of translation, we can trace how newness and difference enter our world, how they are manipulated, assimilated, appropriated, contested, shared, and renewed. As a visible trace and testimony of change, which refuses to erase its constitutive difference, translation is a reminder of the contingent nature of all forms of identification and an invitation to construct communities and societies on an ethics of hospitality that starts but does not end with linguistic hospitality.[9] Translation, as a continuum of local and embodied practices, enters our space and reveals its porosity, its receptivity, its diversity. Returning to the metaphor of travel and transfer from this perspective, translation is no longer a narrow bridge between two self-contained territories, regulating who and what is allowed to come in or out. Instead, translation is a pervasive presence and reminder of the tension between different realities, perspectives, perceptions. Translation opens up the space of the nation, exposing its porousness to a transnational dimension of dialogue and transformation that could not exist without translation and that, thanks to translation, is located as much inside as outside any borders, is always already here, wherever we situate ourselves. That porousness and permeability remind us that no boundary can contain us, no wall can 'protect' us: the imperfect translatability of the world with its inherent tensions echoes the need to act both locally and globally and to pay attention to the multiple ecologies (linguistic, cultural, environmental) in which we are inscribed. Far from discouraging translation, untranslatability (that is, the impossibility of perfect translation) demands further acts of translating, a reminder of the ethical imperative inscribed in its equally irreducible and creative difference.

## Translation as Object and as Method

An imperfect as well as productive meaning-making process in a multilingual world, translation is both a fundamental component of cultural interaction and a central approach to the study of languages and cultures. As students of modern languages, we tend to encounter translation either as part of language learning or in the shape of cultural products (books, films, historical documents) that we approach in and through translation. Both activities often carry negative connotations, associated with the first of the two models discussed above. In language classes, prescriptive or 'perfect' translation focuses too closely on vocabulary and grammatical accuracy, diverting attention from communication in the target language. Translated texts allow access to cultural products without (or before) achieving full fluency in the language in which they were first written, but reading in translation is frowned upon since it is believed to give access only to an inferior version of the original.

Broadening the definition of translation repositions it as a central object of study for language specialists. As the ability to move fluidly between languages,

[9] On the notion of linguistic hospitality see Paul Ricoeur, *On Translation*, trans. by Eileen Brennan (London and New York: Routledge, 2006).

translation becomes a defining skill and a distinctive form of knowledge. Taught through a creative rather than prescriptive approach, translation helps develop students' professional profile and their awareness of the ethical implications of linguistic choices. Beyond the language classroom, paying explicit attention to translation as an object of study illuminates the complex networks of production, dissemination, and fruition of information and cultural outputs. Far from providing a limited, defective understanding of 'originals' in their assumed perfection, critical readings of translations (including, where possible, the source text itself as well as multiple retranslations) facilitate a more active engagement with texts and accurate understanding of notions of authorship, intertextuality, and tradition. With its focus on multiplicity and instability, on rewriting and appropriation, on difference and transculturation, translation dethrones notions of canonicity and, eventually, decolonizes the Modern Languages curriculum, moving away from the methodological nationalism and ethnocentrism marking the history of the discipline.

It is along these lines that translation can move from being an object of study to becoming a methodological approach to languages and cultures. Translation as method helps reformulate our take on cultural history acting as a methodological framework, a key hermeneutic tool, opening up the field of Modern Languages and strengthening its relevance to areas such as comparative and world literature, colonial and postcolonial studies, ethnography and anthropology, gender and queer studies, visual studies and multimodality, or eco-critical approaches to cultural production, reception, and consumption. A translation-sensitive approach affirms that knowledge is constructed on the move, that local and global dimensions or national and transnational approaches exist in tension, and that to forget or ignore the porous, dynamic, dialogical relationship between locations, cultures, and languages is always risky. In its imperfection, translation focuses attention on languages, on their plurality and, importantly, on the specificity of their use. Precisely because it is not neutral, translation reminds us that every language operation involves loss and gain, alters power relationships, and reshapes representations – an antidote to the temptation to stop paying attention to language, to assume its transparency, and to adopt an attitude of linguistic indifference. Rather than a problem to be solved or a dirty secret to be kept out of sight, translation – as object and as method – is a crucial research tool and a powerful agent of cultural production and transformation.

Loredana Polezzi is Alfonse M. D'Amato Chair in Italian American and Italian Studies at Stony Brook University

# 36

# Translation

*Zrinka Stahuljak*

What do two major debates that have in the last decade traversed the humanities and modern languages, and specifically literary studies and translation studies, have in common? At first sight, activist translation/interpreting (translator visibility) and world literature (and, its converse, untranslatability) seem at a far remove one from the other, as if without the conceptual tie to bind them. What they share outwardly is their global spread. Activist interpreting can go from anti-globalist movements across the planet to migrant interpreting (for example, medical, legal) in the West; by definition, world literature spans the globe through translation into English, the dominant contemporary lingua franca, and the language of capitalism. Both do depend on global capitalism; neither can therefore disentangle from politics, and both, albeit indirectly, beg the question of what translation is today.

Is translation in highly politicized and political situations (for example, (im)migration, climate change, war) by definition activism, hence possibly tainted with partiality and inaccuracy? How then to define the ethics of translation today? Do Anglophone capitalist markets drive almost exclusively the publication into English of translatable – palatable – works from other cultures? Is untranslatability, conversely, the last line of ethical and practical defence in the name of indigenous and heterogenous discourses and against forms of approximate interpreting, and Google translation to boot? In response, I submit that since we are confronted with globalization, philosophy of literary translation that has been with us since the Age of Romanticism no longer corresponds to different communicative situations in which globalization has thrust us. Nor is the Republic of Letters defined by the expansion of Europe and its rise to global domination adequate to the circulations of translation in multiple discursive forms in the present-day neo-liberal context of minority challenges to classical Western imperialism and its forms of cultural hierarchy. I focus here on translation issues that have had an impact on modern language and transnational studies to argue that translation studies and world literature urgently need to think translation, not as equivalence, but as a form of commensuration acted via the third term of intermediary.

What has driven twentieth and early twenty-first century study of translation in comparative literature, postcolonial, and world literature contexts has been the heritage of the philosophy of translation that began with German Romanticism. The apogee of its expression is the 1923 essay by Walter Benjamin, 'The Task of the Translator':

> Is a translation meant for readers who do not understand the original? This would seem to explain adequately the divergence of their standing in the realm of art. Moreover, it seems to be the only conceivable reason for saying 'the same thing' repeatedly. For what does a literary work 'say'? What does it communicate? It 'tells' very little to those who understand it. Its essential quality is not statement or the imparting of information. Yet any translation which intends to perform a transmitting function cannot transmit anything but information – hence, something inessential. This is the hallmark of bad translations. But we do not generally regard as the essential substance of a literary work what it contains in addition to information … the unfathomable, the mysterious, the 'poetic,' something that a translator can reproduce only if he is also a poet.[1]

In the opening lines of his essay, Benjamin posits what will influence and shape translation studies, literary studies, continental philosophy, comparative and postcolonial literatures: the superiority of literary translation to all other forms of translation. A 'good' translator is also a poet. This elitism comes at the expense of traditional translation theory (since St Jerome), which postulated that translation is less essential than the original because it seeks resemblance of meanings to it. Benjamin contradicts: translation is essential because it serves to attain the central kinship between languages that are part of a greater, pure language. Translation is thus opposed to communication, which is identified as an inessential function of transmitting meaning and information. These were two significant moves: in rejecting communication, Benjamin posited (literary) translation as essential.

[1] Walter Benjamin, 'The Task of the Translator', in *Illuminations*, ed. by Hannah Arendt, trans. by Harry Zohn (New York: Schocken Books, 1969), pp. 69–82 (pp. 69–70).

## Translation–*Translatio*

Benjamin's influence institutionalized the Romantic heritage, namely Friedrich Schleiermacher's 1813 distinction between art and scholarship (literary translation) and commerce (interpreting and technical translation). Interpreting was devalorized as 'a merely mechanical task that can be performed by anyone with a modest proficiency in both languages'.[2] It created a long-standing twentieth-century hierarchy between translation studies and interpreting studies. The predominantly linguistic orientation of interpreting has not intersected with the cultural/postcolonial turn in literary translation; similarly, interpreting limited itself to deontology (an objective, extra-situational professional code), while translation studies took on the ethical role in the critique of postcolonial and transnational asymmetries in translation.

The elitist and high-brow identity of translation as literary is a recent post-Romantic, nationalist development – the exclusionary politics of translation studies its unconscious heritage. Such configuration has failed to recognize that translation was always first about transmission and much broader than our modern (literary) translation. In the Middle Ages, the Latin term *translatio* stands for transfers of power (*translatio imperii*), knowledge (*translatio studii*), physical objects or materials (such as relics in *translatio reliquiarum*), and linguistic translation.[3] The canonical twelfth-century description of *translatio* shows it as an inexorable migration of knowledge and power through space and time in different – transmuted – material forms: from East to West, from Greece to Rome to France or French-speaking England. *Translatio* presented a nexus of a will to knowledge and technologies of power, articulating voluntarily the teleology of the rise and expansion of Europe.

In the Middle Ages, knowledge was seen as the foundation of all power; in the West, its language had been Latin. Translation, into a vernacular, meant transfer of power (empire) away from Latin (the Church). Empire (*imperium*) could be within reach of any ruler who sponsored a translation movement. Thus, it was translation, not authorship, that served as the primary model of cultural and knowledge production, based on a radically divergent notion of fidelity and accuracy defined by content and its transmutation; conversely, the notion of original did not prevail. Translation was adaptation and commentary (gloss of authorities, *auctoritates*), content and form were in a relationship of plurality, and the translating activity itself could be plural.

[2] Friedrich Schleiermacher cited in Moira Inghilleri, *Interpreting Justice: Ethics, Politics, and Language* (New York: Routledge, 2012), p. 125.

[3] Zrinka Stahuljak, *Bloodless Genealogies of the French Middle Ages: Translation, Kinship, and Metaphor* (Gainesville: University Press of Florida, 2005).

It is usually said that on the cusp between the late Middle Ages and the Renaissance (fourteenth to sixteenth century), the hierarchy between the original and translation changed; the emergence of the author is customarily credited with this reversal. There is another way of looking at this. The impetus to vernacularization, the secularization of power through vernacularization, and the simple linguistic fact that anything is translatable (not only the Church authorities), generated in response goals of equivalence and accuracy, embodied by Leonardo Bruni in 1420: 'The full power of a translation resides in the fact that what is written in one language should be well translated into another'.[4] The translational worth of the text was no longer established by authority and access, but by method; thus method created the original.

Method also made room for claims of authorship. Nicole Oresme, translator of Aristotle's *Nichomachean Ethics* (1370) and *Politics* (1374) for Charles V of France, wrote: 'It so happens that, back then, Greek was to the Latin of Rome as Latin is now to our French ... I can therefore correctly conclude that the consideration and intention of our good King Charles, who has good and excellent books translated into French, is to be praised'.[5] Poet Joachim du Bellay asks in 1549:

> If the Romans ... did not devote themselves to this labour of translation, by what means then were they able to enrich their language, even to make it almost equal to the Greek? Imitating the best Greek authors, transforming themselves into them, devouring them; and, after having well digested them, converting them into blood and nourishment ... as shoots ... they grafted and applied to their own tongue.[6]

The two are separated by two hundred years but united in the desire to enable the vernacular; Latin is a model because it was formerly a vernacular in

[4] Leonardo Bruni, 'The Right Way to Translate', trans. by André Lefevere, in *Translation/History/Culture: A Sourcebook*, ed. by André Lefevere (New York: Routledge, 1992), pp. 82–86 (p. 82).

[5] Elisabetta Barale, '"Le Prologue du translateur" des *Éthiques* et des *Politiques* d'Aristote par Nicole Oresme (1370–1374)', *Corpus Eve. Éditions de textes ou présentations de documents liés au vernaculaire* (2013), <https://journals.openedition.org/eve/643?lang=en> [accessed 10 February 2021]; author's translation.

[6] Joachim du Bellay, 'La Défense et illustration de la langue française', in *Les Regrets. Les Antiquités de Rome*, ed. by S. de Sacy (Paris: Gallimard, 1993), pp. 197–267 (p. 214); Joachim du Bellay, *The Defence and Illustration of the French Language*, trans. by Gladys M. Turquet (London: J.M. Dent, 1939), p. 37.

relation to Greek. The difference is that Oresme speaks as a translator and Du Bellay as an imitator (author): the motivation is no longer to make Aristotle speak French to permit access to content, as if extra-linguistic (Oresme translated Aristotle from Latin, not Greek), but to cannibalize and become a French Horace and Petrarch. That is, Du Bellay posits both a (historical) supersession of Greeks and Romans, and a competition among vernaculars: from an indifference to language in Oresme to Du Bellay's language as the tool of domination and marker of origin (property and identity) to linguistic nationalism. Changing attitudes to translation and language perform a retraction from global connectedness (*translatio*, or migration and mutation of content irrespective of language and accuracy) and inaugurate European prominence (translation as method; language as property and instrument of domination; author as origin). Concomitantly, a move towards fidelity and accuracy in translation can be understood as demarcation of property in the colonial mode. Henceforth, translation could only play the supporting role to the property of the original and the name of the author; translation had been content, but authorship was imitation of forms and ultimately development of style autochthonous to language.

Concordant with the idea of European colonial expansion, Pascale Casanova showed that this was also the moment of the constitution of an autonomous, transnational literary space regulated by an inherent – though invisible – European and national aesthetic value system.[7] While the homology between the cultural and the economic was not always the case, the problem of world literature today is not just that it is culturally Eurocentric, but that it is Eurocentric by virtue of an economic system that is capitalist and European. In the globalized world, capitalist book and translation markets erase the heterogeneity of world forms of knowledge and knowledge-systems by conditioning the regimes of writing (themes, styles, genres) and their translation (into English). The colonial nature of European expansion continues to impose the silent national, European model; so much so that world literature itself may be seen as a phenomenon of globalization. This makes the strongest case for a relational analysis of a world: if relationship of power 'acts directly upon objects, terms, languages, texts, peoples, and societies', then a cultural or literary model of analysis is inadequate to the global moment.[8] Centred on literary works, not authors, Shu-mei Shih proposes networks of horizontal (space) and vertical (time)

[7] Pascale Casanova, *République mondiale des lettres* (Paris: Le Seuil, 1999).

[8] Shu-mei Shih, 'Global Literature and the Technologies of Recognition', in *World Literature. A Reader*, ed. by Theo D'haen, César Domínguez, and Mads Rosendahl Thomsen (London: Routledge, 2013), pp. 259–74 (p. 436).

relationality. But this means we can no longer start our analyses in the sixteenth or the nineteenth century.[9] We need to unyoke from this kind of literary history and teleology because the success of literature – defined by aesthetics, authorship, and debasement of translation – has been wedded to European expansion and colonial domination. If we wish to understand translational asymmetries of power, it is not enough that our analyses are transnational and transcultural; they also need to be transtemporal.[10] In jettisoning classical literary history and teleology, we open up transnational and world literatures to other knowledge systems, truth regimes, and modes of enquiry that are not part of the same (Eurocentric) evolutionary model of literature and translation, from the Age of Discovery to present-day neoliberal globalism. We do not even have to seek far: the Middle Ages will do. Moreover, this will disrupt the notion of translation as literary – the silent principle of elite European culture – and expand it to all translational forms, oral and written.

## Translation–Communication

Nicole Oresme can help us mitigate the contempt for communication that Benjamin cemented. He invents the neologism 'communicacion' in his translation of Aristotle's (Latin) *Nichomachean Ethics*. 'Communicacion' replaces 'societas', 'respublica', 'amicitia', 'urbanitas', 'communitas'.[11] That is, Oresme chooses 'communicacion' instead of 'communité', a term he uses only to describe a polity. Before 'communicacion', there was only the term of 'communion':[12] via the language of the Church (Latin), the faithful integrated the body of Christ. As such, an inherence of knowledge corresponded with the universality of Latin. But 'communicacion' posits something else: relationality because of difference. Here is how Oresme translates Aristotle: 'And if there were no commutation, there would be no communication. And there would be no commutation without equality, and no equality without

[9] See Casanova, *République mondiale des lettres*; also David Damrosch, *What is World Literature?* (Princeton: Princeton University Press, 2003).

[10] Zrinka Stahuljak, *Médiéval contemporain: Pour une littérature connectée* (Paris: Éditions Macula, 2020).

[11] Renée Balibar, 'La communication en langue française', *Langage et société*, 83–84 (1998), 15–37 (pp. 17–18); Charles Brucker, 'Aspects du vocabulaire politique et social chez Oresme et Christine de Pizan', *Cahiers de recherches médiévales*, 8 (2001), 227–49.

[12] Antoine Berman, *Jacques Amyot, traducteur français: Essai sur les origines de la traduction en France*, ed. by Isabelle Berman and Valentina Sommella (Paris: Belin, 2012), pp. 29, 54; Balibar, 'La communication en langue française', pp. 23–27.

measure'.[13] In short, human necessity for things creates communication. But there is no communication without commensuration. To communicate is to commute and vice versa, 'communicacions or commutacions', but this only occurs via a common measure: 'One should measure such things by some other thing, whatever it may be'.[14] This measure turns out to be money. As a measure, money is transactional: it is the third term that makes communication possible.

Commutation is a translation. Communication is about two poles of difference that transit via a third term of 'common measure'.[15] In other words, we are not dealing with direct equivalence (communication is not a communion); common measure produces equality, not fidelity. Translation is a commensuration of discourses, and the need for communication its first condition. It is the condition of possibility of communication – and thus of common life.

## Commensurability–Untranslatability

Thinking of translation as a commensuration of discourses endorses the greater visibility of the translator. Moira Inghilleri has made the best case yet for a more formal and recognized interpreter agency. The basis for a new approach to translation is the recognition that situations of communicative exchange, and particularly of conflict (understood broadly along the spectrum from disagreement to armed conflict) that attempt 'to resolve semantic uncertainties [...] involve decisions not discoveries about the meaning of a spoken utterance'.[16] Inghilleri makes two major and important claims: first, that the visibility and agency of interpreters should be more explicitly based on ethical considerations in the meaning negotiation in political and social communicative contexts, in which interpreters are the sole points of access to all sides of the conflict. And, second, that these ethical considerations can close a significant gap that has separated translation studies from interpreting studies especially by activating the ethical function of literary translation and by undoing the elitist claim of artistic creativity as exclusive to literary translation.

In this light, the concept of untranslatability appears as too narrow a question (and too thin a line of defence of heterogeneity of cultural forms and

[13] Nicole Oresme, *Le livre de Éthiques d'Aristote, Published from the Text of ms. 2902, Bibliothèque royale de Belgique, With a Critical Introduction and Notes*, ed. by Albert Douglas Menut (New York: Stechert, 1940), V. 297; author's translation.

[14] Oresme, *Le livre de Éthiques d'Aristote*, V. 295; author's translation.

[15] Oresme, *Le livre de Éthiques d'Aristote*, IX. 450; author's translation.

[16] Inghilleri, *Interpreting Justice*, p. 17.

modes of enquiry).[17] Untranslatability needs to be unmoored from its premise of translation as equivalence, by which it also maintains essentialist and incommensurable positions of postcolonial asymmetries. While there is close inherence of language and thought – how a culture thinks – terms are not only essences but also utterances. And it is as utterance that cultural incommensurability or incommunicability is no longer suspended on meaning but on a decision – that is, on commensuration. In other words, the ethics of translation studies cannot progress unless it opens up to the decision-based communicative approach from interpreting studies. There is a need for the ethics of the intermediary, which can come about only if we study the *dispositif* of the third term, the common measure.[18]

If conflict defines globalization, world literature thus equally needs an ethics of the intermediary.[19] Proponents of world literature have proposed collaboration and circulation precisely as forms of commensuration.[20] But thus far, world literature has remained grounded in a post-1800 notion of what literature is, defined by nation-states and colonialism.[21] The rare exception tethered literary history to the teleology of European domination beginning in the sixteenth century.[22] The definition of world literature – of texts that exist and circulate outside of culture of origin – is based on the boundaries of nation-states.[23] World literature understood only as modernity (hence Eurocentric and increasingly in English translation) faces the legacy of national literatures that are fastened to the name of the author, and an author-name today is both a political and a market phenomenon. The translation market reinforces the author and returns the translation 'profits' to

[17] See Emily Apter, *Against World Literature: On the Politics of Untranslatability* (London: Verso, 2013); Barbara Cassin, *Vocabulaire européen des philosophies: dictionnaire des intraduisibles* (Paris: Le Seuil, 2006).

[18] Zrinka Stahuljak, *Les Fixeurs au Moyen Âge* (Paris: Le Seuil, 2021). The term *dispositif* relates to Foucault's notion of the apparatus or mechanism used to exercise power: see Michel Foucault, 'The Confession of the Flesh', in Foucault, *Power/Knowledge: Selected Interviews and Other Writings, 1972–1977*, ed. and trans. by Colin Gordon (New York: Harvester Wheatsheaf, 1980), pp. 194–228.

[19] Shu-mei Shih, 'World Studies and Relational Comparison', *PMLA*, 130 (2015), 430–38.

[20] Moretti, Franco, 'Conjectures on World Literature' and 'More Conjectures', in *World Literature. A Reader*, ed. by D'haen, Domínguez and Rosendahl Thomsen, pp. 160–75; Damrosch, *What is World Literature?*

[21] Amir Mufti, *Forget English! Orientalisms and World Literatures* (Cambridge, MA: Harvard University Press, 2016); Damrosch, *What is World Literature?*

[22] Casanova, *République mondiale des lettres.*

[23] Damrosch, *What is World Literature?*

the author's nation whose 'symbolic capital' grows. The market thus brings back the nation and the canon, undercutting circulation and reinforcing presentism.

Thinking of translation as commensuration may require a further interrogation of the very presuppositions that have guided Modern Languages departments until now: authorship, definitions of genre and literature, periodization. That can best be done with either transtemporal or transspatial comparisons of *dispositifs*: we need to create encounters of different situated – but spatially and temporally discontinuous – sets of discourses, whose interaction can open up an ethical reflection on the multiple roles and centrality of translation in societies and histories of humanity. What would a literary history of decisions look like? What if we no longer thought of author-names but of literature written by translators, literature as circulation without origin? Translation, the third term of communication, may turn out to be not the metaphor of open communication and translatability that it has long been, but a new method of transnational literary studies and history.

Zrinka Stahuljak is a scholar of the medieval contemporary and of translation, and Professor of Comparative Literature and French at the University of California, Los Angeles (UCLA), where she also directs the CMRS Center for Early Global Studies.

37

# Voice

*yasser elhariry*

I would like to begin with two simple utterances.

They are

'I speak'

and

'I hear what you speak'

Of course, I am not speaking in the sense of moving my mouth and tongue to shape physical sound produced by the vibrations of my vocal folds. Nor is the sound of my voice physically reaching your outer ear, channelled into your middle ear, converted into electric pulses by your inner ear.

I am not *sensu stricto* speaking.

Nor you hearing.

Yet here we are, short-circuiting the electrophysics of speaking and hearing.

Our languages are satiated by aural metaphors such as these slippages from writing to speaking, reading to hearing.[1] At a rudimentary level, the humblest text is a complex study in vocal and auditory layering and exchange. Any piece of writing can assume the role of audio technology.

It is in this first literary sense that I speak of voice in these pages. Through these pages, on them, out of them, my voice emerges. I speak to you. I speak

[1] See Jonathan Sterne (ed.), *The Sound Studies Reader* (London: Routledge, 2012) especially the selection from Franz Fanon, 'This is the Voice of Algeria', and the entire sixth part of the book dedicated to 'Voices'.

to you by writing for you. You hear me by reading these words. Which seem to say that I am speaking. Give expression to what I have to speak. Whatever it is that I may have to speak. From me to you. For you by me.

In these pages, *you* and *me* and *I* are historical, sociocultural, situated enunciations that carry individual and collective significance and meaning (see 'Me' in this volume). The reader's attentiveness to textual modes of enunciation – who writes or speaks to whom, or when, and under which circumstances, and in what form (a poem? a letter? what kind of a letter or a poem?)[2] – defines a second literary sense of voice, which foregrounds a wide range of otherwise latent, coded information. Race. Sex. Gender. Nationality or nationalities. Narrative control. Social status. Privilege. Space and place. The real and metaphorical distances or gaps between us. Foreclosure versus openness. Human and non-human … Like the table of contents for this book, the list could go on.

The second literary sense of voice highlights a basic critical distinction that differentiates 'voice' from 'author' or 'poet': Virginia Jackson and Yopie Prins write, for instance, of the mid-twentieth century's 'anxiety to authorship', its 'worry about the poet's relation to the fictional "voice" of his poem at a time when critics were working to detach that voice from the poet'.[3] A series of probing questions follows: since it is neither by actual fact nor necessity me-the-author – the persona whose voice you hear or imagine – who is foregrounded, well, then, whose, precisely, is it? A question to which we may add: In what language is this voice speaking? And even more apropos: in what language do you read?[4]

As if all these slippages and passages, translations and transitions between our many selves, and the possibilities opened up by textual audio technologies and literary criticism were not sufficiently complicated, an entire range of vocal modulations enter into the game, altering the basic communicative

[2] See Gérard Genette, *The Architext: An Introduction*, trans. by Jane E. Lewin (Berkeley: University of California Press, 1992).

[3] Virginia Jackson and Yopie Prins, 'Anglo-American New Criticism', in *The Lyric Theory Reader: A Critical Anthology*, ed. by Virginia Jackson and Yopie Prins (Baltimore: Johns Hopkins University Press, 2014), pp. 159–65 (p. 163).

[4] The delightful question comes from Abdelfattah Kilito, 'La langue du lecteur' [The Reader's Language], in *Je parle toutes les langues, mais en arabe* [I Speak All Languages, but in Arabic] (Arles: Actes Sud, 2013), pp. 135–40. Indeed, in the name of what language do we even speak at all in the first place? In guise of a response, see notably Abdelkébir Khatibi, *Plural Maghreb: Writings on Postcolonialism*, trans. by P. Burcu Yalim (London: Bloomsbury, 2019), and Jacques Derrida, *Monolingualism of the Other; or, The Prosthesis of Origin*, trans. by Patrick Mensah (Stanford: Stanford University Press, 1998).

relationships intimated by the voice from the page, by 'I speak', and by the eyes on the page, by 'You hear what I speak'.

For example:

> 'This is the first time that I hear what you speak'

> 'I am confident that this is the first time that you hear what I speak'

and

> 'But this is neither the first time that I hear, nor you speak'

What happens with each iteration within this progression? And what happens with the third, in particular?

I agonized over how best to open this entry on 'Voice'. I felt like I was losing my voice, like someone had taken it away from me by giving it to me, or maybe I had already been losing it for a while, maybe I did not have one at all in the first place. So, I felt strongly that I should dramatize the idea of literary voice by speaking more directly than indirectly to you. That I put the opening transcriptions of speech utterances at a distance by opting to place them in-between inverted commas. That the unidirectional mode of my address to you be bent by imaging a deflection ('But this is neither...') conceived as an utterance by either one of us (though likely – perhaps logically – you), or even by a third, imaginary interlocutor or eavesdropper.

Within the circular vocal progressions that go from me-the-author to you-the-reader and then back again, typographical conventions such as those assumed by inverted commas play a crucial role in terms of literary history. They signal rupture: this is transcribed speech that is to be distinguished from the surrounding words. They signal hospitality: the surrounding words' porosities welcome the words of the other, share space, make place, even pass or give voice to the other, *je te passe la parole* in French, *the podium is yours.*[5] They express the hospitable inclusion and integration of the other. They welcome opposition or irony or fear or suspicion or distrust: just think of 'neologisms' and 'scare quotes'.

So, the inverted comma invites exchange and interchange, difference and dissent, a political reclaiming of my voice. For dialogue and exchange, the silencing and the seductions of voices characterize the earliest of humanity's

[5] See Ryoko Sekiguchi, *Héliotropes* (Paris: P.O.L, 2005), back cover blurb; *Heliotropes*, trans. by Sarah O'Brien (Iowa City: La Presse, 2008).

texts in the Western tradition: Homer's sirens,[6] Sappho's lyric,[7] Plato's dialogues. If we were to look at, say, Plato's *Phædrus*, we would observe that it opens with an encounter by a stream and that Socrates is railing in anger against all of the monotony of all of the speeches that people give in all of the cities in the entire world. Because, I think, the speech is the one single voice stabbing the heart of the crowd's collective silence. Seriously, who even has the power and privilege to give a speech at all in the first place? Dialogue, in contrast, suggests the inclusion of two voices. At least. Even if it's just me. Just me speaking to myself. Writing about myself.

The separations or inseparability of textual voices, such as those between speaker and audience, or between the author and the subject of an author's writing, amount to a distinction between the voice of the former that gives life to the latter. And vice versa. Such striations and synchronisms of textual voice correspond to the basic premise behind Philippe Lejeune's *Le Pacte autobiographique* (*On Autobiography*) (1975), a contract wherein the reader concedes an elevated degree of concurrent correspondence between the writer and their subject matter. This, at least, is the conceit of autobiographical voice. Michel Beaujour's *Miroirs d'encre: rhétorique de l'autoportrait* (*Poetics of the Literary Self-Portrait*) (1980) smudges this inseparability...

[naghama]

... because voice is never really just one, a single voice.

Here is a sublime example of the critical smudge of the voice, one among many in *Kitāb al-sāq ʿalā al-sāq fī mā huwwa al-Fāriyāq* (*Leg over Leg or The Turtle in the Tree concerning the Fāriyāq, What Manner of Creature Might He Be*), which I've chosen as a politically informed corrective to the hegemony of the Western tradition in modern languages. Composed by Aḥmad Fāris al-Shidyāq (c.1805–1887), the work marks a watershed moment in the history of Arabic literature for its radically layered lingual, verbal, intertextual, and formal innovation.[8] The text exceeds translational and transnational paradigms: al-Shidyāq oversaw the work's production, executed entirely in Arabic, in Paris

[6] See Maurice Blanchot, 'The Song of the Sirens', in *The Book to Come*, trans. by Charlotte Mandell (Stanford: Stanford University Press, 2002), pp. 1–24.

[7] See Jonathan Culler, 'Nine Poems', in *Theory of the Lyric* (Cambridge, MA: Harvard University Press, 2015), pp. 10–33.

[8] The book heralds the modern literary advent of what may be dubbed 'postlingualism'; see yasser elhariry and Rebecca L. Walkowitz (eds), 'The Postlingual Turn', special issue of *SubStance*, 154, 50.1 (2021).

in 1855. The text was born translated,[9] in the sense that it folds within itself a downward spiral of ludic translational and intertextual excess, inscribed and marked into the various parts of the body – like, notably, the throat and the ear.

Part of *al-Sāq ʿalā al-sāq*'s formal novelty stems from a layering of voices that all but delegitimizes any claim to literary, biographical, textual, or national-narrative authority: the absence of a central, grounding voice, and the constant subversion of anything that may seem to resemble any inkling of a pretence to authority.[10] Here, voice, unequivocally, is never speech. On one level, the titular character's name, al-Fāriyāq, constitutes a form of *naḥt*, a noun composed by splicing two others: the *Fār–* in *Fāris* against the *–yāq* in *Shidyāq* combine to form *Fāriyāq*. It represents a thinly veiled autobiographical allusion to the person of the author, Aḥmad Fāris al-Shidyāq. On a second level, al-Fāriyāq is shadowed throughout the text by a narrator who records and relays his travels, encounters, and many conversations, which not only moves us away from any semblance of autobiography and into a pseudo-fictional world that combines biography and hagiography, but also insists that the doubling of al-Shidyāq and al-Fāriyāq correspond to and mutate and denature the three-way between author and narrator and protagonist.

Narrative voice offers one way of approaching the work's perspectival alternations. For instance, in Chapter 1, Volume Four of *al-Sāq ʿalā al-sāq* ('Unleashing a Sea'), a long reflection on travel and language begins with a sentence composed from the perspective of a seemingly impartial third-person narrator: 'Only one who has traveled the seas and experienced the misery of their tempests and swells can properly appreciate the ease of life on land'.[11] The narrator then proceeds to speak in the first person, directly addresses the reader in the second person, and even imagines a dialogue that goes back and forth between him and the reader by deploying the formula: 'If you say [...] I reply [...]' (*S* 17). About halfway through the chapter, we move

[9] See Rebecca L. Walkowitz, *Born Translated: The Contemporary Novel in an Age of World Literature* (New York: Columbia University Press, 2015).

[10] Jahan Ramazani describes (and contests) how 'Mikhail Bakhtin famously distinguished between the "centripetal", "singular", "unitary, monologically sealed-off" qualities of poetry and the dialogic and double-sided, heteroglot and centrifugal structure of the novel': *A Transnational Poetics* (Chicago: University of Chicago Press, 2009), p. 3; Mikhail Bakhtin, *The Dialogic Imagination: Fours Essays*, ed. by Michael Holquist, trans. by Caryl Emerson and Michael Holquist (Austin: University of Austin Press, 1981), pp. 272–73.

[11] Aḥmad Fāris al-Shidyāq, *Kitāb al-sāq ʿalā al-sāq fī mā huwwa al-Fāriyāq* [*Leg over Leg or The Turtle in the Tree concerning the Fāriyāq, What Manner of Creature Might He Be*], vol. 4, trans. by Humphrey Davies (New York: New York University Press, 2014), p. 11 (hereafter cited as *S*).

into a different third-person modal address, which shifts narratological gears into a prelude that leads to the narrator's giving of (his) voice to al-Fāriyāq: 'When our friend the Fāriyāq made his decision to leave the island for England, someone told him …' (*S* 19).

To complicate matters further, al-Fāriyāq is split into male (Fāriyāq) and female (Fāriyāqiyyah), ego and alterego, modelled after Munkar wa Nakīr (Denied and Denier), the twin angels of posthumous in-grave torture in Islamic eschatology. Al-Fāriyāq and al-Fāriyāqiyyah talk and debate, offend and flirt, goad and annoy, hit on and seduce one another, in an endless round-robin of oral/aural foreplay, sex, and vocal multiplication of self and other. And in a final structural coup, al-Shidyāq divides the entire book into four separate volumes.

Now let's give a closer listen to how voice makes its way into both the work's narrative and its thematic content. In Chapter 4, 'The Rules for Retelling', the quintupled voice (author, narrator, protagonist, antagonist, book) of the four-way book sketches a theory of eroticism that emanates from a vocal economy of exchange. Erotic pleasure, in al-Shidyāq, is split across five divisions. Al-Fāriyāqiyyah, al-Fāriyāq's feminine counterpart, reports that pleasure may be divided in the following way.

> The first is visualization of pleasure before its occurrence. The second is discussion of it before the same. The third is its actual realization accompanied by these two essential elements. The fourth is the visualization of it after the act. The fifth is discussion of it afterward. Whether the pleasure of visualizing it is greater before it takes place or afterward is a matter of debate. Some believe the first is greater because when it hasn't yet happened one's thoughts about it roam more widely, delve more deeply, and do not stop at any limit. Others claim that the actual occurrence provides one's thoughts with a known shape and a specific form as a benchmark against which to measure any replay or repetition. Similarly, there is disagreement over the times of its visualization, as also of its discussion, though the crucial point is the clearness of the visualization and the *foulness of the tongue*. (*S* 44–47; my emphasis)

*Bae you gotta talk dirty*, she wants to say.

Except that she cannot.

Or, for some reason, chooses not to.

The exchange between al-Fāriyāq and al-Fāriyāqiyyah takes place within the context of the former's sojourn in Britain, and his many reflections on all manner of British habits – from dress to sex to food to mood and humour.

In the narrative, the quintupled, structural voice's scrutiny of British habits, as relayed through al-Fāriyāq's travels, extends to Englishwomen by way of al-Fāriyāqiyyah's five divisions of pleasure. You will have glossed from her erotic system that pleasure involves telling and retelling the act. You will have gathered that it enacts a verbal passage from speaking and telling to hearing and retelling. The telling and retelling, in turn, are governed by a complex set of rules, most importantly *whom* to discuss *what* kind of act as performed with *whom* and *when*, and *when* to discuss, and how often, and how much of it to repeat visually. But above all verbally. So, if you engage in dalliance with 'a man of high status at night, it must be discussed with a woman of high status at night' (*S* 65). And vice versa. And so on. And so forth.

With specific regard to the Englishwoman, the pleasure taken in reliving pleasure through its narrativization is mediated through an alternate semiotic system. Elusive *naghama*.

> Every night the Fāriyāq would see [the maid] going up to the room of one of the lodgers. Then after a time not longer than it takes to say 'Good evening!' he would hear her produce *a kineto-penetrative gasp* [*naghama īghāfiyya*]. The mistress of the house used to see her coming down from the man's room at ten or so at night but had no interest in her ascents and descents. In the morning, when the girl came to make the Fāriyāq's bed, he would stare at her and observe her closely but could see no sign to indicate that she was *the gasper* [*ṣāḥibat al-naghama*]. He therefore assumed that it was a delusion born of his fervent desire for penetration. Then night would come and *the gasp* [*al-naghama*] would be there again, and so would his certainty. With morning the staring would be repeated as would the *pretence of virtue*, and the doubt would be there and so would the confusion, and so on and so forth. Things got so bad that the Fāriyāq's mind almost became unhinged and started to spoil the translation, which he had long feared might fall victim to shortcomings and mistakes due to some issue related to women. (*S* 62–65; my emphasis)[12]

The alternation between hearing and seeing, between sound and sight, erects a passage away from issues of mimesis, ekphrasis, and representation – it brings to the fore a pulling out from the Enlightenment West's 'oculocentricity', or 'the figurative framework of literary criticism and its emphasis on representation'.[13] Pleasure, in al-Shidyāq's vocal-textual economy, divorces

12 Like al-Shidyāq in real life, al-Fāriyāq is working on a translation of the gospels.

13 Tarek El-Ariss, *Trials of Arab Modernity: Literary Affects and the New Political*

sight from sound, sex from sight, and eros (drive, charge, want) from lingual and translational success, coupling it instead to failure, lack, abstinence, non-coupling, or decoupling. It is difficult to dissociate voice from a conception of sound (see 'Sound' in this volume), which renders British sexuality – with its 'pretence of virtue', the desire to speak with 'clear and eloquent tongue of everything that happened', and the kind of pleasure that is the logical outcome of the preceding two points – 'incomplete', 'according to the rule pronounced by al-Fāriyāqiyyah', 'because it will lack the element of discussion' (*S* 64–65).

In Arabic, the tongue and voice reign supreme. It is imperative, says al- Fāriyāqiyyah, 'that there be a flirtatious flash to the eyes, floods of saliva [*fī-l-laʿmi fīḍān*], and a moistness to the tongue, and that the hands sketch what the words describe. This being established', she continues, 'you will have gathered that the trait mentioned as present in Englishwomen is an infraction of the rules of pleasure, and it may be said that the pleasure they take in visualization is so strong because it takes the place of two other pleasures, or that they put their heads inside a cask or the like' (*S* 66–67).

Earlier, I said that 'voice is never really just one, a single voice'.

Reading al-Shidyāq, you and I might come to the further realization that voice is really no voice at all.

It can be as understated as it is erotic.

The rasp of a gasp.

yasser elhariry is a literary critic and
Associate Professor of French at Dartmouth College.

(New York: Fordham University Press, 2013), pp. 6–7. For more on oculocentrism, see yasser elhariry, 'Unsound French', in *Sounds Senses* (Liverpool: Liverpool University Press, 2021), pp. 23–55.

# Index

## Concepts

## Language and Languages

## Names

Places

## Practices and Forms

## Times